The Scarlet Woman
of
Wall Street

Jay Gould, Jim Fisk,
Cornelius Vanderbilt,
the Erie Railway Wars,
and the Birth
of Wall Street

JOHN STEELE GORDON

Weidenfeld & Nicolson · New York

Published by Weidenfeld & Nicolson, New York
A Division of Wheatland Corporation
10 East 53rd Street
New York, NY 10022

Published in Canada by General Publishing Company, Ltd.

Library of Congress Cataloging-in-Publication Data
Gordon, John Steele.
  The scarlet woman of Wall Street : Jay Gould, Jim Fisk,
Cornelius Vanderbilt, the Erie Railway wars, and the birth of
Wall Street /John Steele Gordon. — 1st ed.
      p.   cm.
  Bibliography: p.
  Includes index.
  ISBN 1-555-84212-7
  1. New York Stock Exchange—History—19th century.
2. Wall Street—History—19th century. 3. Capitalists and
financiers—United States—History—19th century. 4. Erie
Railway—History—19th century. I. Title.
  HF4572.G67 1988
  332.64'273—dc19   88–230
                                                                 CIP

Manufactured in the United States of America
Designed by Irving Perkins Associates
First Edition
10 9 8 7 6 5 4 3 2 1

To Robert L. Treadway
An uncatchable Guy Fawkes
beneath the Parliament of my serenity

Contents

List of Illustrations

THE illustrations used in this book come from three contemporary sources: *Harper's Weekly, Frank Leslie's Illustrated Newspaper,* and William Worthington Fowler's great best-seller of 1870, *Ten Years in Wall Street.* The engravings in illustrated weeklies and books were the principal means by which the Victorians viewed the world and events beyond their own ken, much as television is ours.

Acknowledgments

MY first thanks must go to the New York Public Library and to its able and ever-helpful staff. The NYPL came into being through the bequests of three men who made their fortunes in nineteenth-century New York and who, like so many other New Yorkers before and since, left a part of their wealth to glorify the city that had helped to make them rich. Today it is one of the three or four greatest research libraries on earth, and even Lenin thought it one of the great glories of capitalism.

My second thanks must go to my aunt, Eleanora Gordon Baird, for so generously presenting me with a computer, a technology I had heretofore worshiped from afar. This miraculous machine has allowed me to finish this book months—if not years—before I otherwise would have, and I now can hardly imagine writing anything longer than a postcard without it. Gibbon, to be sure, wrote his mighty *Decline and Fall* with only a quill pen and an inkpot, so I realize how spoiled rotten I have become, a condition that is just fine by me.

The library of the New-York Historical Society, the New York Society Library, and the library of the Union Club were also extremely obliging in helping me through the history of the city of which they have all so long been a part. Helen Allen, the librarian of the Union Club, was especially helpful.

I would like also to thank:

Mark Ingwer for being a bridge over some very troubled water.

Al Kraus, Bob Mitchell, and Mark Perlgut for early encouragement.

Jill Prosky and all the others at the Boyar-Prosky Insurance Agency for so cheerfully putting up with what must surely be the most-troublesome, least-remunerative account in the history of transferred risk.

David Granger and Kay Healy for helping to keep the wolf from the door or at least keeping its growls from distracting me unduly.

Edmund B. Cabot, M.D., for sharing his expertise on the arcane subject of nineteenth-century trauma management.

Russel H. Beatie, Jr., Esq., for his careful reading, expert legal opinions, and awesome knowledge of the Civil War and its literature. He also rescued this former copyeditor from many errors in grammar, syntax, and punctuation and attempted to rescue him from many more. If this book still does not sound as though it had been written by Douglas Southall Freeman, it is not because Cap didn't try.

John Case for his thoughtful advice and economic expertise. He set me straight on a number of subjects I apparently dozed through in Economics 101 and untwisted my logic more than once.

E. Jeffery Stann for several helpful suggestions, including the startling notion that streets have two sides.

Mark Polizzotti for his intelligent and skillful editing and for his sensitive handling of this opinionated—not to mention frequently tactless—author. He got me off my soapbox when necessary and persuaded me to part with unneeded paragraphs even when they contained sentences of surpassing literary perfection. He has helped this book greatly.

Margaret M. Cheney for her sensitive and expert copyediting. When I asked her to copyedit this book, she put her Depression-era liberalism on a very short leash, concealed whatever trepidation she may have felt, and marched into the tulgey woods of Wall Street history, red pencils her only weapons. There she banished clichés, deleted the word ''enormous'' an enormous number of times, required parallel construction, asked all sorts of intelligent questions, and generally insisted that I say what I mean. She has made this a much better book.

Needless to say, I remain wholly responsible for any errors still to be found in the book.

The past is a foreign country: they do things differently there.

L. P. Hartley
The Go-Between

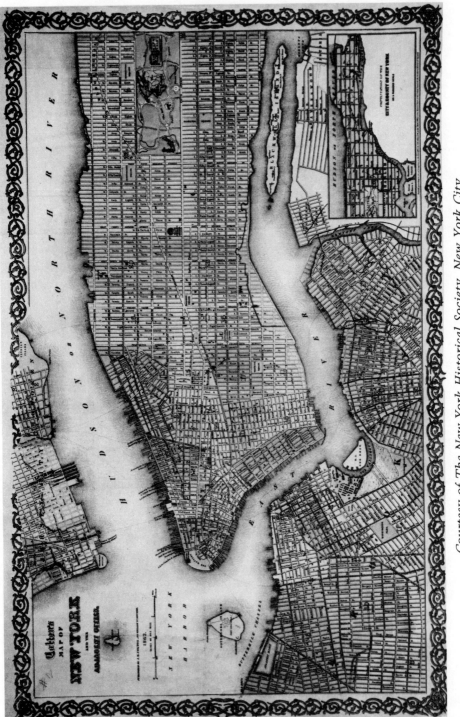

Preface

AS every schoolboy seems not to know, James Watt did not invent the steam engine. Rather he made two fundamental improvements, which changed it from a useful device for pumping water out of mines into a world-transforming machine. Watt's first improvement, the separate condenser, increased the steam engine's fuel efficiency fourfold. His second, a means of converting the steam engine's reciprocating motion into constant rotary motion, which could turn a shaft, allowed its power to be applied to an infinity of tasks.

Until the eighteenth century, work, even in its strict physical sense of transferred motion, could only be performed by men, wind, animals, and falling water. The Watt steam engine was something very new under the sun, and the industrial revolution that resulted from it was characterized by the rapidly accelerating input of energy into the economic system.

The changes wrought by the steam engine came with astonishing swiftness. Although Watt's rotary engine was patented only in 1781, by the first decade of the nineteenth century the poet William Blake was already doubting the presence of God amid England's "dark Satanic mills." And those mills had made Britain the richest and most powerful country on earth.

While there is much about the world of the early industrial revolution that seems foreign, even exotic, to us who live in the late twentieth century, that world and ours share at least two abiding characteristics: ceaseless technological and sudden economic change. In technology, each generation since Watt's has lived to see the world made new. To the people of the twentieth century this never-ending change has become a constant in itself, for it dates to a time before the memory of any of our grandparents. To the early Victorians it was a new and profoundly unsettling phenomenon.

In the 1860's there were still alive many people who had been born into a world that had altered little in its technological aspects over the course of a hundred years and more. Their parents had lived much as their own parents and grandparents had before them. But, as the price of energy began to plummet and its use, therefore, to soar, an ever-increasing flood of inventions to exploit the new resource was unleashed. This in turn shattered the centuries-long economic dominance of land and agriculture, and, for the members of the society that had been based on these sources and repositories of wealth, it ended forever "the noiseless tenor of their way."

The older generation of Victorians thought of themselves as living in a singular era of transition between one world of order and certainty and some new and as yet unknown world of equal regularity and predictability. Thus, in a sense, they felt themselves to be at sea between two continents, being tossed about by new and temporary forces they did not understand. But, as generation succeeded generation and the new world toward which they were supposed to be headed seemed ever farther over the horizon, they began to realize that the sea itself was the new world. If they were to survive and continue to flourish in it, they would not only have to understand the forces at work but also devise new rules to govern the new circumstances in which they continuously found themselves.

Today, once again, there can be little doubt that we are confronting a world-transforming technology, this time the computer. Computers can do at trivial cost many tasks that once could only be done by human beings at great cost, and an infinity of others that formerly could not be done at all. Like energy in the industrial revolution, the gathering, manipulation, and instant transfer of information has suddenly become very cheap, and entrepreneurs are sweeping in to exploit the new possibilities. Like the steam engine before it, the computer has in a single generation changed the world dramatically, given us capabilities quite un-

dreamed of only fifty years ago, and promises now scarcely imag-
ined wonders and changes yet to come. Already the need to discern and adapt to the new sources and repositories of wealth that
are being created by the computer and devise the rules needed by
society to cope with them is obvious.

The old power centers are already crumbling as smokestack America becomes the rust belt and truly multinational corporations and
instant global communications bring the era of the independent
national economy to an end. The economic and technological realities of the computer age are erasing national borders and diminishing the power of politicians over economic affairs far faster than any
political conference could ever hope—or certainly be inclined—to
do.

Luckily, the Victorians faced just such an economic revolution
before us and have much to teach us about how to deal with it. After
all, even many words that seem so apposite to the 1980's, such as
"entrepreneur" and "millionaire," were coined by them in similar
circumstances. Just as we think of our times, the Victorians thought
of theirs as an "age of chaos . . . [a] heaving, tumbling age," and
without a doubt our own times will seem to our descendants as
serene and predictable as the world of Currier and Ives now seems
to us.

•

This book is a history of the search by the Victorians for one small
part of the rules by which they learned to govern their world: those
rules that delimited the great game of Wall Street's financial free
market and maintained its vitality and its immense economic utility
over the course of more than a hundred years.

Throughout history free markets have tended to be ephemeral,
for once they grew to any considerable size, individuals pursuing
their self-interest sought to dominate, and thus destroy them. Indeed, the idea that free markets are a positive good in their own
right—for the game is not a zero-sum one—dates only to Watt's
great contemporary, Adam Smith. That Wall Street succeeded in
establishing rules which maintained its free market was no small
accomplishment and had no small consequences for New York City,
the United States, and the world.

When Watt perfected his rotary steam engine, Wall Street was
nothing more than a short, mostly residential thoroughfare in a
small seaport remote from the centers of world power. A hundred

years later its name was synonymous with the second-largest and fastest-growing securities market on earth. The capital being raised there in the tens of millions was fast building the economy and the civilization that would dominate the affairs of the world to the present day.

Wall Street's financial market today is enormously larger than the market of the post–Civil War era. The value of the securities listed on the New York Stock Exchange now exceeds the value of those listed on all other exchanges in the world combined except Tokyo's. The trading volume of the first ten minutes of a busy day exceeds the trading that took place in any calendar year of the 1860's. But in many ways the situations of Wall Street then and now are similar, as new and only dimly perceived economic realities work their consequences in the marketplace.

Then speculators were bound by no rules beyond the natural ones of the market. They pursued their self-interest by seeking short-term trading profits in the stocks of companies they controlled and without regard to the long-term consequences to the market, to the companies whose securities they manipulated, or to the economic system as a whole. Today, ironically, the vastly elaborated fiduciary responsibilities of pension-fund managers (who now control fully 50 percent of all the securities traded in Wall Street) often force them to do exactly the same, with effects that have proved equally inimical to the well-being of the market.

Then speculators manipulating securities for their own profit would suddenly add or withdraw quantities of stock that were beyond the ability of the market to handle in an orderly fashion. Today computer trading programs, with an equal lack of regard for the consequences, can and do fling vast quantities of securities onto the market in seconds without the intervention or approval or even knowledge of a single human mind, providing the market with days of excitement unseen since the 1920's.

Then, after the Exchange had closed for the day, trading in listed stocks continued out on the street until nightfall and at the informal exchanges uptown until the small hours of the morning. Today, with a similar lack of coordinated regulation, after-hours trading follows the sun to Los Angeles, Tokyo, and London, continuing nearly around the clock. As the events of October, 1987, demonstrated all too vividly, it is now possible for a crash to roll around the world like a financial tidal wave.

No one can doubt that these new realities have the potential for profound and quite possibly catastrophic effects, both on the market itself and on the world economy of which Wall Street is the beating heart. We have, therefore, much to gain from looking at what really happened on Wall Street in the 1860's. At the very least it might help save us all a great deal of money, for forty-seven million Americans now own stocks or mutual funds and well over half of all Americans are the beneficiaries of pension funds.

Until very recently the history of Wall Street, indeed capitalism itself, was largely written by its enemies. These enemies, for the best and the worst of reasons, feared the free market and the very human passions that roil it. They tended, therefore, to emphasize its faults and to treat its denizens as a race apart from the general society in which they lived, indifferent regarding that society and its well-being, and all alike one to another, automatons of greed.

But Wall Streeters in the middle of the last century were, of course, quite as human as their fellow Victorians, as tendentious historians, as Wall Streeters today, or even as you and I. They came to the Street in their infinite human variety, and they flourished or foundered there as their luck, skill, and courage would have it. Enough of them had the wisdom to see that a great market without rules and referees could not long survive, and they managed to supply both when government and the judiciary could not.

I have, therefore, largely ignored the work of those historians and intellectuals who flourished in the anti-Victorian and anti-capitalist tide of the first half of the twentieth century and who imposed, ex post facto, the economic thinking and moral attitudes of that period on their subject. Rather I have sought to look at the Wall Street of the 1860's and its inhabitants through the books, periodicals, and engravings by which the Victorians themselves perceived those portions of their world that lay beyond their own ken. I believe that this is the only way for us to comprehend, in however small degree, that world as it really was. And only thus can we show it the respect that the past, like any foreign country rich in wisdom and human experience, is due.

•

This preface would not be complete without a word regarding my grandfather Richard H. Gordon, who so powerfully influenced the value system that lies behind this book. In 1898, at the age of sixteen, he left his native Nashville, Tennessee, and like millions of others before and since he set out for New York, the city of dreams. There, on Wall Street, he sought and found his fortune. He last went downtown in 1976, two years before his death at ninety-six, and thus had a Wall Street career that spanned almost eighty years and that ranged from runner to senior partner of a large broker-age house.

When I was still young enough to sit in his lap he began to tell me stories of this great and mysterious place he called the Street. He told me of his many victories there and his not infrequent defeats. He told me what he had seen with his own eyes: the Northern Pacific corner of 1901, the explosion outside the Morgan Bank, the great crash, and the disgrace of Richard Whitney. He had a Southerner's gift for storytelling, and soon I had learned about Uncle Daniel Drew and the Commodore, about the days before the rules had been invented, when it was every man for himself. Almost before I was old enough to ride a bicycle I knew what it meant to sell short and what had happened to the customers' yachts.

I have never worked on Wall Street, for it was my fate to inherit my grandfather's love of history, not his financial acumen. But I have in full measure his belief in the free market and its power to improve the lot of mankind, a belief that permeates this work. To the extent that it has been within my power to make it worthy of him, this book is a memorial to this learned, wise, and honorable man, who knew the great game of Wall Street so well, and loved it so much, and first told me of its ways when I was young.

John Steele Gordon
North Salem, New York
October 19th, 1987

A Note on Money and Time

ONE of the more intractable problems facing historians is that of translating the value of money over time: What was an 1869 dollar worth in today's terms?

All too often this has been handled as though it were nothing more than a matter of inflation and the reader is advised simply to multiply antique monetary sums by a given factor. This might have worked well enough in the pre-industrial era, but the coming of the steam engine greatly exacerbated the difficulty of comparison.

Essentially, the industrial revolution introduced three new problems for historians. The first is rapidly rising real wealth. All segments of modern society have enjoyed immense real growth in per-capita income since the dawn of the industrial age two centuries ago. Consequently, if the price of a commodity has stayed the same, net of inflation, the percentage of real income needed to purchase it has been dropping steadily and so, therefore, has its perceived cost. Buying a luxury at a price that represents 25 percent of average annual per-capita income (such as a television set in 1946) is out of the question for most people, but when the same price comes to represent only 2½ percent, that luxury will long since have become a necessity.

The second problem is that while many commodities have remained relatively stable in terms of the percentage of real income that they cost, they have become much cheaper in other economically significant terms, such as time. In 1869 a second-class passage to London and return from New York could be bought for about $150, a significant fraction of what tourist-class airfare costs today. But in 1869 the round-trip took about four weeks, and regular vacations for workers were unknown. So while many Americans could have afforded the price of a trip to London, few could have afforded the time. Today, with England only five or six hours away and paid vacations the norm, the situation is wholly different and foreign travel is a commonplace.

The third problem is that technologies serving the same function at different times often cannot be readily compared. In the nineteenth century, housework was done by hand or by servants (which is to say by hired hands). Today washing machines, driers, dishwashers, vacuum cleaners, microwave ovens, and a host of other appliances have changed matters completely. While the real cost of a maid has increased greatly, the need to have one has drastically diminished.

Consider an extreme example, for this is the nub of the problem. In the middle of the eighteenth century Prince Nicholas Esterhazy, a Hungarian nobleman, had a passion for music. Being one of the richest men in Europe he could afford to indulge this passion with a state-of-the-art music reproduction system. He maintained his own private orchestra, chorus, and five-hundred-seat theater. Presiding over this establishment was the great composer Franz Joseph Haydn. While Esterhazy still lived, however, the mechanization of music reproduction began with the invention of the music box, and today any kid with the price of a Walkman can possess a system that would turn Esterhazy green with envy.

The two systems are not the same, of course. The fidelity of Esterhazy's was, by definition, perfect, while that of the Walkman is only superb. And Esterhazy's system could compose original masterpieces on request, which is no mean feature. But the Walkman has a few advantages of its own that Esterhazy would have greatly admired. It is a lot easier to take to the beach, it requires no maintenance, and it can be relied on not to get the upstairs maid pregnant.

And the Walkman has one capacity that would boggle Esterhazy's mind: it can summon the dead. Do you want to hear Judy Garland sing "Over the Rainbow"? Just insert a cassette, put on the earphones, push a button, and the voice of an artist who has been dust for twenty years fills your head with music.

How has the price of music reproduction changed in two hundred years? I don't know, for the truth is that the two systems cannot be meaningfully compared in economic terms. They are, quite literally, incommensurable. In trying to compare two periods of the industrial era, the problems of comparing these two commodities must be multiplied by the problems presented by thousands of others.

The fact of the matter is that in a period of swift technological change, prices, wages, and the value of capital sums cannot be meaningfully translated over any great distance in time and another means must be found to make economic sense of a past era. It is money, perhaps as much as any other single factor, that makes the past a foreign country.

Because the money of the past cannot be meaningfully translated into a modern economic idiom, the reader must learn to understand the economic language of the past. This is not nearly so difficult as it might sound, for I have tried to provide plenty of signposts along the way.

As this book deals frequently with capital sums of money, it might be noted here that a thousand dollars in mid-Victorian times was a skilled worker's annual wage, sufficient to allow him and his family to live in dignity. A hundred thousand dollars, prudently invested (in government bonds, for instance), was enough to provide an income that would have maintained a family in upper-middle-class comfort, while a million dollars would have made that family a very rich one indeed in the eyes of its contemporaries. Five million dollars was sufficient to make its possessor a major figure on Wall Street if he chose to be. The more than one hundred million dollars that Commodore Vanderbilt left at his death in 1877 made him incomparably the richest man in America and the richest self-made man in the world. Had he ever wanted to, he could easily and single-handedly have precipitated a panic on Wall Street greater than any experienced in the nineteenth century. No man on the Street today approaches that sort of power with his own assets.

The national debt of the United States, vastly increased by the Civil War, stood at about $2.5 billion dollars in 1869, approximately $65 per capita. Today the national debt is nearly a thousand times as large and stands at about $8,800 per capita.

The
Scarlet Woman
of
Wall Street

The Great Game

WHEN the reporter for the New York *Herald* called on Daniel Drew at his house on Union Square on the evening of December 21st, 1870, the latter had been a power on Wall Street for more than thirty years. The reporter had heard that "the Old Man of the Street" had been assaulted near the New York Stock Exchange on Broad Street by an outraged fellow speculator. He had come to get the story.

The winter sun had already set when the reporter made his way through the bustling square, bright with gas lamps and Christmas decorations, alive with the shouts of newsboys and the clip-clop of horses. The handsome house to which he was bound had been built near the corner of 17th Street twenty years earlier, when Union Square had been a newly developed and fashionable residential area. Now commerce was fast overtaking the neighborhood, and Tiffany's, which had already moved uptown several times, had that year opened its latest store on the square itself, just down the block. The wealthy residents already were fleeing to quieter areas farther north.

The reporter was admitted to the house and conducted to the study on the second floor, where he found "Uncle Daniel," as the newspapers often called him, seated in an armchair drawn up close to the fire, deep in a contemplative mood.

Drew's gold-rimmed glasses were pushed up on his forehead. His gray eyes sparkled with the crafty, devious intelligence that still lay behind them. His hair was the same jet black it had been in his youth. In fact, of all his features, only his swarthy skin, deeply creased and wrinkled, revealed his seventy-three years. The reporter thought that the light of the coals burning low in the grate and the dimmed gas lamp just above his head gave Drew "an appearance of venerable dignity quite striking."[1]

Drew admitted cheerfully enough in his odd, reedy voice that Richard Schell, many years his junior, had verbally abused him the other day in broad daylight. "Look at the old rascal," Schell had bellowed to passersby. "He's the villain who's come down here to ruin men by his rascalities. He's the one who's locked up the money so as to bring disasters on others." But Drew only laughed at the idea that he had that sort of power anymore. He knew, if the reporter did not, that his day was nearly done on the Street and that a new breed and new rules were taking over. Still, he could not give up the habits and pleasures of a lifetime and leave the Street to others. Far from it. He would follow the market to the very day he died, for Wall Street was all that Drew really cared about now. Religion may have animated his personality, but it was the Street that stirred his soul.

Daniel Drew had been little more than a boy when he moved to the city from the hillside, hardscrabble farm outside Carmel, New York, where he had been born and where he had received only the most rudimentary education. While he had become one of the most powerful men in New York and moved in its highest business circles, he still affected the clothes, speech, and manners of a country bumpkin and loudly espoused a pious and Bible-thumping form of Methodism. And if throughout his long life Drew had seldom missed an opportunity to praise the Lord, neither had he often forgone a chance to cheat his fellow man. He had founded a major theological seminary, built numerous churches, taught Sunday school, even preached the gospel now and then. But at the same time, by his own proud claim and by common agreement, he had invented and practiced with boundless enthusiasm many of the schemes by which Wall Streeters sought to separate the unwary, and each other, from their assets. If their ways were thought by many to be, in Henry Adams's phrase, both "dark and double," it was

DANIEL DREW   *Courtesy of the Union Club Library*

Daniel Drew who had taught the Street many of the finer points of the game.

•

To a mathematician, a free market such as Daniel Drew and those who followed him found on Wall Street is just another game, featuring rules, players, tactics, and a score. But the score in a free market is kept in money, and while points in football can earn you glory, money can buy you lunch. It is this real-world aspect of the free market that sets it apart from most other games and gives the players a special incentive to cheat.

The little financial market at the southern tip of Manhattan that Drew had found so congenial and profitable in his prime had counted it a busy day when a few thousand shares changed hands. Everyone on Wall Street had known everyone else, and the old market had been almost a private game among friends. The rules had been enforced only by mutual agreement, and no one except the players had paid much attention to it. In this game, dirty pool had been the accepted order of the day and eccentricity had thrived.

Then, almost overnight, Wall Street had become the second-biggest financial market on earth, and by the late 1860's the whole world watched its every move via the telegraph, the newspapers, and the new undersea cable.

Historical forces—the industrial revolution, the telegraph, the Civil War, the geographical advantages of New York City—had suddenly come together to create this great financial free market on Wall Street. The Civil War, like all wars, was largely financed with borrowed money. It expanded the national debt by a factor of ten in only four years, and this money had to be raised in the nation's financial markets. The spread of the telegraph had already allowed these markets to coalesce around the one in Wall Street in the 1840's and '50's, and it was mostly there that this sudden influx of government bonds traded.

In the Wall Street boom engendered by the war and its financing, peer pressure no longer sufficed to keep the players playing by the old rules. But there was no Wall Street institution powerful enough and disinterested enough to devise and enforce a new code of conduct or decide if new strategies developed by the players posed a threat to the game as a whole. The only other possible source of regulation, the government of the State of New York, proved incapable of taking on the task in the postwar atmosphere that enveloped the country.

The American Civil War was the greatest military conflict fought anywhere in the western world in the nineteenth century—the first, overwhelming example of the terrible synergism of war and industrial power. When the rebellion was over, the frightful price that had been paid by the nation (for it cost the lives of fully three of every hundred men) induced a mood of eat-drink-and-be-merry that was strikingly similar to the mood of the world in the 1920's after an even greater and still more terrible war. Nowhere was this spirit felt more keenly or expressed more intensely than in New York, the nation's largest, richest, most glittering city, a city devoted as no other on earth to the gospel of wealth, its acquisition and display.

While foreign immigration and the industrial revolution had profoundly transformed the polity of New York State over the previous twenty-five years, the government had not begun to keep pace. Instead, all three branches of the state government, along with the New York City government, had sunk into a pit of corruption. Politicians and judges succumbed to the easy profits that could be made by selling one's office to the highest bidder. They had little fear of being called to account, for the newspapers were only beginning to discover their power to investigate, and therefore regulate, government. Daniel Drew, when he found himself in a tight place, had been that highest bidder more than once.

•

Thus, for a few short years, Wall Street's financial market was not only free but nearly totally unregulated as well. During this period Wall Street saw capitalism red in tooth and claw, and men found themselves free to play the great game for keeps: all moves were possible, all strategies fair, *caveat emptor* the only reliable guide.

Into this maelstrom of opportunity and peril there swept fools and optimists, crooks and mystics, predators and plungers. Most, of course, were ordinary men who met ordinary fates. But among them were a few of genius, endowed far beyond the common run with sagacity, courage, wit, determination, and élan. These men pursued their perceived self-interests with incomparable skill and zeal, constrained only by the varying extent to which they each possessed a personal sense of honor and by the natural, ineluctable laws of the marketplace. Daniel Drew had been one of the most famous of these men, and reporters called on him regularly to learn what was happening on Wall Street.

"I didn't put much [into the scheme]," he told the *Herald* reporter, explaining the operation that had artificially raised the cost of short-term money and outraged Schell. ". . . I put by some—one or two millions. Why, if what little money I had could raise the devil in Wall Street, what would ten or fifteen millions do?" But Drew was being characteristically disingenuous, for he knew very well what ten or fifteen million could do and had once played with such sums himself when he had been the treasurer of the Erie Railway.

The stocks and bonds of this company had long been a favorite means with which to play the market, and no one had known them better than Uncle Daniel. The battles fought to control this enterprise became known as the Erie Wars, and the tactics and strategies employed by the players—always interesting, sometimes deplorable, often hilarious—were described in newspapers, magazines, books, and poetry.

To most people of that time the world of Wall Street was only a distant, if entertaining, abstraction. But so many investors in Erie securities, whether they had been lured by the mostly illusory speculative charms or by the very real economic potential, found the effects of the wars to be so devastating to their fortunes that the Erie Railway came to be known to history as the Scarlet Woman of Wall Street.

The Erie Wars, however, changed Wall Street. With the whole world watching, and the continued growth and profitability of a by now vast brokerage business at stake, formal rules were fast replacing informal understandings, and treachery was no longer considered just part of the game. The New York Stock Exchange was coming to dominate Wall Street and to enforce its rules on everyone; brokers, not speculators, were beginning to call the shots.

The brokers, who pursued small profits on many transactions, had a stake in preserving the game itself; speculators looked no further than the next big killing. Drew, who had once been a broker but had become a speculator, now deplored "this idea of selling on . . . one-quarter and one-half per cent profit"; to him that was business, not fun. The Wall Street he had known was slipping away into the past, and a new one, greatly larger, more formal, and for the individual investor less perilous, was taking its place.

The great speculator may well have sensed that in this new environment he was playing a long, losing end game. And this winter evening, looking into the fire "as if each burning ember was a Wall Street mystery of the present day which he was striving to solve," Drew seemed at last to be the old man that time said he was.

"Why, just think of it," he said in wonder, half to himself and half to the *Herald* reporter who stood there in the flickering fire-light, "there are at least two hundred millions of stock down there, and, mind you, all of it for sale, and *all of it for sale.*"

Chapter One

The Rise
of
Wall Street

THE financial market in which Daniel Drew spent much of his life was hardly older than he was, but the thoroughfare with which they are both forever associated is far more ancient. The Dutch, at the beginning of the seventeenth century, invented modern financial markets in order to facilitate their burgeoning world trade, and it was the Dutch at nearly the same time who first laid out Wall Street, or at least put up a brush fence "to keep the Indians out and the cattle in"[1] along where Wall Street would shortly run. In 1652 the government of Nieuw Amsterdam decided that a proper wall was required, not so much to defend against Indian attack, for the local tribes had seldom caused much trouble, as to defend against the English settlers of New England, who were beginning to covet the little settlement located in the middle of so splendid a harbor.

The wall that was to give Wall Street its name was paid for, not altogether inappropriately, with money raised by means of an unsecured loan, but it never protected the town from anything. When the crisis came in 1664, Nieuw Amsterdam was attacked by the British from the sea and surrendered without a shot being fired. In 1698, the year that the first Trinity Church was built at the western end of the little street, the wall, already in disrepair, was torn down.

Two years later a new city hall was constructed on Wall Street at the head of Broad, and throughout much of the eighteenth century Wall Street's western end, anchored by Trinity Church and City Hall, was one of the city's most fashionable residential streets. At the other end, where it sloped down to meet the East River, it was already given over to business. Slaves—those staples of seventeenth- and eighteenth-century commerce—were the first commodity to be regularly traded on Wall Street, in a market located at Wall and Pearl streets, where the shoreline then was, before landfill pushed it three blocks farther east.

Until the American Revolution and the establishment of a strong federal government in the 1780's, there were no full-time financial markets in New York or elsewhere in North America because there were few if any financial instruments to be traded. But, when the Constitution came into effect in 1789 and George Washington was inaugurated at the New York City Hall, which had been taken over as a temporary federal capitol, there was an urgent need to deal with the financial chaos into which the country had been sinking. Washington appointed Alexander Hamilton to be the first Secretary of the Treasury. Hamilton proposed to regularize the coinage of the country and to assume the state debts that had been incurred during the Revolution.

These state-issued bonds had depreciated considerably in the inflation that had accompanied the war, as had the paper currency issued by the Continental Congress, which Hamilton also proposed to redeem. Even so there was considerable doubt that any of this paper would ever be redeemed—and much of it had fallen into the hands of speculators willing to gamble on Hamilton's program's being adopted. There was a good deal of sentiment in the country, led and given voice by Thomas Jefferson, that these speculators should not profit at the expense of those who had patriotically bought the bonds or taken the currency and then sold them for much less than their face value.

Hamilton argued that one of the primary purposes in establishing a strong central government was to give people faith in the financial structure of the country and in the soundness of the currency and financial instruments of the government. The only way to do that, he maintained, was to establish beyond doubt the sanctity of the obligations that had already been incurred. If the government could repudiate this debt, the Secretary said, then it would always be thought capable of repudiating later debt, and the country would suffer accordingly. Washington backed Hamilton, and the Congress voted that the Revolutionary War debt be refunded with new federal bonds paying 6 percent interest.

Hamilton had succeeded in establishing a vital precedent for the future of Wall Street: that the United States Government would stand behind its financial instruments and not repudiate them for political reasons. This precedent greatly facilitated the establishment of financial markets in the United States and, perhaps more than any other factor, fostered their growth. Hamilton's program both established a body of rock-solid securities that could be traded and removed a great uncertainty that had been hanging over the country. And it is uncertainty—far more than disaster—that unnerves and weakens markets.

•

Trading in the new federal bonds as well as state bonds sold to finance internal improvements soon began, and markets sprang up to accommodate the buyers and sellers. At first, trading in these markets was handled by brokers who ordinarily dealt in regular commodities. In New York, if the weather was nice, these brokers would meet to talk and trade on Wall Street or an adjacent street such as Pearl, then the city's mercantile center. One of their favorite spots was beneath a buttonwood tree that stood in front of 68 Wall Street. (Buttonwood trees, now much more commonly called sycamores, are the native North American cousin of the London plane tree, so common a present-day feature of New York City streets.)

By 1792 the financial market was growing, and brokers began to specialize in the trading of financial instruments. A group of the more important of them decided that at least a minimum of organization was required, and twenty-four of them drew up an agreement, setting minimum rates and pledging preference to each other, which they signed beneath the buttonwood tree.

The next year the newly formed market—it would not even have a formal name for another quarter of a century—established itself at the Tontine Coffee House at the northwest corner of Wall and William streets. This agreement constituted the first brokers' organization in the country, but there were soon others, and Philadelphia, in 1800, was the first city to organize a real stock exchange.

Philadelphia, then the country's largest city, became the nation's capital in 1790. It was there that Hamilton established the first Bank of the United States, modeled on the Bank of England and intended by Hamilton to function like its model as a central bank. When the federal government moved to its permanent location in the District of Columbia in 1800, the bank stayed behind in bustling Philadelphia rather than accompany the government to the wilderness that was early Washington. The presence of the central bank as well as several of the country's largest commercial banks ensured that Philadelphia, not New York, would hold the early lead as the country's financial center.

But New York was growing quickly, and its financial community was growing with it. By 1817 it was recognized that a formal organization was needed to handle the growing trade in stocks and bonds efficiently, and the leading brokers of the day established the New York Stock and Exchange Board, a title it would bear until the reorganizations of the 1860's transformed it into the New York Stock Exchange. Under its constitution the stock board operated very much like a private club. Initiation fees were minimal, but all members were entitled to vote on new admissions to the board, and three blackballs were enough to exclude an applicant. These applicants were, of course, potential competition, and many more were blackballed than admitted to what was still far more a brokerage trust than a stock exchange. Those brokers who could not or would not join the Stock and Exchange Board simply carried on their business outside of it and were not greatly inconvenienced by their lack of membership.

The sessions of the board were supposed to be held in secret but, because brokerage is a business in which timely information is very nearly everything, it is not surprising that the secrecy tended to be very short-lived. (At one time nonmember brokers even paid for the privilege of listening at the door.) Because of the board's exclusivity, much stock trading on Wall Street took place outside the board itself, not only among brokers who were not members of the board, but among members themselves after hours and in securities that were not listed on the board. Some of the nonmember brokers were insubstantial indeed. "Their offices, when they have offices," William Worthington Fowler wrote in 1870, "are merely desk-rooms in upper lofts or murky basements. More generally the flooring of their office is the sidewalk and its ceiling the firmament."[2]

In boom times, the total volume of stocks and bonds that were traded on the Street—often quite literally on the street—would greatly exceed the volume traded on the board. From time to time rival exchanges would emerge from this activity, and sometimes these were absorbed by the board. More often they just withered away when the financial climate, or even the weather, turned colder. The last of these outdoor exchanges, which was organized only in the 1920's and is now known officially as the American Stock Exchange, is still known to some of the older generation on Wall Street as "the Curb." Today's nearest equivalent to the old curb market is entirely electronic and called the "over-the-counter" market.

In the early days of Wall Street the number of securities traded on the board was very limited, with government bonds dominating the list. Often, the volume was limited as well: the low point in Stock Board activity was most likely on March 16th, 1830, when a grand total of thirty-one shares changed hands. The trading method used by the board was very different from today's continuous auction at a number of trading posts (a system that, in fact, evolved from the trading that took place on the street, where each lamppost was dedicated to the action in particular stocks).

Rather, two formal trading sessions were held per day. The morning session, usually the more important of the two, began at ten o'clock, when the presiding officer rose and read out, one by one, the names of securities that were listed on the board. "The assembled brokers," wrote James K. Medbery in 1870, "with their budget of orders, wait expectant; and the instant a stock is reached that is in their day's book, they spring into the arena with a bid or an offer. When a 'speculative' or favorite stock is called, the excitement deepens, and the air is rent with rival cries. The presiding officer repeats the transactions to the Assistant Secretary at his side, who at once records them, while the 'marker' or blackboard clerk writes off the prices upon the tablet at the head of the room."[3] It was this blackboard that gave stock boards their name. The New York Stock Exchange, once called the Regular Board, has long been known as the Big Board.

•

Daniel Drew was born on July 29th, 1797, five years after the buttonwood agreement was signed and only sixty miles from Wall Street. But at the turn of the nineteenth century sixty miles was a hard, expensive, all-day-long journey by stagecoach, then the fastest means of land transportation. Carmel, New York, located in the part

CURBSTONE BROKERS   In the 1860's at least as much stock trading took place on the street as on the Exchange itself.

of southern Dutchess County from which the present Putnam County was formed in 1812, was then thought to be very deep in the countryside.

Daniel was born when his parents were already far along in life, his father, Gilbert, being sixty-five and his mother, the former Catherine Laurence, thirty-nine and her husband's second wife. While there is not enough data to make firm judgments, it seems likely that the Drew household was not a particularly happy one. Drew's mother had earned her living as a weaver and had married and borne children very late in life by the standards of the eighteenth century. It is possible she married her aged husband only because she realized that he and his hundred acres of poor farmland were the best she was going to do and resented the fact accordingly.[4] But there is no doubt that Daniel much loved his mother, and he spoke of her with affection all his life.

Unlike Westchester County to the south and Dutchess to the north, Putnam was never a rich agricultural area; its short, steep hills were good mainly for cattle grazing. The Drew farm was certainly a hand-to-mouth proposition all during the years that Daniel was growing up (although in 1807 his father managed to exchange the farm where Daniel was born, and where he held only a tenancy, for one that he owned). With little money to pay for schooling— free public schools were still years in the future—Daniel never learned more than reading, writing, and simple arithmetic. And it would seem that neither in school nor at home did Daniel Drew ever learn much about the idea of honor. His mother certainly taught him early to fear damnation and therefore to observe punctiliously the outward forms of Christianity, but the ethical core of his religion appears to have escaped him entirely.

To earn extra money, he worked for the circuses that had their winter quarters in the nearby Westchester towns of Somers and North Salem, and he probably toured with one or more of them as well, learning at an early age the arts of the huckster and barker that he would later put to such profitable use on Wall Street.[5]

In 1812, when Daniel was fourteen, his father died at the age of eighty and war broke out with Great Britain. Drew joined the army as a substitute in order to collect the $100 bonus that was being offered as an inducement. As it happened, the British did not choose to mount a serious attack on well-defended New York, and Drew never saw action. But he had saved his substitution money, and it would prove his ticket out of Putnam County. Over the course of the next fifty years Daniel Drew would turn that $100 into a fortune that at one time amounted—at least by his reckoning—to more than $16,000,000.

Knowing his way around the farms of Putnam County, Drew became a drover, buying cattle from the local farmers and driving them to market in New York City. At both ends of the trail, Drew soon acquired a reputation as a sharp, devious, and frequently unscrupulous trader.

Moving cattle before the development of canals and railroads was a time-consuming, expensive, and, for both the men and the meat involved, toughening experience. It could take as long as a week to drive cattle from Putnam County to New York along the rutted paths that then passed for all but the best of roads. The cattle that were driven from the north usually crossed the Harlem River over the King's Bridge—which gave a section of the Bronx its name—and were then herded down the Boston Post Road, which ran to the city roughly along the route now taken by Third Avenue. Often the drovers would spend the final night of the drive at an inn located on the main street of the village of Harlem, at what is now 125th Street and Third Avenue, which had corrals to handle the cattle. The next day the herd would be driven to market on the Bowery and sold to the city's butchers.

Toward the end of one of these drives, according to a Wall Street legend so ancient and so universally accepted that it might as well be true even though it almost certainly is not, Drew had an idea. The night before the final drive down to the Bowery, Drew gave the cattle all the salt they would lick but denied them any water. The next morning he began the final drive down the Boston Post Road. The herd moved along its thirsty way until it reached a bridge over a stream that then flowed through the meadows of upper Manhattan and now runs somewhere beneath 77th Street. The desperate cattle swarmed into the stream and sucked up bellyfuls of water. When they had had their fill, Drew drove them as quickly as he could into town and sold them, on the hoof and by the pound, to Henry Astor, John Jacob's brother and one of the city's leading wholesale butchers.

Given the fact that cattle have been a staple item of commerce for at least five thousand years, it seems unlikely that no one had thought of this particular scam before Drew. And Drew is unlikely to have sacrificed his reputation with his customers for such a short-term benefit. But he has the credit for it—if that is the term—and his association with it is certainly responsible for bringing the term "watered stock" to Wall Street.

These drives, typically, would start with eight or nine hundred head of cattle, and it was not unusual to lose two or even three hundred along the way to accidents, straying, and casual rustling. "I was rarely in those days off my horse's back," Drew remembered years later. "It was all-day work riding about the country and buying the cattle, and all-night work driving them to the city."[6]

One day, while inspecting some cattle, Drew was caught in a violent storm and very nearly killed by lightning, which did kill his horse. There is nothing like coming close to a lightning bolt to give one the sense of having come close to God or, at the very least, eternity. This experience certainly increased Drew's already intense interest in fire-and-brimstone religion and his equally intense, if much better-contained, piety.

Many among those who knew him doubted the genuineness of Drew's religious beliefs. Henry Clews, a major broker who played the great game for seventy years and left a long, gossipy, and frequently inaccurate memoir, thought it was sheer hypocrisy that animated his old acquaintance.[7]

But E. C. Stedman, who watched Drew at work from an equally close vantage point and was a much more discerning man, could not accept this explanation. "Ethical teachers," he wrote in his history of the New York Stock Exchange, "are frequently known to impress upon those committed to their care the necessity of taking their religion into the routine of daily life. Among the characteristics of 'Uncle Daniel' Drew was the capacity to carry his religion whithersoever he went without any laudable effect upon either his religion or his life. He seemed actually to draw aid and inspiration from his faith for the execution of the schemes in which he appeared at his worst. This was not the fruit of hypocrisy, which, not among the most common of vices, is quite within the range of ordinary experience. But Drew, in the first place, had no practical use for it. If he needed support for any of his commercial or speculative—it would be harsh to say piratical—enterprises, he did not seek it from persons likely to be attracted by his spiritual fervor. That fervor he really possessed. His contemporaries admitted its existence even while loudly exclaiming at its failure to bring forth righteous fruits."[8]

James Medbery, who probably did not know Drew personally but was an acute observer of the Wall Street scene, was equally bemused by the apparent ease with which Drew managed to contain two seemingly incompatible attributes. "Mr. Drew is singularly lacking in popularity," he wrote in 1870. "The belief that he never hesitates to sacrifice his friends, if the necessities of speculation require it, is entertained with such unanimity in the money-quarter, and is illustrated by so many anecdotes, that one is compelled to acquiesce in it. This foible is the more salient on account of the genuine piety of the man. All who have heard him speak at Methodist conferences are struck by the fine religious fervor and earnestness of his demeanor."[9]

Drew always acted exactly as though he truly believed God to be his silent partner in financial speculations and that his loyalty to Him—perhaps even his fiduciary duty—superseded any of his earthly alliances. Drew, wrote Stedman, "seemed unwilling to entrap the public by an ingenious device or to desert an old friend for a new ally without first invoking supra-mundane assistance."[10] He certainly always acted as if he had God's blessing tucked away in his inside pocket. Asked if he had trouble sleeping at night he replied, "Sir, I have never lost a night's rest on account of business in my life."[11]

With or without the assistance of the deity, Drew prospered in the cattle trade for nearly twenty years, ranging farther and farther afield in search of livestock. On one of his later forays he brought two thousand head all the way from Ohio, taking two months to accomplish the drive and selling the herd for a profit of twelve dollars a head when he reached New York.[12]

By 1820 Drew was well enough established to get married and chose for his bride Roxanna Mead, the sister of his brother Thomas's wife. She was a local Putnam County girl—Mead is still a common family name in the area—and even less educated than her husband. In the early days of her marriage she signed her name with an X, a style to which she would revert in her old age. Perhaps because Drew had few if any real friends, almost nothing is known about his domestic situation, though one contemporary wrote that it was a happy marriage and that "his home-life . . . runs like a golden thread through his entire career."[13] The marriage lasted fifty-six years, until her death in 1876, and produced three children, a son and two daughters, one of whom died in infancy.

With a growing family, Drew probably became less willing to lead the hard and semi-vagabond life of a drover, and used some of his accumulating profits in 1829 to buy the Bull's Head Inn, located at what is now Third Avenue and 26th Street. Still a considerable distance from town, the area was then becoming the new center for the growing city's cattle market.

Drew found the occupation of catering to the needs of other drovers even more profitable than being a drover himself, and he soon began to provide services beyond those ordinarily expected of an innkeeper. For one thing he often functioned as their banker to save the drovers the trip downtown to Wall Street, which could easily take an hour each way. It was by acting as an informal banker that Drew first became acquainted with the Street and first felt its fascination. The Wall Street of the 1830's and Daniel Drew were made for each other.

•

Stockbrokers have always tended to be a raucous and rambunctious group, and the members of the New York Stock and Exchange Board, substantial, even important citizens though they often were, were no exceptions.

"No body of men," wrote Medbery, "are to appearance more fond of breaking over minor rules, and promptly meeting the penalty, than New York stockbrokers. The annual dues of the Exchange are only fifty dollars, but the fines of individual members not seldom mount up to nearly ten times that sum. Any interruption of the presiding officer while calling stocks renders a broker liable to a penalty, 'not less than twenty-five cents' for each offense. To smoke a cigar within the Exchange costs five dollars. Non-attendance at special meetings subjects one to a fine of anything under five dollars. A broker cannot stand on a table or chair without being amerced ten dollars. It costs twelve and a half cents to call up a stock not on the regular list, and all the way from one to five dollars to do anything not enumerated in these offenses which may be deemed indecorous by the presiding officer."[14]

Stockbrokers in Wall Street's early days enjoyed a very dubious reputation in the eyes of other Americans. William Armstrong, who wrote one of the earliest guides to Wall Street's ways in 1848, dedicated his book "to the Rev. Orville Dewey, D.D., author of a series of discourses on The Morals of Trade" because, Armstrong felt, here was "a business whose votaries particularly require moral admonitions."[15]

Medbery, writing twenty years later, when stockbroking had become big business and a good deal more awesome, if still not altogether respectable in the eyes of the public, reported that in the beginning "a stock operator was regarded somewhat as lottery dealers are at present. In rural cities and villages the summer visit of brokers was an occasion of suspicion. At watering places solid merchants warned their dames and daughters against these *ignes fatui* of wealth in the same terms of denunciation which opulence assumes toward social adventurers. . . . The great capitalists of the nation . . . so far acquiesced in the prevailing opinion as to seek to cloak their intercourse with what was already known as 'the Street.' The great majority of brokers made it their pride that they performed a purely commission business. However much in the secret ledgers of their offices the outward assumption lacked confirmation, they claimed to be high priests of the ideal in stock market transactions."[16]

There were many reasons why brokers had so low a reputation. One was that it was noticed early on that outsiders venturing into Wall Street in search of speculation were very much more likely to emerge poorer than richer. At a time when there was no regulation of the securities industry, many men on the Street who called themselves brokers were little, if anything, more than con men. The real business of these men was not brokerage but separating fools—then as now not an endangered species—from their money. Even reputable brokers were, from time to time, not above employing tricks "which so often make the outsiders, if not the angels, weep."[17]

Another, more powerful reason was that the ways of Wall Street seemed so mysterious, a word that occurs over and over in early accounts. The stock market did not deal in such commodities as wheat or cotton, whose practical uses were manifest, but in bits of paper, many of which were nothing more than promises of future action. "All the principal values of commerce," Fowler wrote, "are in this mart represented by so many paper certificates. The goods and credit of the merchant are represented by promissory notes, which are bought and sold, and pass from hand to hand, almost like bank-bills. Cotton, pork, grain, sugar, tobacco, and a thousand other bulky and gross products are represented under the form of warehouse certificates. The wealth of banks, of railway corporations, and many other stock companies, are floating about under the guise of certificates, and to the very gold in the vaults of the Treasury, wings are given, and coin and bullion fly in notes of yellow and green."[18]

Today, we are so used to dealing with paper money and checks, not to mention money in all its myriad electronic and plastic forms, that we usually forget the inherently promissory nature of nearly all of it. A hundred and fifty years ago the situation was entirely different. In the 1830's, if it wasn't gold or silver, it wasn't really money.

The prices at which all this paper traded seemed to fluctuate, often violently, without apparent rhyme or reason. A great many people in the dawn of capitalism felt that Wall Street, far from being a vital mechanism of the economic system, was really nothing more than an elaborate game of three-card monte. "The moralist and philosopher," Fowler thought, "look upon it as a gambling den—a cage of unclean birds, an abomination where men drive a horrible trade, fattening and battening on the substance of their friends and neighbors—or perhaps as a kind of modern Coliseum where gladiatorial combats are joined, and bulls, bears, and other ferocious beasts gore and tear each other for the public amusements."[19] It would be the moralists and philosophers, not the brokers and speculators, who would come to write the early history of the Street. Their ignorant, sometimes willful, prejudice about the market would be taken as holy writ by historians until very recent times.

And certainly Wall Street attracted in droves men who today would be called pathological gamblers. "No one who has entered the precincts of the Stock Exchange," wrote Fowler, who himself played the market with enormous enthusiasm (but made his fortune writing about it), "will have failed to notice certain nondescripts who constantly frequent the market. They are men who have seen better days, but having dropped their money in the Street, come there every day as if they hoped to find it in the same place. These characters are the ghosts of the market, fixing their lack-lustre eyes upon it, and pointing their skinny fingers at it, as if they would say 'thou hast done this!' They flit about the doorways and haunt the vestibules of the Exchange, seedy of coat, blackingless of boot, unkempt, unwashed, unshorn, wearing on their worn and haggard faces a smile more melancholy than tears."[20]

•

Although Drew soon began to operate in Wall Street on his own account, he was not yet ready to give his full attention to it and apparently preferred to bide his time while he invested his surplus capital in the steamboats that were beginning to proliferate in New York's many waters. In 1834 he invested a thousand dollars in the *Water Witch*, which ran on the Hudson from New York to Peeks-

THE END OF A SPECULATOR Victorian morality saw poverty, heartbreak, and early death as the inevitable result of all excesses.

kill and back, and by 1836 he was the principal owner of the *West-chester* and the *Emerald.*

Steamboating was an intensely competitive business. The individual owners soon sought to regulate the competition by forming cartels, and the cartels often evolved into full-fledged companies. New competitors would either be forced off the route in a price war or force the cartel to buy them out or take them in. With Drew it was the last, and the Hudson River Association, as the cartel was called—it would soon become the People's Line—made him not only a partner but also one of its directors.

Having joined the club, Drew saw no reason whatever not to swindle the other members. He soon laid on a new boat in competition, with the captain's brother acting as the dummy owner, and urged the board of directors to buy off this new threat. His fellow directors agreed with Drew's proposal, determined on a price, and sent Drew off to negotiate. Having no one to negotiate with except himself, Drew merely walked around the block, it seems, and then reported back that the new competitor insisted on $8,000 more to make a deal. The board of directors reluctantly agreed.[21] Such behavior, while it would certainly have been decried by those adversely affected by it, was not then uncommon, and many thought of it as just part of the game. Drew's reputation in the steamboat business was the same as it had been in the cattle business—that of a tough, shrewd, clever manipulator, but not a crook.

In 1836 Drew formed the brokerage partnership of Drew, Robinson and Company, and for a number of years it was a very successful and respected brokerage house. Three years later he sold the Bull's Head Inn and left the cattle business behind, moving into the city proper to a new house at 52 Bleecker Street, just east of Broadway in what was then the fashionable heart of the city.

Drew's personality and his idiosyncratic morality were already well developed. The ensuing years would only turn them into legend. "He was a curious combination," William Croffut wrote only a few years after Drew's death, "of simplicity and cunning, of boldness and cowardice, of frankness and secretiveness, of honesty and unscrupulousness, of superstition and faithlessness."[22]

Physically he was well above average height, standing five feet ten inches tall, with broad, stooping shoulders and eyes that were notably bright and active, "shining like Bessemer steel."[23] "His form is slender, but lithe and agile," the Reverend McClintock wrote in the *Ladies' Repository* in 1859, by which time Drew was over sixty.

"His head is well shaped, with predominance in the reflective and observing organs; his eye clear and keen; his features strongly marked; his general expression mild, but firm."[24] Henry Clews, who knew Drew well from the course of business and liked him not at all, wrote that "his general demeanor was bland, good-natured and insinuating, with affected but well dissembled humility, which was highly calculated to disarm any resentment and enable him to move smoothly in society among all shades and conditions of men. He has often been mistaken for a country deacon."[25]

Drew's resemblance to a country deacon could only have been deliberate, for in mid-nineteenth-century New York anything rural was the very antithesis of fashion. Men moving to the city worked hard to shed their country clothes, ways, and accents as quickly as possible. But Drew cultivated, even gloried, in his.

And while at one time Daniel Drew "could command more ready cash at short notice than any man in Wall Street, or probably than any man in America,"[26] he spent little of it on personal appearance. His clothes were usually old, and often just plain slovenly. In his old age, when he needed a cane, he sometimes used a broken umbrella. Although he would endow many churches and found a theological seminary, Drew was careful with his charity and was often the unforthcoming target of appeals for funds.

Drew's eccentricities, needless to say, were the subject of endless discussion and amusement. For all his oddities, however, Drew did not seem as peculiar to his contemporaries as he does to us, for there were widely known contemporary precedents, and he looked and sounded like a character that had stepped out of a Dickens novel (although he almost certainly never read one). When something amused him—his enemies thought another person's misfortune to be his favorite joke—he would give vent "to short laughs which sound like the cackle of a hen thrown suddenly off from her propriety."[27] Drew's thin, reedy voice was instantly recognizable, and so was his grammar. " 'Uncle Daniel,' " wrote Stedman, "was not only uneducated but as illiterate as any one could be who mingled with men capable of speaking fair English."[28]

Yet mingle he did, and as early as 1859 he joined the Union Club, which, only twenty-three years old, was already a bastion of the city's business, political, and legal élite, and was ensconced in the grandest clubhouse in the country, at Fifth Avenue and 21st Street.

If Drew's acquaintances made fun of his background, clothes, education, and religion, no one made fun of his brains. "We have said his intellect was subtle," wrote Fowler when Drew had already become the stuff of myth but was still a major player on Wall Street. "The word *subtle* does not altogether express it. It should be *vulpine*. His is the intellect of a fox of the antediluvian period. . . . He covers his tracks and takes to the water, the underbrush or the open country as circumstances may require. Traps innumerable have been set for him, but he generally eludes them, or if caught has broken away, though sometimes torn and bloody, from jaws that thirsted for his blood (or, what is much the same, his money). The hounds of the Street for twenty years have been following his track, now in silence and now baying in deep-mouthed chorus when they run him to earth, but his twistings and doublings and countless devices have foiled them."[29]

Being a great con man, Uncle Daniel was necessarily a great actor. It was part of his stock-in-trade. When several members of "an uptown club"—almost certainly the Union Club—gave Drew a pummeling in the stock of the Chicago & Northwestern Railroad, they kidded him about it unmercifully in the course of the badinage so characteristic of men's clubs. Drew, who did not like to lose and certainly did not like to be kidded, waited for his opportunity.

One evening when several of the brokers were there, Drew walked into the Union Club's new brownstone clubhouse apparently in a state of some agitation. "He appeared to be looking after some man," Clews reported, "and though invited to remain, he seemed to be in a great hurry to get away, and was apparently excited and warm. He seemed to have something important on hand. He drew a big white handkerchief out of his pocket a few times and wiped the perspiration from his heated brow. When he was about to depart there came out of his pocket with the handkerchief a small slip of white paper which floated around apparently unseen by him, and alighted at the feet of one of the bystanders, who quickly set his foot upon it. When Mr. Drew made his exit the white scrap of paper was instantly scanned. It contained these ominous words in his own handwriting, 'buy all the Oshkosh stock you can get at any price you can get it below par.' "

Oshkosh, according to Clews (himself a fellow member of the Union Club), had been rising, and the wisdom on the Street was that it was a good sale. But, reasoned the brokers gathered around the slip of paper, if Drew thought it a buy, then they had no business to argue. They formed a pool to buy thirty thousand shares of Oshkosh the next day. They bought it from a broker they knew

Drew had never used, but (alas for them) he was using then, and the stock tumbled "at the rate of twelve points a day."[30]

Drew had come to be known on Wall Street as the "Great Bear" because of his love of operating in a falling market and because his speculative schemes were mostly designed to make money through other people's misfortunes. "Drew," wrote Fowler, "is a most robust architect of panics."[31] Still, he added, "well too does he deserve the title of the 'merry old gentleman' of Wall Street. In his most earnest operations he never seems to lose sight of 'the fun of the thing.' "[32] Drew's fun, to be sure, was mostly at other people's expense.

While Drew would long continue to have other interests, such as the Stonington Line of steamships, Wall Street more and more became the center of his life as the great game's fascination tightened its grip on his soul. His fortune grew rapidly in these years and so did the Street, for the picturesque little seaport that Drew had known in his youth had disappeared, and a sprawling, raw, brownstone metropolis had risen in its place. Manhattan Island was in the midst of the greatest urban metamorphosis in history.

CHAPTER TWO

The Great Boom Town

THE New York of today is the last city-state, the Venice, writ large, of the western hemisphere, shorn only of sovereignty. Alone of the world's dozen or so cosmopolises New York is not now and, with one trivial exception, never has been a national or even state capital. Thus, while the glories of London and Paris are largely the deliberate expression of the power and majesty of great nations, the glories of New York—its museums, its library, its theaters and opera houses, its boulevards and parks, its architectural magnificence—are solely an expression of the power and majesty of its own citizens.

Like Venice, New York is a bride of the sea. Situated on an archipelago, with only the Bronx a part of the mainland, New York possesses the largest and finest harbor on the North Atlantic. At the turn of the nineteenth century, its citizens found themselves directly athwart a burgeoning trade route connecting the industrial strength of England and the boundless natural resources of the nascent American nation. Battening upon this expanding trade, the city's population began to grow rapidly, and the commercial and financial interests of its people spread ever wider throughout the region, the country, and the world. By the 1820's New York had become the greatest boom town the world has ever known.

•

At the end of his life, in the 1890's, the builder William Torrey remembered that in his childhood, in the first decade of the century, "all above Grand Street was country." It was not thought at the time that that situation would change much for some while to come. But as early as the 1840's Torrey was building the first London Terrace on West 23rd Street, more than two miles north of Grand.

To be sure, it had been thought that New York would grow as the country grew, but no one foresaw just how much more rapid New York City's expansion in fact would be. The city government itself thought that it would be "centuries" before development would extend as far north as the village of Harlem. It was Torrey's own father, a city alderman, who, in 1811, suggested facing the back of the new City Hall with brownstone rather than marble. He argued that the building was so far uptown few would ever see its back and the city could save $15,000 thereby. The Board of Aldermen happily adopted the idea. It would be the 1850's—by which time the city would be built up as far north as 34th Street—before the back of City Hall matched the front and sides.[1]

Most of the elements that were to transform the city so suddenly were already in place. The harbor was beyond compare, with hundreds of miles of shore front, deep channels, easy access, and wide bays. Moreover, it was perfectly positioned, much closer to the open sea than either Baltimore or Philadelphia, and much more centrally located than Boston. In an age when freight moved by water or did not move at all, New York's proximity to Long Island Sound and the Hudson and Connecticut rivers gave it access to the markets and produce of upstate New York, southern New England, and Long Island.

But not yet in existence was the crucial element, the catalyst that would produce New York's commercial hegemony and all that would flow from that hegemony: the Erie Canal, perhaps the most consequential public work ever constructed.

When it was completed in 1825 after eight years of building, the canal gave the city access to the Great Lakes and to the markets and produce of the Middle West, which had been blocked by the Appalachian Mountains and forced to move via the Mississippi River through New Orleans. The economic effect of the canal upon the city was immediate and enormous. It was no wonder: before the canal was built, a ton of flour in Buffalo, worth $40, could be transported overland to New York in three weeks at a cost of $120. The same ton could be transported via the Erie Canal in eight days at a cost of $6, one-twentieth the old cost and in one-third the time. All other commodities benefited similarly.[2]

At the dedication ceremonies of the canal a speaker said, "There will be no limits to your lucrative extension of trade and commerce. The Valley of the Mississippi will soon pour its treasures in this great emporium through the channels now formed and forming."[3] He was right, and New York's share of the country's fast-growing foreign commerce rose from 9 percent in 1800 to 62 percent in 1860.[4] By the Civil War, New York was the leading seaport for the export of all but seven of the thousand different commodities kept track of by the U.S. Customs, and the chief destination for all but twenty-four imports.[5] The Bostonian Oliver Wendell Holmes, Sr., grumpily complained that New York had become "that tongue that is licking up the cream of commerce and finance of a continent."

More and more people moved into the city to exploit the soaring economic opportunities, first from upstate New York, New England, and the other nearby states, and then, from the 1840's on, from Europe. New York's population rose by a factor of twenty between 1800 and 1860. Because of its location at the foot of a long and narrow island, the city could grow only northward, and so it began its headlong rush up Manhattan.

While growth fluctuated with the boom-and-bust cycle that characterized the nineteenth-century economy, it never ceased entirely, and the city grew northward at a rate that averaged two blocks a year. (Given the fact that Manhattan is about two miles wide, that means that the city was adding well over ten miles of developed street front per year.) This colossal building boom can best be seen by following the movement of what might be called the locus of fashion. In 1800 the city's upper class lived on lower Broadway in the area of Bowling Green and on Wall Street. By the 1820's the locus had moved up to the City Hall area, and by the thirties the places to live were Broadway and Lafayette Place in the area of Bond and Bleecker streets, exactly the area to which Daniel Drew moved in 1839.

Just as Broadway angles westward at 10th Street, so did fashion, moving into Washington and Union squares in the 1840's. Toward the end of the decade it began the march up Fifth Avenue that would reach as far as the northern end of Central Park by the turn

THE WEST SIDE DOCKS   Steamships usually used the Hudson River, while sailing ships used the East River, where the prevailing winds made docking easier.

of the twentieth century. As fashion left an area and moved uptown, retail commerce—first-class hotels and fancy stores—followed right behind, tearing down or adapting the old residences. Less-fashionable areas east and west of Broadway and Fifth Avenue were taken over by manufacturing and warehouses or declined into slums. As the hotels and stores followed fashion uptown, the wholesale business area expanded into the areas vacated by the retailers. Thus there were three successive waves of construction and alteration that swept over nineteenth-century Manhattan, giving the city an air of being in a state of perpetual construction, an image it has never entirely lost.

In order to regulate the city's growth in some coherent way, the government in 1811 produced the grid plan for the areas of the city not yet developed. This plan ignored both the better aspects of city planning as it was understood at the time and the nature of Manhattan's hilly, granitic geography. Rather, as the plan itself forthrightly stated, it was adopted because "straight-sided and right-angled houses are the most cheap to build and the most convenient to live in." It was a plan, in other words, that only real-estate speculators could love, and they took it to their collective bosom with a passion.

Real-estate speculation consumed the city's affluent throughout the nineteenth century and was the foundation of many of New York's great fortunes. John Jacob Astor began his career in the fur trade but used his fur profits to buy building lots north of the built-up portion of the city. He would wait for the city to reach his lots and then sell them at greatly appreciated values, reinvesting farther uptown over and over again until he died the richest man in America in 1848. As the city approached an area, the land values could rise with staggering swiftness. In the late 1830's lots in the vicinity of Fifth Avenue and 23rd Street could be bought for $400 to $500 each. Ten years later they fetched $10,000 and even more.[6] In 1818 Robert Lenox bought thirty acres of farmland in the area now called Lenox Hill in the East 70's for $6,000. By 1880, although the area was still only half developed, the land was worth $10,000,000.[7]

By the late 1860's, boom times, the city was building several thousand buildings a year. Streets were piled with bricks and lumber, while, near the city's northern edge, blasting tried to deal with the rock outcrops, often tossing boulders onto, into, and occasionally straight through houses already built.

Philip Hone, a Mayor of the city in the 1820's, moved up Broadway twice as the city pushed northward and noted in his diary in 1836 that many others were being forced to do the same. "The old downtown burgomasters who have fixed to one spot all their lives," he noted with some satisfaction, "will be seen during the next summer in flocks, marching reluctantly north to pitch their tents in places which in their time were orchards, cornfields, or morasses a pretty smart distance from town."[8]

In this tremendous hubbub, buildings that were declared the last word in luxury and style upon completion were, only a few years later, being called inadequate and outmoded. John Cox Stevens built the finest mansion in the city in 1846 at College Place (now West Broadway) and Murray Street. Only ten years later, as the area fell to commerce, Stevens tore down the building and replaced it with warehouses. In 1853, Dr. Samuel P. Townsend, who invented the soft drink sarsaparilla, built at the cost of $250,000 the grandest house in New York, on the northwest corner of Fifth Avenue and 34th Street. Fifteen years later A. T. Stewart, who more or less invented the department store, tore it down to build a house that cost $2,000,000.

Stewart's mansion, everyone thought, would be around for eternity. "There is one edifice in New York," said *Harper's Weekly* in 1869, "that if not swallowed up by an earthquake, will stand as long as the city remains, and will ever be pointed to as a monument of individual enterprise, of far seeing judgment, and of disinterested philanthropy. This is Mr. A. T. Stewart's new and palatial mansion on Fifth Avenue."[9] But *Harper's* proved less than prescient. Stewart's mansion stood for only thirty years before it, too, vanished.

This incessant change, this constant building up and tearing down, had its consequences. While New Yorkers were proud of their city, extolled its grandeur, and heralded its future, few of them loved it. "Why should it be loved as a city?" *Harper's Monthly* asked in 1856. "It is never the same city for a dozen years altogether. A man born in New York forty years ago finds nothing, absolutely nothing, of the New York he knew. If he chances to stumble upon a few old houses not yet leveled, he is fortunate. But the landmarks, the objects which marked the city to him, as a city, are gone."[10]

•

The New York of the mid-nineteenth century bore little resemblance to the monumental New York of today, for the monuments had yet to be built. Modern New York's extreme verticality was utterly lacking. Masonry construction did not allow heights much above ten stories, and the primitive steam elevators first introduced in New York in 1857 were equally limited. It would be 1889 before steel construction and electric-powered elevators would combine to create the skyscraper. In the 1860's it was church steeples that punctuated the city's skyline, and Trinity Church, with its 284-foot steeple, was the tallest building in the city from its completion in 1846 until 1874.

In 1862 Anthony Trollope, touring North America, mourned the lack of monuments. "In other large cities—cities as large in name as New York—there are works of art, fine buildings, ruins, ancient churches, picturesque costumes, and the tombs of celebrated men. But in New York there are none of these things. Art has not yet grown up there . . . but art is a luxury in a city which follows but slowly on the heels of wealth and civilization."[11]

Late in her life Edith Wharton would remember the city of her youth, a place, she wrote, that had been destined to become "as much a vanished city as Atlantis or the lowest level of Schliemann's Troy."[12] ". . . this little, low-studded rectangular New York, cursed with its universal chocolate-colored coating of the most hideous stone ever quarried, this cramped horizontal gridiron of a town without towers, porticoes, fountains or perspectives, hide-bound in its deadly uniformity of mean ugliness."[13]

If few noticed New York's occasional and still modest beauties, every visitor remarked on the extraordinary hustle and bustle of the place. Trollope, who thought that New York was already the most cosmopolitan city on earth, was equally struck by its evident devotion to business. "Free institutions, general education, and the ascendancy of dollars are the words written on every paving stone along Fifth Avenue, down Broadway, and up Wall Street. Every man can vote, and values the privilege. Every man can read, and uses the privilege. Every man worships the dollar, and is down before his shrine from morning to night."[14]

"Every one is obsessed with business," wrote a French visitor at this time. "Broadway, Wall Street and all the downtown area are the universal gathering place for ten hours during the day. Thousands of omnibuses traverse the main streets, filled every morning with a compact crowd which they bring back in the evening. Neither the boulevards, the Strand, nor the Corso of Rome in carnival time can give an idea of this tumultuous movement. Our Parisian strollers hardly resemble this unpleasant, preoccupied, harried throng which elbows its way among the trucks and carts."[15]

James D. McCabe, an American who examined the city in great detail, entirely agreed. "All the world over," he wrote in 1872, "poverty is a misfortune. In New York it is a crime. Here, as in no other place in the country, men struggle for wealth. They toil, they suffer privations, they plan and scheme, and execute with persistency that often wins the success they covet."[16]

As early as the 1840's the newspapers were bemoaning how crowded and noisy the streets were and how slow and tangled the traffic. In 1842 Walt Whitman wrote in an editorial, "What can New York—noisy, roaring, rumbling, tumbling, bustling, stormy, turbulent New York—have to do with silence?"[17] By the 1850's fifteen thousand vehicles a day were counted passing St. Paul's Chapel on Broadway at the foot of City Hall Park. Of all modern New York's most salient characteristics, the only one already in full flower in the mid-nineteenth century was the city's energy and drive.

Unfortunately for those who lived there or even passed through on business, New York had as little to do with cleanliness as it had with silence. The city's attempts at trash collection and street cleaning were erratic at best and often nonexistent. On the more fashionable thoroughfares the store and house owners hired private trash collectors, but even Broadway and Fifth Avenue were still filthy by European standards, especially in bad weather. George Templeton Strong, a New York lawyer and another indispensable diarist of the period, wrote on February 5th, 1857, of "thaw and slop omnipresent and omnipotent."

Europeans were always astonished by the city's four-footed sanitation service, the large and unpenned population of pigs. These pigs mostly inhabited the slums, where the pickings were choicest, at least from their point of view, but they made frequent forays into the nicer parts of town. One English visitor was horrified to see on Fifth Avenue itself a "huge filthy hog devouring a putrid cabbage on a marble doorstep."[18] The pigs were finally banned from the built-up area of the city in 1867. But banning them and actually getting rid of them, of course, were two entirely separate matters. The city found the problem of just hauling off the dead animals difficult enough. In the month of August, 1853, William Reynolds, under contract with the city, cleared from the streets of Manhattan

BROADWAY AT THE FOOT OF CITY HALL PARK   The streets were never this clean.

the carcasses of 577 horses, 69 cows, 883 dogs, 111 cats, 14 hogs, and 6 sheep.[19]

While the major thoroughfares were paved, they suffered from potholes at least as often as they do now, as well as from mud tracked in from the often unpaved side streets and alleys.

Mud, garbage, and even bodies, however, were not the worst problems facing New York City's streets, for every one of those 15,000 vehicles that passed St. Paul's Chapel on an average day was drawn by one or more horses. In the 1860's New York had a horse population of over 100,000, and those horses deposited on its streets 1,000 tons of droppings a day along with 300,000 gallons of urine.[20]

As a result of this vast herd and its equally vast efflux, horses dominated the environment of the city. Just as today it is automobiles that give the air of New York its characteristic essence of engine exhaust, its ambient noise of rumbling engines and swish of tires over asphalt, so in the last century horses filled the city with the smell of their sweat and excrement. The noise of their iron-shod hooves ringing on the paving stones, the endless jingle of their harness formed the urban obbligato behind the shouts and curses of the drivers as they fought their way up and down the avenues amid the other vehicles, the piles of construction materials, and the thousands upon thousands of hurrying pedestrians.

•

The Erie Canal was not the only begetter of this immense transformation. The second major factor was the industrial revolution, which had been radiating out from its epicenter in the Midlands of England since the third quarter of the eighteenth century.

The steam engine made possible the large-scale and much cheaper manufacture of many goods, allowing what had been luxuries for the rich, such as decent clothes, to become the ordinary staples of middle-class life. The costly problem of bringing the raw materials to the new factories and distributing the goods produced in them, however, was still unsolved. The problem was manageable, perhaps, in small and well-developed England, but its solution was critical to the industrial development of vast, raw America.

Overland transportation in the eighteenth century bordered on the nonexistent. Roads were few and in many cases little better than rutted paths, impassable in bad weather. The Great North Road, the major highway through the north of England, had potholes so large that men and horses are known to have drowned in them.[21] And overland transportation was expensive in terms of both money and time. It took a week for a stagecoach to travel from Boston to New York and nearly three weeks for one to make it from New York to Charleston, South Carolina.[22]

The only solution, before the steam engine, was to extend navigable water by means of canals, and numerous canal projects, besides the Erie, were begun in the new United States after the Revolution. But canals had many inherent limitations. They were expensive to build; they required considerable and utterly reliable sources of water, for they were really nothing more than artificial rivers; and they could not operate in winter. Another solution was needed, and the steam engine supplied it.

James Watt's engine was not powerful enough to move more than its own weight, but Richard Trevithick, at the very end of the eighteenth century, had a different idea about how to build steam engines. Trevithick's engine produced much more power for its weight because it used higher pressure than Watt's and because it operated at many more cycles per minute.

Trevithick soon designed a primitive locomotive around his new engine. Miners and iron founders had long used the tramway—a parallel set of rails on which the wheels of carts fitted—to move ore and other bulky commodities for short distances to the nearest navigable water, and Samuel Homfray invited Trevithick to try out his new locomotive on the tramway at Homfray's iron foundry in Glamorganshire, Wales. On February 21st, 1804, the first locomotive pulled the first train along a set of tracks, and the railroad, the seminal invention of the nineteenth century, was born.

The railroad was not a single invention, however, but a complex of inventions and engineering concepts, and it was twenty years before George Stephenson built an entire railroad from scratch as a commercial venture, the Liverpool and Manchester Railway. Stephenson brought together all the essential elements of the railroad, refined them, designed a system in which they could work together, and solved a myriad of engineering problems that no one had ever faced before.

Once the line was built it created great excitement. The Duke of Wellington, then the Prime Minister, and numerous other dignitaries were present at the opening ceremonies for Stephenson's railroad, and Fanny Kemble, the actress and indefatigable journal writer, was thrilled to sit beside Stephenson while "his tame dragon flew panting along his iron pathway."[23] Most important of all, the

Liverpool and Manchester Railway was an immediate financial success. Railroad projects began to blossom in both Great Britain and the United States, and no more canals were planned.

The early trains were not comfortable in the least. In the summer they were extremely hot, and sparks from the engine were a constant menace. Returning from a trip to Montauk, George Templeton Strong damned the Long Island Railroad, as would countless millions after him. "Long detention, rain, smoke, dust, cinders, headache again, all sorts of botheration—home at half-past nine and went straight to bed doubting whether I should ever enjoy the blessing of a clean face again."[24]

Matters were no better in winter, when Strong complained that the cars "with their sloppy floors, red-hot stoves, and currents of chill air from opened doors and windows are perilous traps for colds and inflammations."[25]

But trains were much too practical to do without. Within a single generation the railroads had spread far and had profoundly changed the parts of the world they had reached, for they brought the industrial revolution in their freight cars. By 1844 Philip Hone was complaining in his diary that "this world is going too fast. Improvements, politics, reform, religion—all fly. Railroads, steamers, packets, race against time and beat it hollow. Flying is dangerous. By and by we shall have balloons and pass over to Europe between sun and sun. Oh, for the good old days of heavy postcoaches and speed at the rate of six miles an hour!"[26]

By this time Hone was an old and deeply conservative man, bewildered or at least bemused by the whirlwind of change unleashed in his lifetime by the steam engine. (Hone's nostalgic "the good old days" is the earliest recorded use of the phrase, for only in the 1840's did the remembered past begin to differ markedly from the present.) Still, two years later, he was astounded at how news from Great Britain had been carried by ship to Boston and that "the distance from Boston, 240 miles, was traveled by railroad and steamboat in the astonishingly short time of seven hours and five minutes. What a change from the times when the mail stage left for Boston *once a fortnight,* and consumed a week in going to Philadelphia!"[27]

It was the railroad's speed that so captivated the people of that day. From time immemorial men had been unable to travel at even ten miles an hour. Now it was suddenly possible to travel twice, even three times, that speed for hour after hour, annihilating both time and distance in a way inconceivable to anyone living even a quarter of a century earlier. It is little wonder that the railroad almost immediately acquired a symbolic role for the Victorians. It seemed to them the epitome of their new-found technological prowess and of the progress that they regarded, with every good reason, as the hallmark of their civilization.

Certainly the younger generation had none of Hone's occasional misgivings. "It's a great sight to see a large train get underway," George Templeton Strong, only nineteen, wrote in his diary in 1839. "I know of nothing that would more strongly impress our great-great grandfathers with an idea of their descendant's progress in science. . . . Just imagine such a concern rushing unexpectedly by a stranger to the invention on a dark night, whizzing and rattling and panting, with its fiery furnace gleaming in front, its chimney vomiting fiery smoke above, and its long train of cars rushing along behind like the body and tail of a gigantic dragon—or like the devil himself—and all darting forward at the rate of twenty miles an hour. Whew!"[28]

Probably no invention ever had so profound an effect on the world economy. It could fairly be said that the railroad brought the world economy into being. "Two generations ago," Arthur T. Hadley wrote in his classic work of economics, *Railroad Transportation,* published in 1886, "the expense of cartage was such that wheat had to be consumed within two hundred miles of where it was grown. Today, the wheat of Dakota, the wheat of Russia, and the wheat of India come into direct competition. The supply at Odessa is an element in determining the price in Chicago."[29]

The canals had begun the process whereby freight rates as well as passenger rates fell more or less steadily throughout the nineteenth century, thus lowering the price of everything not locally produced. The Erie Canal had reduced the cost of transporting western produce to the East Coast by a factor of twenty, and Hadley reported that between 1850 and 1880 railroad rates, necessarily competitive with those of canals, "were reduced on an average to about one half their former figures, in spite of the advance in the price of labor and of many articles of consumption."[30]

In the United States there were over a thousand miles of track in use by 1835. By 1840 there were more than five thousand, and by the Civil War, the first major war in which railroads played a significant part, thirty thousand miles of track had been laid.

It was less expensive to build railroads in the United States, with its great stretches of still largely unpopulated country, than in

Europe. But railroads were still very capital intensive, especially by the standards of the day. A railroad of any size needed a great many locomotives, as well as other rolling stock, stations, terminals, and yards. And it cost, on average, about $36,000 to lay a single mile of track at that time.[31]

The earliest railroads were usually local concerns, running only a few miles and designed to alleviate strictly local transportation bottlenecks or connect a town with the existing canal or river transportation systems. These early railroads were often financed with local capital, just as the Liverpool and Manchester Railway had been. But, as the railroads began to expand seriously, and trunk lines running hundreds of miles were envisioned, larger sources of capital became necessary. Railroad builders early turned to the financial market on Wall Street not only to raise the capital needed, but as a place to trade the securities of the proliferating railroad companies.

Government bonds had been the meat and potatoes of Wall Street since the days of the buttonwood tree, but by the 1840's railroad securities were fast overtaking them in importance. In 1835 only three railroads had the price of their shares regularly quoted in the newspapers. By 1850 thirty-eight railroads were being regularly traded, and by the middle of that decade railroads accounted for half of all the negotiable securities in the country, while the volume of trading on the Street expanded to a level ten times as high as it had been twenty years earlier. It was to prove a fateful congruence of economic interests. Wall Street and the railroads were destined to grow up together, and their wild and exuberant adolescence would often be the talk, and sometimes the despair, of the nation.

But in the beginning only the promise, not the problems, could be seen. With the development of the railroad, New York's commercial reach was unlimited, the world the source of its greatness. "Situated as our city is—" wrote a New York newspaper in 1836, "commanding, as it does, the trade of the western continent—with all the wealth of the world rushing into its bosom by means of railroads, canals, steamers and packet ships—will not this become one of the most wealthy, populous, and splendid cities of the globe?"[32]

•

New York was not alone in becoming wealthy, for the industrial revolution generated wealth wherever it reached and gave to the middle class a standard of living that only the very rich had known two generations earlier. The newly affluent throughout the western world were the most rapidly growing segment of the population. While the number of poor people, in absolute numbers, increased greatly with the rapid increase in total population in the nineteenth century, the percentage of the population that was at or below the subsistence level fell continuously.

Nowhere was this increase in wealth and its spread through the population more marked than in New York, however. In 1828, when the city's population was 185,000, there were only 59 New Yorkers with property assessed at more than $100,000. By 1845, when the city's population had more than doubled to 371,000, the number of citizens with property worth more than $100,000 had quintupled to 294, and the word "millionaire" had been coined to describe the newly affluent.[33] The number of those who were, in the Victorian phrase, merely "comfortably fixed" far more than kept pace with the number of the very rich.

This dominant class of the Victorian age, the *nouveau riche*, had a profound impact on the appearance of mid-nineteenth-century New York, just as the corporate culture of the twentieth century would, in its turn, make the city its own. Except for the greatest palaces on Fifth Avenue and its immediate environs, New York's houses were erected almost entirely by real-estate speculators, who built them in blocks of six, eight, or more identical units and sold them off to individual families. This produced a formidable uniformity in the appearance of New York's streetscapes.

The speculators were very conservative in taste, each unwilling to be even a little out in front of the pack in style for fear that their equally conservative and socially insecure *nouveau riche* customers would be scared away. By the 1850's the Italianate style, with its brownstone front, elaborate bracketed cornice, carved lintels, high stoop, and double front door beneath a small but ornate portico was virtually the only style of rowhouse being built.

The New York *Herald* in 1869 praised the "wonderful uniformity" these houses produced, but Edith Wharton, who disliked New York and most New Yorkers while she mined their foibles for her novels, did not think much even of "Fifth Avenue with its double line of low brownstone houses, of a desperate uniformity of style, broken only—and surprisingly—by two equally unexpected features: the fenced-in plot of ground where the old Miss Kennedy's cows were pastured, and the truncated Egyptian pyramid which so strangely served as a reservoir for New York's water supply" (and was located on the present site of the New York Public Library).[34]

The insides of these houses were quite as alike as the outsides. "The twenty thousand drawing rooms of New York," wrote Nathaniel Parker Willis in the 1840's, "are all stereotyped copies of one out of three or four styles—the style dependent only on the degree of expensiveness. The proprietor of almost any house in New York might wake up in thousands of other houses, and not recognize for half-an-hour that he was not at home."[35]

The appearance of mid-Victorian décor was determined by the wondrous capacities of gaslight. For the first time in human history interior brightness was cheap. Until the advent of gaslight in the 1820's, there were only candles and whatever glow could be coaxed from fireplaces to keep away the gloom of night. But candles were quite as expensive in real terms then as they are now, and gas was cheap. By the 1850's its faint hiss and odd, dank smell filled the houses of the middle and upper classes.

Gilding and mirrors abounded to catch and multiply its twinkling glow. Walls that had perforce been light-colored in all but the richest houses to reflect what light there was were covered in dark and often elaborately patterned wallpapers that newly invented presses were able to grind out by the acre, while the floors were covered with equally elaborately patterned wall-to-wall carpets, made possible by the new looms developed in the 1840's.

The industrial revolution, which had transformed the décor of these houses by bringing the price of such luxuries as wallpaper, carpeting, and light within the reach of the middle class, also transformed their technology. In 1840 New York, technologically speaking, was a vastly overgrown medieval village. The houses were heated by open hearths, while people bathed—when they bathed—in the kitchen and used backyard outhouses or chamberpots, whose contents as often as not were later emptied into the streets. There rain or the wandering pigs, it was hoped, would cope with the mess. New York's water supply, drawn from thousands of wells and natural springs, was grossly contaminated by this sewage and was the source, although it was not known at the time, of the city's frequent epidemics of water-borne diseases such as cholera and typhoid.

But when water from Westchester's Croton River first came into the city by aqueduct in 1842 the situation began to change very rapidly. Croton water gave New York City its undying and richly deserved reputation for having the finest municipal water in the

"THIS CRAMPED HORIZONTAL GRIDIRON OF A TOWN"   A much idealized view of Fifth Avenue, looking south from 38th Street. In the 1860's only church steeples rose above the five-story city.

world. Soon new houses could not be sold unless they had water closets and bathrooms, and the city was forced into a crash program of sewer and water-main construction. The drop in demand for well water caused the water table to rise alarmingly and forced the city to construct storm and drainage sewers to overcome an epidemic of flooded basements. All this sewer construction—as much as fifty miles a year—added greatly to the city's appearance of being one huge, never-completed construction site.

Two inventions transformed the kitchen at this time as well. The cast-iron cookstove replaced the open hearth and the icebox came into use. Soon the stoves were fitted with water tanks, and hot running water—undreamed of only a generation earlier—became a commonplace, while the icebox made a cold glass of milk in July a marvelous reality.

The third domestic improvement was central heating. Primitive forced-air furnaces were first installed in the 1840's, but these worked fitfully and as often as not provided more soot and fumes than heat. By the 1860's steam heat, with all its efficiency and technological, if not aesthetic, advantages, was being installed in the latest rowhouses.

By the end of the Civil War the newest dwellings more closely resembled those built a hundred years later than those erected only twenty years earlier, for technologically housing had advanced half a millennium in a single generation. To the middle and upper classes of that generation, it was nothing short of a miracle.

•

Still, for all the recent improvements in living standards, death, sudden or early, was no stranger even in the better parts of town. The sick and the elderly were very seldom institutionalized and were cared for by their families, to die at peace or in agony at home. In the 1850's children under five years of age accounted for more than half of all the mortality in New York City, and it was frequent even for people in their prime suddenly to sicken and die. Every day's obituary column held commonplace tragedies:

McMahon—On Saturday, January 2, at half-past six P.M. Mary F. McMahon, the beloved daughter of William and Sarah F. McMahon, after a painful illness, aged 2 years, 10 months and 6 days.

Darling—Suddenly, on Friday, January 1, Clarence A., second son of A. A. and G. W. Darling, aged 11 years and 2 months.

Reilly—On Friday, January 1, Margaret R., the beloved wife of James W. Reilly, in the 21st year of her age.[36]

The obituary column was itself still another innovation. As the number of people who lived in affluence increased, their need for information about their civilization, its perils and opportunities increased also. Just as the railroad had made possible the spread of material goods, so the newspaper, the other sublime invention of the early industrial revolution, made possible the spread of ideas and information.

Newspapers had begun in the eighteenth century as the narrowly based instruments of various political factions, devoted not to providing the public with information of interest, but to selling a particular political point of view. They were, in effect, nothing but editorial pages wrapped in a little tendentious news.

But in the 1830's the steam engine and the printing press were combined, greatly lowering the price per copy and greatly increasing the number of copies that could be printed in a short period of time. Suddenly newspapers were available that could be afforded and read by the masses as well as the élite, and many intellectuals and politicians, such as Horace Greeley and Henry J. Raymond, moved to exploit the new possibilities. Of all the pioneers of mass journalism no one deserves to be remembered more than James Gordon Bennett, who was neither intellectual nor politician, and who created nearly out of whole cloth the greatest newspaper in the country, the New York *Herald*, and with it the profession of journalism itself.

On May 6th, 1835, Bennett produced the first issue of the *Herald*, selling it for a penny a copy. "It is my passion," Bennett later told his first biographer, "my delight, my thought by day and my dream by night to conduct the *Herald*, and to show the world and posterity that a newspaper can be made the greatest, most fascinating, most powerful organ of civilization that genius ever dreamed of."[37]

Bennett was the first regularly to report social gossip, to give daily listings of stock prices, to print weather reports and sports news. He soon signed up correspondents in Europe and in Washington. He was the first editor to make extensive use of the new telegraph and often printed news of the Civil War before the War Department learned of it. He was the first editor to have his reporters interview people at the scene of news events, a practice that gave the *Herald* a powerful sense of immediacy that is the very heart of good journalistic writing.

Bennett made the newspaper indispensable. "The daily newspaper," wrote the *North American Review* in 1866, only thirty years after the *Herald*'s founding, "is one of those things which are rooted in the necessities of modern civilization. The steam engine is not more essential to us. The newspaper is that which connects each individual with the general life of mankind."[38]

It was the newspapers that unified the Victorian age, quite as television unifies ours, and gave to the people their sense of the world in which they lived, a world that had become in their lifetimes far wider, richer, and more interrelated than any ever known before.

This age was marked by prosperity, social conformity, piety, hypocrisy, and a profound sense of progress in human endeavor, all characteristics of the dominant class of the time, the *nouveau riche.* The great rise in the standard of living and in opportunities for gaining wealth that had been provided by the industrial revolution engendered an atmosphere not altogether dissimilar to an extended gold rush. The yearning for more seemed universal.

Nowhere in New York could wealth be gained—or lost—more quickly than on Wall Street, and many men who had made their fortunes elsewhere came to the Street to try to increase them further. "The mass gaze at the gorgeousness with which the 'shoddy aristocracy' surrounds itself," wrote the London *Times,* no fancier of things American, "and admire and envy the winners in the reckless game that goes on all day long and all the year round in Wall Street."[39]

In 1857, the eccentric George Francis Train described the get-rich-quick frenzy that held New York in its grasp:

> *Monday,* I started my land operations;
> *Tuesday,* owed millions, by all calculations;
> *Wednesday,* my brownstone palace began;
> *Thursday,* I drove out a spanking new span;
> *Friday,* I gave a magnificent ball;
> *Saturday,* smashed—with just nothing at all.[40]

To single-mindedly pursue a fortune was, to the Victorian, an honorable calling. To find it was considered by most to be a sign of

God's grace, for the gospel of wealth was an article of faith throughout the western world.

As early as 1828 the English social critic John Sterling—aptly named—wrote, "*Wealth! Wealth! Wealth! Praise to the God of the nineteenth century! The Golden idol! the mighty Mammon!* such are the accents of the time, such the cry of the nation. . . . There may be here and there an individual who does not spend his heart in laboring for riches; but there is nothing approaching to a class of persons actuated by any other desire."[41]

Money—who had it and how much—was a subject of abiding interest to the Victorians, an interest they made little if any effort to conceal. The cost of everything, even churches, was among the details regularly given in guidebooks to New York. Thanks to James Gordon Bennett, the newspapers had discovered early how much money gossip could add to circulation, and by the middle of the century New Yorkers could read the most intimate, if not always the most accurate, financial details about people of genius and wealth whom they could seldom expect to meet in real life. The costs of people's houses, their net worths, and even their reported taxable incomes, then a matter of public record, were regularly listed in the newspapers and published in pamphlets, which sold briskly.

Of these New Yorkers, none was richer than Daniel Drew's long-time friend and rival Cornelius Vanderbilt, for he possessed not only the genius to see the opportunities that abounded in the new industrial age, but the courage to take them as well.

THE FRUITS OF WALL STREET SUCCESS   They have not
changed much in a hundred years: a house at the beach, a
fancy place in town, theaters, restaurants, and luxurious
transportation.

CHAPTER THREE

The Commodore

WHEN Cornelius Vanderbilt, known to the world as the Commodore, died on January 4th, 1877, a few months short of his eighty-third birthday, he left to his heirs more than $105,000,000, the greatest fortune yet created in the burgeoning American economy. His principal and worthy heir, William Henry Vanderbilt, would double this sum in the next eight years, and the Commodore's progeny, nestled in the bosom of his fortune, would go on to build the most sumptuous private residences ever erected, raise the fastest racehorses in the world, buy the finest European titles, defend the America's Cup, invent contract bridge, and design blue jeans. In the years after the Commodore's death, the Vanderbilts would come to epitomize the life of the American rich, and money, for better or worse, would be the axis of all their lives.

But money itself, or even what it could buy, did not greatly interest the founder of this huge fortune. While hardly averse to living well, what the Commodore loved above all else was to win. Throughout his life, whether he was at the whist table or on Wall Street, behind the wheel of a steamboat or driving a pair of fast horses, he was always fiercely, passionately competitive. Possessed of an immense and entirely justified self-assurance, Vanderbilt always believed that, whatever it was, he could do it better, sail it faster, run it cheaper. Far more often than not, he proved that he could.

•

The Vanderbilt family first arrived in the new world from Holland in the middle of the seventeenth century, while the Dutch still ruled Nieuw Amsterdam. In 1715 the Commodore's great-grandfather was the first of the family to settle on Staten Island, on a seventy-eight-acre farm at the island's northern end. The community the Vanderbilts lived in remained very Dutch, very rural, and not terribly prosperous. For another hundred years, its farmers supplied produce to the small city on Manhattan across the bay and spoke Dutch, at least among themselves, as late as the 1820's.

The Commodore's father, for whom he was named, farmed the family land and owned a boat, which he hired out on odd jobs around New York Harbor. It was Cornelius, Sr., who first conceived the idea of a boat service between Staten Island and Manhattan that would run on a regular schedule and thus, in a sense, was the originator of the Staten Island Ferry. But, while he was a hard worker and possessed a creative mind, the Commodore's father was also very careless about money, too sanguine about the future, and nearly always on the brink of financial disaster. It was Vanderbilt's mother who held the family together and was the principal influence on her remarkable son.

Phebe Hand, as she was named, had come from a good family in New Jersey, though their patriotic investment in Continental bonds during the Revolution had considerably reduced their circumstances. She was tough and she was smart, and in sharp contrast to her husband, there was nothing whatever of Mr. Micawber in her makeup. When the family farm was on the verge of foreclosure, she produced at the last minute $3,000 in gold that she had hidden in the grandfather clock in the hall and saved the place from her husband's creditors. When she died in 1854 at the age of eighty-six, she left an estate of more than $50,000. That was an insignificant sum compared to her son's by then enormous fortune, but nonetheless remarkable for having been accumulated by a woman who spent her life on a Staten Island farm raising the fourteen children of an improvident husband.

Vanderbilt's mother had little use for formal religion, and her son would have none at all, but she read the Bible to her children and thoroughly discussed its teachings. At the end of his life the Commodore would remember that "his mother had got the maxims of the Bible implanted so firmly in his heart that nothing could eradicate them."[1]

Cornelius, his parents' fourth child and second son, was born on May 27th, 1794. When he was little more than an infant the family moved to Stapleton, on the east side of the island. The family's new house was not two hundred feet from the shores of the Narrows, the entrance to New York's Upper Bay, through which all the deepwater shipping of the port passed. Before long the young Cornelius knew all the various types of vessels that plied these already busy waters and could identify on sight most of the ships whose home port was New York.

From the beginning he was strong and active. At the age of six he nearly drowned a horse while riding it bareback in a race with a neighboring slave boy two years older than he. (At the end of his life, seventy-five years later, the Commodore would encounter his playmate once again. Never in the least a snob, still less a racist in an age when racism was taken entirely for granted, the richest man in America invited the old black man, now a Methodist minister, to his house at 10 Washington Place and entertained him there.)[2]

Cornelius did not like school and attended it as seldom as possible. While he had a first-rate mind, the plodding, rote-learning, knuckle-rapping education that was the norm in the eighteenth century must have been torture to one so active and bright. Abstractions for their own sake would never interest him in the slightest. His spelling, even by the notions of an age when English orthography was just beginning to be standardized, was always to be erratic. His grammar was not much better, and, not surprisingly for one who began his life on the sea, Vanderbilt was to be famous for both the quality and quantity of his profanity, a habit he would never manage to break, although he occasionally tried. (In Vanderbilt's old age, a clergyman called on him and found the Commodore uncharacteristically despondent. Asked why, he replied, "Oh, God-damn it, I've been a-swearing again, and I'm sorry."[3])

Near the end of his sixteenth year, Cornelius decided that he had had enough of working on his parents' farm and helping his father on the boat about New York Harbor. He wanted to be his own master. At Port Richmond, where he had been born, he found a periauger that was for sale for $100 and he resolved to buy her.

Periaugers were the workhorse vessels of New York before the age of steam. Flat-bottomed, two-masted vessels up to sixty feet long and twenty-three feet wide, they drew very little water and thus could sail anywhere in the nooks and crannies of New York Harbor's endless waterfront. The design had originated in Spain, and the Duke of Alba brought them to the Netherlands to fight the rebelling Dutch, who promptly adopted them for their own use, while corrupting the Spanish name, *periagua*, which means water elf. Later in the nineteenth century, no longer of any economic use, they would evolve into the famous catboat.

Vanderbilt asked his mother to lend him the $100. She might well have turned him down flat, but he had been dropping hints of late about running away to sea, and with that threat in mind she made a deal with him. If, before his sixteenth birthday, about four weeks away, he would clear, plow, harrow, and plant an eight-acre field that had never been used for anything more than rough pasturage, he could have the $100.

"Mother thought she had the best of me on that eight-acre lot," remembered the Commodore in his old age, "but I got some boys to help me and we did the work, and it was well done, too, for mother would not allow any half way of doing it. On my birthday I claimed my money."[4]

He took his mother's $100 and bought the boat. "I didn't feel as much real satisfaction," Vanderbilt recalled, "when I made two million dollars in that Harlem corner as I did on that bright May morning sixty years before when I stepped into my own periauger, hoisted my own sail, and put my hand on my own tiller."[5] But, while sailing it back to Stapleton, he ran the boat onto a rock or an old wreck and only just made it to shore. Despite this inauspicious start, the boat was soon repaired, and Vanderbilt set out to make his fortune.

While he would own or have an interest in well over fifty sailing ships, river steamers, and ocean-going steamships in an age of frequent maritime disasters, Vanderbilt had had his last accident. Not one of his ships, while owned by him, ever fell victim to fire, explosion, or shipwreck. He didn't even insure them. "Good vessels and good captains are the best sort of insurance," Vanderbilt said. "If corporations can make money out of insurance, I can."[6]

•

Vanderbilt began by carrying cargoes and passengers, at eighteen cents each, between Staten Island and New York. Before long he had earned a reputation for being the most reliable captain operating in

New York waters. He was always punctual, he always sailed regardless of the weather ("Yes," he once said to a request to carry a boatload of soldiers in the midst of a furious storm, "but I shall have to carry them under water part of the way"[7]), and before long he had all the business he could handle. When the periauger was laid up at the end of the first season, he was able to repay his mother the $100 and give her $1,000 more besides—not a bad return on her investment.

Vanderbilt's reputation for reliability was soon augmented by his reputation for hard work. When the War of 1812 began, the demand for ferry services such as Vanderbilt's greatly increased; they were needed to move soldiers and military supplies to and from the various forts around New York Harbor. The army asked for bids on a contract to deliver a boatload of supplies a week to each of six forts that protected the approaches to New York, and Vanderbilt, although he had not submitted the lowest bid, won the contract because the army wanted someone who they knew would not fail. He delivered these boatloads usually at night so that he could continue his regular traffic during the day. He seemed to sleep only on Sundays and in odd moments between sailings.

Most of the time the freelance boatman's business was not a matter of contract, but rather a question of getting to the cargo first and keeping it. It was a game for the tough and Vanderbilt soon made it clear that he was among the toughest. When he was carrying a boatload of soldiers across the bay one day, a rival boatman came alongside with an army officer aboard who told Vanderbilt to transfer the soldiers. Vanderbilt realized that this was nothing more than a naked attempt to steal his cargo and told the officer, in effect, to drop dead. "The military man, almost bursting with rage, hastily withdrew his sword, as if about to avenge his insulted dignity, when young Vanderbilt quickly brought him, sword and all, to the deck."[8]

By no means the least of Vanderbilt's assets were his physical size, appearance, and strength. Six feet one inch tall and broad-shouldered, he cut a fine figure, with his black eyes, handsome face, and florid complexion. All his life he carried himself erect, and his immense physical strength stayed with him long into old age. In 1844, when he was fifty, the Commodore led a parade of supporters of Henry Clay for President up Broadway. Suddenly his horse's reins were seized by "Yankee" Sullivan, a Tammany henchman and the leading boxer of his day. The enraged Vanderbilt leaped off his horse and proceeded to savage Sullivan so thoroughly that he was "in a nearly senseless condition when finally rescued."[9]

Vanderbilt lived as simply as he could, plowing his profits back into other vessels and building his capital. When he was not yet twenty, he felt himself well enough established to get married, and on November 19th, 1813, he married Sophia Johnson, his first cousin on his mother's side and his first cousin once removed on his father's, a degree of consanguinity that was unusual, perhaps, but by no means unheard of in those days.[10]

In the winters, when weather and business were at their worst, Vanderbilt interested himself in ship design and showed a considerable talent for it. As his first biographer put it, "He began earnestly to plan methods of improving the shape and build of ships. He allowed himself to be hampered by no precedents, and he introduced such innovations and modifications as attracted the attention of ship-builders and made 'Vanderbilt models' and 'Vanderbilt methods' discussed even among the experienced and practical men of his craft."[11]

At the end of 1817, Vanderbilt figured that he was worth $9,000 besides being the owner of a respectable fleet of small and middle-sized sailing ships. He was not yet twenty-four and was already clearly a man to be watched. But Vanderbilt had been doing some watching himself.

The waters around New York had been the scene of many of the early experiments with adapting the steam engine for use on water. In 1798 John Fitch had launched one of the first steam-powered vessels in the Collect Pond, a small body of fresh water located where Foley Square is today, just north of City Hall. In 1807, Robert Fulton put the *Clermont*, the first commercially practical steamboat, on the New York–Albany run, which the vessel covered in thirty-two hours, far faster than the trip could be made by land or, with any certainty, by sailing vessel.

There were only a few steamboats launched in the decade after the *Clermont*, but Vanderbilt was quick to note that their independence of wind and tide gave them formidable commercial advantages over sailing vessels, despite the amount of cargo space that was lost to engines and fuel storage. Vanderbilt "went and carefully examined Fulton's craft, took passage to Albany and back, studied the engines and machinery, and reluctantly made up his mind that the future of navigation belonged to the steamboats."[12]

•

Although Vanderbilt had been earning $3,000 a year from his sailing vessels, a very substantial income at that time, he sold them all and went to work as a captain for Thomas Gibbons for $60 a month plus half the profits from the bar of Gibbons's steamboat *Stoudinger.* (In that hard-drinking time, when the per-capita consumption of alcohol was several times what it is today, the bar profits on steamboats often exceeded that from fares.) The *Stoudinger,* which because of its diminutive size was known to New Yorkers as the *Mouse,* ran between New York and New Brunswick, New Jersey, the first leg of the fastest route to Philadelphia. The second leg was by stagecoach to Trenton and from there by steamboat again down the Delaware River.

There was one big problem. The New York State Legislature had granted a monopoly of steamboat navigation in New York waters to Robert Fulton and Robert R. Livingston and had, moreover, arrogantly defined "New York waters" as running up to the high-tide line on the New Jersey side of the harbor. All steamboats operating in defiance of the monopoly were subject to being confiscated. New Jersey countered this by declaring that anyone who tried to enforce the monopoly would be jailed if they chanced to fall into New Jersey's jurisdiction.

This monopoly was extremely unpopular with everyone, whether they lived in New Jersey or New York, unless they benefited directly from it or worked for the Livingston political machine. Gibbons vowed to break the monopoly and Cornelius Vanderbilt was just the man to help him do it.

Vanderbilt persuaded Gibbons to build a larger steamboat, one designed by him and constructed under his supervision. At 142 tons she was greatly admired for her beauty, and most people caught the implication when Gibbons chose to name her *Bellona,* after the Roman goddess of war.

Vanderbilt, endlessly resourceful and as cheeky as could be, delighted in playing cat-and-mouse with the New York State authorities who sought to enforce the monopoly. He flew a flag from the masthead proclaiming that "New Jersey Must Be Free!"[13] and he would boldly steam to Manhattan and land his passengers at whatever pier seemed to be free of authorities trying to serve him with an injunction. New York did not dare seize the vessel itself for fear that New Jersey would retaliate against the first monopoly steamboat it could lay its hands on, and immediately after landing, the captain would disappear into the city. At sailing time he would sneak back as close to the ship as possible and make a dash for it, while the crew, with steam already up, would cast off the instant he was aboard so that any deputy sheriff who happened to be lurking in ambush would have to choose between waiting for another day and risking being carried off to New Jersey and to jail.

While never knowing which pier the *Bellona* would tie up at must have been something of a strain on her passengers, so unpopular was the monopoly that they were willing to put up with the inconvenience and, anyway, Vanderbilt's role as David to the monopoly's Goliath was vastly entertaining. When New York authorities couldn't catch Vanderbilt on land, they tried to catch him by sea, boarding the *Bellona* as she steamed across the middle of the harbor. When they entered the wheelhouse they found neither Vanderbilt nor any other member of the crew at the wheel. Rather they found a young female passenger—one imagines her all ribbons and frills and bonnet—while the captain hid in a secret compartment that he had had the foresight to have installed below decks. The rest of the passengers hooted their derision at the frustrated minions of the monopoly.

Gibbons was so pleased with Vanderbilt that he raised his salary to $2,000 a season and gave him the use of the inn in New Brunswick where passengers en route to Philadelphia stayed overnight. Sophia raised her growing brood of children there and ran the inn efficiently and profitably. Both would long remember these times as the happiest of their lives together. The monopoly tried to get Vanderbilt to come over to its side, offering him the then colossal salary of $5,000 a year, but he declined. "No," he replied to their blandishments, "I shall stick to Mr. Gibbons till he is through his troubles."[14] Vanderbilt, who when crossed and especially double-crossed could be as ruthless and as vengeful as any Old Testament God, would never lose touch with honor.

As feisty and disputatious as his captain, Gibbons fought his way through the courts for more than five years, first in New York State, where he met only with defeat, and then in federal court, where he claimed that the monopoly was contrary to the Constitution's grant of power to Congress to "regulate Commerce . . . among the several states." He hired two of the best lawyers in the country, Daniel Webster and Willard Wirt (who was then Attorney General of the United States; it did not seem to bother anyone that the nation's chief law-enforcement officer should also have a lucrative private law practice).

Webster's argument before the Supreme Court, which took all day, was immediately regarded as one of the most dazzling and brilliant legal arguments ever delivered. John Marshall delivered the unanimous opinion of the Court, holding in the case of *Gibbons* v. *Ogden,* 1824, that the monopoly was indeed unconstitutional and that Congress's power to regulate interstate commerce was both sweeping and exclusive. It soon proved to be one of the most significant decisions ever handed down by the great Chief Justice, as important to the economic development of the country—and New York City—as Hamilton's decision on the guarantee of the debt had been. It ensured that the United States would be a true common market and that New York's commercial advantages could be utilized to the full by the entire country. The proof was not long in coming. In the year that followed *Gibbons* v. *Ogden* the number of steamboats operating in New York waters increased from six to forty-nine.[15] And the next time Vanderbilt steamed into New Brunswick he was saluted with cannon, fired "by citizens desirous of testifying in a public manner their good will."[16]

For the next five years, Vanderbilt continued to work for Gibbons while he slowly built enough capital to strike out on his own. In 1829 he decided the time had come. Gibbons, who had turned over all management of his steamboat interests to Vanderbilt, was devastated by the decision. He asked Vanderbilt to name his own price or make his own deal if only he would stay with him, but Vanderbilt declined. For the next forty-eight years, until his death, Vanderbilt would be wholly in charge of his own destiny.

•

Vanderbilt designed and built the *Caroline,* seventy feet long and named for his sister. (Several years later, during the Canadian Rebellion of 1837 and after he had sold her, the *Caroline* would suffer the singular fate for a ship of going over Niagara Falls.) Vanderbilt put her on the run between New York and New Jersey that he knew so well. Shortly after Vanderbilt left his employ, Gibbons sold his steamboat interests to the Stevens family of Hoboken, early pioneers in both steamboats and railroads. The Stevenses thought that Gibbons must still be backing his protégé, who was underselling them in fierce competition, and so they paid Vanderbilt to withdraw from the route. Vanderbilt was glad to oblige for he was nearly out of money, and what the Stevens family paid him was enough to allow him to build a steamboat large enough to operate on the Hudson River run.

This was to be Vanderbilt's tactic in the steamboat business, and it was simplicity itself. He would look to see where steamboats were paying the best rate of return on the investment in them. Often this would be where there was a cartel in operation that limited the competition, such as the Hudson River Association, to which Daniel Drew belonged and which one year declared a dividend amounting to 70 percent of its invested capital. Vanderbilt would compete against the cartel, figuring that he could operate more efficiently and still turn a profit, or at least lose less, at rates that would ruin the others.

Vanderbilt first started on the Hudson, running to Peekskill in competition with Daniel Drew's *Water Witch*, cutting the fares to as low as twelve and a half cents. Drew, encountering Vanderbilt for the first time, but by no means the last, soon withdrew the *Water Witch* from the run. A few years later the Hudson River Association was only too happy to pay Vanderbilt $100,000 plus $5,000 a year for ten years to get him to withdraw from the river.

Vanderbilt, whose interests were always purely and cheerfully selfish, did not mind in the least being paid not to operate. Steamboats, unlike canals and railroads, could operate anywhere there was water enough to float them. If he was paid to leave the Hudson, his boats could operate on Long Island Sound. Often he was accused of extracting "blackmail" by these tactics, and the *New York Times* in an editorial first used the image, if not quite the words, of the robber barons in decrying Vanderbilt's behavior.[17] But in truth the effect of these tactics was quite as happy for the public as they were for Vanderbilt.

"It has been much the fashion to regard these contests as attempts on his part to levy blackmail on successful enterprises," *Harper's Weekly* wrote in 1859. "It is hardly fair for any man to undertake to decide what are the particular motives of his neighbor in undertaking a specific work, if the work be in itself legitimate and fair. He must be judged by the results; and the results in every case of the establishment of opposition lines by Vanderbilt has been the *permanent reduction of fares.* Wherever he 'laid on' an opposition line, the fares were instantly reduced; and however the contest terminated, whether he bought out his opponents, as he often did, or they bought him out, the fares were never again raised to the old standard. This great boon—cheap travel—this community owes mainly to Cornelius Vanderbilt."[18] Even the *Times* would soon come to adopt this view.

While Vanderbilt, like anyone else operating in a free market, sought to maximize his profit and to charge what the traffic would bear, he realized that his long-term self-interest lay in catering to the passengers and that a full boat at low fares was ultimately more profitable than a half-empty one at high fares. Drew, for all his cunning, could never discern the goose that laid the golden eggs.

These tactics certainly proved profitable for the Commodore, a title first bestowed upon him by the *Journal of Commerce* in 1837. By the 1840's Vanderbilt was the greatest shipowner in the country and had a fortune estimated at $1,200,000 by the owner and editor of the New York *Sun,* Moses Y. Beach. Beach, in his *Wealth and Biographies of Wealthy Citizens of New York,* a wickedly hilarious (and often quite inaccurate) guide for nosey parkers, estimated Daniel Drew's fortune at $300,000.

•

By this time Vanderbilt had developed the public persona that would be so familiar to the world in his latter days and indeed would remain familiar until historians of a generation that had never known him would twist it to their own ends. As a young man he had often appeared to be one in a hurry. William A. Croffut, the Commodore's first biographer, wrote that he had not been "blessed with popular manners. He was not conciliatory and never seemed to care what people thought or said of him. He lacked affability and suavity which are born of a love of approbation—the desire to please. . . . He was sometimes harsh, abrupt, unceremonious, and even uncivil."[19]

With increasing age, fortune, and public recognition, Vanderbilt mellowed, although he was never able to learn patience with people less capable than himself, especially if they were oblivious of their own limitations. In business, the Commodore was forthright and not in the least given to extended bargaining. Offered a deal or a property that interested him, he would decide what he was willing to pay for it and the other side could take it or leave it. As Matthew Hale Smith, a contemporary of Vanderbilt on Wall Street, wrote, even "those who call him sharp, shrewd, unscrupulous in carrying his points admit that he is fair, true and reliable when men treat him

CORNELIUS VANDERBILT *Courtesy of The New-York Historical Society, New York City*

well, and never turns his back on his friends. He has made a fortune for more persons than any other man in Wall Street."[20]

It was the quality of invariably meaning what he said, together with his fortune and his potent physical presence, that gave the Commodore an aura of power unmatched by any of his contemporaries. Everyone knew that "the Commodore's word is as good as his bond when it is freely given. He is equally exact in fulfilling his threats."[21]

At home, Vanderbilt was the undisputed lord and master. Sophia bore him thirteen children altogether: nine daughters, to whom Vanderbilt paid scarcely any attention at all—although he would find his sons-in-law endlessly useful as legal entities through which to operate on Wall Street—and four sons, one of whom died in childhood. His oldest son, William Henry, was early dismissed by the Commodore as a dolt and sent to work for Daniel Drew at his brokerage firm. After William Henry's marriage his father banished him to a Staten Island farm. William worked patiently over the years to change his father's opinion of him, and finally the Commodore came to realize that, while possessed of a very different personality and temperament, his son had a capacity for business that was every bit the equal of his own.

The Commodore's second son was named Cornelius and was a deep disappointment to his father. Epileptic and emotionally unstable, he was always in trouble, and Vanderbilt more or less disowned him. From time to time Cornelius, Jr., would borrow money from Horace Greeley, founder and editor of the New York *Tribune* and notoriously the softest touch in town. When the Commodore found out about it, he stormed down to the great editor's office on Park Row.

"Greeley, I hear you're lending Corneel money," Vanderbilt said.

"Yes," replied Greeley, "I have let him have some."

"I give you fair warning," thundered the Commodore, "that you need not look to me; I won't pay you."

"Who the devil asked you?" responded Greeley, who knew quite as well as Vanderbilt the uses of abruptness.[22]

Despite his warning, when Greeley died in 1872, the Commodore sent each of the editor's daughters a check for $10,000.

His youngest son, as so often happens, was his father's favorite. Named George Washington Vanderbilt after his father's boyhood hero, he grew to be as tall, strong, and good-looking as the Commodore himself had been as a young man and far better educated, graduating with distinction from West Point. But in the Civil War's Corinth campaign, he contracted tuberculosis, the Victorians' "dreaded, dark disease," and his magnificent body slowly wasted away. Before the end of the war he was dead, causing his father the deepest grief he was ever to know in a long and largely unanguished life.

As the Commodore's career developed and his horizons expanded, he began to draw apart from his wife, whose interests were almost entirely those of home and old friends. In 1846 Vanderbilt, who had been living on Staten Island, decided that he had to move to New York to accommodate the press of business and his rising importance in the community. He had a house built at 10 Washington Place, just west of Broadway in the Washington Square area, which was then the height of fashion. Sophia did not want to move and grew more and more tearful and even hysterical as the day neared. Vanderbilt, furious at her unwonted opposition to his plans, had her committed to an asylum, where, in Stewart Holbrook's phrase, "she was given several months in which to reflect."

Although the asylum was private, and not one of the unspeakable hellholes to which the less affluent were consigned, this unforgivable act on the part of Vanderbilt severed the last cords of his intimate relationship with his wife. While they would live together for the rest of her life and maintain the show of a living marriage (on their fiftieth wedding anniversary he would give her an exquisite model steamboat made of gold), in fact the marriage had become little more than a shell. The Commodore would look elsewhere for the satisfaction of his considerable sexual appetite (indeed, his virility would make the task of recruiting and keeping housemaids a thankless one until the very end of his life).

The house that Vanderbilt erected at 10 Washington Place would be his home for the rest of his days. He was comfortable there and saw no reason whatever to join the headlong rush of fashion up Fifth Avenue. By 1870, only twenty-four years after the house was built, it was thought almost eccentric for a man of Vanderbilt's wealth and importance to live so far downtown. "Mr. Vanderbilt lives in a downtown location," Matthew Hale Smith wrote that year. "It was once very fashionable. It is near the New York University; a very large but very plain brick mansion; a good type of the dwelling of the millionaires of the old school, before jaunty freestone houses, with their florid painting and gaudy trimmings, came into vogue.

Everything about it is solid, substantial, comfortable. But there is no North River steamboat about the fitting up."[23]

Sometime after the Commodore's death, the house would be torn down and replaced by a handsome loft building, which now houses part of the university. The spot, so typically of New York, is quite unmarked as having long been the home of one of the great city's most remarkable citizens.

Once established at 10 Washington Place, his life settled into a routine. While he maintained an office downtown at 5 Bowling Green, where the details of his shipping empire were handled, he transacted most of his business in an office located behind his house, on West 4th Street, where he also maintained his stables.

Beyond the outer office was the Commodore's inner sanctum. "The room was furnished somewhat more than the front room," reported the *Herald*. "The walls were covered with pictures and models of boats and ships, and on a high old desk in one corner was a stuffed 'tabby,' of large size, and with such a good-natured face that it seemed to impart an air of comfort to the place which the fire crackling in the grate could not do alone."[24]

In the afternoon, Vanderbilt would often go driving with a team of fast horses on Broadway north of 59th Street, then called the Bloomingdale Road. Trotters had become the rage. "It would seem as if all New York had suddenly become owners of fast horses, and were all out on Bloomingdale on a grand trotting spree. This rushing to and fro of ship commodores, book and newspapers publishers, bankers, merchants, gamblers, and fast men generally, continues until the sun in its daily course has gone to visit the antipodes."[25] Vanderbilt, of course, was one of the fastest drivers along Bloomingdale Road's unpaved and often rutted way, to the terror of his passengers. There were few who could beat him regularly in the impromptu races that were held.

In the evening Vanderbilt loved to play whist or poker, games that allowed him both to be sociable and to exercise his formidable powers of deductive reasoning and psychological dominance. These games often took place at the Manhattan or Union Club when he didn't play at home.[26]

•

In 1849 gold was discovered in California and tens of thousands of people set out to make their fortunes. At that time there were three ways to get there. One was the long, dangerous, and difficult overland route. Another was to sail around Cape Horn at the southern tip of South America, a trip that often took six months and even more. The third was to sail to Panama, trek across the fever-ridden isthmus on muleback, and then take ship to San Francisco.

While the hopes of almost all who went to the gold fields of California would come to nothing, the gold rush would be the means of transforming Commodore Vanderbilt from a man who was merely very rich into one who was rich almost beyond the comprehension of his contemporaries. Not that he went to California, of course; he knew that to be a fool's game. What Vanderbilt did was to find a much better way of getting there.

The Commodore noticed on a map that Lake Nicaragua emptied into the Atlantic through the San Juan River. He reasoned that if a steamboat could ascend the San Juan and cross the lake, the trek to the Pacific would be both shorter and far less miasmal than the isthmian route. He ordered the construction of the *Prometheus,* which at fifteen hundred tons was one of his first ocean-going ships. Sneaking out of town—he didn't even tell his wife where he was going—he sailed her to Nicaragua, towing behind him the small steamer *Director,* in which he proposed to work his way up the San Juan.

When he arrived in Nicaragua, he dispatched a team of engineers ahead to survey and report back to him. They said that the whole idea was impossible, the river was too full of rapids and other obstacles and could not be navigated. "This report," wrote Croffut, "disgusted the Napoleon of navigation, who felt that he was losing $5,000 a day by the delay."

Vanderbilt had the *Director's* boilers fired up and announced that he was going up to the lake "without any more fooling."

"Sometimes," Croffut reported, "he got over the rapids by putting on all steam; sometimes this did not avail, and he extended heavy cables to great trees upstream and warped the boat over in that way. Every device was resorted to. On returning to New York the engineers reported that he 'tied down the safety valve and "jumped" the obstructions, to the great terror of the whole party.' "[27]

The *Director* and her party, terrified and not, made it to the lake, and before long the route was established. It was immediately and hugely profitable. The route was six hundred miles and two days shorter than the Panama route, which meant that Vanderbilt could charge a lower fare and make a higher profit. By 1854, according to Croffut, the Commodore was netting $1,000,000 a year from the

Nicaragua route. That year Vanderbilt himself reckoned his net worth at $11,000,000, on which he was receiving a return of 25 percent per year.

He decided, at the age of sixty, that it was time for a vacation. He built the *North Star,* 270 feet long and fitted with every luxury. Gathering his family and several friends he set sail for Europe, the first of what would become a seemingly endless parade of American millionaires to visit the glories of the Old World while coddled in comforts provided by the wealth of the New.

To handle the Accessory Transit Company, which controlled his Nicaragua interests, he put Charles Morgan, a well-known ship-owner, in charge of the Atlantic end while he hired Cornelius K. Garrison at the huge salary of $60,000 a year to run the Pacific side of the business. Morgan had a good reputation in the New York commercial world while Garrison, a former Mayor of San Francisco, was thought so clever and ruthless that it would take "twenty men to watch him."

Hardly had the *North Star* steamed over the horizon before Morgan and Garrison took over the company. Vanderbilt was removed from the board, new company offices were set up, Morgan had himself elected president, and several of Vanderbilt's enemies—of whom, by this time, he had a goodly number—were given places on the board. The *Herald,* in detailing these developments, laconically noted that "trouble is anticipated upon the return of Commodore Vanderbilt."[28]

When he did return to New York, the first thing he did was to anchor off Staten Island and pay his mother (who was soon to die) a visit. The second was to fulfill the *Herald*'s prophecy. The Commodore wrote a short and soon famous letter:

> Gentlemen:
>   You have undertaken to cheat me. I won't sue you, for the law is too slow. I'll ruin you.
>
>   Yours truly,
>   Cornelius Vanderbilt[29]

Morgan and Garrison proved unusually tenacious and resourceful opponents. But in the end, if they were not ruined, they were most heartily sorry that they had taken on the Commodore.

Vanderbilt continued to expand his shipping empire. While

fighting Morgan and Garrison, he put his steamers, including the *North Star,* on the Panama route until he was paid $40,000—later $56,000—a month not to. He even tried the North Atlantic route, which had been dominated up to then by the heavily subsidized British Cunard Line and the equally heavily subsidized American Collins Line. Steamers designed by the Commodore soon snatched the Atlantic Blue Ribbon for the fastest ocean crossing.

But ideas were beginning to stir in his mind as once, forty years earlier, other ideas had stirred when he sensed the coming power of steamships.

Vanderbilt had had a long and understandable antipathy to railroads. They lacked the mobility of steamships, which could be sent where the competition was most vulnerable, and in 1833 he had been involved, and very nearly killed, in the first serious railroad accident in the United States. The car ahead of his had broken an axle while traveling at the then high speed of twenty-five miles an hour. The train jumped the tracks and everyone else in his car was killed while he was thrown out and dragged along before being flung down an embankment. He had suffered several broken ribs and a punctured lung, which caused terrible pain. He was months recovering.

But his personal dislike did not matter to him. As early as 1854 he was inspecting the Harlem Railroad as once he had inspected the *Clermont.* He would pack a lunch and a bottle of cider and ride the road from one end to the other and back again. "After I had made my collection," a conductor remembered long afterward, "the Commodore would ply me with questions about the Harlem road. How many gallons of milk did we haul a day? How many engines had we? Were they good? Did the farmers patronize the road?"[30]

In his sixties and already rich beyond compare, Cornelius Vanderbilt decided that it was in railroads, not his beloved steamboats, that his future lay. He was right, of course; the Commodore's greatest days were yet to come.

CHAPTER FOUR

The Early Skirmishes

VANDERBILT was never as wholly innocent about railroads, or their economics and financing, as he liked to pretend. Transportation was his business, and as one of the richest citizens of the country's richest city he had often been called upon to invest in various railroad projects and help out in financial rescue operations. When the Harlem Railroad was first proposed in 1831, the founders had turned for capital to Vanderbilt, then just beginning his independent steamboat career. All they had gotten, however, was short shrift. "I'm a steamboat man," he told them, "a competitor of these steam contrivances that you tell us will run on dry land. Go ahead. I wish you well; but I never shall have anything to do with 'em."[1]

But by the 1840's, as the railroads spread across the country, Vanderbilt had slowly and inexorably become involved with them despite himself. He had been a director of the Long Island Railroad in that decade as well as the New Jersey Central and the hybrid Stonington Line, half steamboat line, half railroad, controlled by Daniel Drew.

Nor was he ignorant of the ways of Wall Street, where any major investments in railroads would have to take place. In May of 1857 the Commodore had bought 1,001 shares of the New York and Harlem for between $10 and $15 a share and was elected to its board of directors. A few months later, the panic of 1857 swept over Wall Street, and Harlem stock could be bought for as little as $3 a share. Vanderbilt seized the opportunity to increase his holdings.

Panics such as the one that hit the Street that year are the most spectacular and by far the most widely known feature of financial markets. Essentially they are a psychological, not economic, phenomenon and occur when a trend in prices, either up or down, suddenly reverses on extraordinarily high volume. While the great market-wide panics that are long remembered beyond the Street itself can take months to develop, smaller ones can develop in a matter of minutes, even seconds.

Buyer panics, when prices that have been falling suddenly shoot up, happen just as often, but it is seller panics that tend to live on in the folk memory of the Street. Sometimes these have few long-term consequences—except, of course, to those who are wiped out in the process. But the great seller panics in Wall Street history have usually marked major turning points in the development of the national economy, and the scope of the Street has altered fundamentally in consequence. Throughout the nineteenth and early twentieth centuries, they happened roughly every twenty years.

The first great panic on Wall Street had ended the Street's first real bull market in 1837. The crash and the ensuing depression, which lasted well into the 1840's, were extremely painful on the Street. Philip Hone, himself badly burned, wrote in his diary that "the immense fortunes which we heard so much about in the days of speculation have melted like the snows before an April sun."[2]

But, if New York had been hurt, its rival Philadelphia had been hurt much worse. Philadelphia had already fallen behind New York both in population and commercial activity, but had held on to its financial supremacy thanks to its large banks. Among the major casualties of the crash of 1837, however, was the state government of Pennsylvania, and the Philadelphia banks, holding large amounts of their state government's paper, were crippled by the inability of the state to pay the interest due. New York State was able to meet its financial obligations and the New York financial community soon outstripped that of Philadelphia and never looked back.

Still, Philadelphia maintained its status as a major financial center because markets can never be larger than the area in which communication is instantaneous. Buyers and sellers must know what the current prices are and what the latest news is. Thus in a very real sense it was Samuel F. B. Morse who ended forever Philadelphia's days as a serious rival to Wall Street.

Until the 1840's the speed of communication had been effectively limited to the speed of human travel, but Morse divorced thought from flesh when he found a way for communication to move in huge amounts at the speed of light. His great invention, the precursor of the electrical revolution that would begin in earnest in the last two decades of the century, very quickly affected the way people lived and the size of their world. Its effect on Wall Street was almost immediate, for once the telegraph began to spread through the country in the mid-1840's, Philadelphia capital flowed through its wires into New York just as surely as the electric current.

"Money," James K. Medbery wrote in 1870 as the undersea cable laid in 1866 was just beginning the long process of uniting the New York and London markets, "always has a tendency to concentrate itself, and stocks, bonds, gold, rapidly accumulate at those points where the most considerable financial activity prevails. The greater the volume of floating wealth, the more conspicuous this peculiarity. It resulted from this law that New York City became to the United States what London is to the world. Eminent before, this chief metropolis of the seaboard now assumed an absolute financial supremacy. Its alternations of buoyancy and depression produced corresponding perturbations in every state, city, and village in the land."[3]

Unlike the earlier panic, the panic of 1857 proved very short-lived on the Street, thanks to the outbreak of the Civil War. To be sure, the sudden division that the country underwent following the election of Abraham Lincoln to the Presidency severed the close financial and commercial bonds that had grown up between New York and the South in the previous half-century and shook the Street and the city momentarily.

But any crisis long enough sustained becomes routine, and before very long Wall Street adjusted to the withdrawal of Southern capital and business, which in any event was more than compensated for by the economic prosperity caused by the war. By the beginning of 1862 Wall Street found itself in the middle of a bull market far larger and more frenetic than any it had known before, or would know again until the 1920's.

"The speculative fever reached a height unequalled at any previous or succeeding stage of the national history," wrote Medbery in 1870 as the bull market and its consequences still swirled about him. "Many brokers earned from eight hundred to ten thousand dollars a day in commissions. The entire population of the country entered the field. Offices were besieged by crowds of customers. At least a hundred millions of dollars were realized in sales. New York never exhibited such wide-spread evidences of prosperity. Broadway was lined with carriages. The fashionable milliners, dress-makers, and jewelers reaped golden harvests. The pageant of Fifth Avenue on Sunday and of Central Park during week-days was *bizarre,* gorgeous, wonderful! Never were such dinners, such receptions, such balls. Anonyma startled the city with the splendor of her robes and the luxury of her equipages. Vanity Fair was no longer a dream."[4]

Wall Street, like the city itself, had changed completely in appearance from the time when trading first began and federal-style houses lined most of its length. The great steeple of the third Trinity Church now lorded it over the five- and six-story commercial buildings that had replaced the houses, but sunlight still flooded its gently crooked way.

The rules by which the Street lived had hardly changed at all since the days of the buttonwood tree. Federal securities laws were nonexistent. State law was very limited and could, when it proved inconvenient, usually be ignored or circumvented by the action of a friendly judge. When the Commodore decided he wanted the New York and Harlem Railroad, the Street was still very much a private club.

And, thanks in large part to Daniel Drew's bag of tricks, it had become even more mysterious to outsiders. Before the reforms of the 1930's outlawed most means by which security prices could be artificially manipulated, speculators could, and very frequently did, cause prices to temporarily fluctuate in ways that suited their purposes but had nothing whatever to do with the underlying value. (After the stock ticker was invented, in 1867, these activities would come to be known as "painting the tape.")

But prices on Wall Street, as in every free market, have nonetheless always been subject to the natural law of the marketplace, a law that is every bit as ineluctable as those of physics but, even today, far less profoundly understood in its implications and, unhappily for the world, far less widely accepted.

A free market is composed of all potential buyers and sellers of a given commodity, with each individual seeking only to make a profit. Without exception—and whether its participants be a group of ten-year-olds exchanging baseball cards or multinational corpora-

WALL STREET IN 1866

tions trading the wherewithal of modern industrial states—free markets respond to the same fundamental reality, and prices are determined by the interaction of supply and demand.

If the supply of a commodity available to a market increases while demand remains the same, prices will fall, as traders who wish to sell compete among themselves for buyers by seeking to offer better terms—that is to say a lower total cost—than the next man. Conversely, if demand increases while supply remains constant, the buyers must compete for sellers and the price will rise.

While the law of supply and demand operates inexorably in all free markets, its effects are most immediate and obvious in markets such as Wall Street's, known as auction markets, where buyers and sellers are in intimate and continuing contact.

In such a free market there have always been only two ways to make money, or for that matter lose it. If the trader thinks that prices are on their way up, he will "go long," purchasing the commodity at the current price, hoping to sell it later at a higher one. If, on the other hand, he thinks prices are about to fall, he "goes short." In this case he sells a commodity that he does not own, either borrowing it to complete the transaction or promising to deliver it at a future date. Then, if the price does fall, he is able to buy the commodity, called covering his short, and return it to the person from whom he borrowed it or deliver it to fulfill his contract, pocketing the difference in price.

There is one important difference between being long and being short in the market. If a trader holds a commodity that falls in value to zero—Christmas trees on December 26th, for instance—he loses his entire investment. But a short seller can lose everything he owns if the market turns against him, for while a commodity cannot be worth less than nothing, its price can rise almost indefinitely. And a speculator must fulfill his contracts regardless of the cost or he is out of the game. Wall Street tradition says that it was Daniel Drew, the Great Bear himself, who expressed the short seller's essential nightmare in a couplet:

> He who sells what isn't his'n
> Buys it back or goes to prison.

Since supply and demand will always determine the price of a commodity in a free market, speculators have always sought to control the supply and thus control the price. While the means they employed in these manipulations are almost beyond number, Wall Street's favorite and most elaborate ploy was the device known as the pool.

The members of a pool would try to affect the price of the targeted stock by artful rumor mongering and carefully planned purchases and sales among themselves (known as wash sales). In all cases, however, the object was for the pool to end up already short the stock when the outsiders were beguiled into selling or to be long when heavy buying began. Pools, despite their enduring popularity with speculators, were actually seldom very profitable. It was not easy to achieve the exquisite timing that was necessary to make them pay commensurately with the effort and risk involved.

The more ambitious pools, the sort that made it into the newspapers, required achieving a corner, a device that when successful paid very handsomely indeed. A corner in a market is nothing more than a temporary monopoly of supply.[5] A trader with a corner owns all of a commodity that is available for sale—whether it be shares in a corporation, rights to an invention, or tickets to a hit show—and thus any potential buyer must buy from him or do without. But the short seller, if the time to fulfill his contract is at hand, has no choice but to buy from the holder of the corner and at the price the holder sets.

In a corner, a short seller who has borrowed stock discovers—too late—that he has borrowed from and sold to the same man. In one reported case, the same certificate for six hundred shares of Harlem Railroad was loaned by the pool manipulating the stock no fewer than six times and sold right back to it six times through different brokers by short sellers who did not know what was afoot. When a true corner is achieved, the short sellers, caught in a financial pincers, are said to be squeezed, an exciting, often noisy, sometimes messy event.

But the price level that is set by supply and demand affects in its turn both supply and demand. If the price is thought to be high, more sellers will be tempted into the market, while more buyers will seek substitutes or do without as they wait for the price to fall again.

For this reason corners can be held, in many cases, for only a brief period of time before the price level imposed by the holder of the corner attracts supplies from the hinterland and the desperate shorts have somewhere else to turn. And, in addition, assembling a corner in the first place requires the most delicate timing and artful deception. Somehow, every last drop of available supply must be mopped up, either purchased or neutralized, without driving the price to infinity or having others catch onto the game and flee before the trap can be sprung.

Corners have occurred since markets were invented—the first corner in New York was in 1666 when Frederick Philipse, the colony's richest citizen, cornered the wampum market[6]—and by the mid-nineteenth century it seemed that "hardly a week goes by without a recurrence of these singular phenomena."[7] But they have become increasingly scarce as markets have grown larger and communications swifter. Today, with instant worldwide communications and a host of governmental and stock exchange regulations that firmly discourage if they do not explicitly forbid them, corners are effectively extinct in securities markets, although not in commodities markets. There has not been a true corner on the New York Stock Exchange since the early 1920's.

•

The New York and Harlem Railroad, which had brought the Commodore to the Street, had never been a particularly prosperous enterprise. Chartered by the New York State Legislature in 1831, it was originally intended to operate wholly within Manhattan Island, being authorized to "lay down a single or a double pair of rails from any point north of 23rd Street to any point on the Harlem River between Third and Eighth Avenues, with a branch to the Hudson River between 124th and 129th Streets."[8]

It was soon realized that 23rd Street, which in 1831 was still considerably north of the built-up area of the city, was too far north to be useful as a terminus, and the railroad received an amended charter allowing it to run its tracks as far south as Union Square on 14th Street and to operate horse-drawn streetcars wherever the Common Council and Mayor should allow. The Harlem elected to use Fourth Avenue, now Park Avenue, for its route and it moved more or less steadily northward, tunneling 596 feet from what would one day be 92nd Street to 94th Street through what is now called Carnegie Hill. On October 10th, 1837, the year the Harlem began to use steam engines rather than horses for motive power, it reached the Harlem River.

The railroad established a terminal for steam engines just south of Murray Hill at Fourth Avenue between 26th and 27th streets, at what is today the site of the New York Life Insurance Building. After the engines were detached at 26th Street the cars were hauled down to Union Square by horses. The rapidly growing population of the area complained of the noise and smoke of the engines—even after the railroad had built a tunnel through Murray Hill itself, a tunnel now used by automobiles. The residents succeeded in getting the southern limit for steam power set first at 32nd Street and in 1858 at 42nd Street, which is why Grand Central Terminal is located there.

The Harlem had been an expensive railroad to build, costing $1,100,000 or about $137,500 a mile, almost four times the average cost of railroad construction in the country at that time.[9] One reason for this high cost was the difficult nature of Manhattan's geography and another was the necessity of ignoring that geography and adhering instead to the rigid geometry of the grid plan, although the grid plan existed, above 23rd Street, only on paper.

In 1841 the Harlem was authorized to extend its rails as far north as Albany. It could have utilized the sea-level route along the east bank of the Hudson River—the route developed a few years later by the Hudson River Railroad—but the Harlem apparently feared the competition of the steamboats. It opted instead to meander northward east of the river through an area of small towns and farms whose prosperity was to come to an abrupt end when the railroads connected the lush farmland of the Middle West with the Eastern Seaboard. By December 1st, 1844, the Harlem had reached White Plains, and on January 10th, 1852, it reached Chatham Four Corners, now called simply Chatham, and the junction with the Boston and Albany Railroad.

Because the area through which the railroad ran was bereft of towns of any size or manufacturing of any consequence, its passenger revenues were always at least as important as its freight revenues, although neither was very large even by the standards of the day. Annual passenger revenues, with one exception, never amounted to more than half a million dollars until 1863, and its freight earnings only reached that figure in 1859.

But the Harlem made it possible for the first time to live in the country and work in the city. In a sense it was the Harlem and the Long Island Railroad that invented New York's suburbia. One of the first, and by far the most prominent, of the regular commuters was Horace Greeley, who lived in Chappaqua in northern Westchester County and who was by no means above using his paper to complain publicly about the frequent lapses in service he suffered on the Harlem line.

Its territory losing population everywhere except at its southern end by the early 1860's, the Harlem did not look like much of an investment. In its thirty years as a going concern it had managed to pay dividends amounting to only 13 percent of the capital that had been invested in it. As late as March 25th, 1863, the New York *Herald,* the paper usually most attuned to what was happening on Wall Street, wrote that "of all the railroad shares dealt in, the Harlem probably possesses the least intrinsic value." But the Commodore was steadily buying the stock, and some in Wall Street were wondering if the old man—he would turn sixty-nine in May of that year—was beginning to slip.

While Vanderbilt was immensely rich, he had as yet no real reputation on Wall Street, and its habitués had seen many an entrepreneur arrive with a new-minted fortune and promptly lose much or all of it. But the brokers and speculators did not realize what Vanderbilt was really about. He was not in the least interested in speculation but rather in investment, and he, if almost nobody else, saw great possibilities in the New York and Harlem Railroad.

The Harlem had never been particularly well managed. Although Vanderbilt had never run a railroad, he had no doubt whatever that he could run the Harlem a lot more efficiently. A second reason for investing in the Harlem was that, of all the railroads that served New York City, only it and the Hudson River Railroad, in which the Commodore was also quietly and increasingly investing, had direct access to Manhattan Island. The railroads from the West were blocked by the Hudson River, then unbridged south of Troy, and the New York and New Haven Railroad had to pay to use the Harlem's right of way into the city. A third and compelling reason was the paragraph in the amended charter of the railroad allowing the City of New York to grant streetcar franchises to the Harlem as it saw fit.

The bartering and corruption in the granting of streetcar franchises in New York and other cities around the country was one of the continuing scandals of the mid-nineteenth century. The legislators who controlled these rights were usually far more concerned with feathering their own nests than with providing transportation to the citizens or revenues to the government. There was little, beyond personal honor, to stop them from soliciting and accepting bribes. Most New Yorkers would certainly have agreed with George Templeton Strong in 1857 when he wrote in his diary, "Heaven be praised for all its mercies, the Legislature of the State of New York has adjourned."[10] Matters had become so flagrant by 1860 that Horace Greeley wrote in the *Tribune* that he did not think it possible "that another body so reckless, not merely of right but of decency—not merely corrupt but shameless—will be assembled in our halls of legislation within the next ten years."[11] But Strong, Greeley, and New York City had seen nothing yet.

George Law, who had built the Croton Aqueduct, had secured franchises from the Legislature for streetcar lines on Eighth and Ninth avenues and was now after the biggest franchise of all, the right to operate on Broadway, the city's busiest, grandest thoroughfare. "When we reflect," wrote Fowler in 1870, "that from one to two hundred millions of people pass up and down that roaring thoroughfare every year, the value of this grant may be estimated."[12] A bill was introduced in Albany that would have granted Law the franchise in return for nothing in the way of revenues for the city. Law was spending heavily to see that passage was assured.

The Harlem went to the Mayor and Common Council, the equivalent of today's City Council, and suggested that they use the powers granted under the Harlem charter to give the railroad the franchise in return for 10 percent of the revenues and an annual $25 license fee for every car. There can be little doubt that this offer was accompanied by a good deal of bribery, but at least the Common Council, a far smaller body than the Legislature, could be bought more cheaply.

When the bill was introduced in the Council, Harlem stock began to rise in anticipation of its passage, and many members of the Council itself were among the heavy purchasers. By early April the stock had risen to the low 50's. It had been a speculative favorite all winter and, as Fowler noted, "It seemed to have quicksilver in it, and hobbled up and down without apparent cause, as though some strange atmosphere was at work on it. The stock was the favorite one of the whole catalogue, and was operated in boldly, both on the long and short side, in amounts so large that the whole capital stock sometimes changed hands in a single day. Vanderbilt was known to be buying it for investment, and some of the sharp ones were chuckling at the idea of 'sticking' him with big 'jags' of it at 58 and 60. The idea that he was buying it for *investment* seemed intensely funny to the brokers. They sold it right and left, in the most dashing style, amid the laughter of their associates. Still he kept buying it."[13]

"The Commodore moved about through the turbid waters of the Street, making no secret of his doings and quietly absorbing into his vast financial maw the huge slices of Harlem fed out to him by the frolicsome and infatuated bears."[14]

On April 22nd, 1863, the Common Council passed the franchise bill and Mayor Opdyke announced that he would sign it. The next day the *Herald* reported that "Harlem opened at 64, against 58 last evening, advanced on the Broadway Railroad Ordinance to 75, reacted to 68 . . . and closed at 68. The short interest in this stock has been very large and the bears have suffered very severely indeed. They seem, however, to be quite as anxious as ever to put out contracts."[15]

The Harlem lost no time in exercising its new-won rights. The very next morning it had crews at work tearing up the cobblestones in Union Square. At 15th Street and Fourth Avenue a *Herald* reporter found that "a small army of laborers, supplied with crowbars and pickaxes, were tearing away at the pavement in magnificent style, under the direction of an energetic supervisor." At Broadway and 14th Street an even larger crew was at work, while a crowd of citizens gathered, in the best New York City fashion, to watch them work and debate the merits of the franchise. One man firmly declared, "I'm opposed to this damned swindle. This is a regular outrage upon the city. Talk about being a free city. Bah! Free! Free to be robbed and fleeced by a pack of ignorant boors and unprincipled pothouse politicans. I tell you, sir, the people here ought not to stand for it."[16] But, if the Harlem franchise was a damned swindle, the Law franchise, most of the sidewalk superintendents agreed, was a far worse one.

Anticipating injunctions from Law and his allies, the officers and directors of the New York and Harlem made themselves scarce that day, and it was seven in the evening before an injunction could be served, on a foreman of one of the crews, and work halted. The Legislature then passed the Law franchise and sent it to Governor Horatio Seymour, who was "now sitting upon and cogitating over it like an old hen in a fearful dilemma," the *Herald* wrote. "The excitement over this extends throughout the city, and bets are freely made on both sides. Even Wall Street is running wild over it, and is betting upwards of ninety on the stock of a railroad that but a few months ago was on the market somewhere in the teens."[17]

Once the Legislature passed the bill, Law sent his own crews onto Broadway, and it appeared for a while that the crews of the rival franchises might come to blows until another flurry of injunctions stopped all work. On May 7th Seymour vetoed the Law franchise, calling it a violation of the state constitution's home-rule provisions, and on May 8th the stock of Harlem closed at 98½. The *Herald,* not normally as concerned with the ethical and moral issues as the *Tribune* and the *Times,* was disgusted with Albany. "The Legislature," James Gordon Bennett wrote, "showed by its recent action that it was bought up almost to a man by the money of these concerns, and that the rights and interests of the city had not the slightest weight with it."[18]

On May 19th Harlem hit 116⅝, nearly six times its price only a few months earlier. Then a wave of heavy short sales began to batter the stock. Word spread that "The Aldermen and Councilmen of the City of New York *were selling Harlem,* the pet of the Commodore, the life of the Street."[19] A prime mover behind this short selling, apparently, was one of the Harlem's own directors, Daniel Drew. E. C. Stedman, writing forty years later of events to which he was an eyewitness, reported that "the spiritual Mr. Drew is said to have been a partner in this scheme, which he no doubt regarded as an agreeable pleasantry at the expense of his good friend Vanderbilt."[20]

Vanderbilt, it was rumored, had warned the Council—doubtless in no uncertain terms, for the Commodore was no diplomat—against the folly of their actions. For a while the stock "vibrated between 90 and 105. But someone was always ready to buy it, particularly when the sellers wished to *go short of it.* A great hand was always extended to receive the stock and pass it away out of sight, in a deep, broad iron chest."[21]

On June 10th Harlem stood at 88½ and two weeks later was down to 80 at the afternoon call of the Regular Board. Ignoring the Commodore's warning, "the Common Council, who had fattened their purses some weeks before with profits made on the long side of Harlem, now prepared to take further profits by covering their extensive shorts. As a means to that laudable end, at four o'clock on the afternoon of June 25th they passed a resolution rescinding the Broadway grant."[22] It was too late for the action of the Council to affect the price on the Regular or Open boards, but the price on the Curb fell "like a shot partridge" to 72, and the bears were licking their chops in anticipation of the Commodore's impending embarrassment.

The price of Harlem the next day did not fall further, however. Far from it: it rose to 97, and on Saturday morning, June 27th, it hit

THE REGULAR BOARD   The brokers at the New York Stock Exchange did not lose their actual seats until the 1880's.   *Courtesy of the Union Club Library*

106. The reason was soon obvious to everyone, even the stunned members of the Council. "The chief owners of the Harlem property," the *Times* explained on that date, "are Mr. Cornelius Vanderbilt and his immediate friends, and that portion of the capital stock which they have not already paid for and transferred to their names they have the cash means in bank to pay for, whenever the short sellers—who have contracted for more than the entire capital—are ready to make their deliveries. The public sympathies are wholly with Mr. Vanderbilt in this transaction, and there are the most hearty congratulations exchanged in the Street today that the shameless trick and fraud of the City Council and their stock-jobbing co-conspirators have been paid off with compound interest."

On Monday, June 29th, while the *Herald* was gleefully reporting that as many as fifty thousand shares had been shorted "by parties who had the misfortune to be in the secret,"[23] the much-chastened Council rescinded its rescission of the grant. Vanderbilt magnanimously permitted the price of the stock to fall to 94, at which price, according to Stedman, the Council members were allowed to fulfill their contracts. But Vanderbilt had no intention of allowing the professionals of Wall Street, as opposed to the potentially useful Council members, off the hook so easily. No sooner had the Council members covered their shorts than the price bounced back up. As summer advanced, so too did the price of Harlem, "amid the execrations of the whole ursine tribe. No mercy! Still up, 120, 125, 130, 140. The bears loosed their hold by dozens as it rose. At 150 most of them had covered. Some hard heads still kept their positions. But when it touched 180 there was not a single man of them left."[24]

The first Harlem corner was over. By year's end the price of the stock had settled back to 89¾.

•

While the Harlem corner would have been enough to occupy the mind and fortune of the Commodore that summer, his other major railroad interest, the Hudson River Railroad, was also the subject of speculative manipulation on the Street.

The Hudson River Railroad had been chartered in 1846 to exploit the route along the river's east bank that the Harlem had spurned. By 1849 it was running from New York to as far north as Poughkeepsie, from where the initial impetus to build the road had come, and in 1851 it completed its route to East Albany. From there, through passengers and freight were ferried across the Hudson to connect with what would soon become the consolidated New York Central.

While the engineering difficulties of building the Hudson River route had been considerable—the land often slopes precipitously down to the water's edge—once it was done its advantages over the Harlem's route were obvious. It was sea level all the way, making the trains much cheaper to operate than those that traveled over the Harlem's many grades. And the railroad connected substantial towns such as Yonkers, Peekskill, Beacon, and Poughkeepsie with both Albany and New York City. In winter the railroad had the route to itself, but even in other times of the year it proved able to hold its own against the competition of the steamboats on the river. Better managed than the Harlem, the Hudson usually made a profit, and in 1861 the railroad completed its new terminal at 30th Street and Tenth Avenue just in time to receive President-elect Lincoln on his way to Washington.

Vanderbilt, possibly already envisioning what would soon be known as the Vanderbilt system—the combination of the New York Central, Hudson, and Harlem railroads—bought Hudson stock steadily. By 1863 he was on the board and was one of the principal stockholders.

Just as the members of the Common Council were about to double-cross the Commodore on Harlem, a bear raid was organized on Wall Street against Hudson stock. The bears, perhaps, were counting on Vanderbilt's preoccupation with Harlem for a free hand in manipulating his other interests. According to Henry Clews, Vanderbilt had taken to his yacht and was sunning himself on a pile of logs on the New Jersey side of the Hudson when news of the raid reached him. "The Commodore," wrote Clews in his most flowery manner, "arose and shook off his lethargy as a lion may be supposed to shake the dew from his mane."[25] He went down to Wall Street and ordered his brokers to buy all the seller's options that were offered in the stock.

At this time, stock was often sold for future delivery within a specified time period, usually ten, twenty, or thirty days, with the precise time of delivery at the discretion of either the buyer—in which case it was called a buyer's option—or the seller. Short selling was usually accomplished by use of seller's options rather than by actually borrowing the stock.

These options differed from modern options—puts and calls, which existed then but were seldom important tools of stock speculation—in that puts and calls convey only a right, not an obligation, to complete the contract. But a person who bought stock "buyer thirty," as a thirty-day buyer's option was called, was obliged to take title to the stock within the time period regardless of any movement in the stock price in the interval. By buying up all the seller's options that were offered, Vanderbilt was, in effect, announcing his intention to corner the stock. But the Commodore had something far more elegant in mind than an ordinary corner. "The prolific brain of the Commodore . . . [had] invented a new move in the game,"[26] and he was about to demonstrate, in Russell Sage's words, that "he was to finance what Shakespeare was to poetry and Michelangelo to art."[27]

The Street, indeed the whole city, knew that he was heavily involved in the action in Harlem, and with this new threat to his fortune to be countered, it was easy to believe that Vanderbilt, rich as he was, might be pressed for ready cash with which to finance the corner. The Commodore made no moves to dispel the rumors and probably helped to noise them about. His brokers certainly acted as if the attempt to corner Hudson was underfinanced, for they approached other brokers and asked them to "turn" the stock, a move that would have been known nearly instantly all over the Street.

Turning was a means whereby, with a maximum of luck, a corner might be achieved with a minimum of cash. The would-be cornerer would buy stock from outsiders and immediately turn around and sell it for cash to another party, buying back from that party a buyer's option at a slight advance in price, thus preserving his cash while increasing his control. The trouble for the cornerer with turning a stock was that the party who had bought the stock was under no obligation to hold it until the cornerer exercised his buyer's option. If he felt that the corner would fail, and the vast majority of corners did fail, he could sell the stock, confident that he could buy it back cheaper when he had to fulfill his buyer's option.

As it was widely thought that the Commodore was in over his head, many of the brokers who had turned the stock immediately sold it and waited for the corner to break. But Vanderbilt, in truth, was not cash short; he and his friends had plenty of it. The brokers did not know it, of course, but they were selling to intermediaries of the Commodore, for cash, stock they had already contracted to sell to the Commodore himself later.

In the first ten days of July, 1863, as Grant triumphed at Vicksburg and Lee failed at Gettysburg, as fifteen hundred bodies piled up in the streets of New York in the greatest riot in the city's history, the Commodore closed the trap. When the seller's options that he had been buying from the shorts began to fall due, the sellers went into the market to buy Hudson stock in order to make their deliveries, only to discover that there was none to be had, for the Commodore owned every share of the floating supply and a good many more besides. Then he called for the stock he had bought on buyer's options, and those unfortunates as well discovered that Vanderbilt was the only seller and that the price was not cheap, for he put it from 112 to 180 virtually overnight.

The Commodore did not insist that the bears fulfill their contracts right away and was happy to lend the necessary stock, albeit at 5 percent interest per day. When it was clear that he could hold the corner as long as necessary, the bears were forced to cover and the Commodore and his allies were richer by more than three million dollars.

Vanderbilt's double envelopment of the bears, Wall Street's Battle of Cannae, was immediately recognized as a masterpiece of financial manipulation, the *Herald* declaring flatly that "Wall Street has never known so successful a corner."[28]

•

Vanderbilt had of necessity become deeply involved in the workings of Wall Street and from the first had shown a total mastery of its ways. But speculation still did not interest him; it just wasn't his game. After one panic on the Street, he was visited at his office by an earnest young reporter.

"Good morning, young man," said the richest man in America.

"What do you say about the panic, Commodore?" asked the reporter.

"I don't say anything about it."

"What do you think about it, then?"

"I don't think about it at all."

"What would you say about it," asked the now slightly desperate but still determined journalist, "if you thought about it, Commodore?"

"How can I tell?" replied Vanderbilt. "See here, young man, you don't mean to go away till I say something. Very well, I'll say something. Don't you never buy anything you don't want, nor sell anything you hain't got!"[29]

Unlike many givers of sound financial advice, Vanderbilt practiced what he preached. "The Commodore," wrote his first and greatly admiring biographer, William A. Croffut, "did not believe in buying and selling invisible things. And he did not believe in selling the same thing he bought. He bought opportunities and sold achievements. He bought nest-eggs and sold chickens."[30] In this way Vanderbilt on the Street was the exact opposite of Drew. In the steamboat business Drew had been as tough and as shrewd as the Commodore, although far more unscrupulous. But on Wall Street Uncle Daniel never rose above the level of speculator, pure and simple; Vanderbilt was seldom less than a capitalist.

Uncle Daniel could not have cared less about the long-term interests of the publicly held companies he dominated, except as they directly coincided with his own short-term interests. Rather, he controlled companies only to be in a better position to manipulate their securities. The game had become for him an end in itself—an addiction that, like all addictions, had come to control its victim. The Commodore, however, had bought Harlem stock not in order to play the great game—although he played it, when challenged, with both gusto and genius—but in order to control the railroad.

On May 19th, 1863, a week before his sixty-ninth birthday and a month before the first Harlem corner, Vanderbilt was elected president of the company. He intended to make the Harlem a paying concern, telling his son William Henry, after he had become master as well of the Hudson River Railroad, "If these railroads can be weeded out and cleaned up and made shipshape, they'll both pay dividends."[31]

The Commodore was sure how to proceed. As he testified later to a committee of the New York State Senate, "My system of railroading is . . . to take care of it just as careful as I would of my own household affairs, handle it just as though it was all mine; just the same as I would if it was my house, to the best of my ability, and take good care of its income; that is my aim, you know, and give that to the stockholders. I am president of three roads, but I have not received a dollar yet from any of them or anything like pay in any form; no commission or any other way you can fix it. I have not got a dollar from any railroad I am in for any fees or anything else."[32] Vanderbilt, in other words, perceived his self-interest to be identical with the interests of the other stockholders and proceeded from there.

Vanderbilt made William Henry, now his most trusted lieutenant after the years of exile, vice president and, in effect, chief operating officer, a task at which he excelled. The younger Vanderbilt introduced immediate reforms, dismissing incompetent and superfluous employees, starting to double-track the line, and building new stations. He increased the rolling stock and "checked extravagance and looked after small economies whose aggregate was large. Before anybody suspected it, the road was a paying investment."[33]

Horace Greeley, the long-suffering commuter from Chappaqua, noticed the change. "The Harlem Railroad," he wrote in the autumn of 1867, "this day puts its train on a winter footing and we, as a paying customer, return thanks to the managers for the excellent accommodations we have enjoyed throughout the past summer, and especially for the Mount Kisco train. We lived on this road when it was poor and feebly managed—with rotten cars and wheezy old engines that could not make schedule time; and the improvement since realized is gratifying. It is understood that the road now pays, and, if so, we are glad of it."[34]

The Vanderbilt philosophy for running a railroad was as simple as it was effective: "1, buy your railroad; 2, stop the stealing that went on under the other man; 3, improve it in every practicable way within a reasonable expenditure; 4, consolidate it with any other road that can be run with it economically; 5, water the stock; 6, make it pay a large dividend."[35]

Stock watering had a very bad press during the late nineteenth century, thanks largely to Daniel Drew, drover and speculator. Journalists like Charles Francis Adams, Jr., and his brother Henry never tired of denouncing the practice. But Vanderbilt—who almost certainly never heard of David Ricardo, perhaps even Adam Smith—knew what he was doing.

Stock watering consists of nothing more than increasing the number of shares outstanding without increasing the paid-in capital or reducing the par value. To many, this amounted to cheating the stockholders by diluting their equity. But the Adams brothers, Medbery, and other "moralists and philosophers" failed to make a crucial distinction. In the hands of people like Drew, chronically short the stock of companies he was supposed to be managing, the practice was indeed nefarious, with Drew the company treasurer creating and issuing new shares for the convenience of Drew the speculator, without bothering to inform the real stockholders.

But Vanderbilt was the dominant stockholder in the railroads he ran, positions he increased year by year by buying in the open market. Vanderbilt's new issues were publicly announced and fairly distributed. If he was cheating the stockholders, he could only have been chiefly cheating himself.

Vanderbilt in reality simply had a twentieth-century notion of the worth of a stock. He knew, as most of the self-appointed financial reformers seemed not to, that it was not the paid-in capital or even the book value that determined the price but rather the earning power of the corporation. As railroads that came under Vanderbilt's control invariably became far more profitable, and their price on the Street tended to rise far above par, increasing the number of shares outstanding and distributing them to the stockholders only tended to keep the price from going through the roof. In fact, Vanderbilt was guilty of nothing more heinous than paying out what were often lavish stock dividends. Along with the stock dividends came equally lavish cash dividends financed by Vanderbilt's improved management, not by raising tariffs. Journalists may have objected to Vanderbilt's stock watering, but there was nary a peep from the contented stockholders.

Today, the term "stock watering" has disappeared from the Wall Street lexicon, not because the practice has disappeared but because it has become universal. A stock's par value, which once determined its initial price, is now a nearly irrelevant technicality, and many stocks are issued with no par value at all.

•

The spate of injunctions that had halted construction of the Broadway streetcar line had eventually resulted in a court decision that the Common Council in fact lacked the power to grant franchises to the Harlem Railroad beyond what it had granted thirty years earlier. If Vanderbilt was to have his streetcar line, he would need an act of the Legislature in Albany. In February, 1864, he traveled there and secured a pledge from the legislators and the Governor to pass the bill, a pledge for which he undoubtedly paid good money. On March 9th Daniel Drew, Augustus Schell, and other members of the Harlem board also went to Albany and testified in favor of the franchise.

But Drew, it would seem, had other fish to fry while in the state capital: he met privately with some of the legislators to suggest a course of action that was, at the least, at variance with his public testimony before them. He told the Assemblymen and Senators that Harlem stock had been rising swiftly in anticipation of the bill's passing and that if it were suddenly to fail those who had shorted the stock at the recent highs would make a killing. It was, of course, a near carbon copy of what the members of the New York City Common Council had tried the year before with such disastrous consequences for themselves.

One is at a loss to explain how the legislators could have been tempted by the scheme. "The statesmen at Albany," Stedman wrote, "in the spring of 1864, were well aware of the misfortune into which the statesmen at New York had plunged themselves, less than a year before, by their bear campaign against this stock. Yet they rushed fatuously into a similar attempt, as if Vanderbilt had proved an easy victim. Perhaps the public treasury, the customary object of their conspiracies, had lately been too well guarded. Perhaps the opportunities for fleecing corporations were more restricted than they are today. Or perhaps they had achieved such success, in raids of one sort or another, as to become intoxicated by good fortune and reduced to the mental condition of a beast of prey which has tasted blood."[36]

To be sure, Drew was a persuasive talker. If his genius had not expressed itself in stock speculation, there is little doubt that he would have made a first-rate flimflam man; his days as a circus barker could only have honed what was already a considerable native talent. And Vanderbilt's financial position at this time, while equally formidable, was not as comfortable as it had been the year before. Holding huge blocks of Hudson and Harlem stock, he was not nearly as liquid as he might have wished. Drew, who had the instincts of a ferret, probably sensed the Commodore's relative weakness.

Drew had certainly been telling the truth about the stock rise. Harlem had started the year at about 90. By the end of January it was over 100, and a month later it stood at 137½. The legislators went into the scheme with their boots on, and Clews reported that some of them mortgaged their houses to raise money to sell Harlem short. "They advised all their friends that it was such a sure thing that failure was impossible, and brought all their acquaintances whom they could influence into the speculative maelstrom of Harlem."[37]

On March 26th, with Harlem selling for about 140, the committee that had been hearing testimony reported the franchise bill unfavorably. The stock fell immediately to 101. The legislators could have covered their shorts at this point and made a lot of money, but they waited for the stock to fall to 50. The legislators, along with their mentor Daniel Drew, apparently had forgotten one of the oldest of Wall Street truisms: "Bulls make money and bears make money but pigs don't make money."

Obviously they had also forgotten just who it was they were dealing with. Vanderbilt believed in the golden rule. But he also believed firmly in what might be called the Vanderbilt corollary to the golden rule: Do unto others as they have done unto you. The Commodore had no scruples whatever about buying the corrupt New York State Legislature if that was what was required to do a legitimate business. But, being himself a man of honor, he expected the Legislature, once paid for, to stay bought.

According to Clews, "This was probably the darkest hour in the Commodore's life. He hardly knew which way to turn. He was on the ragged edge."[38] While this was certainly a considerable exaggeration, Vanderbilt was indeed in trouble, but he was also furious. He summoned his old friend John M. Tobin. Long active on the Street, Tobin had been an ally of the Commodore in the first Harlem corner and Vanderbilt had known him since he was little more than a boy, having hired him to run the Staten Island end of the Staten Island Ferry. (Tobin had impressed Vanderbilt immediately: being instructed by him that the ferries were always to leave on the dot and were never to be delayed to wait for stragglers, Tobin the next morning dispatched the ferry while the Commodore himself was strolling down the hill toward it.)

"They stuck you too, John," the Commodore said, for Tobin had been holding Harlem stock. "How do you feel about it?" Tobin, not surprisingly, did not feel too good about it.

"Shall we let 'em bleed us, John? Don't these fellows need dressing down? Let's teach 'em never to go back on their word again as long as they draw breath. Let's try the Harlem corner."[39] Tobin put in a million dollars, and others, notably the speculator Leonard Jerome (Sir Winston Churchill's grandfather), brought the sum to five million.

Tobin went into the market and began to buy. "Every day, at the Public Board or in the street, John M. Tobin could have been seen bidding for and buying thousands of shares, his face pale with excitement and his opalescent eyes blazing like a basilisk's."[40] The effect of this mammoth increase in demand was immediate. On the first call of the Regular Board on March 29th, Harlem stood at 109. On the second it rose to 125½, and by the end of the week it was back up to 137½. By April 9th it had reached 175, and the end of the month saw it at 224.

"The members of the Legislature were paralyzed," Clews reported. "They could expect no mercy from the Commodore. He owed them none and though a good Christian prior to his death, he was then practically a stranger to the doctrine of the great Nazarene."[41] When the brokers informed the pool that it held 27,000 more shares than existed (there were only a total of 110,000 shares outstanding), Vanderbilt was asked what to do. The Commodore, Fowler wrote, was taking his revenge. "Five hundred strong men, hard of head and deep of coffer,"[42] were in his grasp.

"Put it to a thousand!" he bellowed. "This panel game is being tried too often."[43]

But Leonard Jerome persuaded the Commodore to temper justice with a little self-interested mercy. He pointed out that while the bears were deep of coffer, no one was that deep. With Harlem at a thousand, Jerome said, half the houses on Wall Street would fail, and the resulting panic would be like nothing known before and would have consequences no one could predict. "The Commodore," Clews relates, "yielded to that touch of nature that makes all the world akin, and under the magnetism of Jerome's prudent entreaty, like Pharaoh with the Israelites, agreed to let the Legislature go—at 285 for Harlem."[44]

Vanderbilt could not have been more delighted. "We busted the whole Legislature," he chortled, "and scores of the honorable members had to go home without paying their board bills!"[45]

The Commodore had not only made millions for himself and his allies—taking those millions out of the hides of people whose misfortunes were entirely self-inflicted—but he had made a reputation such as no man on Wall Street has enjoyed before or since. An Englishman describing Vanderbilt only a few years later wrote that among professional speculators "he assumes the royal dignity and moral tone of a Gaetulian lion among the hyenas and jackals of the desert."[46]

The second Harlem corner was over. There would be no need for a third. For a generation and more on Wall Street the phrase "short of Harlem" would mean much the same thing as "up the creek."

A BROKER'S OFFICE IN THE 1860'S   The customers cut right across class lines.

The New-York and Erie Rail Road

PROBABLY the worst hit in the Harlem débacle was the man who had dreamed up the idea. Daniel Drew owed the Commodore and his friends about $1,700,000.

By no means too proud to snivel and grovel, Drew paid a call on the Commodore and sniveled and groveled with a vengeance, reminding Vanderbilt of their old steamboat days and how he had given William Henry his first job. The Commodore, well aware that magnanimity was hardly Drew's long suit, asked him what mercy Drew would have shown if the stock had fallen to 75 instead of rising to 285. Drew than tried a different tactic, telling the Commodore, if Fowler can be believed, that "these contracts merely say that you may *call* upon me for so much stock; they say nothing about my *delivering* the stock. *Call* then, and keep *calling*, I am not obliged to *deliver* any stock."[1]

This distinctly novel doctrine in contract law would certainly in the long run have proved a slim reed with which to defend a lawsuit. But Vanderbilt and his allies realized that Drew, who knew his way around New York State's all too mercenary judiciary, could postpone the final reckoning almost indefinitely, and they settled for an even $1,000,000. Daniel Drew needed to repair his fortunes. To do that he turned, as he so often would, to his favorite stock, the Erie Railway.

•

That the Erie Railway should have become a "scarlet woman" would not have surprised her Victorian contemporaries, for she was born a bastard. Although the Erie was one of the largest economic enterprises of the day—at completion in 1851 it was, briefly, the longest railroad in the world—the original route and much of the financing were decided by political, not economic considerations. While virtually all railroad projects at the dawn of the era were short local lines, such as the Liverpool and Manchester Railway, the Erie was designed from the beginning to be a trunk line that would run from the Great Lakes to New York City through the Southern Tier, the counties of New York State that border on Pennsylvania.

That the railroad was finally completed at all is a monument to the perseverance and tenacity of two major figures of early American railroading, Eleazar Lord and Benjamin Loder. But some of the decisions they made—many of which were forced upon them by politics and circumstance—would haunt the history of their beloved railroad for a hundred years and more and drive her again and again into bankruptcy and the arms of the unscrupulous.

Like so much else in New York State's economic development, the Erie Canal was the father of the Erie Railway. Governor De Witt Clinton, in order to secure the political support of the Southern Tier for the building of the canal, promised those sparsely populated counties an "avenue" of their own once the canal was finished, to be built by, or with the substantial aid of, New York State. The immense success of the canal, and the boom it immediately engendered along its whole length only accentuated the desire of the people of the Southern Tier for the building of an avenue through their own "sequestered counties."

A canal was out of the question across the rugged Catskill and Allegheny mountains. Thinking at first, therefore, was largely in terms of a toll road, and preliminary surveys were made with that in mind. But the success of the Liverpool and Manchester Railway turned everyone's attention toward the new technology. It was soon clear that what the Southern Tier wanted was a railroad, and residents began to organize in order to push Albany to keep its promise. Meetings were held in many of the towns in the area; petitions were drawn up, debated, and forwarded to Albany.

While the enthusiasm within the Southern Tier was growing quickly, the enthusiasm in Albany even to grant a charter for the railroad, let alone help finance it, was not. Again, the Erie Canal was at the heart of matters. The canal had had an enormous impact on the economy of New York State as well as New York City and thus had had an equally profound impact on the state's politics. The "Canal Ring," a political group dedicated to protecting the advantages enjoyed by the area served by the canal, was in control in Albany and would remain so for some time. It was only with the utmost effort that the politicians from the Southern Tier were able to redeem Governor Clinton's old pledge. The charter that was so grudgingly granted, on April 24th, 1832, made both the building of the railroad and its eventual profitability as dubious as possible. The railroad, which was to be known as the New-York and Erie Rail Road Company, was permitted to raise capital to the extent of $10,000,000, but it was not to organize formally until half the stock had been subscribed to and 10 percent of the purchase price of the stock had been paid in.

Further, the line was to be located wholly in New York State and was to have no connection with any out-of-state railroad without the Legislature's specific permission. In 1832 the ignorance of basic railroad economics was, of course, nearly total. Some even thought that they would operate like a toll road, the owners allowing anyone's trains to operate on the line for a fee. The apparent purpose of the Legislature's seemingly bizarre requirement was to protect the Erie from having traffic siphoned off by other railroads. (In 1850, having learned much in eighteen years, the State Legislature would pass a General Railroad Act requiring all New York State railroads, the Erie included, to connect wherever possible with out-of-state lines.)

To further discourage interconnection with other railroads the charter specified a gauge of six feet. At first, railroads had been built to whatever gauge suited the engineer in charge, but by the late 1840's American railroads were being built either to the Erie's "broad gauge" or, much more commonly, to what was already known as the "standard gauge": four feet, eight and a half inches. (The exact origin of this curious width is one of the mysteries of railroad history.) When it became economically imperative to switch to the standard gauge in the 1880's, the expense proved disastrous for the Erie Railway.

As the railroad could not hope to attract $500,000 in paid-in capital without a precise route already surveyed (for it was expected that the individuals along it would be the major investors) the new corporation turned to the federal government, hoping that it would foot the bill for the surveying. President Jackson, as a man of the frontier, almost always looked with favor upon internal improvements, and at first he promised that the army would make the survey. But he changed his mind after the "Canal Ring" persuaded him through Martin Van Buren, a New Yorker who had been his Secretary of State and would soon be his Vice President and later his successor.

Without a survey it was impossible to raise money, and the committee seeking to do so could do no better than $9,800 of the $500,000 they needed before the charter permitted them to organize officially. The committee appealed to the counties involved to fund the survey, but only Rockland, Orange, and Sullivan counties responded, and not nearly enough money was forthcoming.

There was no choice but to return to the Legislature and ask for an amended charter. After a very considerable political struggle one was granted, permitting organization when only $100,000 had been raised. The subscription books were opened on July 19th, 1833, and ten days later the money was in hand. Among the first directors of the corporation were Stephen Whitney, a cotton broker and one of New York's most prosperous citizens, and Samuel B. Ruggles, a New York real-estate entrepreneur who, two years earlier, had laid out Gramercy Park. The first president was Eleazar Lord.

The New-York and Erie Rail Road, after a protracted labor, had been born. It was very feeble, and its future was problematical at best, but it was alive.

•

Eleazar Lord, who would be president of the New-York and Erie no fewer than three times in the course of the vicissitudes that attended its construction, had been born in Franklin, Connecticut, in 1788 and attended the College of New Jersey (now Princeton University) in order to study for the Presbyterian ministry. Eye disease, however, forced his withdrawal before graduation, and while he gave up his ambition to be a minister, he never lost his interest in missionary work, writing a number of books on the subject, including a *History of the Principal Protestant Missions to the Heathens.*

Moving to New York, Lord founded the Manhattan Fire Insurance Company and prospered with the city. He built a large stone house, as a country seat, in Piermont, New York, located on the west side of the Hudson River's Tappan Zee, just north of the Palisades and the New Jersey state line. Because the charter required that the eastern terminus be in New York State, Lord soon convinced himself that Piermont, twenty-five miles north of New York City, was the best possible place. From there freight and passengers would be taken by steamboat to the company's dock at the foot of Duane Street in Manhattan.

The state was induced to appropriate $15,000 to make a survey, not nearly enough for a thorough job but enough to identify the major problems that lay before the company, and an engineer named Benjamin Wright was hired. He soon determined that geography virtually compelled the line to make two short incursions into Pennsylvania, and the New York State Legislature eventually acceded to necessity and amended the charter to allow it. The State of Pennsylvania, for its part, was happy to allow the Erie to use its territory, however briefly, provided that it receive $10,000 a year in compensation.

Lord insisted, with all the stubborn righteousness of the missionary he had longed to be, that Piermont be the eastern starting point. So Wright worked his way from there northward through the rich agricultural lands of Orange County and into the highlands of the Catskills to Port Jervis on the Delaware River and then to Binghamton, the largest town on the projected route, with a population of about three thousand. From Binghamton, the road ran west through the Southern Tier to the shore of Lake Erie. It was decided that Dunkirk, which had a good harbor but was hardly larger than Piermont, with a population of just four hundred, would be the western terminus.

As Benjamin Wright surveyed the route, the New-York and Erie Rail Road was to extend 483 miles from a town of no importance whatever on the shores of Lake Erie to a town of equal obscurity on the shores of the Hudson, running the whole way between them through territory that was among the least populated in New York State. It was an economic undertaking, in other words, that could only have been planned by politicians. But, as the Erie Canal had amply demonstrated in the previous decade, and as countless railroad projects were to demonstrate in the ensuing ones, good transportation is often all that is needed to induce spectacular growth.

Wright estimated that with bridges and grading for the double track line, but with initially only a single track, the line could be built for $4,726,260. Not even the ever-optimistic directors of the

New-York and Erie were willing to use Wright's estimate unhedged. In their first report, issued at the end of 1835, they wrote that they were "convinced that the whole work can be completed upon the plan recommended in the report of engineers (including vehicles to the amount of $500,000) for a sum not exceeding, and probably falling considerably short of $6,000,000; that the road when finished will admit the use of locomotive engines throughout its entire length drawing weights of at least forty tons net and at a rate of speed which will reduce the time of passage [to] within forty hours from the Hudson River to Lake Erie; and, if necessary funds shall be secured without delay, the whole work can easily be completed and put in operation within five years."[2]

The Committee on Railroads of the New York State Assembly didn't think Wright's estimate worth the paper it was printed on. "Discarding estimates founded entirely on conjecture," the Committee snootily, if wisely, reported in 1834, "and adhering to the practical results from construction of these roads in Pennsylvania, 375 miles of the road in question . . . for a single track will cost $12,327,000. But it is apparent to your committee that this road, with a single track and of so great a length, cannot be advantageously employed for general transportation, nor in any manner accommodate the numerous villages through which it would pass, nor to any extent compete for or accommodate the trade and business of the great West. If constructed at all, it should therefore be constructed with a double track and will in all reasonable propriety cost $16,435,875."[3]

Even the cold-eyed realists who were the authors of the committee report—none too anxious to see the road built at all—proved in the long run to have been as optimistic as their estimates were precise. The Erie would cost a total of $23,500,000 before it was completed, with only sixty miles of double tracking, and it would take not five years but seventeen before a train would run clear through from the Hudson to the Lakes.

In the summer of 1835 the directors asked the stockholders to pay in part of their subscriptions, and the Erie took in $2,362,100. On November 7th, 1835, groundbreaking ceremonies were held at Deposit, New York, a few miles east of Binghamton.

Hardly had the groundbreaking ceremonies been completed, however, when the great fire of December 16th, 1835, erupted in Manhattan and wiped out not only seventeen square blocks of the heart of New York's business district but the fortunes of many of

the Erie stockholders, whose subscriptions were by no means paid
up in full. With the fire and the tightening credit markets that were
beginning to signal the end of the boom of the mid-thirties, it
became increasingly difficult for the railroad to raise new capital as
needed. In 1838, however, it did manage to complete a four-thou-
sand-foot pier that is still a prominent, if no longer functioning,
feature of the Tappan Zee. (Washington Irving, whose house, Sun-
nyside, is directly across the Hudson from Piermont, complained
bitterly that the pier had so altered the usual pattern of currents in
the river that his shoreline was being eroded.)[4]

As the depression that gripped the country after the panic of 1837
deepened, it was soon clear that if the New-York and Erie was ever
to be completed, or even reach the stage where revenues might start
coming in, much more state aid would be needed. One bill passed
the Legislature in 1836 that promised $600,000 in state aid after the
Erie had spent an additional $1,750,000 of its own money. Since the
railroad was already broke and had little prospect of raising more,
this bill was not much help.

The Erie asked its New York stockholders to pay in more on their
subscriptions, but fewer than half did so. The state then passed a
new state aid bill that promised, far more realistically, $100,000 in
state money (later $200,000) for every $100,000 raised by the corporation in the market. Much of this money was raised locally along
the right-of-way from people who had a direct interest in seeing the
completion of the railroad. Even with this local money and the state
aid, however, the New-York and Erie was never far from the brink
of insolvency.

Alexander S. Diven, a long-time director and later a Congressman
and Civil War general, remembered: "We were building a railroad
to cost millions and we hadn't enough money to buy candles. There
was positively not one cent in the treasury. Every director in the
company had endorsed for the last cent he was worth. There was
no gas in those days and we used to pass the hat among us to get
money to pay for the candles which lighted us at our work."[5]

Slowly and erratically, the Erie crept northward from Piermont
through Rockland and Orange counties. On June 30th, 1841, five
and a half years since groundbreaking and seven months after the
date first estimated for the completion of the entire railroad, the first
commercial train ran on the Erie. In September of that year service
was extended as far as Goshen, the county seat and center of commerce for central Orange County.

Almost as soon as service had begun between Goshen and Piermont, cutting the time needed to travel between central Orange County and New York City from the better part of two days to a few hours, the railroad became a major beneficiary of the serendipity that is one of capitalism's greatest and least-appreciated virtues.

Orange County was New York State's leading dairy county, as it would remain for many years to come. But, though it was only about fifty miles from the city, there was no way for the milk produced there to reach New York before it spoiled. Consequently most of it was churned into butter, and "Goshen butter" was famous throughout the country for its high quality. New York City, meanwhile, had to make do as best it could. The wealthier citizens could afford to keep a cow or two in their stables for their own use or pay the price demanded by nearby farmers in Brooklyn, upper Manhattan, and the Bronx, many of whom catered to the city's carriage trade.

Most New Yorkers, however, had to use milk from cows that were kept by brewers and distillers. These poor creatures were fed the mash after it had been fermented and most of its nutrients extracted. Besides having an impoverished diet, the cows were kept in crowded, miserable, and unhealthy conditions. The largest such establishment on Manhattan housed two thousand animals and its stench could be smelled a mile away. And as New Yorkers were just beginning to suspect, "swill milk," as it was called, was a major source of tuberculosis, cholera, and other potentially milk-borne diseases. Swill milk was a prime contributor to New York's appalling rate of infant mortality.

Thomas Selleck, who had been appointed by the railroad to be its agent in Chester, not far from Goshen, had an idea. He saw a product in abundant supply at one end of the Erie Railway and a vast market for it at the other. Why not, he thought, move the milk by railroad? At first the local farmers refused to take him seriously—everyone knew that milk could not be transported any distance without going sour—but in the spring of 1842 he persuaded Philo Gregory, a local dairy farmer, to ship 240 quarts of milk via the Erie to New York, where it sold out instantly. Soon lines a block long were forming to meet the Erie steamboats bringing fresh country milk down from the Piermont terminal. By July, 1843, the *New York Railroad Journal* could say that "At this moment fine and wholesome milk is sold all over the city at four cents a quart. The price for swill and adulterated milk was six. This wonderful revolution has been wrought through the agency of the New-York and Erie Rail Road."[6]

Soon the Goshen *Independent Republican* could report happily that "Orange County milk is driving swill milk from the city."[7]

Although it would be more than thirty years before swill milk disappeared altogether from New York, in 1842 the Erie shipped between 600,000 and 700,000 quarts of milk to New York. In the next year it shipped 4,000,000, and by 1845 milk accounted for 40 percent of the Erie's freight revenues. (By 1900 the Erie would be shipping 73,000,000 quarts of milk into New York City every year.) Almost as if to keep all this milk company, the Erie also became a major shipper of berries to the city, and in 1846 carried over 400,000 boxes of strawberries, about one box for every New Yorker.

The milk trade's entirely unanticipated revenues did not develop quickly enough to solve the corporation's soon chronic cash-flow problems. Perhaps because of its money problems, or more likely because Eleazar Lord, again president of the Erie, feared for the status of his precious Piermont, the Erie passed up at this time a golden opportunity that would almost certainly have made it the most important railroad in the Northeast.

When the New York and Harlem began to build northward through Westchester County, its president, Samuel R. Brooks, wrote the Erie and suggested that it lay tracks from a point opposite Piermont to connect with the Harlem's own. This would have given the Erie, with only a short ferry connection, direct access to New York City at a cost estimated at less than $90,000, a pittance compared to what the Erie had already spent west of the Hudson. While Brooks's suggestion is preserved in the archives of the Erie Railway, no reply, if there ever was one, has survived, and certainly no action was taken regarding it.

As E. H. Mott, the great historian of the Erie, wrote in 1899 in his monumental *Between the Ocean and the Lakes,* "The great Vanderbilt system of today is centered where the Erie might have been and should have been. It is idle to speculate on how different the country's commercial affairs and individual power and fortune would have been if short-sightedness, incompetence, or what you will, had not reigned in Erie management two generations ago."[8]

•

The Erie's financial situation went from bad to worse in the darkling economic conditions of the early forties. In the spring of 1842, less than a year after trains had first begun to run on the line, the New-York and Erie Rail Road Company defaulted and went into liquidation. The state aid bill of 1838 specified that, if the Erie went bankrupt, the state was to foreclose, and the comptroller accordingly advertised that the Erie was for sale and that the sale would take place on December 31st, 1842.

All summer the fate of the Erie was a major issue in the political campaign of that year. The state had already spent far too much money for the politicians to be willing to abandon the project, so how the railroad could best be completed was the issue. The Whigs felt that more state aid should be granted. After all, whatever the faults of Erie's management, and they were not nearly as misfeasant as they were depicted in, for instance, the Democratic *Evening Post*, it was certainly not the fault of the Erie that the depression had caused such havoc with the economy. The Democrats on the other hand felt that the state should take title to the Erie and complete it as a state enterprise, just like the Erie Canal. In August, 1842, the Legislature postponed any sale for six months, and in April, 1843, it passed yet another Erie relief bill. The sale was postponed until July 1st, 1850, provided that construction began again within two years. The bill forgave the Erie all that it already owed the state and authorized it to issue $3,000,000 in bonds that would have a first lien on the company's assets. But, even as the senior security of the company, the bonds could not then be sold in the very tight and depressed financial climate.

In February, 1844, the Erie was still far more dream than substance. It ran for only fifty-three miles, between Piermont and Middletown, New York; four miles west from Corning—which lay at the middle of its projected route; and seven miles east from Dunkirk. The Erie project was moribund.

Then, as the national economy began at last to improve in the mid-forties, the Legislature passed a fourth and, it turned out, final Erie relief bill on May 14th, 1845. It released the company from its debt to the state provided that it complete a single track of its line within six years of the passage of the bill. It authorized the issue of $3,000,000 in bonds of the company, which the state would take and resell to private purchasers provided that the company raise an equal sum by stock subscription. The state reserved the right to buy the New-York and Erie within one year of its completion for its cost plus 14 percent.

New blood was needed if this enormous enterprise was ever to be brought to fruition. The old management, especially the aging and increasingly stubborn and inflexible Eleazar Lord, was tired. A new president and a new board were required.

Benjamin Loder agreed to become the railroad's new president. Loder had been born in South Salem, in northern Westchester County, in 1801. At first a schoolteacher, he entered the wholesale dry-goods business in the city and prospered, amassing a fortune of more than a quarter of a million dollars. His reputation was considerable, and the New York *Herald* wrote in connection with his election as president that "he now, while yet in the prime of life, comes into the direction of the Erie Road with all the shrewdness which characterized the architect of his own fortunes, and the observation gained from his own daily intercourse with all classes of men lead them to believe that he is the Hercules, aided by a most able board, who will, if any man can, drain the present miry slough."[9]

The new board was indeed most able, as well as perhaps the most distinguished in the long history of the Erie. It included among its members Stephen Whitney, a holdover from the old board; James Harper, former Mayor of New York and one of the founders of the publishing house of Harper & Brothers; Daniel S. Miller, a wholesale grocer; Henry Suydam, Jr., of the old Knickerbocker aristocracy; and William E. Dodge, the founder of Phelps Dodge and one of New York's most notoriously rectitudinous men (his statue, by John Quincy Adams Ward, stands today in Bryant Park just behind the New York Public Library).

The first order of business for Loder and the board, obviously, was to find an effective way to sell the newly authorized stock issue so that money for construction would be in the till and the state's commitment to take the bond issue would be activated. Loder met with twenty-two of New York's richest and most prominent citizens at a hotel shortly after taking office.

The very real threat of the newly completed Boston and Albany Railroad to divert much of the traffic of the Erie Canal away from New York City and to the port of Boston had already concentrated the minds of the New York merchants. But Loder knew that a grand and compelling gesture would be needed if the public was to be made to believe that the Erie, already well known as the graveyard of investors' hopes, would at last be finished and would be upon completion a viable, money-making railroad. Loder's gesture was as risky, personally, as it was simple: he announced to the assembled group that he would pledge his entire fortune to the purchase of the new Erie stock and he hoped that the others present in the room would make substantial commitments as well. The meeting was stunned. Stephen Whitney tugged at Loder's coattails and warned him, "It will ruin you."[10] But Loder stuck by his decision and it had the desired effect, for the stock issue sold out. The Erie project began to lumber forward once again.

By November 1st, 1846, the Erie had reached Otisville, some miles beyond Middletown. The hardest part of the construction on the whole line now lay directly ahead, for the southern ridges of the Catskills had to be breached. The thirteen miles that lay between Otisville and Port Jervis on the Delaware River would require fourteen months of great effort to complete.

Just one of the engineering problems confronted was the cutting through of the crest of the Shawangunk ridge, a cut 2,500 feet long and often 50 feet deep. The New York *Herald* asked its readers "to think of a force fully as large as our army that stormed and took the Mexican capital, and still holds it, battling away here among the rocks, with picks, spades, hoes, hammers, axes, and all manner of instruments, not excepting even the celebrated 'excavating machine' patented by Otis F. Carmichael."[11]

Building the railroad between Otisville and Port Jervis would require altogether 317,000 pounds of gunpowder and the removal of 210,000 cubic yards of solid rock and 730,000 cubic yards of earth. Fourteen thousand yards of sloping wall had to be constructed, and 3,000 laborers worked a total of 300,000 man days while horses toiled their way through 30,000 days' worth of labor.

When Loder was not in New York raising ever more capital, he was out on the line moving things along. There was a lot to coordinate. As the Erie was building its way northward from Port Jervis to Binghamton there were a total of twenty-two contractors involved (each of whom had agreed to accept one-third of the cost in company stock). On February 24th, 1848, Loder wrote in a letter home: "I have just arrived at this place after a fatiguing journey on horseback—on foot—on lumber wagon—etc. Yesterday all day on horseback riding through snow, rain, hail and slush; muddy and disagreeable underfoot. I feel quite well though and shall continue on this afternoon and hope to reach a shanty about seventeen miles ahead by night."[12]

Great excitement was demonstrated in town after town as the symbol and reality of the progress of their age reached them, along with the happy prospect of economic boom. The boys of the various villages and towns were quite as fascinated with locomotives as their twentieth-century descendants would be with automobiles. In Narrowsburg, when the first Erie engine pulled into town they promptly surrounded it. Awestruck at first with its size and implicit power, they were soon climbing all over it until the mischievous engineer suddenly blew the steam whistle and they all "tumbled off like a lot of mud-turtles dropping off a log."[13]

Just before the railroad reached Binghamton, at the end of 1848, the Binghamton *Democrat* wrote that "great numbers of our citizens have been attracted to the railroad to see the first locomotives on the track. Some who have often seen this spirited animal before, and been conveyed by its wonderful speed, are delighted to witness his antic gambols among the hills of Broome [County]. Others who have never ventured beyond the limits of the 'sequestered counties' are amazed at the gigantic power of the steam horse, while he snorts and snuffs the fresh breeze of our valleys, and vanishes away to the morning fogs of the Susquehanna. The boys throng the track to see which way the *bull*gine is coming. All are exceedingly gratified to realize the beginning of the long-waited-for completion of the New-York and Erie Rail Road."[14]

As Binghamton was the largest town on the route of the Erie, it decided to throw a considerable bash in honor of the first train, due to arrive on the day after Christmas, 1848. The celebrants had every reason to congratulate themselves so heartily, as Mott explained with some exaggeration: "They had accomplished the most stupendous undertaking in engineering and construction that up to that time had ever been attempted in this or any other country. They had carved and hewn a place for a railroad in miles of the solidest rock; bridged many wide and rapid rivers, yawning chasms and deep defiles; surmounted obstructing and frowning hills, and, in spite of them all, carried the greeting of the Hudson to the Susquehanna within the appointed time."[15]

In so doing they had spent every dime that the New-York and Erie had raised both on its own behalf and with the help of New York State. The Erie, hardly for the first time and by no means for the last, was broke. Loder and the board decided to issue $4,000,000 in second-mortgage bonds, which were to pay 7 percent interest and were convertible into stock anytime within the next ten years. These bonds were sold both upstate to individuals and on Wall Street, where they were discounted 10 or 15 percent to brokers who promptly resold them to the public at or near par. This was one of the earliest instances of underwriting (and at a handsome profit) on the Street. But the money raised only sufficed to build the railroad as far as Corning, some seventy miles past Binghamton. Two more series of mortgage bonds totaling $7,000,000 were issued before the Erie was completed. This mountain of debt, which would grow with nearly every passing year as the Erie struggled to expand with its market, would haunt the railroad for the rest of its corporate life as the interest gobbled up operating profits.

While Binghamton was only a little more than a third of the way along the Erie's projected route to the Lakes, the railroad was in fact, both figuratively and literally, over the hump. The rest of the way presented nowhere near the engineering difficulties that the Erie had faced between Middletown and Binghamton, although the bridge over the Genesee River, 900 feet long and 230 feet above the surface of the river, would require all the lumber produced from "three hundred acres of close grown pine."

Under Benjamin Loder's relentless prodding, progress was steady, and it became clearer and clearer that the Erie would be completed, and completed within the six-year deadline of the last relief act.

•

As the New-York and Erie Rail Road neared completion after seventeen years and $23,500,000, the company planned a mammoth four-day, 469-mile-long party to celebrate. President Millard Fillmore, his cabinet, and everyone else of any importance in the federal, state, and local governments were invited, and most of them, it seems, accepted.

On May 15th, 1851, a huge parade was held up Broadway and down the Bowery, and the next morning everyone piled aboard the steamer *Erie* (commanded by a man with the wonderfully Dickensian name of Captain Maybee) for the trip to Piermont. The *Herald* reporter covering the event noted that so many important politicans were aboard that, should something happen to the *Erie*, government would be paralyzed at all levels for weeks.[16]

Two trains awaited the steamboat at Piermont. So glorious was the weather that Daniel Webster, then Secretary of State and in the last year of his life, decided against sitting in one of the passenger cars and opted instead to sit in a rocking chair placed on a flatcar, in order, he explained, to have a better view of the countryside (and perhaps in order to give the inhabitants of that countryside a better view of the ever-hopeful presidential possibility).

The first day the trains made it as far as Elmira, having stopped frequently for speeches and celebrations. The next day, through towns bedecked with banners, through cannon salutes and band music and clouds of oratory proclaiming a great and prosperous future, the trains rolled westward to Dunkirk and the shores of the Great Lakes.

At Dunkirk a fireworks display was held and a mammoth barbecue served, featuring "chowder, a yoke of oxen barbecued whole, ten sheep roasted whole, beef a la mode, boiled ham, corned beef, buffalo tongues, bologna sausage, beef tongues (smoked and pickled), head cheese, pork and beans, fifty roast turkeys, one hundred roast fowls, hot coffee, etc."[17]

Conspicuously uninvited to these festivities, however, were the stockholders who had helped pay for them. Instead, the company fobbed them off with a public announcement: "It would have afforded the President and directors great pleasure if they could have extended their invitation to the stockholders and other friends of the road, but the disappointment in receiving their passenger cars, and the limited accommodations at Dunkirk, rendered it impossible to do so. At an early day arrangements will be made to furnish excursion tickets to stockholders, giving them an opportunity to examine the road at their leisure, and at a reduced price."[18]

This was only the earliest incidence of what would soon become the standard fare served up to the stockholders of the Erie by its management.

CHAPTER SIX

Uncle Daniel's One-Stringed Chinese Lyre

FROM the first, business on the Erie had been brisk, and it became steadily better. In the parlance of today's Street, the Erie was a major growth company. From 1841, the year when the company first had revenue, to 1856, gross revenues increased from $29,689 to $6,349,990, an average annual growth of 49.6 percent. Net operating earnings, which first appeared on the company's books in 1842, grew from $31,732 to $3,189,592, an annual growth rate of 47.9 percent.[1]

One of the primary reasons for this rapid growth, of course, was that the territory served by the road constantly enlarged as the line pushed its way westward. And, even after the main line was completed in 1851, the company's trackage continued to expand. A side branch was acquired to connect the Erie with Buffalo, and it soon became the main line, when, to nobody's surprise, Dunkirk proved very unsatisfactory as a western terminus. Even before the main line was completed, the Erie acquired leases on the Paterson and Hudson and the Paterson and Ramapo railroads, which together provided a connection between Jersey City, located just across the Hudson from downtown New York, and the New Jersey border just south of Suffern, New York, on the Erie main line.

When the Paterson and Ramapo was completed in 1848, passengers to New York soon discovered that by switching lines at Suffern they could save twenty miles and perhaps an hour and a half over what was required to travel via Piermont. The Erie tried to counter this by charging the same to Suffern as it did to Manhattan by way of Piermont but to no avail.

When the Erie leased the New Jersey roads, over the anguished protests of Eleazar Lord, Piermont began immediately to fade back into the obscurity from which Lord had worked so hard to raise it. While the Erie continued to maintain repair yards there for some years and to move freight, if not through passengers, over the old main line, by 1870 Piermont was once again the small backwater it had been forty years before and which it continues to be today, its long pier virtually the only reminder of its brief glory days as the terminus of a great railroad.

A second reason for the rapid growth of the Erie was the equally rapid economic expansion of the territory it served. Partly this was due to the synergistic relationship between the railroad and the surrounding area: the vastly improved transportation within the territory—and between the territory and outside markets—stimulated economic activity. This in turn contributed to increasing the revenues of the Erie.

The milk trade that the Erie had discovered continued to grow, and many other agricultural products that had formerly moved by canal, river, or their own four feet began to be shipped by the railroads more and more. When anthracite coal from the mines of northern Pennsylvania began to come into use in the boilers of steamboats and locomotives, replacing wood, the Erie found itself perfectly situated to exploit this new traffic.

Still another reason was that the Erie developed technological innovations that lowered costs and increased convenience. Because its very long road was almost entirely single-tracked, the Erie had severe scheduling problems that delayed many trains. To avoid collisions, trains could not leave a station if another train traveling in the opposite direction was expected. Instead, it would wait an hour, and if the oncoming train still had not appeared, a flagman would be sent out ahead and the train would limp along behind him to the next station. If it met the oncoming train before a siding was reached, one of them had to back up.

In the fall of 1851, Charles Minot, the general superintendent of the Erie, found himself stuck at Turner's, New York (now Harriman), waiting for a delayed train. Suddenly he noticed the telegraph line running along the right-of-way, and the problem and the solution came together in his mind. He telegraphed ahead to the next station, asking if the other train had passed yet. Informed that it hadn't, he ordered it held and proceeded on his way. Before long an elaborate system of telegraph signals had been developed and quickly spread to other railroads, most of which were still single-tracked at this time.

But, if the Erie was a rapidly growing company, it was not a well-managed one, as so many young companies are not. The Erie had to raise capital continually to finance its expansion in trackage and rolling stock. (In 1841 the Erie had been a railroad of five locomotives, four passenger cars, and three freight cars. By 1856 the numbers were 203, 97, and 2,810, respectively.) The General Railroad Act of 1850 permitted the boards of directors of railroad companies to issue bonds on their own authority, but not stock, to finance expansion. The market much preferred these bonds to Erie stock anyway. The bonds paid a fixed interest, which was as high as any dividend that might or might not be forthcoming on the stock. And, because the board made the bonds convertible for the first ten years of their existence, the bondholders had a free ride in any event.

So most of the railroad's expansion was financed by bonds rather than stock, a fact that made the company peculiarly vulnerable to any unexpected expenses or to a downturn in the economy that might affect its revenues.

But there was one person on Wall Street, at least, who was much more interested in the stock than the bonds of the Erie, and that was Daniel Drew. Drew was interested in the voting power a stockholder had in the company and the proxies by which the stockholders could then sell that power to someone else. In 1853 Drew was able to maneuver his way onto the board. In March of the following year, just as the company was beginning to experience severe cash-flow problems—not that the phrase would be invented for another century—he was elected treasurer. The fox of Wall Street was now in charge of the Erie's henhouse.

In the fall of 1854 the credit market was tight and money hard to find. The credit of the Erie, big as it already was, was not enough. Drew was forced to ask his old friend the Commodore to endorse a loan for $400,000, an endorsement Vanderbilt was willing to make, although he took a mortgage on the rolling stock to cover his risk. Drew himself endorsed loans totaling $980,000, taking as his security a mortgage on everything in the railroad's possession not already nailed down by previous hypothecation.

When the Erie had survived this close call, steps were taken to remedy the debt situation. A sinking fund was established to reduce and, it was hoped, soon eliminate the floating debt—unsecured, short-term loans—that had been growing dangerously. But the company often proved unable to keep up payments to the sinking fund because of a continuing flow of unanticipated costs.

The Erie, despite having cost $23,500,000, had been built on a shoestring. Its cost per mile was not out of line with that of other railroads at that time, especially considering the engineering difficulties that had had to be overcome. Its tracks were often in a sad state of repair, and while railroad accidents at this time were both frequent and bloody, the record of the Erie was particularly appalling. In the year 1852, the line had a total of thirty accidents, sixteen of them in the space of only two months, a rate of better than one every four days.

Hemmed in by the vagaries of New York State law, the Erie made no serious attempt to deal with its debt-heavy capital structure. Rather, it kept piling it on, and the company's financial situation became ever more precarious. It ceased to pay dividends on its common stock after 1854, and the stock price became more and more volatile. This was partly because the stock, shorn of its dividend, had become more speculative, and partly because its treasurer was frequently manipulating it on the Street for his own account.

In October, 1856, the engineers struck for better work rules, and the loss of revenues that resulted from the strike was very damaging. The winter of 1856–57 proved to be particularly severe in the area served by the Erie. Snowstorms at the western end blocked trains for days at a time, while in January an ice jam on the Delaware River destroyed bridges and miles of track. Hardly had the bridges been repaired when another flood in February took them out again.

The company not only had to meet these unanticipated expenses, but others it had contracted for as well. It was building elaborate terminal facilities in Jersey City, including a mile-and-a-half-long tunnel through Bergen Hill, which had to be bored 4,300 feet through solid rock and which took the lives of 57 men before it was completed.

By the summer of 1857 the condition of the national economy was deteriorating as fast as the Erie's, and money was harder than ever to find. Drew loaned the company $1,500,000, again taking a mortgage on everything mortgageable, and helping himself to a $25,000 finder's fee as well. But he took care to resign as treasurer, though not from the board, on July 20th, 1857, perhaps to avoid any blame for what he could see was coming. (Two days earlier, William E. Dodge had resigned from the board itself, giving as his reason that he objected to the railroad's policy of allowing work on the Sabbath. Since he had somehow managed to contain his horror at this violation of the Fourth Commandment during the previous twelve years, one can only wonder if he, too, saw the handwriting on the wall.)

In October, 1857, as panic once more hit Wall Street and depression briefly returned to the nation, Erie revenues declined for the first time in its history. Somehow, by borrowing from Peter to pay Paul and leaving its employees unpaid for weeks at a time, the Erie managed to avoid a default for almost two years. But on August 16th, 1859, its bag of tricks exhausted, the Erie staggered into bankruptcy for the second time, with more than $700,000 in unpaid bills, its bonds' coupons uncashable, and its 4,400 employees unpaid.

Over the following three years the Erie was reorganized. In 1862 the New-York and Erie Rail Road Company disappeared forever and the Erie Railway took its place, with a much-improved capital structure and much-improved prospects because of the great boom brought on by the Civil War. Daniel Drew remained on the board during this time, and now that the company had emerged from bankruptcy he was quite as prepared to manipulate the new stock as he had been the old.

The Commodore had also been on the board since 1859 to protect his interests during the reorganization. But he took little if any interest in Erie's day-to-day affairs as he moved to take control of the Harlem and Hudson railroads, and to teach his old friend Uncle Daniel a thing or two about the hazards of speculation.

•

In the midst of the new bull market that developed with the outbreak of the Civil War, the Regular Board still held its two sit-down auctions at 10:30 A.M. and 1 P.M., but they were no longer nearly adequate to handle the Street's business. Even here speculation was intense and the volume swelled to many times what it had been only ten years before. The Open Board, which had organized early in the war when the Regular Board was too slow to expand to meet the sudden surge in volume, at first held its sessions in a basement room called, with no great affection, the Coal Hole. It was open from 8:30 A.M. to 5 P.M. and it featured a continuous auction. Its volume soon exceeded that of the Regular Board.

The speculative fever was stoked not only on the Regular Board (which in 1863 changed its official name, the New York Stock and Exchange Board, to the New York Stock Exchange) and on the Open Board but on the new and often ephemeral exchanges that sprang up alongside them. The Mining Exchange, which had first been organized in the previous decade, was reorganized in 1863 and did a brisk business in such stocks as Woolah Woolah Gulch Gold · Mining and Stamping Company and the Dry Digging and Gold Washing Company. Some of these enterprises were legitimate, if risky; others were nothing but plain frauds. Many were a little bit of both. North State Gold and Copper, which had assets totaling $1,200, issued 200,000 shares of stock, and much of this was sold for $4 a share, giving the stock a price-to-book-value ratio of better than 666 to 1.[2]

Medbery reported that the Garner Hill Company issued a million shares and that these were marketed at a price that "would have made the mine worth $1,600,000, giving the promoters, who had paid only thirty thousand dollars in cash, the net profit of a million and a half, with seventy thousand thrown in as contingent expenses!"[3]

Besides the Mining Exchange, the Petroleum Exchange was also organized in 1863 to trade shares of the new companies that were beginning to exploit the oil that had been discovered in Pennsylvania in 1859. Petroleum was so new that many considered its main contribution to civilization would be medicinal. Speculation, which always flourishes best where hopes can most easily outrun reality, was rampant.

Trading on the street came to a halt only with nightfall. But "the days were too short for the fervid haste of the speculators,"[4] so an evening exchange, called Gallagher's, was organized. It operated at the Fifth Avenue Hotel, uptown on Madison Square, and then in its own quarters, until after the war was over. While Gallagher's lasted, it was possible to trade securities twenty-four hours a day in New York City, a circumstance that would not recur for more than a hundred years.

The London *Times* hardly knew what to make of this financial bacchanalia that had come into being overnight. "In the great cities

BUBBLE COMPANIES   Companies and the brokers who dealt in their stock often disappeared abruptly.

of the United States," it said in 1872, as the bull market was only beginning to tire, "the web of human life is woven in colors so glaring and diversified as to strike with painful effect on eyes accustomed to the more subdued tints and graduated shades of European existence. In the New World everything seems to spring into being with unnatural speed, and to expand in its mushroom growth to gigantic dimensions. Vast fortunes are built up in a few years by frauds surpassing the wildest dreams of our old-world criminals and the wealth thus amassed is lavished with a contempt for appearances and a careless reveling in the enjoyments of the senses unparalleled even in the imaginative extravagances of Parisian fiction."[5]

E. C. Stedman, a broker as well as a writer, had himself been treasurer of the Petroleum Exchange. He wrote forty years later that "men were not satisfied with normal working hours. They rushed into the arena from a hurriedly snatched breakfast, shouted and wrestled throughout the day, stealing a few moments to sustain vitality and encourage indigestion at a lunch counter or restaurant [lunch counters, the first fast-food restaurants, were invented in New York at just this time to handle the sudden demand for instant nourishment], and renewed the desperate tension in the evening, prolonging it till long past the hour when wearied bodies and shocked nerves demanded respite and an opportunity to prepare for the next day's trials. It was a killing pace, and the marvel is that it was kept up so long."[6]

Certainly one way the killing pace was sustained was with frequent interruptions for horseplay and practical jokes. While the Regular Board was more staid and decorous than the Curb or the smaller exchanges—for its members were both older and richer—it was still notoriously rowdy. "That men whose fortunes, or whose customers' fortunes, depend upon the earnest attention to every phase of shares," wrote Medbery, "should break out into the effervescence of a schoolboy recess, tossing paper darts, jerking off hats, singing 'So Say We All of Us,' 'Shoo, Fly,' opera bouffe, 'John Brown'; extemporizing mock markets; forsaking the regular call in order to be onlookers in a fracas between two irate brokers, who commence their 'mill' at the Board, and adjourn to an upstairs committee room, where the fight is carried to the bitter end amid the cheers of a hundred friendly bystanders;—that such scenes should be so frequent as to be an admitted feature of broker life is a puzzle that we will not venture to solve. It is one of the mysteries of Providence, and, like other mysteries, has, perhaps, a wholesome and saving element behind it. In an insane asylum, dancing and theatrical exhibitions are sanitary measures. And the tense brain fibers of these soldiers of finance would paralyze under the incessant strain of business, were it not for these occasional outbursts."[7]

•

It was in this frenzied atmosphere that Drew had taken his drubbing at the hands of the Commodore and in which he sought to repair his still very considerable fortune. If he had been badly shellacked in Harlem, he was still the master of Erie, the favorite speculative stock of the small fry. "The mania seemed to possess everybody," *Fraser's Magazine* informed its readers. "Old-fashioned merchants abandoned the principles of a lifetime and *'took a flyer,'* or in other words, bought a few hundred shares of Erie. Professional men, tired of their slow gains; clerks sick of starvation salaries; clergymen, dissatisfied with a niggardly stipend, followed fast in the same course. Even the fair sex, practically asserting women's rights under the cover of a broker, dabbled in Erie shares."[8]

Drew began a campaign of manipulation in Erie, "a campaign in which," Fowler reported, "he took revenge on old enemies, wiped out old losses, filled his treasury with plunder . . . Erie was like a one-stringed Chinese lyre in his hands, on which he played two tunes: when its price was high, he sang 'who'll buy my Erye? Who'll buy my valuable Erye? Buy it, oh buy!'

"When it was low, he sang 'who'll sell me Erye, who'll sell me worthless Erye? Sell me Erye, sell, sell!'

"And the Street listening entranced to his mellifluous voice, bought it of him at a very high price, and sold it to him at a very low price. Every night Uncle Daniel dreamed of money-bags, and every day his dream turned out true. He coined money out of his musical performances on his one-stringed Chinese lyre—Erie."[9]

Drew, by his mastery of the psychology of speculation, was indeed entrancing. He was able time after time to lure speculators into Erie, and time after time he snatched away their dreamed-of profits and turned them into real profits for himself.

It is not possible at a remove of well over a hundred years to reconstruct in detail all the ins and outs of Drew's complex speculations in Erie. He kept his accounts in his head and used dozens of brokers in order to conceal what he was up to. These brokers in turn traded not only on the Regular and Open boards but on the Curb, at Gallagher's Evening Exchange, and in the corridors and lobbies of the Fifth Avenue Hotel. To keep track of this trading was difficult in the extreme even then. To regulate it was quite impossible.

Over the course of the years 1864–1868, the price of Erie moved up and down between 40 and 120, and these moves in price were correlated neither with the market in general nor with the fortunes of the Erie Railway. Rather, as the brokers said, it was a case of

> Daniel says up—Erie goes up.
> Daniel says down—Erie goes down.
> Daniel says wiggle-waggle—it bobs both ways.[10]

In the fall of 1864, Leonard Jerome and John Tobin, fresh from their triumph in Harlem, moved heavily into Erie stock, seeking to corner it. They borrowed money from Drew to finance the corner and got his agreement not to sell Erie above a certain price so as to lessen the selling pressure when the stock was high, making their corner much easier to achieve. The price rose to 102 in early November, moving against a declining market, but Jerome and Tobin could not keep it there, and it sagged to 80 early the next year.

Drew, according to Fowler, had been violating his agreement with Jerome and Tobin (" 'Love laughs at locksmiths,' " Fowler explained. "Daniel Drew laughs at contracts."[11]) and was shorting the stock heavily. Having done so, "he arose and saddled his coal-black steed named Panic" and got a friendly judge to issue an injunction forbidding the Erie Railway to pay any dividends, for the Erie had been paying regular dividends of as much as 7 percent since its reorganization, although it had had to borrow the money more than once to do so.

Erie sagged further with the news of the injunction, and Drew then suddenly called in his loan to Jerome and Tobin, who were forced to sell their Erie stock to pay back Drew. "Grant and Sheridan were pounding at the gates of Richmond," wrote Fowler, "and another great stampede now took place. Wall Street then might have been taken for Landseer's picture of Highland bulls in a storm. They who had bought Erie at 80, and thought it cheap at that, now sold it at 45 and said it was not worth 20. It was offered and sold in blocks of five thousand and ten thousand shares. As fast as it reared itself upwards fresh blows threw it back lower than before. It found bottom at 42."[12]

Having found bottom, Erie rebounded quickly, selling at 81 by the last week in April, only four weeks later, and spending most of the year in the 90's. For Jerome this would be only one of the many downs in an extraordinary up-and-down career; for Tobin it was the beginning of the end.

It was not that Drew operated in secret. Far from it; the newspapers were often hot on his trail. On August 2nd, 1865, the *Herald* reported that "Erie cash stock has been so abundant today that it was very difficult to loan it, and the reports manufactured by the speculative director"—as Drew was by now often called in the newspapers—"and his clique, to the effect that it would remain scarce for delivery, have produced only 'a delusion and a snare.' The reports were promulgated while the promulgators were saddling the Street with their own stock, and a more unscrupulous 'confidence' game was probably never practiced in Wall Street."[13]

A month later the *Herald*'s financial editor gave out some excellent advice on how to avoid being caught by the likes of Drew. "It is generally safe to act upon the supposition that when a clique is most strenuous in 'bulling' the market and most copious in its arguments in favor of a rise, that then the clique is most anxious to sell and pass on to other shoulders the weight resting on its own."[14]

In 1866, Erie stock sank steadily throughout the first half of the year. The *Herald* had no doubts as to the cause. "It is supposed on the Street," its financial editor wrote, "that a person connected with the management of the road and occasionally a large holder of its stock has sold out with a view to buying back at a lower price."[15]

The *Times,* which editorially was far less indulgent of the maneuvers that went on in Wall Street than was the much larger and more influential *Herald,* thought that Drew's shenanigans were necessarily self-limiting. "As his influence now stands," the *Times* wrote on April 6th, 1866, "and with the prevailing feeling against his conduct in Wall Street, it seems doubtful whether he will be suffered to have things his own way much longer, even in the Erie direction, blind and devoted as the majority of that board have been to his financial lead and arbitrary control for years. The question is one of self-respect for their own determination."

The *Times,* unfortunately for the small stockholders of the Erie, considerably overestimated the need felt by most of the members of the Erie board of directors for self-respect. The Commodore, consistently outvoted, had had more than enough, however, and resigned his seat. He maintained his investment in the Erie, but his first concern was now the New York Central.

NIGHTTIME STOCK TRADING AT GALLAGHER'S EXCHANGE Although Gallagher's was soon suppressed by the downtown exchanges, informal night trading continued at the Fifth Avenue Hotel for years.

•

While Drew had been working his one-stringed Chinese lyre on Wall Street, the Commodore was maneuvering to expand his railroad interests beyond the Hudson Valley. The Central had been assembled out of nine small local roads in 1853 and ran between Albany and Buffalo, roughly along the route pioneered by the Erie Canal. In the winter it shipped its considerable freight traffic to New York via the Hudson River Railroad, which was now controlled by Vanderbilt, but in the nine warm months of the year the Central used the steamboats on the river for this through freight.

The result was that the Hudson River Railroad was forced to maintain a very large amount of rolling stock—it had eighty-five locomotives at the end of 1866—that remained idle most of the year. Vanderbilt thought this quite unfair, as well as very expensive, and determined to do something about it.

Having acquired several thousand shares of New York Central stock, Vanderbilt supported Erastus Corning, who controlled the Albany County political machine, for president. Vanderbilt was represented on the Central board by James A. Banker. When Corning resigned the next year he was succeeded by Dean Richmond, whom the Commodore had known for years in the steamboat business. Richmond was soon elected to the Hudson River board, while Horace F. Clark, one of Vanderbilt's sons-in-law, was added to the Central board.

The two increasingly friendly roads negotiated a settlement that called for the Central to pay the Hudson River a bonus of $100,000 a year to compensate it for keeping so much rolling stock available for what was only a seasonal business. (The Commodore thought $100,000 to be much too low and testified that $300,000 to $500,000 would have been a lot more like it. But William Henry had accepted the lower figure, and his father felt obliged to back him up.)

Unfortunately for Vanderbilt, Dean Richmond died suddenly in the summer of 1866, and the new president of the Central was Henry Keep, a successful Wall Street broker and no friend of the Commodore. Keep and others assembled a pool that pushed the price of Central stock from 90 to 132, and in the fall election Keep and the pool threw Vanderbilt's representative out. The new board almost immediately, and unanimously, abrogated the agreement with the Hudson River Railroad. Attempts to negotiate a new contract were stalled, and the Commodore felt himself to have been badly treated.

But Henry Keep had chosen the wrong time of year to pick a quarrel with Vanderbilt. On January 16th, 1867, there appeared in the New York and Albany papers the following notice:

President's Office
Hudson River Railroad Company
New York
January 14th, 1867

The Hudson River Railroad Company gives notice that the arrangement heretofore existing between this company and the New York Central Railroad Company having been terminated by the directors of the New York Central Railroad Company, this company will, after Thursday the 17th day of January, instant, only sell tickets and check baggage over their own road, and will only recognize tickets sold at their own offices and by their own agents.

Passengers will after that date be ticketed and baggage checked to and from Greenbush, or East Albany, the terminus of the road.

The same rule will be observed as to freight.

C. Vanderbilt
President[16]

This meant that passengers who wanted to transfer from the New York Central to the Hudson River Railroad, or vice versa, had to walk across the new railroad bridge that Vanderbilt now declined to utilize, and cope with their baggage during the two-mile trek as best they could. But it also meant that the New York Central freight bound for New York City, by far the bulk of its business and the source of most of its profits, could go exactly nowhere. The New York Central suddenly found itself 150 miles up the creek.

On January 19th the *Herald* reported that "The general freight agent of the New York Central Railroad issued a circular today announcing that the road would not receive any New York freight because it had not the ability to deliver it at its place of destination. Seventy-five carloads of cattle were refused yesterday at Buffalo and were compelled to take the Erie Railroad. It is estimated that one-third of the freight from Chicago reaches tidewater by the New York Central, but none of it can take this route while the difficulty is unadjusted."

God, it would seem, was on Vanderbilt's side as the worst winter weather in a dozen years pounded into New York with back-to-back blizzards on the 18th and 20th. The *Herald* reported on the 21st that "for some days past the North and East Rivers have been literally jammed with floating masses of ice and frozen snow, so completely that all traffic by water, unless the most indispensable, has been entirely suspended."

There was an immediate outcry in the press about the railroads' damning the public interest in ruthless pursuit of their own, and an Assembly committee was ordered to investigate and devise legislation to prevent such an outrage from occurring again. But the New York Central did not have time to wait for the committee to come to its relief. It capitulated completely, promising Vanderbilt that it would send its through freight via the Hudson River Railroad all year long.

While the dispute ended in only four days, the Assembly committee continued to hear testimony, including that of the Commodore. When the Assemblymen wanted to know why he had refused to let his trains cross the railroad bridge, Vanderbilt pointed out to the legislators that they had long ago passed a law, years before the bridge was actually built and presumably at the behest of the New York Central, that forbade the Hudson River Railroad from running trains across the river, a law no one had paid attention to for years until the Commodore put it to his own uses.

"But why did you not run the train *to* the river?" one of the Assemblymen asked.

"I was not there, gentlemen," said the Commodore, all innocence.

"What did you do when you heard of it?"

"I did not do anything."

"Why not?" asked the exasperated legislator. "Where were you?"

"I was home, gentlemen, playing a rubber of whist, and I never allow *anything* to interfere with me when I am playing that game. It requires, as you know, undivided attention."[17]

Asked whether or not he felt an obligation to serve the public, Vanderbilt replied, "I have always served the public to the best of my ability. Why? Because, like every other man, it is my interest to do so, and to put them to as little inconvenience as possible. I don't think there is a man in the world who would go further to serve the public than I."[18] The regular passengers on the Hudson River and Harlem railroads, except, perhaps, those who had recently had to transfer to the New York Central, might well have agreed with him. The Commodore, after all, knew how to run a railroad quite as well as he knew how to get what he wanted.

When asked why he had chosen to take matters into his own hands rather than seek a remedy at law, the Commodore told the Assemblymen: "I for one will never go to a court of law when I have got the power in my own hands to see myself right. Let the other parties go to law if they want, but by God I think I know what the law is; I have had enough of it."[19] Given what the Commodore had already seen of the corruptibility of the New York State judiciary, let alone the Legislature before whose members he was presently testifying, these remarks would seem to be no more than common sense. But these words of the Commodore are the only ones recorded in his lifetime that come anywhere close to the famous phrase so often attributed to him, "Law! What do I care about law? Hain't I got the power?"

The Commodore began to buy New York Central stock and to seek alliances with other major stockholders. The common economic interests of the Hudson, Harlem, and New York Central railroads were so obvious that their eventual merger began to seem inevitable.

The other major stockholders of the Central, including Edward Cunard and John Jacob Astor III, were in favor of the consolidation and it seemed to them that Cornelius Vanderbilt was just the man to run such a railroad. They gave him their proxies, publicly announcing the fact in newspaper advertisements, and when the election for the board was held in December of that year, the Commodore was the only man to vote and the only one who needed to, for his own stock and the proxies he held gave him a majority. The Central was his.

•

During the course of 1867, as his eventual control of the New York Central became ever more certain, the Commodore began to look on New York City's railroads from a different, and larger, perspective. As Fowler was to write a few years later, "The wealth of the richest valley shone upon by the sun—the Valley of the Mississippi and its tributaries—is poured into the lap of the Queen

City of America through three grand trunk railways—the Pennsylvania Central, the Erie, and the New York Central."[20] Vanderbilt, of course, would run the New York Central with his customary efficiency and attention to profits. But the Commodore, already intuitively understanding the peculiar nature of railroad economics, was fearful of the consequences of railroad rate wars on a grand scale.

As the economist Arthur T. Hadley would note twenty years later, in his most-fundamental contribution to theoretical economics, the reason that railroad freight rates had been falling more or less steadily since the earliest days was that "the profitableness of a railroad as a whole, or of any particular parts of its business, depends quite as much upon the volume of traffic secured as upon the absolute price charged."[21] Railroads, in other words, were inherently a volume business. Because of their high capital and maintenance costs, which continued whether business was brisk or slow, railroads benefited more than most mid-nineteenth-century enterprises from economies of scale. Because of this, Hadley wrote, railroad price wars were inevitable as the companies fought for business, even to a point below costs. The economic consequences of this inescapable fact would dominate the railroad industry and American railroad politics in the last decades of the nineteenth century, but had profound effects from the very beginning of the industry.

The Pennsylvania Central—it would soon be called just the Pennsylvania Railroad—under its creators, J. Edgar Thomson and Thomas Scott, could be counted on to be sensible and to keep its side of any agreement that was reached, or at least keep its cheating within reason. The Erie was another matter altogether. An agreement on rates that had been made among the three railroads in 1863 had never proved workable, thanks to the Erie's erratic management.

"In the minds of the American public," *Fraser's Magazine* wrote in 1869, the Erie Railway "seems to be a very peculiar compound of two distinct entities. There is the Erie Railroad, physical, and the Erie Railroad, financial; two parts which in other railway corporations are wont to be inseparably intermingled in the complete unity of the 'company' like the body and soul of a human being. But in the anomalous Erie an unnatural divorce has been effected between these component elements; and, as a severed worm is said to be able to do, each sundered portion wags along the way of its existence happily indifferent to the paths and fortunes of its own other half."[22]

The Erie, the Commodore knew, was the wild card in the game of New York railroading. Vanderbilt could not count on its being operated in the interests of the stockholders, which Vanderbilt, or anybody else, could easily discern. Rather it would be operated in the interest of a majority of the members of its board of directors, and who could tell what that might be at any given moment? If Drew and his allies were substantially short of Erie stock, a financially ruinous rate war might suit them just fine.

A perfect example of the cheerful indifference that Drew and his followers on the board habitually exhibited toward the interests of the railroad they controlled but did not own is the Erie's acquisition of the Buffalo, Bradford & Pittsburgh Railroad. The Erie bought this small, derelict, and nearly worthless enterprise from a group of its own directors.

Relying on information given him by one of the directors involved, Charles Francis Adams, Jr., described this classic, if something less than arm's-length deal in "A Chapter of Erie," published in the *North American Review* in 1869 and one of the early masterpieces of investigative reporting. "The road . . . cost the purchasers, as financiers, some $250,000; as proprietors, they then issued in its name bonds for $2,000,000, payable to one of themselves, who now figured as trustee. This person then, shifting his character, drew up, as counsel for both parties, a contract leasing this road to the Erie Railway for four hundred and ninety-nine years, the Erie agreeing to assume the bonds; reappearing in their original character of Erie directors, these gentlemen then ratified the lease, and thereafter it only remained for them to relapse into the role of financiers and divide the proceeds. All this was happily accomplished, and the Erie Railway lost and someone gained $140,000 a year by the bargain." It would subsequently cost the Erie $1,000,000 more to put the road into usable shape.

Drew was never in charge of the Erie in the sense that the Commodore was in charge of the Hudson and Harlem lines. He had no interest in running railroads, but only in manipulating their securities to his personal advantage. Unfortunately for the Erie and its true stockholders, a majority of the board was perfectly content to allow him to do so, and make a buck for themselves in the process. "It is one of the most unaccountable and lamentable facts in Erie history," wrote Mott in 1899, "that there were men associated with

Daniel Drew in the directory of the company who made boast then, as they make boast today, such of them who live, of their personal probity and business integrity, yet who looked on in unprotesting acquiescence at his raids on the credit of the company, the honor and good name of which he as well as they were bound as sworn trustees to protect."[23]

The Commodore decided that in order to protect his own interests in the New York Central, he would have to be, at the least, a powerful voice on the board of the Erie. He did not choose to return to the seat he had quit in 1866, however, feeling that getting rid of Drew and putting his own reliable man in his place would be sufficient. He soon found others who were interested in the Erie as well: the directors of the Boston, Hartford and Erie Railroad.

This "malodorous New England enterprise,"[24] as Stedman termed it, ran between Boston and Hartford, Connecticut, and was projected to run to Fishkill, New York, on the Hudson River, where it would connect with the Newburgh branch of the Erie by ferry, an extension it was not destined to make. The Boston, Hartford and Erie was burdened with no fewer than ten mortgages, and its financial history was such that "its name was synonymous with bankruptcy, litigation, fraud, and failure. If the Erie was of doubtful repute in Wall Street, the Boston, Hartford and Erie had long been of worse than doubtful repute in State Street."[25]

Moribund for years, the road had been revived by a group of investors and speculators headed by Eben D. Jordan and John S. Eldridge, who was president of the company and "a financier bred in the school of State Street, Boston. . . . His subsequent career in Erie affairs proved that the State Street school of finance was not far behind that of Wall Street in the teachings of methods that kept always in view the best way of caring for Number One, no matter what the consequences might be to the other person."[26]

In the spring of 1867, the Boston, Hartford and Erie secured from the Commonwealth of Massachusetts a loan of $3,000,000 provided it raised $6,000,000 elsewhere or had that amount of its existing debt guaranteed by another railroad. As the road had long since lost its allure to even the most gullible investors, the company could hardly hope to enter the financial market; it would have to look elsewhere if it expected to raise so large a sum. Eldridge thought that the Erie Railway was exactly what he was looking for. After all, his road had been planned all along with the idea of serving as a Boston connection for the Erie, and the two railroads had been in frequent touch with each other and had seven common directors, Drew being one.

On March 28th, 1866, President Berdell of the Erie had appointed a committee of board members, including Drew, "to confer with the Boston, Hartford and Erie Railroad Company in regard to the arranging of traffic between the two railroads." The duties of this committee could not have been very onerous, for the tracks of the two roads did not come within a hundred miles of each other.

While Berdell was willing to appoint committees that had nothing to do, he was not willing to saddle the Erie with massive new obligations for the sake of another railroad. Drew and a majority of the Erie board, however, were not so fastidious. On June 3rd, 1867, a meeting of the executive committee of the board was called to consider the Erie's guaranteeing the payment of interest on $6,000,000 of the Boston, Hartford and Erie's debt. In exchange for this backing, the Boston railroad proposed "to set aside a certain amount of the receipts from its coal traffic to secure the Erie in its guarantee."[27]

There was one thing wrong with this collateral: the Boston, Hartford and Erie *had* no coal traffic and would not have any until it succeeded in connecting with the Erie and took on part of the Erie's very considerable traffic in coal. In other words, the Erie would incur immediate and substantial risks and take as collateral future, and dubious, revenues. Berdell was adamantly opposed to this nefarious scheme, but General Diven, a board member since the railroad's earliest days, proposed that the Erie guarantee a total of $4,000,000 of the Boston, Hartford and Erie's debt, a proposal that carried, although with certain provisos.

Eldridge and his allies realized that President Berdell would prove a continuing problem with regard to any future plans they might have for the Erie and its treasury. In order to get rid of him, they would need a majority on the board. They began to buy stock and proxies while looking around for allies in the coming struggle. They and the Commodore soon agreed to make common cause.

The annual meeting and election of directors of the Erie was scheduled for October 8th. On September 30th, the *Herald* reported that "Erie was in particularly active demand, with sales as high as 65, owing to an impression on the Street that the Great Mogul of the company [that is to say Drew] is a buyer of the stock. Whether he is or not would be difficult to say, for he sometimes swims in very deep waters so that it is no easy matter to keep him in sight."

Regardless of how deep he was swimming, however, it was soon obvious to Drew that Vanderbilt and the Boston group had the votes.

By the Sunday before the election, Drew knew that he was in serious trouble, and he paid a call on the Commodore at 10 Washington Place. It is not known what was said, but it is safe to assume that Drew felt it was time to snivel and grovel again—only this time he succeeded. He apparently pleaded with Vanderbilt that he would vote on the board in Vanderbilt's interest and that he would cease his speculative bear raids in the stock and indeed would work with Vanderbilt's allies to bull Erie upward.

The Commodore, needless to say, would not have trusted Drew out of his sight with a five-dollar banknote, let alone a great railroad. But, in a rare slip from self-assurance into arrogance, he evidently felt that Drew would be so beholden to him that he would be able to control his wily old friend, and that Drew in turn might prove very useful in keeping the Boston group on a short leash.

Whatever his exact reasoning, and in retrospect the Commodore would certainly if ruefully have agreed it was faulty, Vanderbilt decided to keep Drew on the board. He summoned the Boston men to a second meeting at his house and announced his about-face. Eldridge and the others were flabbergasted—Vanderbilt had been bad-mouthing Drew all over town in anticipation of throwing him off the board—but they were perfectly happy to accept the new situation. Besides, they had little choice, for Vanderbilt held the balance of power.

At a third meeting, this time held at Drew's house on Union Square, they agreed to Drew's remaining on the board, and a face-saving diversion was devised. The original slate that had been agreed to by the Commodore would be elected and then one of Vanderbilt's men, Levi Underwood, former Lieutenant Governor of Vermont, would resign and Drew would be elected to replace him.

The morning after the election the *Herald* was delighted with Drew's apparent defeat. "The stock market has been in a state of effervescence all day," it crowed, "and Erie has been the cynosure of all eyes. The annual election of the board of directors took place at noon, and the speculative director, poor old Dan, *drew* a blank. His name was left out of the majority ticket by the so-called Boston party that won the day, and finding that he could not help himself, he gracefully voted to elect his rivals."[28]

By the next day the *Herald* had learned why Drew had been so calm and so uncharacteristically gracious. Underwood had duly resigned, and the board had not only elected Drew to replace him but welcomed him back into the fold by giving him once more his old job as treasurer, which he had not held for ten years. It elected Eldridge as president. The *Herald* was left hoping only that one day the Erie Railway would not be run by "a pack of financial vultures."[29]

Certainly the *Herald* was not impressed with the other members of the new board. "The speculative director and his pack of cormorants," wrote the *Herald*'s financial editor (who seems to have had a weakness for bird images) before learning of Drew's reaccession to power, "have given place to a batch of nobodies who have elected themselves by a stock-jobbing operation and will certainly benefit themselves more than the Erie Railway Company, and the stock of the Erie Railway is likely to continue as it has been, the shuttlecock of Wall Street; for what can be expected from speculators but speculation and mismanagement to suit their own corrupt ends?"[30]

Two of the nobodies who had been elected to the board, nobodies to the point where several of the newspapers misspelled their names, were Jay Gould and James Fisk, Jr. They would not be nobodies for long. In agreeing to their election to the board—and there is no evidence that either had thought much about it one way or the other—both the Commodore and Drew had made the biggest mistakes of their lives.

CHAPTER
SEVEN

A Formidable Pair

"BOLDNESS! boldness!" wrote Fowler while Fisk still lived, "twice, thrice, and four times. Impudence! cheek! brass! unparalleled, unapproachable, sublime!"[1] Neither the Street nor the world at large had ever encountered anyone like him, for such as James Fisk, Jr., had not been possible before his own time.

Born at the very dawn of the age of the media, Jim Fisk had both a genius and a passion for making good copy. An editor's dream, he was among the first to achieve international fame at least as much for the grandeur of his personality as for the magnitude and notoriety of his deeds.

Fisk's deeds alone would have been enough to assure him a major place in Wall Street history, for he possessed, and utilized to the fullest, not only a first-class mind but great executive ability, tactical skills, sure speculative instincts, and the easy, almost heedless, financial courage necessary to put them to use. But his financial talents would never receive their due. Great as they were, they were no match for "the blond, bustling, rollicking James Fisk, Jr., who in 1865 came bounding into the Wall Street circus like a star acrobat, fresh, exuberant, glittering with spangles, and turning double summersets apparently as much for his own amusement as for that of a large circle of spectators. He is first, last and always a man of theatrical effects, of grand transformations and blue fire. All the world is to him literally a stage and he is the best fellow who can shift the scenes the fastest, dance the longest, jump the highest, and rake in the biggest pile."[2]

One of the most interesting aspects of Fisk's Wall Street career was his intimate, fruitful, and mutually respectful association with Jay Gould, who was his opposite in nearly every way that two human beings can differ from each other. In a sense Jim Fisk never really grew up, looking upon the world to his dying day with a child's wonder, enthusiasm, and sense of fun. But Jay Gould was never really a child. Rather, one of those human beings who are somehow born middle-aged, he always felt the hot breath of mortality upon him. It would be Jay Gould's tragedy that he never felt he had time to be anything except rich.

When he was only about fourteen years old he wrote, in his only known poem, "Time is flying past, night is coming fast," and to his niece, who knew him well, the words were "indicative of a feeling that seems to have been always in the mind of Jay Gould from his boyhood on, a feeling which apparently, though perhaps unconsciously, spurred and drove him . . . seldom permitting him pleasure in leisure or relaxation. Again and again he came to speak of the shortness of life and the necessity of doing while there was yet time to do."[3]

Small and frail, haunted by illness, he devoted his limited physical resources, as well as his matchless intellectual ones, almost exclusively to the pursuit of a fortune. It is a measure of his financial genius that when he died he was worth over $70,000,000. But it is equally a measure of the single-mindedness with which he acquired it, and of his seeming indifference to the good opinions of others, that he also died possessed of the most malignant reputation of any major figure in Wall Street history.

That reputation in many respects is undeserved. But Joseph Pulitzer, who bought the New York *World* from Gould and knew him personally, called him "one of the most sinister figures that has ever flitted bat-like across the vision of the American people," and the newspapers never tired of depicting him as financial evil incarnate. Once the newspapers had cast Gould in the role of the "Mephistopheles of Wall Street" they diligently maintained that image, and he did nothing to change it.

Ironically, Gould was one of the very first men to understand the concept of the public image in the age of mass media and to seize

JAMES FISK, JR.   *Courtesy of the Union Club Library*

upon the techniques needed to create and alter one. He was quite probably the first company president to hire a public-relations expert to change a corporate image, but he never expended the energy or the time necessary to change his own. He seems not to have cared what others thought of him. While he had some sincere admirers among his contemporaries, even a few close friends, it was only within the bosom of his own family, who loved him as dearly as he loved them, that Gould seemed emotionally alive.

Jim Fisk wore his heart on his sleeve; Jay Gould guarded his as though its privacy was the greatest of all his treasures.

•

Fisk came from old Yankee stock and was born in the tiny town of Pownal, Vermont, just north of the Massachusetts line, on April Fool's Day, 1835. His mother died before Fisk could have had any memory of her, and his father soon remarried. His stepmother, Love B. Ryan, reared the "chubby, roly-poly"[4] little baby as though he were her own and Fisk returned that love always, remembering her generously in the will he would write in agony during the last few hours of his life.

He was always a healthy child, taking in easy stride the childhood diseases that killed so many of his contemporaries. "He was also a good-looking little fellow, the envy of all the other boys around and the admiration and pet of the girls."[5] From an early date he exhibited the exuberant, good-humored nature that was always his most salient feature and to which the least trace of introspection was foreign, for "the phenomenon of his existence didn't trouble him a bit, but simply titillated him as a continual joke."[6]

When Fisk was still very young, the family moved across the Green Mountains to Brattleboro, in the southeastern corner of the state, and it was that town that Fisk would always think of as home.

His father made his living as a peddler. R. W. McAlpine, who wrote one of the better of the many biographies that were rushed into print upon the son's death, described the father as "an old-fashioned country peddler . . . a very plain, commonplace man, with no education, and imbued with very little more taste than that acquired in a life directed to petty trade and in a country inhabited mainly by people more given to manual labor than to intellectual culture."[7]

But if Fisk, Sr., lacked polish, he seems to have been both shrewd and adaptable. On one peddling trip, when he had run out of shawls, he convinced his customers that some tablecloths he had in stock were in fact the latest Boston fashion in shawls and sold them out. He was also inventive, designing among other things a quick-release mechanism for runaway horses.

Young Fisk attended the village school in Brattleboro, where he demonstrated a marked talent for both arithmetic and making friends and no inclination whatever to bother with anything that bored him. McAlpine was shown by Fisk's stepmother a copybook that Jim had used when he was about twelve years old, about the time he quit school for good. "To say that it is a literary curiosity," wrote McAlpine, "is to do meager justice to one of the most original of all the written results of schoolboy labor ever examined by the critic. Hardly a page but shows the antipathy of the boy to every-thing like set forms, and hardly a line but bears evidence of his natural contempt for uniformity."[8]

Like the Commodore, and unlike Gould, Fisk had no use what-ever for the theoretical or abstract. When he first rose to fame, the *Herald* described him as "quick and sharp to perceive, and, possess-ing a remarkable memory, he seldom forgot anything once learned by experience, particularly if it promised to be of any practical advantage to him, and it is, perhaps, to this quality more than any other that he is indebted for his peculiar success in life."[9]

When he left school his father set about teaching him the ped-dling business. The son showed such a natural aptitude for sales-manship that before long the father was sending him out on the road alone, while he stayed behind in Brattleboro and built the Revere House hotel, which opened in 1850. When the younger Fisk was not out on the road he had to make himself useful around the hotel waiting on tables. There, apparently, he learned of and began to hone his talent for entertaining others, telling the customers jokes and feeling in his veins for the first time the sweet rush of the drug that is applause.

Many sources report, and others flatly deny—there are few facts about Fisk's early life that are beyond doubt—that he traveled for a while with Isaac Van Amberg's circus, first as an animal keeper (he was always to be immensely fond of animals and birds, especially canaries) and later as a ticket salesman.

In November, 1854, when Fisk was only nineteen, he married Lucy D. Moore of Springfield, Massachusetts, who was four years younger than he, not then an unusually early age for a girl to marry. Theirs was to be a curious, and curiously successful, union. In the seventeen years it lasted, the longest period that they lived continuously under the same roof was six months. In the early years Fisk was continually on the road. For the last six years Mrs. Fisk lived a life of genteel respectability in Boston, while he lived one of ever-increasing notoriety in New York. And yet their relationship has every appearance of having been one of mutual affection and support.

"She is no hair-lifting beauty, my Lucy," Fisk told the actress Clara Morris when he had been living in New York for several years and his troubles with his mistress there had become the talk of the nation, "just a plump, wholesome, big-hearted, commonplace woman, such as a man meets once in a lifetime, say, and then gathers her into the first church he comes to, and seals her to himself. For you see these commonplace women, like common sense, are apt to become valuable as time goes on!" It was Lucy's common sense, perhaps, that most endeared her to him, for he added that "Never, *never*, does Lucy surprise me with a visit, God bless her!"[10] Certainly their contemporaries did not doubt that her grief upon his death was genuine or that he had loved her in his fashion and even been true to her in his way.

Fisk took a more and more active role in his father's peddling business. He wanted to put into effect some ideas he had gleaned from the traveling circuses, but his father demurred, feeling, apparently, that as he had been in the business for years he knew very well how to sell calico and notions to New England housewives and didn't need any advice from whippersnappers.

So Fisk went out and bought his own wagon and painted it red with yellow wheels and dressed himself up in striped trousers and a top hat. He put on a little act for the housewives, and business boomed. Not long thereafter, as Fisk father and son were riding together on the box of the father's wagon south from Putney to Brattleboro, Fisk, Jr., made a startling suggestion: he would buy out his father's interest in the peddling business and take him on as an employee.

"Well, James," asked the father, taken aback, "how much of a salary will you give me?"

"I will give you $3000 a year, father," said Fisk, if the New York *Herald* can be believed, for that was a very large salary for that time and place.

"It's a bargain, then."

"All right," the son responded, "but I want you to understand distinctly that you are my clerk, and I don't want you to put on any of your damned airs."

Jim Fisk, Jr., loved to laugh and joke and wring from life all that was in it, but he never forgot for a moment that business is business.[11]

Fisk lost no time in expanding the enterprise far beyond what his father had ever dreamed of. He bought more wagons and hired drivers to man them. He would give each a particular route and arrange a rendezvous for them all at the end of the week. There Fisk would meticulously go over their accounts with them and supply them with fresh goods that he had previously arranged to have shipped in to the rendezvous by railroad. By using the railroads, which would shortly make the Yankee peddler all but extinct, he was able to cover far more territory than any peddler had before. It extended from southern Vermont and New Hampshire, through most of Massachusetts, and into eastern New York State.

Before long "James Fisk, Jr., was the heaviest dealer outside of [New York]; and the matrons and maids from one end of his route to the other could never have been brought to admit that Jim Fisk was not the most captivating peddler, the most stylish driver, and the most princely traveler that ever measured silk, cracked whip, or settled tavern bill."[12]

By no means the least of the reasons for his success was Fisk's undoubted way with women. He delighted in their company and found them irresistibly attractive, a compliment that a satisfactory percentage of them hastened to return. Wit, flattery, and flirtation, Jim Fisk soon found, sold a lot of calico. He was "always jocose, scattering pennies and candy among the children, bewitching smiles among the sweet-sixteens, and consternation among their mamas."[13]

Fisk would always be nostalgic about this period of his life, when he first enjoyed success and first began to sense and to use the powers that were his. Years later, world famous, he was asked if he had been happy as a Yankee peddler. "Happy!" he replied, "by George, them was the happiest days of my life! I had everything I hankered after, money, friends, stock, trade, credit, and the best horses in New England. Besides, by God, I had a reputation. . . . I'd rather be driving that wagon than managing the Erie Railway."[14]

If in later years Brattleboro looked very different to Fisk from the vantage point of New York and the great world, so had they, in turn, looked very different from the vantage point of Brattleboro. Successful as the peddling business was, after a few years Fisk realized that it had reached the limit of its possibilities. Fisk had to choose between continuing what he was doing, running a very successful small business in a remote corner of the country, or moving on to bigger things.

Fisk had obtained most of his stock in trade from the fast-rising Boston dry-goods firm of Jordan, Marsh and Company, and his conspicuous success had come to the attention of Eben D. Jordan, one of the firm's founders. In 1860 Jordan offered Fisk a job as a wholesale dealer for the firm. He was to go around to dry-goods merchants and sell them merchandise that Jordan, Marsh in turn bought from mills in England and, increasingly, New England as well.

Fisk accepted Jordan's offer, sold out his peddling business, and moved with Lucy to Boston. It was soon obvious that Fisk had no talent whatever for the wholesale dry-goods business. At the retail level he had been able to count on his bonhomie, flirting with the women and joking with the men. But at wholesale, his particular brand of salesmanship was ineffective. His customers here were professionals who could count quite as well as Fisk and could not be joked into buying what he had to offer.

Eben Jordan, who was already fond of his young protégé and would remain his friend until the end of Fisk's life, when he was named an executor of Fisk's will, suggested gently that perhaps Fisk ought to go back to the peddling business, at which he had proved so good. But Fisk, who disliked failure as much as he enjoyed success, wanted another chance and asked for six months in which to prove himself, promising Jordan: "I'll make my light shine like a bushel of firebugs."[15]

Very shortly afterward, Fisk had one of the many strokes of great good fortune that would come his way, when the looming crisis of the Civil War broke with the firing upon Fort Sumter and Lincoln's call for 75,000 volunteers to suppress the rebellion. Fisk realized immediately that those soldiers, and heaven only knew how many more after them, would have to be supplied with clothing, blankets, and tents. Further, while he had been unsuccessful with the dry-eyed, penny-counting shopkeepers of New England, he had no doubt that he would fare far better with army supply officers, who would, of course, be spending other people's money as fast as they could in the emergency. Fisk headed for Washington and set up what would today be called a hospitality suite at Willard's, the capital's leading hotel.

At Willard's, Fisk dispensed hospitality lavishly. "It is unnecessary to say," wrote McAlpine, "that his wines and cigars, his delicate lunches, his jokes, and, perhaps, a little of his money judiciously distributed, gained the point for which he had been striving."[16] The contracts began to roll in. Fisk was able to sell at a profit of more than $200,000 a warehouseful of blankets that Jordan, Marsh had despaired of selling at all. Contracts for cotton and woolen shirts and underwear poured into the Boston firm, which soon earned a reputation in Washington of delivering what it promised, unlike many others who unloaded on the army whatever they thought they could get away with in the scandal-plagued early days of procurement.

Fisk's expenses at Willard's were said to run upward of a thousand dollars a day, but Jordan, Marsh did not quibble. Indeed, so pleased was the firm with the performance of the man they had so nearly fired a few months earlier that they took him in as a partner.

Jordan, Marsh, like nearly every other firm in the North, was flourishing as never before in the economic boom of the Civil War. But, while it could sell every yard of cloth it could get its hands on, acquiring that cloth was proving more and more difficult. The North, anxious to prevent the South from obtaining the gold it desperately needed to buy war matériel in Europe, blockaded the Confederacy and forbade all commercial intercourse. The South, equally anxious to prevent the North from having the cotton it needed to clothe and house its troops, forbade the export of cotton to the North. The Southern cotton planters and the Northern mill owners had a common interest in evading the war measures of their respective governments, and evade them they did.

In 1862 Jim Fisk began to send agents south on behalf of Jordan, Marsh to buy cotton and get it north somehow. His father was among those he sent, and it was on one of these expeditions that Fisk, Sr., suffered a mental breakdown of some sort, from which he never recovered. He would spend the rest of his life in and out of mental institutions. While Fisk, Jr., was a most forgiving man and sloughed off the most grievous insults as just part of the game, he would always exhibit an implacable hostility to anyone who attacked him by means of his father's illness.

In May, 1862, Fisk himself went to Memphis, Tennessee, by then safely in Union hands, to coordinate the purchasing and shipping of cotton to the insatiable northern mills. These purchases, according to McAlpine, sometimes amounted to as much as $800,000 a day.

In September, 1862, Fisk was in Boston when the news of the Battle of Antietam reached that city. While it was counted a northern success—although General McClellan had, as usual, managed to snatch only equivocal victory from the jaws of total triumph—the cost in lives had been staggering. At least 110,000 soldiers fought at Antietam on both sides, and by the end of the day fully 20 percent, 22,000 men, were dead or wounded, more casualties than had been suffered in the entire American Revolution.

The American Civil War was the first great war fought in the new industrial era, and the extraordinarily sanguinary nature of warfare in such an age was now becoming apparent. Antietam would prove to be the bloodiest one-day battle of the war, and its carnage came as a profound shock. The news reached Boston on a Saturday, and Fisk, a spontaneously generous and warm-hearted man, was deeply moved. Characteristically he sought to do something to help the survivors. Almost single-handedly he organized the churches of Boston, and the next day, Sunday, ordinarily a compulsory day of rest in that most rectitudinous of American cities, was given over to assembling food, blankets, bandages, and other supplies and comforts for the troops.

One man who watched Fisk at work was awed by both his titanic energy and his ability to organize so large an enterprise on such short notice, a talent he would later put to far less eleemosynary uses. "I was with Fisk all day," he wrote, "and all that night, and never in my life have I seen anyone throw his whole soul into his work as that man did. He seemed to do more in an hour than any three other men. He had an eye to everything, controlled everything. Everybody deferred to his judgement; in short, the movement was Jim Fisk's, and it was so recognized and acknowledged."[17]

Fisk continued with Jordan, Marsh until 1864, when, with the end of the war in sight, the flood of government contracts began to ebb. With so much of the cotton-growing area of the country back in Union hands, the cotton crisis, too, had passed. Fisk, quite possibly, was already restless and Jordan, Marsh probably felt that his special talents were more suited to wartime than to the daily grind of the dry-goods trade in peace. They parted amicably, the firm buying out his interest for $65,000. Fisk briefly opened his own dry-goods business in Boston, but closed it down after a few months.

Having terminated his business interests in Boston and with a small fortune in his pocket, Jim Fisk looked around for opportunities. He soon found himself irresistibly attracted to Wall Street at just about the time that Jay Gould first came there.

•

Called a "complex Jew" by Henry Adams—through whose vast intellect ran a rich vein of anti-Semitism—Jay Gould in fact was descended from a line of New England puritans that was quite as ancient, if not in latter days quite as distinguished, as Adams's own. Shortly after the Revolution they migrated with a group of other Connecticut families to Roxbury, New York, in Delaware County on the western slopes of the Catskills, and it was there, on the farm carved out of the wilderness by his grandfather, that Gould was born on May 27th, 1836, the only boy of six children. (If the Commodore and Gould ever realized that they shared a birthday, the fact appears to be unrecorded.) Although the boy was christened Jason, his name was almost immediately shortened.

The farm, of about 150 acres, ran "far up a hill back of the house and far down a hill in front . . . on the other side of the highway. The nearest neighbor is a quarter of a mile away. Stone fences run hither and thither, losing themselves in clumps of beech and maple trees. There is an apple orchard, and down at the bottom of the hill the Creek, as it is called, winds its way through the thick dingle." Jay's father, John Burr Gould, who was, as his son would be, "a little man with a very dark complexion" and who walked with a cane because one leg was shorter than the other, grew buckwheat and oats and kept a herd of about twenty dairy cows.[18]

The Goulds were better off than most of the farmers in impoverished Delaware County. The naturalist John Burroughs, who was one of Jay's close boyhood friends, said that the "Goulds were very prosperous, and naturally stiff-necked; they lived in a little better style than the other farmers."[19]

They were, however, in no sense rich, and Jay, despite being very young, had to do his share of the chores. "As I was the boy of the family," Gould testified years later to a committee of the U.S. Senate, "I generally brought the cows in the morning and assisted my sisters to milk them and drove them back, and went for them again at night. I went barefooted and I used to get thistles in my feet, and I did not like farming in that way."[20]

Gould's mother died when he was only four and a half. His father remarried almost immediately, only to be widowed again within

JAY GOULD

four months. He married a third time, but this wife too, having borne him another son, soon died. Widowed three times in less than five years, he apparently gave up on matrimony, and Jay's older sisters took over the job of running the household.

When Jay was old enough he attended the district school and took at once to learning. While physically undersized and often ill, mentally he was more than a match for anyone in the neighborhood. John Burroughs described him as "a brilliant student [who] stood easily at the head of his class. He was doing algebra when I looked upon it as something strange and mysterious, although he was only one month older than I."[21]

Jay seems to have been as popular with his schoolmates as he allowed himself to be, although John Burroughs remembered that "he seldom engaged in the sports of the school, because he was proud and exclusive, and would not put himself on an equal with the other boys. One winter the boys were seized with the wrestling craze. It was all the rage at recess and noontime. Jay would wrestle with no boy but me. He and I wrestled by the hour. He was very plucky and hard to beat. I frequently went home with him and stayed all night but he would never go home with me."[22]

One of Jay's sisters said that it was not pride that kept him from sports but a love of study. "In the winter he would sometimes ride down on a sled, perhaps once or twice, but he really didn't have any time for sports, because he was always either studying or reading. He never played baseball, checkers or cards. When he was twelve or thirteen years old, he was studying geometry and logarithms."[23]

Jay attended Hobart Academy, eleven miles from Roxbury, for a year, earning his room and board and walking back home every weekend. The next year John Gould helped establish the Beechwood Seminary, where his son had the last two years of his formal schooling. But this was not the major part of his education. Like most people of notable intellect and a love of learning for its own sake, Gould was a self-educated man, devouring books on subjects that interested him.

In 1851 Jay's father exchanged his farm for a hardware store in the village of Roxbury, and Jay clerked for him. "My duties in the store," he testified to the Senate committee, "occupied me from six o'clock in the morning until ten o'clock at night. In the mean time I had got quite a taste for mathematics, especially surveying and engineering. I took that up after I left school, and as I was pretty busy during the day, I used to get up at three o'clock, and I very soon found that I got a pretty good idea of that branch, so I concluded I would start out as a surveyor."[24] Jay found a job helping to survey Ulster County for $20 a month plus board. He resolved to burn his bridges behind him and left home with only enough money to pay his fare.

His employer had told him that while surveying he should mark down in a little book what expenses he incurred for room and board and the employer would come along afterward and pay them. The first night Gould stayed at a farmhouse. When the farmer asked for payment, Gould explained the arrangement his employer had instructed him to use; but the farmer would have none of it. "He has failed three times," the farmer said. "He owes everybody in the county, and you have got money and I know it, and I want the bill paid."

"There I was," remembered Gould. "I hadn't a cent in my pocket; so I just pulled my pockets out and said to him: 'You can see that I tell the truth. There are my pockets.' " Finally the farmer said, "I'll trust you, but I won't trust that man."[25]

The sixteen-year-old Gould was devastated by this incident. It "had such an effect on me," Gould testified, "that it seemed to me as though the world had come to an end. This was in the morning, and I could not have the heart that day to ask anybody to give me dinner, so along about three o'clock in the afternoon I got faint and I sat down for a few minutes. . . .

"I debated with myself whether I should give up and go home, or whether I should go ahead. I came to a piece of woods where nobody could see me, and I had a good cry. Finally I thought I would try my sister's remedy—a prayer."[26] Whether it was the prayer or not, Gould soon found a way to earn his keep while surveying, for many farmers were willing to pay a dollar to have Gould construct a noonmark so that, in an age when clocks were still very expensive, they could keep better track of time. A noonmark, really a primitive sundial, is nothing more than a line that runs due north and south, so that a stick placed vertically at its southern end will throw a shadow on it exactly at noon.

Gould's employer failed a fourth time that summer, and Gould and two other surveyors took over the job of completing the map. Gould sold out his interest in the project for $500, and he would never be broke again. He used the money to finance his own surveys of Albany County and his native Delaware County.

In 1853 Gould took enough time from his surveying of Albany

County to visit the Crystal Palace Exhibition in New York City, his first visit to the metropolis. As one might have already expected of him, it was not purely a pleasure trip. His grandfather Alexander More had invented an improved mousetrap, and Gould was taking that traditionally surefire fortune maker to the Crystal Palace to be exhibited. (Emerson's famous phrase, quite coincidentally, dates from just this period.) Years later even Gould thought it was funny. "I was ambitious," he told the Senate committee, "and had brought a little thing with me which I was sure was to make my fortune and revolutionize the world, and you will smile when I tell you that it was a mousetrap."[27] But on the omnibus headed uptown, as Gould gawked at the sights, an Irishman stole the mousetrap.

"He was a great strong fellow," Gould reported, "but I collared him." Gould, only seventeen, might be thought brave to have accosted so large a man, especially given the fact that the immigrant Irish, who were pouring into New York at this time, had already acquired a vast and richly deserved reputation for street brawling. Actually some of Gould's bravery was involuntary. Always honest about himself if not his activities, he told the Senate committee that once he had grabbed the man, "I really regretted that I had done so and tried to let him go, but the fact is one of my fingers caught in a button hole of his coat, and before I could get off there was a crowd around us and a policeman, who took us off to a nearby court."

The judge ordered the box opened and there, as the New York *Herald* reported—this was Gould's first mention in the press—"was a tin mousetrap, on a new plan, painted up in colors to look pretty for the Crystal Palace. The owner of the trap exhibited a certificate showing that he had a stand for his trap in the Palace and no humbug."[28]

Gould remembered that when the box "was opened to verify the truth of my statement, and the purloiner of my great invention found that it was only a mousetrap, his face assumed such an expression of disgust that I could not help laughing at him." Neither could the rest of the courtroom, and the judge, dispensing with judicial impartiality for the sake of a *bon mot,* observed that he appeared to be the largest rat ever caught with a mousetrap and bound him over for trial.

While the trap was presumably exhibited at the Palace, the world did not beat a path to Gould's front door, and the device disappeared from history. But Gould had been deeply impressed by the great world beyond the Catskill Mountains, and he told a friend when he got back, "I'm going to be rich. I've seen enough to realize what can be accomplished by means of riches, and I tell you I'm going to be rich."[29]

After Gould returned upstate he continued his surveying and gathered material at the same time for a history of Delaware County. He worked at this mapmaking as hard as he could. "He was all business in those days," said Oliver J. Tillson, one of his partners in the surveying business. "Why, even at meal times he was always talking map. He was a worker, and my father used to say: 'look at Gould; isn't he a driver?' "[30] He was such a driver, of himself more than others, that he became seriously ill with pneumonia.

Gould's maps of upstate New York are exquisite examples of the draftsman's and surveyor's art, both accurate and beautiful, and the originals are now very rare and valuable. Gould later led surveys in counties as far west as Ohio and Michigan, and did engineering surveys, picking up the necessary skills as he needed them. In April, 1856, Gould, not yet twenty, delivered the manuscript for his *History of Delaware County*, written in his spare time, to his publisher in Philadelphia.

But for Gould the nightmare of all authors, at least before the invention of the Xerox machine, came true. The publisher's building caught fire and his manuscript was destroyed. He set immediately to work rewriting it from surviving fragments and memory. The 450-page book was finally published in September of that year, and it is still an invaluable resource for the early history of the area. Gould had exhausted himself, and shortly after finishing the manuscript for the second time he collapsed with typhoid fever. He needed months of careful nursing before his always limited strength returned.

•

Gould had saved about $5,000 in his three years of surveying and history writing, a substantial sum for so young a man from so poor an area, and he looked about for an opportunity to invest it.

One of the leading citizens of that part of New York State was Zadock Pratt, an early pioneer and founder of Prattsville in Greene County. He had made a fortune in, among other things, the tannery business, and had served in Congress for ten years. By the 1850's he was nearing seventy and was in partial retirement. But he had been mightily impressed with the up and coming Jay Gould, who had taken care to cultivate the old man. Gould had noted that there were extensive stands of hemlock trees along the Lehigh River, across the border in Pennsylvania, and that while the wood was being lumbered, the bark, which provided the tannin for tanning leather, was largely going to waste. He proposed to Pratt that they form a partnership to exploit this wasted resource. Pratt agreed that Gould would run the tannery and he would put up most of the capital. The partners were to share equally in the profits.[31]

In less than two years Gould had created a thriving tanning business, a business in which he had made himself expert. But something was wrong. Exactly what happened and whether or to what extent Gould was to blame is not known. Certainly Zadock Pratt was a man of large vanity, used to being deferred to. As Gould became more and more knowledgeable about the tanning business it is possible that he was less and less inclined to ask his partner's opinion or even permission before taking action as he saw fit.

In any event, Zadock Pratt wanted Gould out. The old man made his young partner an offer: he would buy Gould's share for $10,000, or Gould could buy his for $60,000. Pratt knew perfectly well that Gould had neither the money nor the extensive credit necessary to raise such a large sum, but Pratt, like many others afterward, had underestimated him. The young man went to see Charles M. Leupp, the biggest leather dealer in the New York market.

Leather was one of the primary commodities of the nineteenth-century economy, necessary not only for shoes but for horse harness, machinery belts, and a myriad of other uses. Leupp was therefore one of New York's most prominent citizens, and he agreed to a deal. Gould returned upstate and, much to Pratt's astonishment, bought him out. The next day he sold a one-third interest in the tannery to Charles Leupp and one-third to David W. Lee, Leupp's business partner and son-in-law.

From the start the partners disagreed about nearly everything. Leupp's and Lee's interests as leather merchants conflicted with their interests as tannery owners, and Gould's interests conflicted with theirs, for Gould had already set up a business as a leather merchant at 39 Spruce Street in New York. Before their disagreements could be ironed out, Charles Leupp, who had been increasingly unstable for the past several years, suddenly committed suicide by shooting himself through the heart on October 6th, 1859.

On December 19th Gould agreed to buy back the two-thirds interest from Lee and from Leupp's heirs for $60,000, to be paid at the rate of $10,000 per annum. The executor of the estate, William Maxwell Evarts, already distinguished and soon to be perhaps the most famous lawyer in the country, objected to a minor point and before a final agreement could be negotiated David Lee decided to take matters into his own hands.

Knowing that Gould was in New York, Lee went to Gouldsboro, the town that had grown up around the tannery, on February 29th, 1860, and simply took over, ordering the leather in stock to be made ready to be taken away. As soon as Gould found out about Lee's action, he followed him, arriving on the evening of March 3rd, and demanded the return of the tannery. Lee, who had a force of twelve or fifteen men, refused.

Gould was quite popular with the employees of the tannery and other townspeople—he was always to be popular with those who worked closely with him—and they were more than willing to help him regain possession of the tannery. "I burst open the door and sprang in," Gould wrote in a letter to the *Herald.* "I was immediately saluted with a shower of bullets, forcing my men to retire; and I brought them up a second time and we took a second broadside, compelling us a second time to fall back. Up to this time not a shot was fired or a word spoken by one of my men—a third time and pressed them into the building, and by this time the company at the upper end of the tannery had succeeded in effecting an entrance and the firing now became general on all sides, and the bullets were whistling in every direction. After a hard-contested struggle on both sides we became the victors, and our opponents went flying from the tannery, some of them making frightful leaps from the second story."[32]

Despite the uproar, the net result was almost exactly the same as if nothing had happened. The agreement reached by Gould, Lee, and Leupp's heirs was slightly amended to meet Evarts's objections and filed with the county only three weeks after the battle. In 1865 the tannery burned down, and in 1868 Gould sold all his interest in what remained to David W. Lee.

The immediate consequences of this episode were almost nil. But Gould's enemies and their journalist allies would find the Gouldsboro tannery a rich source of misrepresentations with which to vilify both him and, later, his memory. Nearly a decade after the event, an irate mob would gather outside of Gould's brokerage house, thinking him to be inside, and shout over and over, "Who killed Charles Leupp?"

•

The record of Gould's career between the tannery battle and his election to the board of the Erie Railway in 1867 is scanty. We do know that when Gould was in New York he usually stayed at the Everett House, a hotel located on the north side of Union Square. Somehow he made the acquaintance of Helen Day Miller, who lived in style with her father, Daniel S. Miller, at 30 East 17th Street, across Broadway from the Everett House and down the block from Daniel Drew's house. Daniel Miller had made his fortune in the wholesale grocery business but had sold it and interested himself in Wall Street. He had been a director of the New-York and Erie Rail Road for a decade before its second bankruptcy. Gould and Helen Miller were married on January 27th, 1863.

Helen Miller was a very considerable catch for the ambitious farmer's son from Delaware County. Not only was her father rich even by the standards of the country's largest and richest city—the Millers would soon abandon fading Union Square and join the parade of fashion to Fifth Avenue—but on her mother's side she was intimately interconnected with many of New York's old Knickerbocker families. The Knickerbocker aristocracy, whose names—Kip, Rhinelander, Livingston, Schermerhorn, Beekman, De Lancey, Bleecker—still fleck the map of the city, was rapidly losing its economic and political dominance in the flood tide of the *nouveau riche* and Irish immigration. Perhaps as a result, it was enjoying ever greater social prestige.

However convenient her father's money and her mother's social connections, the marriage of Jay Gould and Helen Miller was a love match and was an entirely happy one, lasting twenty-six years, until Mrs. Gould's untimely death in 1889. While Gould was to be accused of nearly every crime it was in his capacity to commit, and more than a few that weren't, adultery was not one of them. What few pleasures he allowed himself as he husbanded his time and energy for business were domestic in nature. He came home every night when he said he would, indulged his children, ate dinner with his family as often as possible, and read in the library until it was time for bed.

There were six children born in the first fourteen years of the marriage, four boys and two girls, and they grew up greatly loving their father. He in turn greatly valued their love, certainly for its own sake but surely also as an antidote to the endless stream of vilifications and calumnies from the world outside his door, which he refused to notice.

At some point in this period Gould became interested in a short railroad line, the Rutland and Washington Railroad, which ran for sixty-two miles between Rutland, Vermont, and Troy, New York, located across the Hudson from Albany. Typical of the short lines of the early railroad era, it was by this time in a dilapidated condition and nearly bankrupt. Gould was able to buy its bonds at about ten cents on the dollar and its stock at equally depressed prices. Before long Gould had become president of the line, and he learned the railroad business as he had learned about engineering and tanning leather: on the fly.

"I gradually brought the road up," Gould explained twenty years later to the Senate committee, "and I kept at work, and finally we made the Rensselaer and Saratoga consolidation. . . . In the meantime my bonds had become good, and the stock also; so that I sold my stock for about 120."

Gould spent much of his time upstate running his railroad, but he also spent time on Wall Street, learning the ways of the dog-eat-dog stock market that was flourishing there as never before. And it was sometime in 1865 or 1866 that he first made the acquaintance of Jim Fisk.

Fisk had become active in New York as early as 1863, but it was only late in the following year that, free of his connections with Jordan, Marsh, he opened a broker's office at 38 Broad Street, directly across the street from the New York Stock Exchange. There he tried to imitate the tactics that had proved so fruitful in Washington. "When he rented an office in Broad Street," reported McAlpine, "he fitted it up in the most extravagant manner, giving *carte blanche* to the artists and workmen employed to make it the most attractive den ever dreamed of by bear or bull."[33]

But Wall Street was not Washington, and the players were not army supply officers and politicians. To be sure, they crowded into his offices. They ate his food and drank his champagne. They laughed at his jokes. They took him to the cleaners. "He was mercilessly hugged by the bears and unceremoniously tossed by the bulls, but with indomitable pluck and a blind trust in the possibilities of the future, he held his ground until the Street had swallowed every dollar of his money and he was ruined."[34]

Fisk had lost every cent of the modest fortune he had garnered in the Civil War. But, if his fortune was ruined, his personality most decidedly was not. Medbery, writing only a few years later, noted that "then, according to veracious rumor, occurred one of those dramatic passages which lend grandeur to human existence. Seating himself upon the stoop overlooking the Stock Exchange and surveying the eager sea of faces which on that day heaved and billowed upon the Broad Street pavement, Mr. Fisk swore a mighty oath, that since Wall Street had ruined him 'Wall Street should pay for it.' "[35]

Asked what his plans were, Fisk replied, "I'm going to dog Boston a little. Then I propose to come back to this den of iniquity and boss Wall Street a little. Then I expect to pick my teeth and enjoy myself a little. But I've got to hurry up, for my school teacher used to tell us, 'thecrastination is the proof of time,' or something to that effect. I'll be back in Wall Street inside of twenty days, and if I don't make things squirm I'll eat nothing but bone button soup till Judgment Day. Damn 'em! they'll learn to know Jim Fisk yet!"[36]

Fisk took the train to Boston. No sooner had he boarded it than the serendipity that was so often to bail him out of a tight spot came into play. On the train was a man named John Goulding, who had been trying unsuccessfully to market a patent for a device used in textile weaving that had been invented by his father. Fisk, who knew a great deal about textiles by this time, examined the device and recognized immediately its potential value. He persuaded Goulding to accompany him all the way to Boston, where he soon organized a syndicate of his friends to buy the patent. After a number of infringement suits were successfully prosecuted, the Goulding device would prove extremely remunerative.

But the Goulding patent did not solve his short-term problems, and while in Boston Fisk raised money from his former dry-goods partner, Eben Jordan, and others in order to mount once more an assault on Wall Street. His credit was excellent, for although he was a spendthrift by nature, he was always punctilious about paying his bills.

While in Boston he learned of a group of investors who were interested in buying the Stonington Line. In New York Fisk had heard a rumor that the owner of the line might be happy to sell. The owner was Daniel Drew, and Fisk smelled a deal.

Within a month, he was back in New York and he called on Uncle Daniel. Apparently the two took to each other, perhaps they reminisced about their old circus days, and Drew authorized Fisk to negotiate the sale of his money-losing steamboats, a deal that Fisk arranged for $2,300,000. Drew was delighted and was soon helping Fisk set up again on Wall Street, introducing him to William Belden, a son of an old friend, and the new firm of Fisk, Belden and Company was soon doing much profitable business with the speculative director.

Fisk, always an apt pupil when the subject interested him, soon learned the art of speculation from the master himself. Whereas on his first foray into Wall Street Fisk had been an outsider, and treated accordingly, now he was inside, allied to one of the Street's most influential and dangerous forces. Fisk was soon rich once more. With increasing frequency he was seen at Delmonico's and the theater. He built Lucy a $75,000 four-story mansion at 74 Chester Street in Boston, while he moved into a suite at the Fifth Avenue Hotel, the city's largest and most fashionable, located on Madison Square, which was then the heart of midtown.

At this time also he became deeply infatuated with a young woman known to the newspapers, and to history, as Josie Mansfield.

Like the value of money, beauty does not translate readily from one age to another, for different human attributes move into and out of fashion. In the case of Josie Mansfield, at least to judge from her one surviving photograph, it is especially difficult to see what all the fuss was about. Even by the standards of an age that valued the Rubenesque, she appears to have been somewhere between zoftig and fat. But whatever it was, Josie Mansfield had it in spades. She not only ensnared Jim Fisk, she fairly knocked the socks off a *Herald* reporter who called to interview her.

"She was tall and shaped like a duchess," he wrote. "Her skin was as fair in fibre and hue as the lily itself. Over a fair white forehead hung a mass of jet, silky black hair, and from her small seashell-like ears depended a pair of hooped earrings. Her hand, white and smooth, which she offered to the reporter as she rose gracefully from the table, was a hand from which a cast could be taken. The lady's eyes were of a peculiar gray, and lambent like the phosphorescent streaks of light that follow the wake of a ship in mid-ocean. When she rose the folds of her dress fell in undulating waves to the richly carpeted floor."[37]

Helen Josephine Mansfield had been born in Boston on Christmas Day, 1847. In 1863 she moved with her mother and stepfather to San Francisco, where she soon became involved with a man who, it seems, was blackmailed by her stepfather as a result. (She would

JOSIE MANSFIELD   *Courtesy of The New-York Historical Society, New York City*

admit in open court that her stepfather held a gun to the man's head while he wrote a check, but vehemently denied the man was wearing only a shirt at the time.) In September, 1864, not yet seventeen, she married Frank Lawlor, later a well-known actor, and with him moved to New York in January, 1865.

Josie Mansfield was not cut out for the simple domesticity that Lawlor insisted upon, and they parted the following year. After the breakup of her marriage, Josie boarded with several women, including a Mrs. Bishop at 42 Lexington Avenue and Miss Annie Wood, described as an actress, who lived on 34th Street, both fashionable addresses. How respectable they were is another question, for ladies' boardinghouses, regardless of the neighborhood, ran the gamut from perfectly proper establishments to bordellos. An inevitable consequence of the double standard, the demimonde was in its heyday, and brothels ranging from unspeakable dives to opulent palaces were scattered throughout the city.

Josie Mansfield met Jim Fisk at Annie Wood's house and he fell under her spell almost at once. Soon they were seen together at the theater and restaurants, and it was obvious that Fisk was infatuated with her. While she was content to have him pay her bills and maintain her in style, there is no evidence whatever to suggest that she cared for any aspect of him besides his money. Jim Fisk, who was very lucky in so many ways, was not, in the end, to be lucky in love.

•

Gould, meanwhile, joined the brokerage firm of Smith, Martin in 1867, although he was to use it only for his own speculative convenience. He apparently foresaw the impending struggle for control of the Erie and bought stock and proxies. John S. Eldridge invited him to join the new board that the Boston men and the Commodore were getting up, while Jordan presumably saw to it that Jim Fisk was added to the list.

Fisk was in his prime. Of about average height for the time, he was already of well above average girth, although obesity was not nearly so unfashionable then as it is now. He had a florid complexion, with blue eyes and auburn hair; altogether it was a pleasing if less than handsome face. His mustache and dress would become ever more elaborate with the years. Fisk was already a decided dandy; before long his clothes and uniforms would be the talk of the country.

But it was not his physiognomy or his clothes that most attracted the attention of those who knew him. "Perhaps the strong point of this man is his physique," wrote Fowler. "So robust, so hale, so free from the shadow of every peptic derangement. His boldness, nerve, and business capacity are supplied by his physique, which also supplies him with animal spirits beyond measure. He is continuously boiling over with jokes, good, bad and indifferent."[38]

Jay Gould could not have been in greater contrast. "Uncle Jay," his adoring niece Alice Snow remembered in her old age, "was exceedingly quiet. His words were both few and carefully chosen. He was perfectly poised, always. In my many months of residence as one of the family I never once saw him give way to anger. Self-control, I should say, was one of his most pronounced attributes."[39]

As for his clothes, they were "invariably the same; of good quality and cut; they were either black or, on occasion, deep blue. . . . He never wore jewelry of any description, unless that term can be applied to his modest watch and chain. When you looked at him your impression was that of a small, dark, yet somehow strikingly powerful man, who, unlike many commanding men of slight stature, had neither need nor taste for display."[40]

Physically, Gould could hardly have amounted to less. He was always sickly, with poor digestion and scant interest in food. "He was almost the thinnest man I ever met," remembered William A. Croffut in his memoirs. "I saw him take the plunge in the Turkish bath at Saratoga. His arms were small, his chest was hollow, his face was tawny and sallow, and his legs! Well, I never before saw such a prominent 'bull' that had such insignificant calves. Perhaps—perhaps you could not put a napkin ring over his foot and push it up to his knees; I am not certain."[41]

Whatever Jay Gould lacked in physical strength, sartorial panache, or *joie de vivre,* he more than made up for in sheer brain power. He was soon to prove the most intellectually gifted player of the great game at this time, perhaps any time, with an astonishing ability to comprehend the totality of the economic forces at work in any given situation. There is no doubt that Jay Gould could have been one of the greatest economists of the nineteenth century. But he was interested in applied, not theoretical, economics.

Jay Gould and Jim Fisk were the most unlikely of friends, for to the outside world they seemed to have nothing in common. But they shared one attribute at the very least, a ferocious determination to be masters of the game: Jim Fisk to assuage his powerful thirst for life at its fullest and Jay Gould to make a great fortune. Each was more than smart enough and self-honest enough to realize that the other had what he himself lacked.

With Gould's genius and Fisk's personality, they made a formidable pair. Together they would ride the Erie Railway into history and turn Wall Street upside down in the process.

CHAPTER EIGHT

The War Breaks Out

VANDERBILT was represented on the newly constituted Erie board not only by Drew but by his nephew Frank Work, who would prosper mightily by his unswerving devotion to his uncle's interests. By the time of his death during the First World War, Work would have amassed a fortune that amounted to more than $15,000,000. (Unlike the apparent majority of his fellow American millionaires of the Gilded Age, Work had little use for Europe and none whatever for its aristocracy. He forbade his children to marry anyone not an American citizen, but his daughter defied him and married the heir to the first Lord Fremoy. It was through the issue of this marriage that Work would become in time the great-great-grandfather of Diana, Princess of Wales.)

Vanderbilt thought that he had achieved a stable balance of power on the Erie board. Drew, however, had other ideas, and so did Fisk and Gould, who moved swiftly into the Erie's leadership and were soon appointed to the all-important executive committee. Drew had known the Boston men for years and was already close to Fisk. Perhaps Uncle Daniel filled their heads with notions of the riches that awaited them from speculating from the inside in Erie stock, just as he had once charmed the Legislature into speculating in Harlem. Gould, too, must have been attracted by Drew. While better educated, infinitely better read, and much more intelligent, Gould recognized Drew's immense native cunning and surely appreciated his lack of scruples. The Commodore's interests were soon being short-changed on the Erie board.

Hardly had the new board assumed office when a pool was formed by some of its members and several outsiders to bull the price of Erie upward. Because Drew was universally acknowledged to be the master speculator of Wall Street, he was put in charge of handling the pool's funds. But the price of Erie did not respond as the other members of the pool thought it would under such presumably heavy buying pressure. Drew counseled the clique not to worry, telling them that everything was in hand. He was, as always, persuasive, so much so, in fact, that one member of the pool even borrowed pool funds from Drew in order to speculate on the coming rise in Erie on his own, a move that would greatly increase his profits, provided, of course, that Erie did indeed rise. At last it began to move upward.

By January, 1868, Erie had managed to get as high as 79, but then it broke suddenly to 71. On the evening of the break the trading in Erie went on long after the Stock Exchange and Open Board had closed and twilight had faded from the Curb. "The whole strength of Wall Street," Fowler reported, "seemed to have poured into the halls of the Fifth Avenue Hotel. Daniel Drew, with his face pushed into an expression more than usually somber and solicitous, stood near the grand stairway, watching the writhings of his victims, the late exultant bulls."

"Well, Mr. Drew, is Erie going down?" a prominent broker asked.

"Other folks think it is," he replied, cackling happily, " 'though I can't give you any points in it."[1]

The behavior of Erie stock in the marketplace made it look more and more as if one of Drew's classic bear raids was in progress rather than the bull movement he was supposed to be managing, and the *Herald* reported that "the emissaries of the speculative director exerted themselves all day to create a panic, and told more false-hoods than usual about stocks in general and Erie in particular."[2] Finally the pool member who had borrowed funds from Drew in order to buy Erie on his own became so desperate—and suspicious—that he checked on just where it was that the Erie he had bought had come from. He was horrified to find out that the stock had come from the pool's own brokers. He went to the other members of the clique and asked their help in dealing with the speculative director.

They went to Drew in a body and demanded that Drew put up the price of Erie as he had agreed to do.

"I sold all our Erie at a profit," Drew responded deadpan to his assembled partners, "and am now ready to divide the money."[3]

As Charles Francis Adams explained it, "The controller of the pool had actually lent the money of the pool to one of the members of the pool to enable him to buy up the stock of the pool; and having thus quietly saddled him with it, the controller proceeded to divide the profits, and calmly returned to the victim a portion of his own money as his share of the proceeds."[4]

Frank Work—who may well have been Drew's principal victim in this scheme—was, of course, disgusted with it and kept the Commodore fully informed as to what was going on. The Commodore was getting more and more uneasy.

Vanderbilt was not interested in speculating in Erie stock but in protecting the profits of the New York Central. He and the Pennsylvania wanted the Erie to come in with them and pool the earnings on their New York City business, dividing them evenly. This, at a stroke, would have eliminated any possibility of a ruinous rate war among the three trunk lines serving New York City. Vanderbilt fully expected the new Erie board to go along with this plan (it seems likely that it was an explicit part of the deal by which the composition of the board had been decided). So did almost everyone else, the *Herald* reporting on January 9th the rumor on the Street "that the contemplated running arrangement with a view to the consolidation of earnings between the Erie, the New York Central and the Pennsylvania Central will shortly be completed, after which the stock of the Erie Company will range permanently much higher than it has done hitherto."

Vanderbilt was stunned, therefore, when the Erie board voted down the proposal, with only Frank Work voting for it. The board said that the scheme was unfair to the interests of the Erie Railway and that the Erie's share should be larger. Vanderbilt recognized the vote for what it was: a declaration of war. Drew had betrayed him and seduced the other members of the board into betraying him likewise. Control of the Erie had slipped from his fingers, and it was once more the loose cannon of New York railroading.

Since the Commodore had found out he could not control the Erie through others, he set out to buy it. "Vanderbilt was not accustomed to failure," Adams wrote, "and in this case the sense of treachery, the bitter consciousness of having been outwitted in the presence of all Wall Street, gave a peculiar sting to the rebuff. A long succession of victories had intensified his natural arrogance, and he was by no means disposed even apart from the failure of his cherished plans, to sit down and nurse an impotent wrath in the presence of an injured prestige. Foiled in intrigue, he must now have recourse to his favorite weapon—the brute force of his millions."[5]

For the ensuing battle Vanderbilt could count on most of his old allies on the Street, such as Richard Schell (who had been part of the recent Erie pool) and Leonard Jerome, but the Commodore surely counted on public opinion's being strongly on his side as well. He had every reason for thinking so as the papers had been praising him and excoriating Drew and the rest of the Erie board since the day it had been elected. On February 8th, 1868, the *Herald* declared flatly that there was no one "so well fitted for the trust [of running the Erie] as Commodore Vanderbilt . . . although any change could hardly fail to be for the better."[6]

But even with public opinion solidly on his side—and in the event the Commodore was to be deeply disappointed in this regard—Vanderbilt was undertaking a mammoth task. While the Erie may have been "in ruins," in the words of its own superintendent, and "running on it . . . a flat defiance of Providence,"[7] it was still, by the corporate standards of the day, a very large ruin. With slightly more than 250,000 shares outstanding, nearly all of them in the floating supply, the market valued the Erie Railway at about $17,500,000. To buy a majority of that stock, which is what Vanderbilt intended to do, would take as much as $10,000,000, possibly more, since the buying itself would drive up the price. This was a vast sum even for the Commodore, whose immense assets were tied up in the stock of the Hudson, Harlem, and New York Central railroads.

But that was not Vanderbilt's biggest problem; he was after all the best credit risk in town. Rather, "the peculiar difficulty of the task . . . lay in the fact that it had to be undertaken in the face of antagonists so bold, so subtle, so unscrupulous, so thoroughly acquainted with Erie, as well as so familiar with all the devices and tricks of fence [on] Wall Street, as were those who now stood ready to take up the gage which the Commodore so arrogantly threw down."[8]

While officially there were 251,050 shares of Erie outstanding, that figure did not include a few things. In May, 1866, the Erie had once more found itself seriously short of money. Drew, ever helpful, had proposed a solution to the problem. He would lend the company $3,480,000 for two years at 7 percent interest. As collateral, the company would turn over to him 28,000 unissued shares from its treasury and $3,000,000, face value, in bonds convertible into 30,000 shares of stock. (One can hardly help noticing the difference between Drew's idea of collateral when his own assets were at risk and when it was those of the Erie Railway that might go down the tubes.)

The convertible bonds he received were among the more curious securities ever to trade on Wall Street. Not only were they convertible into stock at par, but the stock could be subsequently reconverted into bonds.[9] This made it possible for Drew to expand and contract the floating supply of Erie stock by more than 20 percent whenever it suited his speculative purposes to do so.

Before Vanderbilt could hope to buy control of the Erie he would have to do something to neutralize not only the phantom 58,000 shares of stock that Drew could conjure up out of thin air, but he would also have to prevent Drew from manufacturing even more stock out of new convertible bonds, using his position as treasurer. Drew's reputation for creating stock was mythic in its proportions. "How manifold and ingenious," wrote Adams, "were the expedients through which the cunning treasurer furnished himself with Erie, when the exigencies of his position demanded fresh supplies." The Commodore would have to do something about the "apparently inexhaustible spring from which such generous supplies were wont to flow."[10]

Vanderbilt, who only a year before had told the committee of the New York State Assembly, "I for one will never go to a court of law when I have got the power in my own hands to see myself right," now decided that he had no choice but to go into court. The Commodore must have known full well how dangerous an enterprise he was undertaking when he chose "to play the double game of manipulating the courts and the stock market at the same time, and against wily opponents, who were experts in both operations."[11]

•

The court whose help he sought was the New York State Supreme Court. Despite its name, which has confused generations of non–New Yorkers and not a few natives, it is not the state's highest court but rather its court of first instance, the first, not the last, rung on the judicial ladder for serious cases.

The Supreme Court dates to the new state constitution of 1846, which was written in the full flush of Jacksonian democracy. The prime attribute of Jacksonianism was a profound trust in the wisdom of the people and a faith that that wisdom could be usefully expressed by means of the ballot in all cases. Coupled with this idea was an equally profound distrust of the executive. The Governor, therefore, had to submit to reelection every two years, while most of the important state officials, such as the Secretary of State, the Canal Commissioners, and even the Prison Inspector, were elected as well and thus independent of the Governor.

Unfortunately, the result of all these good intentions was not to put power in the hands of the people but into the hands of political parties, the only way in the nineteenth century to "get out the vote." To be elected it was necessary to be nominated, and to be nominated one had to secure the approval of those who controlled the political machinery, none of whom took Cincinnatus for his model. Supreme Court judges were also elected—as they still are, providing the last real political power wielded by what little is left of the New York City Democratic political machine.

In the mid-nineteenth century, the state was divided into eight judicial districts, with four judges sitting in each district, except in Manhattan, where five judges tried to cope with the city's huge caseload. The judges of each district, sitting *en banc,* constituted the appellate division of that district, which meant that judges frequently had to judge the decisions made by their closest judicial colleagues, with whom they were often politically allied.

The results of this system, based on a political ideology rather than the realities of human nature, were predictable. "The system of electing judges by the popular vote," wrote Adams, "had at last brought forth bitter fruit, and men had been elevated to the bench who should have ornamented the dock."[12]

The procedure by which Supreme Court judges sought to adjudicate commercial disputes was spelled out in the Code of Civil Procedure that had been adopted by the Legislature shortly after the new constitution came into effect. Until then New York State judicial procedures had been a hodgepodge of statutory and common law that had grown unchecked since the days of King Richard the Lionhearted. The new code, a model of order and clarity, was the work of David Dudley Field, a prominent New York City lawyer.

It would be difficult to overestimate the influence of the Field codes (in addition to a code of procedure, he wrote criminal and civil codes) upon subsequent legal history. They were adopted in whole or in part by twenty-six states and the federal government. In 1873 they were adopted as the basis for reforming the laws of England and from there spread throughout the English-speaking world and far beyond. It is ironic that Field's codes should be least honored and perhaps most abused in the state where they originated.

"This single reform [the Code of Civil Procedure] was the greatest ever accomplished in the remedial law of an English-speaking people," wrote David McAdam in 1894. ". . . Unfortunately, the symmetry and excellence of Mr. Field's legislative work have been much marred either by the action of the Legislature or by its failure to adopt the entire scheme of reform as reported by the codifiers."[13]

One weakness of the Code of Civil Procedure was that, while the judges were elected only by the voters of the district in which they sat, their powers in law and equity ran to the borders of the state, and they were entirely free to make rulings on any case brought before them regardless of its status in any other court. Until the coming of the railroad and telegraph, this had been of no consequence; time and distance kept the judges from interfering with each other. The new technology, however, changed matters entirely, and the denizens of Wall Street and their well-paid attorneys were swift to discern and exploit the new possibilities. This overlapping jurisdiction would make the ensuing legal fracas between Commodore Vanderbilt and the Erie board extraordinarily complicated.

A second weakness of the code was the almost unlimited power of judges to issue injunctions and appoint receivers in ex parte proceedings and the difficulty the defendant might encounter in trying to vacate these orders. In such proceedings only one side of the case is heard, and the judge decides only if there is enough evidence and legal standing to order a full hearing.

In ex parte hearings, judges are usually extremely cautious in issuing injunctions, which can have very expensive real-world consequences. But the justices of the New York State Supreme Court in the 1860's, many of whom made politics and profit their first priorities, were not nearly so fastidious. "An injunction is the favorite weapon in all contests," wrote Jeremiah Black, who had been President Buchanan's Attorney General and had failed to win a seat on the U.S. Supreme Court only because his acid tongue had made him too many enemies in the Senate. "Its simplicity commends it to the professional mind, as the simplicity of the knout and

DAVID DUDLEY FIELD   A cartoon from *Harper's Weekly* after the death of Fisk. *Courtesy of the Union Club Library*

the bastinado makes them dear to the heart of the Muscovite and the Turk."[14]

Although George Templeton Strong was a lawyer by profession, he had nothing but contempt for the court where so much of his business took place. "The Supreme Court is our *Cloaca Maxima*," he wrote in his diary in 1870, "with lawyers for its rats. But my simile does that rodent an injustice, for the rat is a remarkably clean animal."[15]

Strong was worried about New York's economic future, and thus his own. "Law does not protect property," he lamented. "The abused machinery of law is a terror to property owners. No banker or merchant is sure that some person calling himself a 'receiver,' appointed *ex parte* as the first step in some frivolous suit he never heard of, may not march into his counting room at any moment, demand possession of all his assets and the ruinous suspension of his whole business, and when the order for a receiver is vacated a week afterwards, claim $100,000 or so as 'an allowance' for his services, by virtue of another order, to be enforced by attachment. No city can long continue rich and prosperous that tolerates abuses like these. Capital will flee to safer quarters."[16]

Field worked hard to correct these weaknesses in his code as they were discovered, for he realized fully their disastrous long-term consequences. But the Legislature, ever attentive to the short-term interests of its members and their friends, resisted any reforms.

While Field was a great codifier he was also a great lawyer. As long as these anomalies remained on the books he not only fought vigorously to have them removed but exploited them fully for the benefit of his clients. It is one of the ironies of history that, while David Dudley Field's influence upon the law as it is daily encountered by lawyer, judge, and defendant alike exceeds that of almost any jurist and codifier who has ever lived, he is almost wholly forgotten today for his great achievement. Field is remembered now, when he is remembered at all, for using his mastery of the code he created to defend and advance the interests of his two most famous clients: James Fisk, Jr., and Jay Gould.

•

None of this, however, greatly concerned the Commodore, who did not seek to reform the world but only to flourish in it. His lawyer was Charles Rapallo, already distinguished and soon to be named to the state's highest court, the newly reorganized Court of Appeals.

His judge was George G. Barnard, whom Stedman described as "a Tammany Helot, numbered among the Vanderbilt properties."[17] Explaining matters to the English readers of *Fraser's Magazine,* its reporter wrote that "in New York there is a custom among litigants, as peculiar to that city, it is to be hoped, as it is supreme within it, of retaining a judge as well as a lawyer. Especially in such litigation as that now impending, it was absolutely essential to each party to have some magistrate in whom they could place implicit confidence in an hour of sudden emergency."[18]

George G. Barnard had been born in Poughkeepsie in 1829 and graduated from Yale when only nineteen, entering the practice of law in New York City shortly thereafter. Working his way up through the Tammany political organization, he was appointed to fill a vacancy on the Supreme Court and was subsequently elected to the bench. "During the eight years he has served in that high position" of Supreme Court judge, said *Leslie's Illustrated* the following November, "Judge Barnard has probably been more severely criticized than any of his colleagues, and yet even his most bitter opponents concede that he possesses some of the most important qualifications for a good judge, among which may be mentioned unquestioned ability, a most remarkable quickness of perception, untiring industry, and a thorough indifference to newspaper attack or public clamor."[19] Among the attributes conspicuously absent from this list of Barnard's judicial qualities were honesty and impartiality.

The *Herald* picked up rumors of impending court action on the 16th of February, and on Monday the 17th Frank Work appeared before Judge Barnard and asked through counsel for an injunction against Drew and the Erie Railway.

Having heard the argument, Judge Barnard lost no time in granting, at least provisionally, all that Work asked for. He temporarily enjoined the board of the Erie from paying either interest or principal on the loan from Drew or making any settlement of the loan, and further enjoined it from releasing Drew from any liability or from any cause of action it might have against him. Drew was personally enjoined from any legal proceeding against Erie. The judge set Friday the 21st as the date for formal argument, but on Wednesday, Work, this time seconded by the New York State Attorney General—clearly the big guns were being brought out—asked Barnard to remove Drew from the board, alleging misconduct with regard to the leasing of the Buffalo, Bradford and Pittsburgh Rail-

JUDGE GEORGE G. BARNARD *Courtesy of The New York Public Library*

road. Barnard obliged by temporarily suspending Drew from the board.

Although Frank Work, as a member of the Erie board, was the plaintiff in the case, there was no doubt whatever regarding who was behind it all. On February 20th, the *Herald* noted that "it may be shrewdly suspected that the defendant has been simply entrapped by Vanderbilt, who is, no doubt, the operating strategist of the whole transaction, Mr. Frank Work and others being simply component parts of the trap, the pawns and knights of the controlling mind."[20]

Drew duly appeared in court on the 21st, but argument on the merits was postponed until the 26th and then until the 3rd of March. On that day, argument for Drew's removal was postponed until the 10th of the month, but Barnard enjoined the Erie board from any further conversion of bonds into stock or any new issue of stock beyond the 251,050 already acknowledged to be in existence, and from guaranteeing the bonds of any other railroad. Drew was personally enjoined from "selling, transferring, delivering, disposing of or parting with"[21] any of the Erie stock in his control, and from fulfilling any contracts already entered into until he had returned to the corporation the 58,000 shares it had hypothecated to him two years earlier as well as the 10,000 shares he had acquired as a result of the Buffalo, Bradford and Pittsburgh deal.

Vanderbilt apparently thought that he had Drew thoroughly hogtied, for he ordered his brokers to go into the market and buy all the Erie that was offered. But, as the *American Law Review* would explain later that same year, "if . . . they counted upon an easy victory, Commodore Vanderbilt and his friends showed a profound ignorance both of the resources of their opponent and of the character of New York law."[22] As the *Herald* explained on the day the injunction was handed down, Drew, "although suspended from the board by the Supreme Court, is, in fact, as much its controlling spirit as he ever was and on the same principle that love laughs at locksmiths he laughs at injunctions."

The *Herald* was putting it mildly, for Drew had been busily converting bonds into stock regardless of any injunctions and, what is more, issuing brand-new bonds and converting them instantly into stock as well. "On the 29th of February," Fowler reported, "Uncle Daniel might have been seen scuttling into the office of William Heath & Co., No. 19 Broad Street. A few moments later, that office was resonant with the rustling of fifty thousand shares of fresh, crisp, Erie certificates, like the chirping of locusts at noontide in July."[23]

Vanderbilt did not yet know it, but the floating supply of the stock he was seeking to corner had just increased by 20 percent. Rumors began to spread on the Street of newly printed shares, and the price of Erie began to fall, while banks became more and more reluctant to lend money on Erie stock.

Drew and company were equally active on the legal front. On March 5th, attorneys appeared before Supreme Court Judge Ransom Balcom, who sat in Cortland, located some sixty miles beyond Binghamton, in the heart of Erie country, to ask for an injunction against any further proceedings in Barnard's court. This compliant justice promptly issued a show-cause order and set the 7th of April as the date to hear testimony in Cortland. While he was at it, he suspended Frank Work from the board.

The spectacle of a rural Supreme Court judge enjoining any further proceedings in the courtroom of another Supreme Court judge sitting two hundred miles away in New York City disgusted Bennett, who wrote in the *Herald* on March 10th that "while there may be legal warrant for the course pursued by the defendants in this matter and for the action of their judicial friend from the rural districts, it is nevertheless a most singular proceeding, and one which, however reconcilable with Wall Street ethics, appears to be in conflict with all our preconceived ideas of professional courtesy and public justice."

In order to counter this attack from the far left field of upstate New York, Richard Schell now applied to Supreme Court Judge Daniel P. Ingraham, who sat in Barnard's district and who promptly enjoined the board from transacting any business whatever without Frank Work present and voting. Thus, three co-equal judges, sitting in two widely separated districts, had all issued injunctions that were squarely in conflict and equally binding. There was more to come.

On Wall Street the excitement was steadily mounting, and its rumor mills, in perfect working order as always, spewed forth stories. "The Street is afraid to hold Erie," reported the *Herald* on March 6th, "and the clique supporting it [that is, Vanderbilt and his allies] has to bear its full weight, and there are rumors afloat that the amount of common stock is far larger than is generally supposed, owing to the conversion of old bonds into stock and the issue of new convertible bonds to an extent which is at present difficult to estimate." The next day the *Herald* reported that the Commodore and his friends held 100,000 shares of Erie.

But the bankers now refused to lend the Commodore any more money on the collateral of Erie stock. "We can't lend on Erie," Croffut reported one as saying. "There is an illegal issue of stock, and Erie isn't worth anything." Richard Schell, dispatched to deal with the recalcitrant bankers, knew just how to handle them and asked, if they would not lend on Erie, what would they lend on. New York Central, they told him, would be fine.

Schell, of course, knew that most of the big houses on Wall Street had large positions in the gilt-edge stock of the New York Central, then selling for about a third over par. "Very well, gentlemen!" replied Schell. "If you don't lend the Commodore half a million on Erie at 50, and do it at once, he will put Central at 50 tomorrow and break half the houses on the Street! You know whether you will be among them."[24]

The bankers caved in at once, and Vanderbilt had his money. He went on buying Erie steadily, and the price began to rise once more. Ignoring the rumors, for he apparently believed still that Judge Barnard's injunctions had Drew effectively neutralized, the Commodore must have felt that control was nearly in his grasp.

He also, it seems, churned out a few rumors of his own in hopes of calming the market. On March 10th the *Herald* reported that "the Street is still more demoralized on the subject of Erie than it was last week, and the full weight of the stock is thrown upon the bull clique; but the latter still confidently predicts that it will sell at par before the next annual election, and asserts that the new certificates of stock already referred to do not represent new stock, but were issued in exchange for old ones, the exchange having been made for the purpose of creating the impression that new stock was being thrown on the market."

Barnard had enjoined the secretary of the Erie from issuing any further shares of stock, and that injunction had not as yet been contradicted by any judge loyal to Drew. If the secretary were to issue stock, therefore, he could be held in contempt. Jim Fisk solved this minor problem with his customary dispatch. When the secretary told a messenger to take the new shares of stock to the transfer office on Pine Street, Fisk was waiting outside the Erie offices on West Street at the corner of Duane and simply seized the certificates when the messenger appeared, running off down the street with them while the thoroughly baffled messenger returned to tell the secretary what had happened. Now, since the stock was in unknown hands, at least officially, those hands could not be enjoined from issuing it.

On the morning of March 10th, as the buzzing crowds began to surge into the financial district, William Belden, Fisk's brokerage partner, appeared before Judge Gilbert of Brooklyn and asked for a writ of mandamus, compelling the issuance of convertible bonds. Belden alleged a conspiracy among the Commodore, Schell, Work, and Judge Barnard. Gilbert declined to issue the writ, which ordinarily only applies to a public official, but he added to the growing pile of conflicting injunctions, enjoining "all parties to all previous suits from further proceedings, or from doing any act in furtherance of said conspiracy."[25] In addition, he ordered all Erie directors, except Frank Work, to continue the discharge of their duties and, all important, ordered that they continue to convert bonds into stock.

The *American Law Review,* whose contempt for the New York State judiciary bordered on the total, noted that "the New York community is not apparently unaccustomed to seeing one justice of its Supreme Court enjoining another on the ground that his respected associate has entered into a conspiracy to use his judicial power in a stock-jobbing operation."[26]

Barnard immediately voided all injunctions except his own, but Drew and his friends were now in a nearly perfect legal situation. As Stedman observed, "Since they were forbidden by Barnard to convert bonds into stock, and forbidden by Gilbert to refuse to do so, who but the most captious could blame them for doing as they pleased?"[27]

As these injunctions were flying back and forth, the excitement on Wall Street reached a crescendo. "The whole market hung on one word—Erie," wrote Fowler the following year. "The strident voice of George Henriques, the Vice President of the Open Board, was heard calling off in quick succession, government bonds, state bonds, Pacific Mail, New York Central, then a pause, a shadow rippled across his face and a shiver ran through the hall as he ejaculated in a tone still more strident—Erie! For ten minutes bedlam seemed to have broken loose. Every operator and broker was on his feet in an instant, screaming and gesticulating. The different Vanderbilt brokers stood each in the center of a circle, wheeling as on a pivot from right to left, brandishing their arms and snatching at all the stock offered them. As the presiding officer's hammer fell and his hoarse voice thundered out 'that will do, gentlemen. I shall fine any other offer,' Erie stood at 80. The crowd, leaving the other stocks not yet called, poured into the street, where nothing was heard but Erie. Vanderbilt's brokers had orders to buy every share offered, and under their enormous purchases the price rose, by twelve o'clock, to 83."[28]

And if on the street all that was heard was Erie, it was the same once more inside the offices of William Heath & Company, where Jim Fisk had appeared with still more new stock for immediate sale. Once more came the sound of "the rustling of fifty thousand fresh shares, as they dropped from the plump, jeweled fingers of James Fisk, Jr."[29] Fisk was heard to remark of Vanderbilt, "If this printing press don't break down, I'll be damned if I don't give the old hog all he wants of Erie."[30]

As reports of newly dated certificates raced through the market, the price of Erie dropped "like lead to 71." The Commodore's position had suddenly become perilous in the extreme, "loaded as he was with ten millions of fresh stock . . . to say nothing of the huge blocks of Central, Hudson, and Harlem, which he was carrying on his aged shoulders. Any lack of nerve would have produced a financial collapse, which would have involved himself and thousands of others in frightful loss, and perhaps ruin. But he never flinched."[31]

In his finest hour, and "in spite of the fact that he had spilled over seven millions like water, the Commodore managed to sustain the market through it all."[32] Putting at risk his entire fortune, the Commodore ordered his brokers to keep on buying all that was offered, and the price lumbered heavily upward once more, closing at 76⅛. The Commodore and his allies held almost 200,000 shares of Erie. But was it a majority of the stock outstanding?

Nobody, certainly not the Commodore, knew for sure.

•

What the Commodore did know was that his attempt to use the courts as a means to pin down his financial enemies had been a complete, indeed ignominious, failure. The richest man in America had been made a fool of by a couple of newcomers and a man whom Vanderbilt had been pleased to think he owned only six months earlier. Drew, Gould, and Fisk now had $7,000,000 of Vanderbilt's money—which they had prudently converted to greenbacks, draining New York of much of its money supply and causing short-term interest rates to rise sharply. All Vanderbilt had to show for this sum was 100,000 dubious shares of Erie stock with the ink hardly dry on the certificates. He could not even sell them, for two days later the New York Stock Exchange and the Open Board both ruled that certificates of Erie dated after March 7th, 1868, would not constitute good delivery.

While Barnard's injunctions had miserably failed in their purpose, the courts were now Vanderbilt's only weapon. He would have to unleash his bloodhounds, as he called the lawyers, and early in the morning of March 11th, Vanderbilt, certainly in a towering rage, the air thick with his profanity, sent them to roust out Barnard.

Drew, Gould, and Fisk, meanwhile, were in fine fettle, thoroughly pleased with themselves and their accomplishments. "The executive committee of the Erie board," wrote Fowler, "were holding high festival over their triumphs at the offices of the company at the foot of Duane Street, on the morning of the 11th of March. Uncle Daniel's corrugated visage was set into a chronic chuckle. Jay Gould's financial eye beamed and glittered and the blond bulk of James Fisk, Jr., was unctuous with jokes."[33]

The party spirit evaporated abruptly when it was learned that "process of the court had been issued to punish them for contempt of its mandates, and would soon be placed for service in the hands of the high sheriff's spongy officers."[34]

The effect of this news was electric. They realized that, once they were clapped into jail, the courts would belong to Vanderbilt. And the Commodore, they well knew, would have no mercy whatever. The only thing to do right then was to get beyond the reach of New York law before the Sheriff's minions could arrive. That they did. "In fact," reported the *Herald,* which like all the other newspapers was having a field day, "so complete a clearing out has not taken place since the Fenians fled from Dublin on the night of the suspension of the *habeas corpus.*"[35]

Within minutes of the arrival of the news, "the policeman on that beat observed a squad of respectably dressed, but terrified looking men, loaded down with packages of greenbacks, account books, bundles of papers tied up with red tape, emerge in haste and disorder from the Erie building. Thinking perhaps that something illicit had been taking place, and these individuals might be plunderers playing a bold game in open daylight, he approached them, but he soon found out his mistake. They were only the executive committee of the Erie company, flying the wrath of the Commodore, and laden with the spoils of their recent campaign."[36]

Drew, who at seventy years of age had no stomach for a spell in the Ludlow Street jail, and most of the others took the first ferry across the Hudson to Jersey City, where they and the loot were safe. Gould and Fisk, however, stayed behind in New York for a while, as did a few of the other directors. Three of them would be caught and arrested for contempt, including General Diven, who was arrested just as he was boarding a train for Albany.

That night Gould and Fisk dined at Delmonico's with lookouts posted in all directions. In the middle of dinner they learned that arresting officers were on the way. Fleeing the restaurant, the pair hailed a carriage and took it to the foot of Canal Street, where the steamer *St. John* was docked. After brief negotiations a boat was lowered and two seamen engaged to row them across to New Jersey.

The Hudson, crowded at all hours with boat traffic large and small, was always a dangerous place. The night of March 11th found it at its worst, with no moon and a thick blanket of fog muffling the whistles, bells, and running lights of the vessels. Fisk, always the take-charge type, ordered the seamen to row up the river in order to avoid the ferries, but the fog was so thick that they soon lost their way and apparently rowed in circles for a while. A large ferryboat suddenly loomed out of the fog and only "the vigorous use of their lungs" saved them from being run down. They escaped from that one "only in time to see another bearing down upon them. Ultimately," *Harper's Weekly* reported, "they determined to get some assistance, and for this purpose hailed a Pavonia ferryboat but could get no response, and therefore made a clutch at the supports of the guard [the housing of the giant and very dangerous paddlewheels] and were drawn so near to the wheel as to nearly wash the whole party out of the boat. They however saved her from swamping, and climbed aboard, arriving shortly afterwards at Jersey City, safe and sound, but thoroughly drenched."[37]

The Hudson River and the limited reach of state law now separated the antagonists, and the first battle of the Erie Wars was over. In a sense it was a standoff. While Drew, Fisk, and Gould held the Erie Railway and Vanderbilt's $7,000,000, the Commodore held New York. They could not come home until they had settled matters with him, and the Commodore was hardly in a forgiving mood.

CHAPTER
NINE

Fort Taylor

FISK soon organized a temporary headquarters for the fugitives at Taylor's Hotel, which stood right on Jersey City's waterfront, conveniently near both the Erie Railway depot and the slips for the ferryboats to and from New York City. The Erie's Duane Street headquarters was closed until further notice, and by March 14th the *Herald* was able to report that "Mr. Fisk appeared to have established a regular bureau for the transaction of business" in New Jersey, and "couriers were flying between Wall Street and the 'camp' every hour during the day."

The directors of the Erie, meanwhile, settled in for the siege, making themselves at home at the hotel. "They dined and wined during the day, and patronized the hotel so liberally that at the next report of financial affairs [of the company] an unusually large item may be expected opposite the 'incidentals.' "[1] Among the creature comforts Fisk provided for himself was Josie Mansfield, whom he installed in a suite at the hotel.

Public interest in the Erie War, as it was dubbed by the newspapers, was intense, and "Jerseymen and New Yorkers crowded around Taylor's Hotel with as much interest as though another Chancellorsville were being fought."[2] The *Herald* reported that "the impeachment proceedings at Washington [of President Andrew Johnson], with which the morning papers teemed, were almost entirely eclipsed by the new phase which the struggle for power between the two millionaires assumed."[3] Even *Harper's Monthly*—not given to journalistic hysteria—agreed that the Erie War "entirely superseded public interest in the impeachment of the President."[4]

While Drew and the other directors were safe from the hands of New York law as long as they stayed in New Jersey, they had reason enough to fear extralegal attempts to return them to New York State and the tender mercies of the Commodore. Judge Barnard announced that he would hold on contempt charges, and $500,000 bail, any of the fugitives who strayed or presumably could be dragged into his jurisdiction.

To guard against any sudden raids Fisk set about transforming Taylor's Hotel into what the newspapers promptly christened Fort Taylor. By March 16th it was guarded by three twelve-pounder cannon, which, according to the *Herald,* peered "grimly from the dock dividing the ferry and Cunard wharves, and the Hudson County artillery forms a powerful reserve to the little garrison. Fifteen picked men of the Jersey City police force, armed with revolvers and locusts [nightsticks, which are usually made of locust wood] under the command of Chief of Police Fowler, command the approaches to Taylor's Hotel, and a large force under Inspector Masterson, who is special superintendent of police on the Erie Railway, comprise the garrison under the command of Daniel Drew. Mr. Fisk, who ranks as lieutenant colonel, has been transferred to the command of the navy, which comprises four small boats, three of which are manned by fifteen men, the fourth by six men armed with Springfield rifles. Eleven detectives occupy positions at the Erie Railway depot and the ferries along the river on both sides, and five others are posted in certain parts of New York where the roughs are known to congregate."[5]

The government of Jersey City was anxious to be as helpful as possible to the Erie Railway. The Erie dominated the economy of the town, where its New York terminal was located, and it is safe to assume that its management had taken care to shower largess, such as free passes, on the local holders of power. The president of the Jersey City Police Commissioners assured the directors that "the entire police force of Jersey City would be held in readiness at their

FISK AND GOULD FLEEING TO NEW JERSEY   *Courtesy of the Union Club Library*

service if required."[6] A system of signals was coordinated with the police, using fire by night and guns by day in case Fort Taylor was suddenly attacked.

Apparently no rumor regarding Fisk's preparations for defending the holdout was too ridiculous to be printed. The *Herald* reported that a last-ditch defense had been prepared whereby "underneath the box containing the valuable deposits, including bonds, was placed a pan of nitro-glycerine, in order that if the brave directory should be stormed in the upper room of a Jersey hotel, and should there find the last entrenchment of liberty, they should emulate the Spartan heroes at Thermopylae, and on the last survivor would devolve the fearful alternative of consigning his body and the treasure to a common perdition."[7]

All these comic-opera precautions seemed, briefly, to have been justified on the 16th, when fifty men "organized," said the *Herald,* "at a disreputable gin mill in New York,"[8] took the Pavonia ferry, and at four o'clock in the afternoon appeared at the Erie Depot. They were looking, they said, for Daniel Drew. Inspector Masterson, head of the Erie detectives and forewarned of their approach, was able to deal with them, mainly by convincing them that Drew was not at the depot and that they could hardly hope to pry him out of Fort Taylor.

Rumors buzzed that $50,000 had been promised to anyone who could deliver Drew into Vanderbilt's clutches, and it was widely assumed that this gang had been organized by the Vanderbilt forces. But Charles Francis Adams, for one, doubted this. "To suppose," he wrote the following year, "that the shrewd and energetic Commodore ever sent them to go gaping about a station ignorant both of the person and the whereabouts of him they sought would be to impute to Vanderbilt at once a crime and a blunder. Such botching bears no trace of his clean handiwork."[9]

But if not Vanderbilt, then who? It might very well have been Fisk himself who organized the gang and sent them on a wild-goose chase in order to get a point firmly across with Drew.

All the newspapers at this time still assumed that Drew was as much the dominant power in Jersey City as he had been on Wall Street, as thoroughly in command of his side as Vanderbilt undoubtedly was of the other. But Drew was out of his element now, for he was really at home only in the murky depths of the Street, where he could use his many different brokers to keep his right hand from learning what his left was up to. Cooped up in a New Jersey hotel

under the constant eye of his fellow directors, Drew found his room
for maneuver, and treachery, greatly restricted, and he chafed
severely under the restraints. "Hardly had the Erie confederates
been installed in Taylor's Hotel," wrote Fowler, "when his younger
and more robust associates noticed the workings of his timid, vacil-
lating nature. He had been borne along by their stronger wills and
now felt painfully his trying position. He missed his pleasant fire-
side, where he had so often toasted his aged limbs and dreamed of
panics."[10]

What his associates feared most was that Drew might attempt to
make a separate peace with Vanderbilt that would protect his own
position at the expense of theirs. They were well aware that Drew
was quite incapable of honor, even among thieves, and had managed
to wheedle forgiveness out of Vanderbilt more than once before. He
might well seek to exploit again the fact that "the only soft spot that
the Commodore had in his nature was a sentimental willingness to
help Drew out of scrapes."[11]

The directors had more than just their reading of Drew's character
to go on, for the company treasurer soon took to disappearing from
the hotel on solitary walks. And, "taking advantage of that blessed
immunity from arrest which the Sabbath confers on the hunted of
the law,"[12] Drew began secretly visiting New York on Sundays. His
associates put detectives on his trail to confirm this, and they spied
him boarding the Weehawken ferry bound for New York.

From that point on Drew was never without a tail. The treasurer
went so far as to withdraw the cash held by the directorate in New
Jersey banks and deposit it in New York ones, where, if the Commodore had found out about it, it could have been attached. Fisk
promptly attached Drew's own securities that had also been brought
to New Jersey for safekeeping and compelled Drew to return the
company money. Drew was now watched continuously, and Adams
wrote that "his orders on the treasury were no longer honored, and
that he had, in fact, ceased to be a power in Erie."[13] As early as the
20th of March, when the directors had been in Jersey City only a
week, the *Herald* reported that "Mr. Drew has been kidnapped, not
by the New York roughs, but by the directors."

While Fisk organized and directed the defense of Taylor's Hotel,
the Erie War continued to rage in the courts. On the 12th the *Herald*
had pointed out just what was at stake: "The great Erie Railway
stock litigation, at present going on in this city, promises to assume
proportions of the most extensive and complicated character ever

brought before the civil courts of any country, it being virtually a contest in which the actors are the two greatest stock speculators in the United States; the weapons about $120,000,000 of capital, on both sides; and the prize the control of two great railway systems."

On March 14th Judge Barnard appointed Charles S. Osgood to be receiver of the proceeds of the stock sale that his own previous orders had forbidden to take place at all. Osgood was a close personal friend of Barnard, a common enough circumstance in judicial appointments at that time, and hardly unknown in our own. In addition, Osgood just happened to be one of the Commodore's ever-useful sons-in-law. The lawyers for the Erie directors, not surprisingly, objected to the appointment as receiver of a close relation of one of the principal litigants and got Judge T. W. Clerke, who sat in Ulster County, to stay the appointment. Barnard promptly voided his colleague's stay, but Osgood soon declined the appointment and Barnard named Peter Sweeny to take his place.

Sweeny was not without his own connections, being a major power in Tammany Hall and bearer of the title of City Chamberlain. While Sweeny was appointed receiver, what he was supposed to receive had already been carried out of the court's jurisdiction in a carpetbag, and consequently there was nothing for him to do. This fact, however, did not stop Judge Barnard from rewarding him with $150,000 of the Erie Railway's money—a considerable fortune in the middle of the nineteenth century—in compensation for his nonexistent efforts.

Barnard's habitual generosity with other people's money was well known and much appreciated by the New York legal establishment. "There are few lawyers," wrote *Leslie's Illustrated* that year, "even of opposite political views that would not prefer to argue a motion before him than before any of his colleagues. His liberality in granting counsel fees to lawyers in cases where the law allows them, has made him very popular with the whole profession."[14]

On March 18th Judge Gilbert, whose injunction commanding the continued conversion of bonds into stock had so perfectly suited the interests of Drew and his allies, voided his own injunction, saying that he had been deceived into issuing it in the first place. Gilbert, whom Charles Francis Adams called "one of the most respected [judges] in the State of New York," is very nearly the only one involved in the Erie Wars to emerge with so much as a shred of honor. The others involved in this "saturnalia of bench and bar . . ." Adams thought, "all seemed to vie with one another in their efforts to bring their common profession into public contempt."[15]

But Adams, typically, was being unduly harsh on the lawyers if not the judges. While judges and certainly legislators have a primary responsibility to serve the public who elected them, lawyers do not. As David Dudley Field would so passionately argue in the newspapers a few years later, a lawyer's duty is to his client. If "the law is a ass," it is nonetheless a lawyer's obligation to exploit that condition for his client's benefit.

As suit followed suit and judge after judge issued injunctions, voided those of others, and reinstated their own, the legal tangle compounded upon itself until finally "a good-sized wheelbarrow would have been called into requisition to carry the briefs and papers to the court."[16]

At last the judiciary seemed to sense what a spectacle it was making of itself in this case, and on the 26th of March Bennett was able to editorialize in the *Herald* that "the judges appear to have come to the wise conclusion that they are doing the bench no service in interposing between the opposing forces, and by common consent they have ceased firing their paper bullets and await the result of the bill now pending at the state capital."

The next phase of the Erie Wars was to be fought not in the courts or on Wall Street but in the legislatures of New York and New Jersey. By comparison, the courts and the Street were models of rectitude. As Adams wrote at the time, "Probably no representative bodies were ever more thoroughly venal, more shamelessly corrupt, or more hopelessly beyond the reach of public opinion, than are certain of those bodies which legislate for republican America in this latter half of the nineteenth century."[17]

If the exiles in New Jersey were to win the Erie War, or even come home again, the decisive battles would have to be fought in Albany and Trenton, and that was going to be expensive. "Under our modern forms of government and in the advancing strength and intelligence of the people," The *Herald* informed its readers, "men no longer attempt to rule by the sword, but they find in money a weapon as sharp and more effective; and having lost none of the old lust for power, they seek to establish over their fellows the despotism of dollars."[18]

Of dollars the Erie directors had a plentiful supply, including seven million they had swindled out of the Commodore with new-minted stock. Those, conveniently enough, were in cash, for the legislative phase of the Erie Wars would have to be fought not with paper bullets, but with silver ones.

•

President Eldridge of the Erie was fearful that Vanderbilt would get the New York courts to give him control of all Erie property that lay in New York State, a move that would have left the directors a head without much of a body, and the Erie board moved to forestall this possibility. The directors petitioned the New Jersey Legislature to grant them a charter making the Erie a corporation of that state.

New Jersey has long suffered from an inferiority complex caused by its giant neighbor across the Hudson. Consequently, anything that New Jersey could do to injure the prestige or economic interests of New York its legislature almost invariably hastened to do, and a charter for the Erie Railway seemed tailor-made for this purpose.

On March 25th it was reported that "in less time than a man would take to travel from Albany to Poughkeepsie a bill conferring on the Erie Railroad Company all the rights and privileges they enjoyed in New York was passed by both houses of the Legislature at Trenton and placed in the hands of the Governor. The Legislature then adjourned and nothing could be done till Monday night." While the Legislature was adjourned, several members visited Fort Taylor and "assured the directors of the support and protection of the laws of New Jersey, and that if necessary new measures would be enacted for their security."[19]

But the New Jersey legislators, in their zeal to injure New York's economic interests, had also quite inadvertently injured their own personal ones, as they were quick to realize. When Vanderbilt learned of the impending action he instantly dispatched lobbyists to Trenton in hopes of reversing the action of the Legislature, a move that he could only expect to obtain by bribery. "Such a rush to Trenton," wrote the *Herald*, "such bustle in the State House and such lobbying as was witnessed that evening the Trentonians avow beat anything of the kind before. To recover the bill—that is withdraw it from the executive chamber—reconsider and finally kill it; there was the rub."[20]

The next day the *Herald* reported that "the Legislature and lobby at Trenton are in despair at finding that by the hasty passage of the bill granting large powers to the Erie Railway Company in that state they have unconsciously deprived themselves of as promising and profitable a contest as that now being waged in Albany. An attempt was made in one of the New Jersey houses to get back the bill; but to the dismay of the lobby it could not be done, and it remained with the Governor for his action." The Governor subsequently signed the bill into law.

The Erie therefore became, at least for the moment, a New Jersey corporation and thus gained a measure of legal breathing room (for no one, certainly, wanted to drag the Erie Wars into the comparatively honest arena of the federal courts), but it still had grave problems. The vast majority of the company's property lay in New York State, not New Jersey. Besides, Jersey City was the home of only one of the directors and was certainly not where the financial action was. As the *Herald* explained, with typical New York contempt for all things trans-Hudson, "New Jersey is a very good place to grow cranberries, but hardly suited to the great business demands of the Erie Railway direction."[21]

The day after the New Jersey Legislature acted with such alacrity, a bill was submitted in the New York State Assembly by a friendly legislator.

Section 1. The issuing of the bonds of the Erie Railway Company for the purpose of completing, furnishing and operating its railroad, convertible into the common stock of said company by authority of the board of directors of said company, and the conversion of the same into such stock, shall be deemed to be within the powers of said company.

Section 2. Whenever said company shall hereafter issue any stock it shall, on the 1st day of January next after such issue cause a certificate of the same, stating the number of shares and the time when the same was issued, to be filed in the office of the Secretary of State.

Section 3. The guaranteeing by the Erie Railway of the bonds or coupons of any other railroad company, necessary or proper, in order to secure a connection of said Erie Railway with other railroads, for the purpose of securing better facilities for the traffic of said Erie Railway, shall be deemed and taken to be within the powers of said Erie Railway Company.

Section 4. It shall be lawful for the Erie Railway Company to contract with any other railroad to provide a track with a gauge corresponding to the present gauge of the track of the Erie Railway, and to run the engines and cars of the Erie Railway Company on the same, in order to facilitate the transportation of freight and passengers on the Erie Railway.

Section 5. The acts of said company in issuing bonds and
stock respectively, and in entering into such contracts and guar-
antees prior to this date, are hereby ratified and confirmed.[22]

To put it simply, the bill confirmed the board of directors in all
that it had already done and gave it *carte blanche* to do what it liked
in the future without having to bother with anything so confining
as the interests of the stockholders. Even Judge Barnard, hardly a
stranger to the art of selling his office, was astonished by the sweeping nature of the bill's language, calling it the equivalent of "an act
to legalize counterfeit money."[23]

Everyone not hopelessly naïve knew that such a bill could only
be passed with the help of a great deal of real money. The legislators
certainly knew it and, as *Fraser's Magazine* reported, "flocked to
Albany like beeves to a cattle-mart. All were for sale, and each
brought a price proportioned to his *weight.*"[24]

The *Herald*, reflecting the deep cynicism that New Yorkers felt
about their government at this time, editorialized that the legislation "comes as a Godsend to the hungry legislators and lobbymen,
who have had up to this time such a beggarly session that their
board bills and whiskey bills are all in arrears and their washer-
women and bootblacks are becoming insubordinate. As the Erie bill
promises to carry the fight up to the Capitol, the whole army of
strikers, inside and out, are in ecstasies; and numbers of experienced
lobbyists, who had left Albany in despair, are packing up their paper
collars and making the best of their way back, in the hope of sharing
in the anticipated spoils. It is whispered about that Vanderbilt is
determined to defeat the bill, and fabulous sums are mentioned as
having been 'put up' for that purpose. Upon its merits the bill ought
to go through and become law; but its fate will probably depend
upon the comparative amounts ready to be paid for its success or
defeat."[25]

The *Herald* was in favor of the Erie bill not because it was good
for the Erie Railway, its stockholders, or its customers, but only
because it would keep the railroad out of the hands of the Commodore, for the publisher had changed his mind about Vanderbilt's
suitability to run the Erie.

Bennett had lost none of his respect for the Commodore as a
manager of railroads, but he had suddenly grown to fear that New
York could only suffer in the long run if so many of the city's
railroad connections were to fall into the hands of a single entity.

"So far as the contest for the control of the [Erie] company is concerned," he wrote, "it is obviously contrary to the interests of the public that any one party should have control of the Erie, the New York Central, the Hudson River and the Harlem. Such a monopoly could exact its own rates of fare and freight, except where restricted by legislative enactments, and the results would be deplorable."[26]

The Erie board, almost certainly at the urging of Jay Gould, who from the start understood the power of public opinion, had worked hard to get it on their side. A report of the board released to the newspapers had stated: "The motive for the otherwise unaccountable change of front on Mr. Work's part is to be found in the well-known fact that he was put into this board in the interest of the Hudson River and Central Railroads; and that when we refused to become parties to the schemes of Mr. Vanderbilt and his friends to create a gigantic monopoly for the benefit of the Central line, Mr. Work's interests were exposed."[27] Gould was to spend his entire career in Erie casting the railroad in the role of David standing up to the transportation Goliath that Commodore Vanderbilt had become. For a while it proved a powerful and rewarding image and one that Vanderbilt was never able to counter effectively.

The *Commercial and Financial Chronicle,* the *Barron's* of its day, had as much respect for the Commodore as the *Herald* and as many reservations about the outcome if he were to gain control of the Erie. "The question that concerns our great trading interests is this—shall the main avenues of our commerce be under the control of a gigantic monopoly, or shall they be stimulated and expanded under the wholesome competition of transportation companies?"[28]

With such papers as the *Chronicle* and especially the mighty *Herald* opposed to Vanderbilt's gaining control of the Erie, public opinion began to shift away from the Commodore. As early as the 12th of March the New York City Chamber of Commerce voted for a resolution that called for the Erie and the New York Central to be under separate ownership. And by the middle of that month "memorials against monopoly began to flow in at Albany."[29]

Neither the *Chronicle* nor anyone else had any illusions about what would determine the outcome in the Legislature. "The record of corruption at Albany and elsewhere," it said, "is too plain and voluminous to admit of any hope that legislation in these matters would not be dictated by the parties who controlled the roads."[30] The venality of this "Sanhedrin of rascality,"[31] as George Templeton Strong called the Legislature, was exceeded only by the brazenness with which its members pursued their private gain at the public expense. For, if the legislators had been having "a very beggarly time" that session, it cannot be said that they were unprepared to take advantage of any opportunities that might come their way.

That year the Legislature had changed the law as it applied to bribing public officials. "No *conviction,*" said the new law, "shall be had under this act on the testimony of the other party to the offense, unless such evidence is *corroborated* in its material parts by other evidence."[32] In that pre-electronic age, this meant, of course, that as long as a legislator took care to be out of earshot of third parties and took his bribe in cash, there was no possibility whatever of his being convicted of a crime. As wrote Hudson C. Tanner (secretary of the Assembly for many years before he wrote his tell-all book, *"The Lobby," and Public Men from Thurlow Weed's Time*), "The political cry of 'an honest ballot and a fair count' has been perverted so as to apply more to an honest count of the boodle than an honest count of the ballot."[33]

The Erie directors at first sent John E. Develin to handle their interests in Albany. But Develin very considerably underestimated the going rate for malfeasance in the State Capitol, a matter that had been a subject of much discussion there as the Erie War moved to Albany. "The prices to be demanded," wrote the *Herald,* "occasioned a great deal of debate. Some cheap-rated fellows suggested $1000 a head, but they were smiled at for their lack of boldness and for their unsophisticalness. The rate vibrated between $2000 and $3000, and some were unwilling to say anything less than $4000. The Drew men promised $1000—$500 down and $500 when the bill became law. The latter proviso was too old a trick, many had 'been there before,' to quote their mystical way of expressing themselves. The words are not very luminous to people generally but the lobbyists understood them. The Drew men at the outset thus won for themselves a reputation for cheapness that was fatal to their cause. The paltry offer of $1000 (only half cash) was contemned in view of the magnificent proportions of the wealth of Commodore Vanderbilt. The friends of the latter, however, had not entered this portion of the field of battle; but they were expected, and so the first offer was nonetheless refused."[34]

While the Commodore's forces perhaps had not yet begun wholesale bribery, they had been most active in the Assembly's Railroad Committee, and the *Herald* reported a rumor that half a million dollars had been spread around the committee to kill the bill.[35] Whatever the sum, it proved quite adequate, for on March 27th the committee reported out the bill unfavorably and the Assembly agreed to the committee report on the 28th, by a vote of 83 to 32. "The hint," wrote Adams, "was a broad one; the exiles must give closer attention to their interests."[36]

The Erie directors were quick in taking the hint and, "after the retreat of the discomfited and routed forces that fought under the Drew banner, the leaders held a council of war, and the result was the deposition of the previous managers of the lobby and the substitution of no less a personage than Jay Gould himself as generalissimo."[37]

Gould proceeded to Albany, where he arrived on the 30th and installed himself in Parlor 57 of the Delavan House, Albany's leading hotel. Among his luggage, according to the *Herald,* whose reporter was working the Capitol lobby for the latest rumors, was a trunk "literally stuffed with thousand dollar bills which are to be used for some mysterious purpose in connection with legislation on the subject of the bill now before the Legislature. Mr. Gould has already secured himself the reputation of an excellent 'manager.' "[38]

As soon as Vanderbilt's forces got wind of Gould's arrival in Albany they sicced the sheriff on him. Judge Barnard was asked to issue a warrant for Gould's arrest to Sheriff Parr of Albany County, who was to hold him pending a bail of $500,000. Sheriff Parr received the warrant about one o'clock on the 31st and served it on Gould at the Delavan House at three. But Gould surprised him by immediately producing the bail money, while the Commodore's old ally, Erastus Corning, stood as his surety. The warrant was answerable in New York City on Saturday, April 4th, and Gould duly appeared before Judge Barnard, who scheduled a contempt hearing for the following week. Gould took the eleven o'clock train back to Albany, now in the custody of James Oliver of the New York City sheriff's office.

Once Gould was safely back in the Delavan House he came down with a cold—a cold that rendered him "not too ill to go to the Capitol in the midst of a snow storm, but much too ill to think of returning to New York."[39] Meanwhile, Adams wrote, his pen fairly dripping sarcasm, "Pending the recovery of his health, he assiduously cultivated a thorough understanding between himself and the members of the legislature."[40]

The Erie bill had been reintroduced, this time in the Senate, and

the directors did not repeat their previous error, the *Herald* reporting that "they seem determined to make amends for their recent
shabby conduct in leaving the lobby and the 'rings' [legislative
cliques] in the lurch. They are plentifully supplied with funds, and
while they are entertaining all who honor their quarters with a visit,
dispensing champagne and cigars *ad libitum,* they do not forget the
arguments which are most convincing."[41]

A great deal of money was being distributed in Albany. Adams
passed along, but did not quite vouch for, a report that one individual received $100,000 to influence the legislation and then took
$70,000 from the other side to get lost, which he promptly did, "and
thereafter became a gentleman of elegant leisure." Meanwhile,
"other senators were blessed with a sudden accession of wealth, but
on no case was there any jot or tittle of proof of bribery."[42]

On April 15th the Erie suffered one of its frequent disasters when
a broken rail sent three cars tumbling down an embankment in Port
Jervis, killing twenty-six people. (George Templeton Strong wrote
in his diary that the way to stop these accidents was to hang a few
railroad directors on a charge of murder, suggesting that Drew or
Vanderbilt would do nicely for starters.) Despite the accident, or
perhaps because of it—for the bond issues ostensibly were to finance
improvements—the Senate voted in favor of the Erie bill on April
18th, by a vote of 17 to 12.

"The Erie men," reported the *Herald,* "have succeeded admirably
under the skillful direction of Jay Gould, who in this respect has
undone all the bungling work of John E. Develin and his *coterie*
who came here to initiate the first Erie campaign. Some idea may be
formed of the rich placer which the 'ring' are about to work, when
it is known that the Erie men have already spent over eight hundred
thousand dollars to accomplish their purposes."[43]

But something was in the wind, as an acute reporter for the *Herald*
had noticed as early as the 15th when he saw the directors in Jersey
City no longer skulking about with armed guards but walking
"abroad with as much freedom and apparent indifference as though
they were in Wall Street or Broadway."

While the silver bullets had been flying in Albany, quiet talks had
been going on in New York.

•

Vanderbilt was hardly oblivious of public opinion, although he
would only seldom, and usually with unhappy results, try to manip-

ulate it himself. And he knew, even if Charles Francis Adams doubted it, that not even the New York State Legislature could totally ignore it. Clearly, pressure was building to prevent his gaining control of the Erie while he already held the New York Central, Hudson River, and Harlem lines.

The Commodore could be a notably stubborn man, but he was stubborn only so long as he thought he could win. Probably he decided that any victory he might win in the Legislature this time around would be both very expensive in the short term and to no avail in the long.

In any event, he decided to cut his losses and sent a note to Drew to come see him. Clews reported that the note was delivered by a waiter at Taylor's Hotel, who was instantly fired for his treachery and then hired by Vanderbilt at an increased salary.[44] Before long the Albany *Argus,* among others, "learned that Mr. Drew was in personal conference with Mr. Vanderbilt, and that on successive Sabbaths the old chief of the Erie came over from his New Jersey retreat to visit and consult with the Commodore of the Central at his residence in New York. It was evident that at any time these two stars now in apparent opposition might move into conjunction."[45]

Once the Boston group on the board had thought about it, they must have realized that Drew no longer had the power to double-cross them, for he no longer had control of the company treasury. If Vanderbilt wanted to talk, they had every reason to listen to what he had to say, and Drew, with his mysterious power to sweet-talk the Commodore, was just the man to hear him out.

Vanderbilt, it turned out, was determined to have three things. First, the stock he had been saddled with would have to be taken off his hands at a price near what he had paid for it. Second, Richard Schell and Frank Work would have to be made whole for the beating they had taken at the hands of Drew in the pool of the previous winter. Third, Drew must withdraw from any further participation in the management of the Erie. What Vanderbilt had always wanted more than ownership was that the Erie be managed in a businesslike manner, with due attention to its corporate and stockholders' interests. He had finally learned that Drew was inherently incapable of doing that. Like the scorpion in the fable, Drew couldn't be trusted even to pursue his own self-interest, for it had become part of his nature to sting.

As for Uncle Daniel, he had many reasons to make a bargain. He was desperately anxious to get out of New Jersey and back to Wall

Street again. And he certainly knew that he had thoroughly fouled his nest with the other directors and would never again be allowed near the levers of power at the Erie. Drew at this point was happy to be able to get out more or less whole and come home.

As for the Boston group, they too were anxious for their trans-Hudson hegira to end. They had only wanted to use the Erie as a catalyst for turning the base metal of Boston, Hartford and Erie paper into the gold of a negotiable security and had found themselves swept up into something much more than they had bargained for.

The only ones left out of this happy coincidence of interests were Jim Fisk and Jay Gould, both of whom opposed the settlement from the first.

While negotiations continued for some time, an agreement in principle was struck on Sunday, April 19th, at the Manhattan Club, to which both Drew and Vanderbilt belonged. The news did not take long to reach Albany. "Suddenly," Adams wrote, "at the very last moment, and even while special trains were bringing up fresh contestants to take part in the fray, a rumor ran through Albany as of some great public disaster, spreading panic and terror through hotel and corridor. The observer was reminded of the dark days of the war, when tidings came of some great defeat, as that on the Chickahominy or at Fredericksburg. In a moment the lobby was smitten with despair, and the cheeks of the legislators were blanched, for it was reported that Vanderbilt had withdrawn his opposition to the bill."[46]

Gould learned of the settlement about nine o'clock Monday morning. "Ere ten o'clock," the *Herald* reported, "there was a perfect rush for Parlor 57 at the Delavan House, where the pecunious Gould has been holding forth. It is said that prices came down wonderfully. Those who had been demanding $5000 were now willing to take anything not less than $100. The great Erie coffers were closed, however. There was no longer any need of votes. . . . The utmost excitement continued until eleven o'clock. The curses against Vanderbilt were loud and deep. His treachery or cowardice had cheated the 'ring' out of thousands, nay, hundreds of thousands of dollars."[47]

The Assembly, in its fury at being denied what its members regarded as their just deserts, suspended the rules and gave final passage to the Erie bill by a vote of 106 to 6. Among its provisos was a prohibition of common ownership for the New York Central and the Erie. The Governor signed it the next day, while in the Assembly "the docket was ransacked in search of other measures calculated to injure or annoy" Vanderbilt.[48]

By the 22nd of April, the *Herald* was in a state of high glee at the discomfiture of the legislators. "The disappointed members of the House, who anticipated heavy bonuses from the railway contestants, must be in a bad way. How are they now to pay their board bills, their washing bills, their brandy and cigar bills, their amusement bills, their gambling debts? Three dollars a day for one hundred days, without roast beef, is their legal compensation. That will not settle the cigar bills of half of them. What shall be done, then, in this extremity for the preservation of the credit of the Solons at Albany?"

Wall Street also sought to do the Commodore an injury that Monday. "When cliques have control of a stock," Fowler wrote, "they rarely select a wet, unpleasant day in which to run up the price. But this rule did not hold good in the case of New York Central. On . . . Monday . . . , at twelve o'clock meridian, the news reached the Long Room that the Erie bill had passed by a large majority. The bears (who generally sympathized with the Erie faction), now sold Central short on every side. The skies grew black and a pouring shower followed, amid which the strong hand of the Commodore, regardless of the elements which were against him, hoisted the enormous bulk of Central to 120."[49]

There were many loose ends to tie up, not the least of which was the opposition of Fisk and Gould to the whole deal. This involved much negotiation and no little gamesmanship. One morning before Vanderbilt was even up, Gould and Fisk presented themselves at 10 Washington Place. "Gould," Fisk testified to the New York State Senate committee investigating the Erie Wars the following year, "wanted to wait until the Commodore should have time to get out of bed, but I rang the bell, and when the door was opened I rushed up to his room. The Commodore was sitting on the side of the bed with one shoe off and one shoe on. . . . I remember that shoe from its peculiarity. It had four buckles on it. I had never seen shoes with buckles in that manner before, and I thought, if these sort of men always wear that sort of shoe, I might want a pair." Having noted for future reference the Commodore's sartorial appointments, Fisk got down to business.

Vanderbilt "said I must take my position as I found it, that there I was and he would keep his bloodhounds . . . on our track; that he

BROAD STREET LOOKING SOUTH FROM WALL STREET   The New York Stock Exchange is the tall building on the right, on the same site as the current building.

would be damned if he didn't keep them after us if we didn't take the stock off his hands. I told him that if I had my way, I'd be damned if I would take a share of it; that he brought the punishment on himself and he deserved it.

"This mellowed him down. I told him he was a robber. [One can only doubt that this had mellowed him down one bit or that even Fisk had the chutzpah to call the Commodore a robber to his face in his own bedroom.] He said the suits would never be withdrawn till he was settled with. I said (after settling with him) that it was an almighty robbery; that we had sold ourselves to the Devil, and that Gould felt just the same as I did."[50]

Early in June, Gould and Fisk arranged a meeting with Eldridge at the Fifth Avenue Hotel to try to come to terms, but Eldridge failed to appear. Finally Gould wondered if the rumor he had heard about a meeting at the house of former Judge Edwards Pierrepont (later U.S. Attorney General under President Grant) a few blocks down Fifth Avenue might be true. To find out, the pair ran down the street and rang the bell of the judge's house. A servant answered the door and shortly Pierrepont sidled out of the back parlor, closing the door behind him, looking, said Fisk, like "a man that was not in; I kept moving along as I had not been invited to take a seat." With characteristic effrontery, Fisk went around the judge and opened the door to the back parlor. There were Drew and the rest of the Erie board, all looking distinctly sheepish.[51]

Finally the details were worked out. Fifty thousand of the Commodore's shares of Erie were taken from him at 70, paid for with $2,500,000 in cash and $1,250,000, face value, of Boston, Hartford and Erie bonds at 80. He was paid another $1,000,000 for a four-month call on his other 50,000 shares.

Drew agreed to resign from the Erie board and, of course, the treasurer's job, and to pay into the Erie treasury $540,000 in exchange for all claims the Erie Railway might have against him. The Boston group exchanged $5,000,000, face value, of Boston, Hartford and Erie bonds for Erie acceptances, and they also resigned from the board. Frank Work and Richard Schell were paid $429,500 by the Erie Railway in exchange for withdrawing their suits against the railroad.

Presumably to get their agreement to this deal, Gould and Fisk were given what was left of the company. Gould was to become the president and Fisk the controller of that now well-plundered enterprise.

"The next thing to be done," wrote Fowler, "was to sell the one hundred thousand shares of Erie. How could it be effected? for one hundred thousand shares is no flea bite. Very easily, thus: Orders were given every day to sell a certain amount of the stock and to hold the market steady meantime. The stock thus sold was borrowed of different parties for delivery, and in this way the impression was created among those not in the secret that a large short interest was being made; this induced the belief that Drew and Vanderbilt were working together to raise the price so as to sell their stock. In a few weeks, one hundred thousand shares were sold. Then the parties from whom the stock had been borrowed, were repaid with the hundred thousand shares held jointly by the Erie Company and by Vanderbilt."[52]

The Scarlet Woman had dropped her handkerchief one more time on Wall Street, and hundreds had once again rushed to her aid.

Meanwhile there was the matter of all those contempt citations Judge Barnard had issued. Barnard's outrage at the affront to his judicial dignity had much diminished by this time, and when Gould, finally restored to health, appeared before him on April 30th, with Fisk, Barnard set the latter's bail at only $11,000. Indeed, as Adams noted, "when the terms of peace had been arranged between the high contending parties, Barnard's roaring by degrees subsided, until he roared as gently as any sucking dove, and finally he ceased to roar at all. The penalty for violating an injunction in the manner described was fixed at the not unreasonable sum of ten dollars, except in the cases of Mr. Drew and certain of his more prominent associates; their contumacy his honor held too gross to be estimated in money, and so they escaped without any punishment at all."[53]

Neither Drew nor Vanderbilt suffered financial disaster in all this. But Drew had lost control of his one-stringed Chinese lyre. Perhaps to console himself, he told Vanderbilt that there was nothing left in Erie anyway.

"Don't you believe it!" replied the Commodore.[54] And the Commodore, as usual, was right, for the very day after the settlement, James Fisk, Jr., was seen on Wall Street decked out in a "nobby velvet coat."

"Erie is going down,"[55] he told his friends there.

Chapter Ten

The Embarrassment of Daniel Drew

IT was not until the 10th of July, 1868, that the settlement under negotiation throughout the spring was put fully into effect. Drew resigned both as treasurer and a member of the board on July 2nd and retreated to Putnam County. Eldridge likewise resigned, returning to Massachusetts with the Boston, Hartford and Erie's $4,000,000 share of the spoils, while Jay Gould was elected in his place as president of the Erie Railway. Jim Fisk took over as controller and, in effect, chief operating officer.

The settlement, when all was said and done, had cost the Erie (which is to say its stockholders) about $9,000,000 and left the company in a state of even greater financial disrepair than usual. As the new management settled in, according to Fisk "the first thing we found was a very well dusted treasury."[1] Even after the stock the Erie had taken back from the Commodore was successfully unloaded on the market, something still needed to be done to replenish it if the railroad was to be of much use to Fisk and Gould, who had certainly not taken on the considerable burdens of managing the Erie for the sake of the salaries involved. The easiest means of doing this, to which they immediately turned, was the tried and true one of the printing press.

The price of Erie had remained steady at about 70 since the end of April, when the siege of Fort Taylor had ended. But in August it began a steep slide, from which it would never recover during the Gould and Fisk regime. At the end of July the stock stood at 68½; by the end of the first week in August it was down to 59⅛. By August 15th it was at 53⅜, and a week later it stood at only 44½. This 35 percent drop had nothing to do with the economic fortunes of the corporation, for receipts that prosperous summer had been better than they had been since the war, but rather resulted solely from the issuance of new convertible bonds that were instantly converted into stock and the stock thrown onto the market. All this was accomplished "without a word of previous intimation to the stockholders."[2]

Nor was the money raised used for capital improvements, as required by the law passed the previous spring and by the General Railroad Act of 1850, or even for desperately needed repairs. The *Commercial and Financial Chronicle* reported that "for the issue of $20,000,000 there is nothing to show beyond $5,000,000 of the bonds of another corporation [the Boston, Hartford and Erie], the interest of which is guaranteed by the Erie Company, the laying of a new line of rails, some minor improvements of no great consequence, and ordinary repairs which should have been covered by the current earnings."[3] In fact, thanks to the years of neglect under the previous regimes, there was a vast amount of repair that urgently needed to be done.

When Gould and Fisk took office in July, they were assured of their positions only until the next regular election of the board, due on October 13th, and rumors abounded on Wall Street that there would be a contest for control. The *Chronicle* even reported, quite erroneously, that "Messrs. Drew and Vanderbilt are now manipulating the market with a view to getting sufficient stock for controlling the next election, and that in order to compass that object, they aim to force a large amount of stock out of the hands of the present president of the road."[4]

Far from hoarding stock, of course, the present president was issuing it nearly as fast as the presses could print it. But, to prevent any struggle for control developing or even the presence on the board of any directors not to his liking, Gould closed the transfer books on August 19th, nearly a month before they were due to close prior to the election. As Adams explained, "The managers were satisfied with the present disposition of the stock and meant by keeping it where it was to preclude any such unpleasantness as an opposition ticket."[5]

Gould was duly reelected president, as was Fisk controller. Elected to the board with them were, among others, Gould's brother-in-law, Daniel S. Miller, Jr.; William M. Tweed, Tammany Hall's Grand Sachem; and Peter Sweeny, New York City's Chamberlain and the man Judge Barnard had appointed receiver just the previous spring. Over the course of the summer Judge Barnard, that judicial windsock, had become one of the closest allies of the new management of the Erie Railway.

Safely reelected, the Erie management immediately made it even more difficult for the stockholders to interfere with their activities. On October 30th it was brought to the attention of the Stock Exchange that the most recent certificates of Erie stock had had added to them the words "this certificate is held subject to the by-laws of the company." Brokers wanted to know just what this meant and whether the new certificates would constitute good delivery. The answer to that question turned out to be yes, for the bylaws had been altered only so as to require stockholders to vote in person at any meeting that might be held. By forbidding proxy votes the new board had, with the stroke of a pen, disenfranchised many local and virtually all foreign stockholders.[6] Before long Gould would rewrite all the bylaws and delete about half of them to suit his convenience.

With the treasury restored—largely at the expense of the stockholders, whose equity had been cut by better than a third by the new issues—and the election out of the way, Gould was ready to play the great game. He and Fisk invited their old mentor, Daniel Drew, to join the fun, although it was by no means an altogether friendly invitation. Uncle Daniel, however, couldn't resist the temptation to speculate in Erie. "Three months of comparative dullness in Erie [had] passed away," wrote Fowler, and "Uncle Daniel took down his rusty and cobwebbed armor, donned his bear-skin cap, and prepared to enter a new campaign against all the bulls."[7]

Henry Clews, who only a couple of years earlier had toasted Drew at a dinner held in his honor when the speculative director had been at the top of his form, now felt that the Great Bear's powers had sadly declined. "Drew might have enjoyed life and the consolation of religion on the few millions he had left," he wrote a few years later, "if he had retired in company with his Bible and hymn book to some lovely, secluded spot in the peaceful vales of Putnam

County; but he was under the infatuation of some latent and mysterious force of attraction, the victim of some potent spell."[8]

Uncle Daniel had long since reached a point where he could no
more forswear speculation than a drunken man can forswear alcohol. But, wrote Clews, "when he returned to the Street after a few
months absence, the scene was greatly changed. His two pupils had
shown themselves to be such apt scholars that in the interim they
had exceeded the wildest dreams of avarice that ever their able
preceptor had conjured up or inculcated."[9]

What Gould, that master analyst of market forces, had in mind
was a bear trap, a device that Drew knew intimately. But Gould's
trap was larger, grander, and far more subtle than anything Drew
had ever tried, for it involved not just one stock on the Regular
Board, but the whole money market, not just New York's Wall
Street but London's Lombard Street as well.

The British, whose domestic economy generated far more capital
than could be usefully employed at home, had a frequently expensive fascination with American railroad securities throughout the
nineteenth century. Gould had been feeding the English market's
continuing and unaccountable appetite for Erie stock with all the
shares it would take, quietly shipping special ten-share certificates
to London, where they would be safely out of the reach of the bears
when the trap was sprung.

In addition, Gould intended to constrict the supply of greenbacks, the immediate effect of which would be to cause interest rates
to soar and the price of stocks, in consequence, to fall. To do this
was a simple matter, provided plenty of cash was on hand. Money
was always tight in the New York market in the fall, when farmers
in the countryside sold their crops and money flowed out to pay for
them, taking some time to cycle back into the money center.

To add to this natural scarcity Gould proposed to add a factitious
one as well by writing checks against the large deposits of the Erie
Railway and then having these checks certified. The banks would
be forced to hold reserves, theoretically 100 percent, against the day
the checks would be presented. But, instead of cashing them, Gould
intended to take the certified checks to other banks and use them
as collateral against which to borrow greenbacks. The greenbacks,
in turn, he intended to lock up in safe deposit boxes, effectively
removing them from the New York money supply.

Gould had perhaps $10,000,000 on hand from the new stock he
had sold in the summer, and he invited Drew to add $4,000,000 to

the pot. Used to being automatically deferred to in matters of speculation, Drew now found the situation very different. "In plain
terms," Clews explained, "he was coolly requested to go into a
'blind pool' in Erie, deposit four millions, shut his eyes and open his
mouth, leaving the Erie sharpers to put taffy or candy into it, just
as they pleased. He was no longer to have the privilege of pulling
the wires, nor the wool over other people's eyes."[10]

Gould had begun the process of locking up greenbacks even before the election of the board of directors on October 13th. At first
the Street was unimpressed, and the *Commercial and Financial
Chronicle* reported on October 10th that "the efforts made through
tightening money last week to depress the stock market were wholly
unsuccessful. The artificial interference was anticipated, and the
brokers consequently had generally protected themselves by time
loans so that prices were comparatively steady."

But as October turned into November Gould tightened the
screws, and Wall Street began to howl. The *Herald,* always sensitive
to the mood of the Street, reported that, "except in times of actual
panic, Wall Street has rarely been in a more disturbed and excited
state than it was all last week, and at the close there was not only
no prospect of improvement but the monetary stringency was more
severe than on any previous day."[11] On the 31st the market finished
a week that saw both a new weekly record for trading volume
established—647,000 shares—and Erie stock sink as low as 38½,
while the *Chronicle* reported that banks that were members of the
New York clearinghouse "have lost $20,000,000 of currency depos-
its and $13,000,000 of legal tenders."

The *Chronicle* knew exactly where to lay the blame for the
troubles. "There has been a mischievous manipulation of the
money market for speculative purposes," it reported. "A combination, not only owning large private capital, but also controlling
several millions of funds in possession of a leading railway company,
have withdrawn from the banks and placed in hoard an aggregate
of money which cannot be estimated below $10,000,000, and by
many is considered to reach $15,000,000. In addition to this with-
drawal of funds, these parties are engaged in reckless and demoraliz-
ing operations embracing a railroad scheme the full scope of which
is not yet apparent, but which it is feared may involve more serious
consequences to holders of securities and to the public confidence
in corporate management than is generally anticipated."[12]

Drew by this time was becoming more and more unhappy with

LOCKING UP GREENBACKS

his own situation. Uncle Daniel was not temperamentally suited to standing aside while others manipulated the market with his money. Besides, he had every good reason to suspect the motives of Fisk and Gould and no reason whatever to suppose that they would hesitate for a second to sacrifice his interests upon the altar of their own. Heaven only knew he would have sacrificed theirs fast enough had the situation been reversed.

Early in November Drew panicked and demanded out. He suddenly withdrew his funds from the combination, losing, according to Clews, a million dollars by his premature withdrawal. It seems much more likely, however, that that sum is all he had yet committed of the four million he had originally pledged. Drew then "undertook the task of bearding these young lions in their den—the den which he had constructed for them, and the young lions which he had so carefully nurtured to destroy him. They were very wroth with him on account of what they regarded as his treachery, which virtually consisted in his refusal to be totally devoured by them."[13]

Drew, like the good Christian only he believed himself to be, sought not only consolation but revelation as well in religion, and "after considering the matter prayerfully, as he always did in such emergencies, he resolved to operate alone, and the oracle told him to go on the short side."[14] Drew shorted Erie to the tune of 70,000 shares at an average price of about 38, convinced, apparently, that Gould and Fisk would continue their plans unchanged and that he could have a free ride with them until instinct told him to jump off the Erie merry-go-round. But the younger men did not prove to be nearly so accommodating. Betrayed, as they saw it, by Drew yet again, they resolved to break him now, once and for all.

To do that, they unlocked greenbacks and allowed the money to flow back into the market, bringing down interest rates. Almost at once the mood on Wall Street began to lighten perceptibly. But, while the rest of the market lumbered upward, Erie did not, and in fact continued to decline, lulling Drew and the other bears into a false sense of security. On Saturday, November 14th, Erie opened at 36⅝.

Suddenly the market exploded, and when the half-day session ended, Erie had accounted for half the total volume of 80,000 shares on the Regular Board, while its price jumped to 52½. Drew, suddenly seeing disaster straight ahead, became desperate. "He tried hard to pray," wrote a wholly unsympathetic Clews, who may or may not have known what he was talking about, "but his irresistible desire to keep constant watch on the tape of the ticker to see the quotations, evidently distracted his devotions."[15] Drew, as he always seemed to do when in a bad way, decided to pay a call on his betters and went to see August Belmont.

Belmont, who had made his fortune picking up the pieces after the panic of 1837, had been one of the great powers on the Street for more than thirty years. He owned four thousand shares of Erie stock personally and had watched the value of his investment be cut in half by the maneuvers of Fisk and Gould when they had still been on the short side of the market. Far more important, Belmont represented numerous English and European clients who were short the stock. Like Drew, they were facing disaster, for the stock with which they intended to fulfill their contracts was on board the Cunard steamer *Russia,* then at sea, and not due to arrive in New York until Monday, November 23rd.

Despite the fact that Belmont could hardly have been ignorant of what had happened to the Commodore when the latter had sought to turn the courts to his use on Wall Street, he nonetheless decided to sue Gould and Fisk for malfeasance and to ask the courts for the appointment of a receiver to run the Erie. Whether this was Belmont's idea to start with or, more likely, had been suggested to him by Drew is not known. Drew agreed to provide proof of Gould's and Fisk's corporate perfidy (as well, inevitably, of his own) by signing an affidavit that revealed in great detail all the shenanigans that had gone on in Erie since the previous fall.

Drew and Belmont were playing for time, hoping, apparently, that the filing of a lawsuit would persuade Gould and Fisk to let them off the hook or at least keep things sufficiently up in the air until the *Russia* could dock and they could break the corner with the stock that was aboard her. But, while Belmont was concerned for his clients, Drew was concerned for himself; and he certainly knew how slim a hope any action in the courts represented. When all was said and done, Drew had still sold seventy thousand shares of what was not his'n.

It is altogether likely that he was playing a double game with Belmont from the moment he entered the latter's front door, and he certainly departed through that door intent on double-cross, for he had the affidavit in his pocket. Drew told Belmont that he wanted to read it more carefully at home and promised to return it first thing Monday morning.

But on Sunday morning, when he might have been more profitably, and certainly more honorably, engaged in the practice of his religion, he called instead on Fisk and Gould at their offices in the Erie building on the corner of West and Duane streets.

Drew pleaded and groveled and wheedled and begged. But if Vanderbilt, and apparently even August Belmont, had a soft spot for Uncle Daniel, Gould and Fisk had none. They had no good old steamboat days to relive fondly with him, but instead only his record of unbroken treachery. The two toyed with the old man all day long and, promising nothing, told him to return at ten that night.

Even then they spared Uncle Daniel no humiliation, keeping him waiting until eleven before they appeared. Drew's bright gray eyes were sunk in his deeply wrinkled face and the gaslight flickered and hissed as once again he begged them to lend him the stock for a week so that he could make his deliveries. "I am a ruined man," he bleated.[16]

But Fisk merely pointed out that Drew "should be the last man that should whine over any position in which you may be placed in Erie."

"You can loan me the stock," Drew continued undeterred. "I will give you three per cent for it." Failing that, he asked that they give the printing press one more crank for his sake. "You have the power to issue more convertible bonds, and I will buy the bonds from you if you are caught, or I will buy the bonds of you with the understanding that I shall not pay for them unless you are caught." But they would agree to none of these schemes.

Seeing that they were adamant, Drew, desperate, played his last trump. According to Fisk's deposition, published in papers all over the country the following week—one can only wonder what Belmont thought as he read it—Drew "then entered into an explanation as to certain proceedings that he said were being got up in the courts; he said that he had been in the enemy's camp, and all that he cared about was to look out for number one."

"You know that during the whole of our other fights," Drew told them, "I objected to ever giving my affidavits, but I swear I will do you all the harm I can do if you do not help me in this time of my great need." He showed them the affidavit that had been prepared and told him he would sign it and it would be before Judge Josiah Sutherland the very next morning unless they came to his aid.

Now forewarned of the impending court action, they stonily refused. "His pupils proved that they had profited only too well by his instruction. Just as he would have acted under similar circumstances, they were perfectly relentless."[17] At last, past one in the morning, Drew realized that it was hopeless. He rose and headed for the door.

"I will bid you goodnight," he said to them.

The Old Man of the Street went out into the chill November night, armed now, at least, with the courage that despair alone could give.

•

The next day Drew signed the affidavit, and Belmont's lawyers, who last time around had been Vanderbilt's lawyers, went into Supreme Court on Monday morning before Judge Sutherland, a magistrate, according to Adams, "of such pure character and unsullied reputation that it is inexplicable how he ever came to be elevated to the bench on which he sits."[18] They asked that a receiver be appointed to handle the affairs of the Erie Railway, alleging innumerable irregularities on the part of the present management. Sutherland agreed to take the matter under advisement, but before he acted it was discovered that Belmont's and Drew's actions had been anticipated. A receiver had already been appointed to handle the affairs of the Erie Railway Company, and his name was Jay Gould.

Very early Monday morning, before Judge Barnard was even out of bed, Gould, Fisk, and their lawyers had called upon his Honor, asking him to hold, in Adams's phrase, a *lit de justice*. The fact that it was Judge Sutherland's turn that month to handle the business of the district and assign new cases did not deter Barnard in the least. An independent party was needed for what they had in mind, a suit against the Erie Railway Company, and Gould provided Charles MacIntosh, the superintendent of the Erie's Hudson River ferries and the owner, so he said, of two hundred shares of the company's stock.

"The policy of the conspirators, resolved as they were to control the proceedings, was prompt and characteristic," reported the *New York Times*, which, like all the other New York newspapers, was giving the latest battle of the Erie Wars blanket coverage. "One Charles MacIntosh, *a hired ferry agent of the set controlling the Erie Company*, was caused to bring suit before Judge Barnard on a few shares of stock, in which he praises 'the management,' declares the public is unreasonably disturbing its policy by making troublesome inquiries about stock issued and to be issued, tells us that it will be best to let things go on as they are going, assures the public that if it was wrong to secretly issue thirty millions of stock in violation of law to pay for bonds of other railroad companies illegally purchased, and for opera houses, real estate, etc., etc., that the true remedy—the one he prays for—is that the chief author of the iniquity be appointed receiver; that his associates remain in power; that they bring such suits as they wish before Judge Barnard alone; that Mr. Belmont and everyone else be enjoined from bringing any suit anywhere; that the other judges attend to other business, while this ferry agent, Mr. Jay Gould, Mr. James Fisk, Jr., and Judge Barnard, aided by the advice of Mr. Lane, counsel to the Erie Railway Company, attend to the whole of that particular business! If anything could surpass the audacious assurance and effrontery of this scheme set forth in the suit of MacIntosh, it would be the fact that Judge Barnard responded instantly to its demands."[19]

While all this was going on, the date when Drew's contracts would come due grew inexorably closer. "It was manifest, however, that by [that] time Drew would have reached the end of his millions, and probably most of his credit would have vanished with his own filthy lucre. His oppressors were bearing down upon him with all their might, and were evidently determined to make short work of him."[20]

The price of Erie rose steadily on Monday and Tuesday as Drew and the other shorts tried to cover. On Wednesday it ran up all the way to 58. "The Broker's Board [that is to say the Open Board] was wild with excitement. High words passed; collisions took place; the bears were savage and the bulls pitiless."[21] By Thursday morning the price of Erie reached as high as 62, and Drew was faced with taking a loss of $24 on every share he managed to buy.

Fisk and Gould were confident that they had Drew hopelessly cornered, as the difference between the price of Erie, deliverable immediately, and that deliverable Monday when the *Russia* was due to arrive, ranged as high as sixteen points. They were sure that there was little Erie stock left in the market and that Drew would soon have to come to them and settle on their terms. But, just to be certain, they had already asked Judge Barnard to deliver the *coup de grâce*.

Upon the petition of the newly minted receiver of the Erie—who, as receiver, now doubted the legality of the stock that, as president, he had himself issued the previous summer—Barnard empowered Gould to buy up that recently issued stock, up to 200,000 shares, at any price up to par without regard to the price at which it had been sold. Gould and Fisk "had sold the property of their wards at 40," Adams wrote; "they were now prepared to use the money of their wards to buy the same property back at 80, and a judge had been found ready to confer on them the power to do so."[22]

New York State law quite expressly forbade the managers of a railroad company to use corporate funds to deal in the company's stock. But Barnard obviously felt that what the law denied to an officer of the corporation he was quite free to give to an officer of the court, and he handed receiver Gould *carte blanche* to use corporate funds to corner corporate stock.

It is little wonder that Gould and Fisk had named the Erie's newest and fanciest locomotive, gleaming with eighteen coats of varnish and adorned with paintings by Jasper Cropsey, the *George G. Barnard.*

But Gould, most uncharacteristically, had blundered in his calculations as to who was holding Erie stock. Gould thought that the ten-share certificates he had sent to England were all still safely in London. In fact, many of them had wafted back across the Atlantic and were right there in New York, in the hands of hundreds of small merchants, housewives, carpenters, and clergymen, anyone with a taste for taking a flier in the great game. These small fry had mostly taken the Erie when the price had been falling over the previous three months, and now they flooded into Wall Street to grab their sudden profits while the grabbing was good. Gould and Fisk were forced to buy all they could to keep it out of the hands of Drew, while Drew in turn snatched at all he could get.

By the close of business on Thursday, Drew had managed to find enough stock to cover his contracts, paying, as near as anyone could tell, about 57. Drew's short sales, therefore, had cost him about $1,300,000.

Once Drew left the market so, of course, did Fisk and Gould, and the price of Erie dropped at once to 42. The party was over for the little guys. As for Fisk and Gould, "the victors had got the spoils," Clews wrote, "but they paid dearly for them, and had come pretty near being destroyed in the moment of their triumph. They had purchased Erie at 'corner' prices, and they were obliged to carry it, for nobody wanted it."[23] For weeks afterward no more than a few hundred shares of Erie changed hands on the Street each day, and sometimes none at all. Of course it was the Erie Railway, not Fisk and Gould, that had to carry the stock.

For the first, perhaps only, time the long-suffering small shareholders had gotten the better of the Scarlet Woman. It is ironic that in doing so they had inadvertently saved from destruction the man who had led her so often and so far astray.

But, if Drew had averted utter ruin, he had taken a frightful licking, and Gould and Fisk had at least accomplished their purpose, for he was mortally wounded as a major power on Wall Street, although that would not become apparent to the newspapers, or even to Drew, for some time.

Uncle Daniel's position in the great game had always depended far more on his reputation as the most artful of speculators than on the "brute force of his millions," which made the Commodore so potent a player on the Street. Drew's mastery of the psychology of speculation, his seemingly magic ability to make Erie move up and down as he wished, had given him his power. Once he was seen to have lost his touch in Erie and, in fact, to have taken a clobbering in the stock himself, his reputation on the Street began to collapse. Like the Wizard of Oz, Drew had suddenly been revealed to be nothing more than an eccentric old man.

•

The public and the newspapers were dazzled by the sheer size of the speculative scheme undertaken by Gould and Fisk. The *Herald* wrote that "the speculations of the last month have been on a gigantic scale such as never were equalled before in Wall Street, while it is doubtful if they have been surpassed elsewhere. Millions of dollars have been handled as if they were thousands, and the capital employed has been such as to make the outside public gape with astonishment at the daring and boldness of the operators."[24]

"Such strategy," it continued the following day, "is on a par with all the operations of the clique who have made Erie a football, and it exhibits the presence of the mastermind which has planned and carried out all the magnificent schemes connected with the speculations in Erie. However questionable these schemes may be, their skill and success exhibit Napoleonic genius on the part of him who conceived them."[25]

The *Commercial Advertiser*, however, like most other newspapers, harbored no such romantic weakness in its editorial soul and

A SMALL-TIME SPECULATOR

wrote forthrightly that "there is nothing in the history of this or any other country that begins to compare with this unblushing scoundrelism of the leaders in the Erie Railway swindle. Their connection with the road has been a history of perjury, fraud and robbery."[26] The *New York Times* also thought Gould and Fisk had no parallel at home or abroad. "England and France," it said on November 19th, "have had their speculative bubbles, their gross violations of trust, their robbery of confiding stockholders by men high in position, and with riches in abundance. But neither England nor France presents a parallel to the infamies of the Erie railroad."

Even the enormously prestigious London *Times* took notice of the doings on Wall Street and wrote, in its best magisterial style, that they "seem likely to create distrust as to the possibility of any legal, equitable control being exercised for the protection of investments in American corporations."[27]

The London financial world was fast waking up to the fact that a serious rival was developing across the Atlantic at the other end of the new cable, in operation since 1866. While listed securities on the London Stock Exchange had a total valuation of ten billion dollars, those on the New York Stock Exchange now amounted to fully three billion, and the total was increasing rapidly. New York brokers and speculators were beginning to be a major force in the London market as well. In 1870 they would run up over a million dollars in cable bills.

The *Commercial and Financial Chronicle,* which had quoted the London *Times* in alarm, put its finger on the heart of Wall Street's problem. The capitalists, it wrote, were not wholly at fault because "the letter of the law is very deficient in its regulation of the management of corporate interests." Because railroads were very capital-intensive, they needed the capital of many investors. For the first time in history, economic enterprises were being managed by people who did not own them, and these enterprises, the railroads, were central to the functioning of the economic system of the new industrial age.

So long as the law was silent and did not forbid such schemes as Gould and Drew utilized, such men would exploit the void for their own short-term profit. It was up to society as a whole, argued the *Chronicle,* to pursue its own long-term self-interests and devise rules that would force managers to act as the fiduciaries they had become. The *Chronicle* even had a suggested law that would eliminate at a stroke most of the abuses that Drew had invented and

Gould had raised to the level of high art. The *Chronicle*'s law would have required:

1) That directors shall make no new issues of stock except by and with the consent of two-thirds of the stockholders in interest.

2) That no new shares shall be issued without first offering them to the existing stockholders, and that all issues shall be made openly and after due notice.

3) That all stock companies shall keep a record of the amount of their stock outstanding, in the office of some well-known financial institution, at all times open to the inspection of the shareholders, or of parties holding the shares as collateral for loans.

4) That these requirements shall apply to stock issued in the way of dividends as well as for other purposes; and

5) Any violations of these provisions should be constituted a criminal offense, subject to punishment and fine.[28]

This proposed statute made admirable sense, and in substance it is the heart of American corporate law today, but there was an obstacle in the way of getting it enacted: the New York State Legislature, which had already shown itself to be as deaf to the public welfare as it was sensitive to the needs of those willing and able to bribe its members.

The *Herald* thought that the regulation of railroad securities, and indeed the whole industry, was a national, not a state, problem and required federal legislation. This idea, however sensible in the abstract, simply did not square with political reality in post–Civil War America. It would be another twenty years before the political situation permitted even ineffectual federal regulation of railroads, and then only of their rate structures, while it would take sixty years and the onset of a great depression before anyone would seriously suggest that the regulation of securities markets might be a federal responsibility.

Charles Francis Adams, who had in full measure the long-standing pessimism of the Adams family regarding the future in general and the perfectibility of man in particular, thought that only the executive veto stood between the republic of the founding fathers and the development of a full-blown plutocracy. The man who contributed so significantly to the development of investigative journalism never came to realize the power of his own invention to force politicians to pursue their own interests by pursuing the public's.

But, if politics made it impossible for the federal government to act, and corruption incapacitated the state government, the self-interest of Wall Street's brokers soon galvanized their private associations, the New York Stock Exchange and the Open Board of Brokers, into meaningful action and reform.

The brokers had made a lot of money from the Erie Wars and the earlier speculative goings-on on the Street. According to William Worthington Fowler, who, as a speculator and not a broker, may well have been less than objective, they had made out best of all. If brokers "are members of the pool, they know exactly when to slip out," Fowler lamented. "If they are merely the manipulators of the stock, they know just when to buy and just when to realize their profit outside of the combination. Their surest source of profit, however, is from the enormous brokerage resulting from the purchases and sales which they make for the pool's account."

Even in the 1860's, the customers' yachts already in short supply, it was widely thought among speculators that there were only two roads to Wall Street success: be lucky or be a broker.

The brokers were, of course, perfectly happy to take their commissions buying and selling dubious stock for their customers' accounts. They still are. But lending money on that stock had now become another matter altogether. If the number of shares of a corporation in existence could be doubled or halved at any time, and if even the very number of shares outstanding at any given moment could be treated as a private matter of the issuing corporation, then how could any meaningful determination of each share's worth be made? Problematical collateral is not collateral; and if stocks could no longer be bought on margin, the boom days on Wall Street would be over. Even the dimmest of the brokers could understand this.

As early as the last week in October, 1868, uneasiness on the part of the brokers caused the New York Stock Exchange to send a delegation to the Erie offices to confer with Gould. The new president of the Erie was forthright, if not necessarily honest with his figures. "Gentlemen," he told them, "since the settlement of the Vanderbilt litigation in July last, we have issued $10,000,000 in Erie convertible bonds. Of these, $5,000,000 have been recently converted into common stock, and the remainder is likely to be converted at any time. The amount of common stock of this company now outstanding is $39,500,000. We are thinking of laying a third rail. If we resolve to proceed with the work we shall be obliged to raise $3,000,000 more by the conversion of more bonds into stock."[29]

Gould declined to say when or even if any more stock than this might be forthcoming. He claimed that only by maintaining the right to flood the market with new stock any time he chose could he keep the Erie out of the hands of Vanderbilt, who otherwise would obtain a monopoly of New York City's railroad lines. A few months later Gould testified before an Assembly committee to this effect.

"With unspeakable effrontery," Adams wrote, "an effrontery so great as actually to impose on his audience and a portion of the press, and make them believe that the public ought to wish him success, he described how stock issues at the proper time, to any required amount, could alone keep him in control."[30] What Adams was describing was Gould's successful use, in the middle of the nineteenth century, of a public-relations technique that would only be named in the middle of the twentieth: the big lie.

Adams was amazed at how well the technique worked. "The strangest thing of all was that it never seemed to occur to his audience that the propounder of this comical sophistry was a trustee and guardian for the stockholders, and not a public benefactor; and that the owners of the Erie road might possibly prefer not to be deprived of their property, in order to secure the blessings of competition."[31]

If the Assemblymen and reporters were taken in by Gould's statements, the brokers certainly were not. As the corner engineered by him and Fisk culminated in the week of November 15th, they became more and more alarmed, and by the end of that week a manifesto was circulating on Wall Street to do something about the situation. "We the undersigned," it read, "bankers, brokers, and dealers in railroad securities, deeming it extra hazardous to deal in Erie Railway hereby pledge ourselves not to make loans upon said stock of said Erie Railway, except in existing contracts, until some registration is placed upon the issue of stock by placing of the transfer books in some respectable institution for registry."[32] The *Herald* reported that fifty or sixty firms had already signed and that "others would like to put their names to it, but they stand in fear of the great financial kings whom it is intended to reach."

On the last day of November the New York Stock Exchange and

the Open Board acted in coordination and adopted identical resolutions requiring the registration of all listed securities before January 31st, 1869.[33] Further, the resolutions required that all listed companies give thirty days' public notice before issuing any new securities.

Many companies already maintained public registries of their shares, and the soundness and long-term benefits of this regulation to brokers, customers, and stockholders alike were so obvious that virtually all unregistered companies traded on the two exchanges complied without complaint. By February 1st, only the Erie Railway and three express companies that, like the Erie, had been the subject of much insider speculation would be struck from the calls for noncompliance.

On February 4th, the *Herald* noted that the Erie was a stock without a home. "Erie, like Noah's dove, is wandering about not finding whereon to place its foot. When driven from the Long Room it made an effort to fold its wings in the Mining Board, but on discovery that the lease of the latter apartment from the Regular Board forbids its use for the sale of railway stocks, it had to go out upon the sidewalk, which is its present uncharitable domicile."

Although Gould established the National Stock Exchange, known as the Erie Board, to handle trading in Erie securities, it was soon obvious that the Erie needed the increasingly dominant New York Stock Exchange more than the Exchange and its members needed the Erie. Gould gave in and complied with the registration requirements on September 13th, 1869, by which time no fewer than 700,000 shares of Erie common stock were in existence, an increase since his meeting with the brokers the previous autumn of 305,000. The National Stock Exchange's brief existence terminated almost at once.

The New York Stock Exchange achieved unquestioned dominance on the Street when it merged with the Open Board of Brokers that year to become the only important stock exchange in the country. For the first time it became really important for a brokerage firm to be a member, and thus for the first time the Exchange could exercise real power over those members.

It was a bare beginning at best, but a vital step in the right direction. As Medbery wrote at the time, "It remains for the brokers of the Stock Exchange to decide whether they will seek the petty profits of a speculation marred by grave faults, or will cast their influence still farther and with more strenuous emphasis against the encroachment of the cliques. The former means isolation. The latter will be prelusive of an expansion in international relations which will make New York imperial, and Wall Street what its pivotal position demands and allows, the paramount financial center of the globe."[34]

The brokers took Medbery's advice. Effective self-regulation of the New York stock market would increase greatly in the next few years as the New York Stock Exchange began to exercise its new power. It would be self-regulation rather than government that would successfully guide Wall Street for the next two generations, as it eclipsed London and grew into the largest financial market on earth.

THE STOCK TICKER AT DELMONICO'S RESTAURANT The ticker first appeared in 1867 and immediately became indispensable to brokers and speculators alike. *Courtesy of The New-York Historical Society, New York City*

Castle Erie

ON November 24th, 1868, the steamer *Russia* had finally appeared in New York Harbor with large quantities of Erie stock on board but several days too late to be of any help to Drew and Belmont. Although the lawsuits were equally too late to help Drew, they continued on their way, snowballing just as they had the previous spring as Gould and Fisk, Drew and Belmont set their judges to doing their very considerable best to compound the legal tangle.

On the 24th Barnard stayed Judge Sutherland's order appointing a receiver. Sutherland immediately issued a show-cause order as to why Barnard's stay should not be vacated, and proceeded to appoint the very distinguished former Judge Henry E. Davies as receiver. On the 25th, Sutherland vacated Barnard's order that had stayed his own and confirmed Davies as receiver, saying that "certain issues of Erie stock might as well be called poetry as stock."[1]

Meanwhile upstate judges were beginning to enter the fray. Judge Balcom of Cortland (an old friend of the Erie), Judge Peckham of Albany, and Judge Boardman of distant Oneida County all would issue orders in the case. While none actually named a receiver, each declared his readiness and intention to do so, and each "declared his to be the only shop where a regular, reliable article in the way of law was retailed, and then proceeded forthwith to restrain and shut up the opposition establishments."[2]

Gould and Fisk thought that they were ready for an assault upon the Erie offices by any unwelcome receiver. The offices were closed to business, and the doorkeeper had orders to admit no one unknown to him. "At the iron gate which bars the entry to the offices," the *Herald* reported, "a clerk was stationed who gave very curt answers to inquiries. He refused to inform several gentlemen who called yesterday morning why the office was closed, and seemed nervously anxious that no intimation of the condition of affairs inside should reach the public through him."[3]

As soon as Judge Sutherland had confirmed his appointment, Henry Davies went to the Erie offices to take command, accompanied by another former judge, Noah Davis, and D. B. Eaton, who had been counsel to the Erie Railway (and was the man largely responsible for creating the city's professional uniformed fire department). Despite the precautions of Gould and Fisk, the clerk at the door recognized Eaton and therefore admitted him and the others to the building. Henry Davies found Fisk and Gould deep in conversation with their lawyers, and, according to the *Herald,* they were "evidently very much astounded at the appearance of the newly appointed receiver."[4] At first both the president/receiver and the controller of the Erie Railway were civil to the unwelcome intruders, but Fisk soon excused himself. When he returned he left the door to the president's office open and "directed Mr. Eaton's attention to a party of ten or twelve rough looking men standing in the hall outside, who, he said, were ready to put into effect his resolution to summarily eject Mr. Eaton and the receiver."[5]

This was the first appearance of what would come to be known as the "Thugs of Erie," headed by Tommy Lynch. Tommy Lynch ran an oyster stand at the Erie docks, but he was soon in the business of supplying Fisk and Gould not only with oysters but with muscles as well, for Lynch headed one of the Irish gangs that infested the West Side waterfront.

The Erie lawyers objected strenuously to this use of goon-squad tactics, however, and Gould apologized for his partner's impetuosity. The lawyers, it turned out, had no need of hired muscle, for when Davies handed them Judge Sutherland's order appointing him receiver, they immediately handed him in return an order signed by Judge Albert Cardozo, which stayed all proceedings upon Judge Sutherland's order. (One of the more interesting aspects of

Cardozo's stay was the fact that it was dated November 23rd. Judge Cardozo, in other words, had stayed on Monday an order that Judge Sutherland had only gotten around to issuing on Wednesday.)[6]

Cardozo sat in the same district as Sutherland and Barnard, and so now three of the five judges of the New York State Supreme Court sitting in New York City were all busily enjoining, staying, and vacating each other with regard to the same case.

A member of one of the city's oldest and most distinguished families, Cardozo was a far abler and more ethical man than Barnard. While he was active politically and used his office to do favors for his political friends (such as naturalizing recent immigrants by the boatload so they could vote Democratic), he never used his office for personal aggrandizement as Barnard did. And if Cardozo sullied the "judicial ermine," a favorite Victorian phrase, with his political activities, he glorified it forever with his paternal ones, for he was the father of Justice Benjamin Cardozo.

Davies protested the backdated order, but the Erie lawyers persuaded him to settle for formal possession while deferring actual possession until Friday. If Davies thought that formal possession would do him any good he was sadly mistaken, for on Friday he "found the directors again fortified within and himself a much enjoined wanderer without."[7]

Sutherland's term as head of the New York City District of the Supreme Court was due to expire at the end of the month, when Cardozo would take over for his turn, and the Erie lawyers must have been betting that Sutherland would be willing to dump the whole mess into Cardozo's lap and not fight his orders as vigorously as he had fought Barnard's. They were right, and Cardozo would remain in charge of the case from that point on.

•

Rumors abounded in the New York newspapers that Fisk and Gould, together with the Erie treasury, were about to or already had "skedaddled to Jersey or Canada," fleeing the jurisdiction of the New York and even federal courts, for a suit—in fact actually instigated by Gould—had been filed in the U.S. District Court.

On the night of Sunday, November 29th, there was so much activity in and about the Erie offices that Superintendent of Police John A. Kennedy sent men over to find out what was afoot. Fisk was noted coming and going several times and was even observed being served with legal papers. Finally a large man who appeared to be

Fisk—he was rather ostentatiously bundled up—left the Erie offices and climbed into a waiting carriage, loudly instructing the driver to take him to the Fifth Avenue Hotel. It was soon discovered that the carriage, instead of going to the hotel on Madison Square, had gone to the Pavonia Ferry, where its passenger had gotten on board and departed for New Jersey.

At the Erie depot in Jersey City an engine had been coupled to a director's car and made ready, with steam up in its boiler. Soon after midnight it was seen departing for parts unknown, and it was widely reported in the papers that Fisk had flown the coop, taking the Erie's negotiable assets with him.

But a few days later Fisk, who had obviously enjoyed himself hugely, telegraphed identical letters from Port Jervis to all the major papers explaining what he had been up to.

Port Jervis, N.Y.
Tuesday, Dec. 1, 1868

To the Editor:

Returning from a journey undertaken in relation to the affairs of the rolling mill of the Erie Railway Company, I am astonished on taking up your paper this morning to find that I am charged with having secretly carried off eight millions of dollars of the company's money. I presume it is to the vivid imagination of Mr. Kennedy, combined with the vigorous pens of the reporters of the press, that I am indebted for this enormous calumny. The facts are simply these: I left New York for the purpose I have stated, without $20, and without a dollar's worth of securities of any name or nature, except the threadbare garments which I usually take with me when travelling.

Although upon an errand of mercy, I did not feel satisfied in encroaching upon the sacred hours of the Sabbath, especially since my Counsel would not use that day to finish up my affidavits. Accordingly I made arrangements to depart as early Monday morning as possible. . . .

The money of the Erie Company is not, and has not been under my charge, but is now in the treasury, where it ought to be, and has been since the present board of directors was entrusted with the charge of the corporation's affairs. The rival receivers can get at the funds just as easily now as they could before I left town. I am not so easily frightened by a lawsuit as to run away either with my own money or that of anyone else.

Both Gould and Fisk always sought to portray themselves as just two misunderstood businessmen, manfully doing their best under difficult corporate and legal circumstances (although Fisk could never stop himself from being amusing about it). "Whenever the facts are fully known," wrote Gould (who could), "and the public becomes aware of what is being done to make the Erie Railway the most magnificent and perfect railway line in the country and the pride of the city and state, then the acts of the present managers will be appreciated."[8]

As soon as Fisk returned from his trip upstate—his alleged mission of mercy had in fact been a call on Judge Balcom—he and Gould embroiled the Commodore once more in the Erie Wars. The two had always publicly denounced the settlement with Vanderbilt the previous summer, and on Saturday, December 5th, Fisk set out through a furious snowstorm, the first of the season, with 50,000 shares of Erie in a carpetbag, intent on tendering them to the Commodore. Riding with Fisk was Thomas G. Shearman, an associate of David Dudley Field and a Sunday-school teacher at Henry Ward Beecher's Plymouth Church in Brooklyn. "I rode up with Shearman," Fisk later testified, "holding the carpet bag tight between my legs; I told him he was a small man and not much protection; this was dangerous property and might blow up."[9]

When they got to 10 Washington Place, Fisk and Shearman went inside and confronted Vanderbilt. "I told the Commodore," Fisk explained, that "I had come to tender 50,000 shares of Erie and wanted back the money which we had paid for them and the bonds." Since he could buy all the Erie stock he wanted—which was none—on Wall Street at 40, the Commodore found Fisk's tender at 70 an eminently refusable offer and did so.

The next day, for reasons known only to himself, Vanderbilt wrote the *Times* a letter.

Sunday, December 6th, 1868

To the Editor of the *New York Times*
  In your paper of the 6th instant is an alleged extract from a paragraph in the *Evening Post* of Saturday as follows:
  "The Erie fight assumed a new and interesting phase today. The Erie Company paid to Mr. Vanderbilt for the stock in his hands last spring, the sum of $3,500,000, and a bonus of $1,000,000, in order to stop the suits instituted by Messrs. Schell and others."

The above statement is altogether false. I have had no dealings with the Erie Railway Company, nor have I ever sold that company any stock or received from them any bonus.

As to suits instituted by Messrs. Schell and others, I had nothing to do with them, nor was I in any way concerned in their settlement.

Very respectfully yours
C. Vanderbilt[10]

One is at a loss to explain this unadorned falsehood on the part of the usually forthright Commodore. Not only was it a lie, it was an easily exposed one.

Fisk had gone to Boston for a few days, but when he returned he fairly leapt upon Vanderbilt's letter and dispatched one of his own, complete with facsimiles of checks that had been endorsed by the Commodore himself. "In as much as it appears from these documents," wrote Fisk, "that someone of the name of 'C. Vanderbilt' received $1,000,000 from the Erie Company, and as it does not appear by any records in the Company's office that Mr. Vanderbilt gave the company any consideration for that sum except the discontinuance of suits over which he now says he had no control, it would seem that some further explanation is needed to relieve Mr. Vanderbilt from the imputation of an enormous fraud upon the stockholders of the Erie Railway Company."[11]

Vanderbilt, thoroughly bushwhacked, would not try to tangle with Fisk and Gould in the newspapers again. (However, the next day the anonymous author of the *Times*'s financial column, presumably C. C. Norvell, the financial editor, wrote exactly what Vanderbilt wanted written, clearly in hopes of making the best of a hopeless situation.) The Commodore would never come to admire Fisk and Gould or their ways, but he learned quickly to respect them, and would soon call Gould "the smartest man in America."[12]

On December 10th, the tender having been refused, the Erie Railway Company sued Vanderbilt for the money.

Jim Fisk did not have the newspapers all his own way. On November 28th, Samuel Bowles, the distinguished editor of the Springfield, Massachusetts, *Republican*, wrote a nasty editorial. "The Erie hero of the hour stands in a precarious position; he has great capacity, now great wealth, certainly great notoriety; all these he can make most useful to himself and the country; it is a pity they should be wasted in destruction alike of character and of values, when the country needs them all, and will reward them all so generously, in measures of construction. Many even of his friends predict for him the state-prison or the lunatic asylum; his father is already in the latter; but we shall hope and believe that he will soon escape them both, and win a more honorable fame than now gathers over him."[13]

The cheap-shot remark about the confinement of Fisk's father, typical of people of self-conscious rectitude like Bowles, enraged the usually imperturbable Fisk. He immediately sued Bowles for libel, and when the *Times,* the *Tribune,* and the *World* all copied the editorial, he sued them as well.

But Fisk soon had a better idea for getting even with Bowles and dropped the suit in Massachusetts only to institute one in New York, which the editor necessarily visited often and where Fisk had friends in high places.

When Bowles duly appeared in the city with his wife just before Christmas and checked into the Fifth Avenue Hotel, Fisk went to Judge John H. McCunn of the Superior Court (in fact an inferior court of local jurisdiction, one rung below the Supreme Court in New York's topsy-turvy judiciary) and persuaded him to issue an arrest warrant for Bowles on the libel charge. Waiting until evening, when the courts would be closed for the night, Fisk had the sheriff serve the warrant on Bowles as the editor was chatting with friends in the lobby of the hotel, one of the most public places in the entire city.

Bowles was dragged off to the Ludlow Street jail with no more courtesy than would have been shown a pickpocket caught *in fla-grante,* not even being allowed a word with his wife. When his friends attempted to make bail for him, not a judge could be found, for they were all off at a party in honor of the newly elected Mayor of New York, A. Oakey Hall, where Fisk as well was enjoying him-self. As the cherry on the top of Fisk's revenge, Samuel Bowles had to pay $19.50 for his room and board because it was a civil jail in which he had been incarcerated.

The next day he was immediately freed, and newspaper editors around the country fell all over themselves denouncing this insult to one of their brethren. It is altogether likely, however, that the majority of the people reading of Samuel Bowles's night in jail felt he had gotten just what he deserved; the public's love affair with Jim Fisk was well under way. Fisk himself, well pleased, wrote a letter to the Boston *Evening Gazette* in which he explained himself; the letter was widely copied. The libel suits, their real purpose accomplished, were never pursued.

All these suits, countersuits, injunctions, stays, and orders were getting the various plaintiffs nowhere and making the lawyers rich ("The lawyers lap up Erie money like kittens lap up milk,"[14] Fisk said). For Drew and Belmont the whole matter had already become painfully academic. Gould and the Commodore soon discovered that they each had business in Albany with the Legislature and it was in their common interest to set aside for the moment their quarrels.

•

When the Commodore acquired control of the New York Central in December, 1867, he brought to it immediately his customary notions of corporate efficiency and attention to profits. Until Vanderbilt's accession, directors had enjoyed the right to issue free passes on the road to anyone they chose, and they had availed themselves of this perquisite liberally. But the Commodore canceled all outstanding passes and decreed that henceforth only he and his son William Henry would decide who was entitled to ride free on the New York Central.

More symbolic was his order that locomotives be stripped of their brass ornaments. He felt that the engineers had better things to do, which is to say more economically productive things to do, than polish brass. In an age when it was widely thought that there was no such thing as too much ornamentation and when locomotives still had both names and the idiosyncratic natures of ships—and like ships were often referred to in the feminine—this was thought a very cold-eyed way of doing business. (Vanderbilt, however, made an exception in the case of one engine, which had been named for him and which was allowed to keep not only its brass but its portraits of the new president as well.)

More important, there was much deadwood among the personnel of the railroad to be gotten rid of, and the new regime hacked away at it ruthlessly, paring the payroll of hundreds of unnecessary workers. Vanderbilt was not out to save money at any cost. Far from it, he believed in paying good men well and bad men nothing. When he had first gained control of the Harlem Railroad a few years earlier, he had taken I. D. Barton, the railroad's general freight agent and assistant superintendent, for one of his terrifying afternoon drives on the Bloomingdale Road in order to get acquainted with him.

"What salary are you getting, young man?" the Commodore asked in the course of the conversation as his magnificent horses trotted smartly up the way.

"Seventy-five dollars [a month]," Barton replied.

"More than you're worth," Vanderbilt grumped and changed the subject. But the Commodore was evidently impressed by the twenty-nine-year-old, for at the next payday Barton found that his salary had been doubled.[15]

Nothing gave Vanderbilt more satisfaction, one could almost say real pleasure, than running an enterprise, any enterprise, at top efficiency. Waste deeply offended him, and the Vanderbilt regimen had an immediate effect on the profits of the New York Central, as can be seen by comparing the last year under Henry Keep with the first year that Vanderbilt was president.

	1866–1867	1867–1868
Gross revenues	$13,979,514	$14,381,303
Operating expenses	$10,653,692	$ 9,238,163
Net revenues	$ 3,325,822	$ 5,143,140

Although revenues increased only 2.9 percent, Vanderbilt's administration reduced expenses by fully 13.3 percent, and this combination increased profits by a whopping 54.6 percent.[16] Profit growth such as this endears management to both stockholders and Wall Street. The *Commercial and Financial Chronicle,* not always admiring of the Commodore, wrote that he and his allies had "administered the affairs of the company with such consummate skill that their stocks are now classed among the best in the country for investment."[17]

By way of contrast, the Erie in 1868 had a nearly identical gross revenue, $14,376,872, but had expenses that totaled fully $14,354,200 (including interest on the funded debt), leaving a net revenue of only $22,672, less than one-half of one percent of New York Central's $5,143,140.[18]

Nor was Vanderbilt's efficiency purchased at the price of public safety. In the same year, while the Erie had suffered twenty-six passengers killed and seventy-two injured, all the Vanderbilt roads combined had had no fatalities and only eleven injuries.

So great an asset to the New York Central was the Commodore that the state of his health was a significant factor in the price of the stock. In January, 1869, a rumored sleighing accident involving Vanderbilt caused Central to nose-dive until the story could be contradicted, which prompted the *Herald* to offer the Commodore some advice. "It is said that one of the best things the great Rothschild did before dying was to direct his family and friends to 'sell Lombardy shares short,' well knowing that his death would produce a panic in those securities. Mr. Vanderbilt should be equally obliging to his friends and give due notice of his intended demise."[19]

The Commodore thought that the increased profitability brought to the Central by his administration should be reflected in the number of shares outstanding. Rumors began to surface on the Street that Vanderbilt was planning a stock dividend, and the price of Central began to bobble up and down as the talk appeared and melted away only to appear again. On September 19th, 1868, the *Chronicle,* unimpressed with what it regarded as deliberate rumor mongering, snidely reported that "New York Central has today sold at 131½, an advance of eight per cent. [Stock moves at this time were still expressed in terms of a percentage of the par value. Today we would say "eight points."] The old report of the purpose of the directors to declare a large stock dividend has been revived in connection with the rise. This story, however, has so often proved convenient for speculative purposes that we presume the company will not spoil its effect by actually making the dividend."

Vanderbilt was biding his time, for he had both a public-relations problem and a legal one. Most people, including most financial writers, still had not grasped the notion that expected future earnings and not past investment determine the price of a stock, and Vanderbilt felt compelled to concoct an argument that met this objection to issuing new stock without altering the par value.

Vanderbilt stated that the improvements to the line had already been made and paid for out of past earnings and that these capitalized earnings should be given to the stockholders in the form of new shares. The *Chronicle,* however, looked into the matter closely and pointed out that either the Commodore was lying now or the previous annual reports of the company had lied in the past. It expressed the belief the stock dividend was purely a speculative ploy, intended to bilk the long-suffering outsiders on Wall Street.

An even bigger problem was that there was no easy way to issue new stock. The General Railroad Act of 1850, the law that governed the corporate affairs of New York State railroads, provided for the issuance of convertible bonds on the authority of the directors, as the Commodore knew all too well, but allowed stock issues only by a vote of two-thirds of the shareholders.

And Vanderbilt had to move quietly. There was a large short interest in the Central, made up of speculators who were betting that the rumors would prove false and who would certainly seek by legal action to prevent any move to issue new stock. Given the still infant state of corporate law and precedent and the corruption that permeated the New York judiciary, the one thing the manager of a publicly traded corporation could be sure of was that someone would seek to enjoin him no matter what he did. The trick was to accomplish the deed first and argue about its propriety afterward. The state of the courts was one of the many reasons that Vanderbilt always advised people to "never tell them what you're going to do until you've done it."

On Saturday, December 19th, he did it. After the close of the market, the board of directors of the New York Central met with no public notice at the home of Horace F. Clark, one of the company's directors as well as one of the Commodore's sons-in-law, and decided to issue a stock dividend amounting to 80 percent of the stock outstanding. Because they could not issue the stock itself without a vote of the stockholders, they voted to issue scrip until the new stock could be authorized. Further, this scrip would receive a 4 percent dividend.

The scrip certificates had already been printed, most conveniently, and the Union Trust Company, the Central's transfer agent, began to issue them to the stockholders the first thing Monday morning. Somebody had moved swiftly, however, because even before dawn on Monday, E. D. Worcester, the treasurer of the Central, was served with an injunction forbidding him to issue the certificates. Worcester calmly replied that he was not issuing them, that it was the Union Trust Company that must be enjoined. He may or may not have bothered to point out that by the time a new injunction could be obtained and served, the scrip would be out and gone.

The market, which had quivered at every rumor of a stock issue, leapt on the actual news, and New York Central, which had closed on Saturday at 134, shot up to 165 before profit-takers knocked it back down to 154½. The shorts had been taken to the cleaners, and they immediately sought the help of the courts. But it was Isaac N. Jenks, who was long a few shares of Central, who sued in Supreme Court to prevent the board of directors from acting as it planned. Jenks's property had increased in value by 15 percent on account of the board's action, so his complaint seemed captious, not to say perverse, but there was a simple explanation.

"In the outside world," the *Herald* helpfully informed its bemused readers, "people seek relief in the courts for damages to property which they are the owners of. In Wall Street they are more philanthropical. They seek to redress the grievances of their neighbors and lay claim for damages to property which is not their own. The friends of the plaintiff in the Vanderbilt suit had no Central stock. In the parlance of the Street they were short of it. The secret of their solicitude for the welfare of all connected with New York Central is that they [had] sold what they did not possess."[20]

Having no stock, the shorts had no standing to complain of management's actions, and they needed Jenks to do their suing for them. It is not known for sure who put Jenks up to his suit, but the fact that the Erie's principal litigator, David Dudley Field—whose large fees Jenks could hardly have afforded on his own—argued in court for the plaintiff lends much credence to the supposition that it was Fisk and Gould who had been sandbagged by the Commodore's sudden move.

The case was tried in Supreme Court before Judge Daniel P. Ingraham, and among the witnesses was the Commodore himself. Field asked the Commodore for particulars as to what exactly had occurred on Saturday, December 19th, and Vanderbilt answered in his usual direct if not overly helpful manner. Then Field, who like any good lawyer surely knew the answer to his question before he asked it, wondered why the proceedings had been so clandestine and why they had not been made known to the public in advance.

"Made known to the public!" bellowed the Commodore. "Made known to a gang of thieves and robbers in Wall Street! That is the reason."[21] Vanderbilt explained his philosophy of running a railroad and why he thought the stockholders were entitled to the full fruits of their successful investments. This argument was disingenuous, but it was honesty itself compared to the criticisms that have been leveled against the Commodore's reasoning and actions since. These are mostly the tendentious ones of later economic writers such as Gustavus Myers in the first decade of this century, who took it as a given that fortunes could only be gained by theft, and who strove hard to provide an economic and moral justification for nationalizing the railroads, an idea that would have been countenanced by no one in the 1860's. Charles Francis Adams argued at this time that because the railroads had been built under the authority of a public franchise, their success should have been accompanied not by increased dividends but by decreased fares and freight rates. Stripped of its unbeatable rhetoric, Adams's argument is nothing more than the idea that the investors should take the risks while the public was entitled to any rewards. Such an economic arrangement would hardly have given managers an incentive to manage well, let alone have gotten many railroads built in the first place.

The Commodore noted that the passenger fares in New York State were already set by law, at two cents a mile, and freight rates by competition, which was true except where, possessing a monopoly, the Central could—and certainly did—charge what it pleased. Even the *Commercial and Financial Chronicle* noted that both passenger fares and freight rates had been falling steadily since the advent of the railroads thirty years earlier, and only argued that their continued fall was necessary to the prosperity of the country.

All this economic philosophy was of no interest to Judge Ingraham, however, who ruled that Vanderbilt could not pay dividends on the scrip or convert it into stock without an act of the Legislature. The Commodore would have to go to Albany, and the capital was looking forward to his visit, for the idea "that Vanderbilt should bleed, because he has unlimited means to do so, is an argument that comes with peculiar force to the minds of the lobby men who surround the halls of Albany legislation."[22]

Ever since Vanderbilt had come into control of the New York Central it had been assumed that it would be just a matter of time before he sought legislation to combine it with his other railroads, especially the Hudson River Railroad, and establish a through route from Buffalo to New York City. Although there were the predictable cries regarding monopoly raised against this idea, in fact the two railroads could not have competed even if they had wanted to, for they lay end to end and not parallel. Vanderbilt decided that, as he had to go to Albany anyway, he might as well work to have both bills passed.

He had no doubt he could handle the Legislature and the lobby if left alone to do so, but he wanted greatly to avoid a repetition of the previous year's bidding war for the Legislature's favor. Happily for all concerned, Fisk and Gould had plans of their own regarding the Legislature and were equally anxious to avoid a fight with the Commodore in Albany.

Gould, seeking a direct connection to Chicago, which would, at a stroke, have made the Erie the dominant railroad of the Northeast, had acquired a majority of the stock of the Pittsburgh, Fort Wayne and Chicago Railroad. The annual election of the company was due in March, but the Pennsylvania Railroad, which Gould had caught napping, could not countenance this invasion of what it regarded as its own turf and went to the Pennsylvania government for relief.

The Commodore and Gould could only have dreamed of having the influence in Albany that the Pennsylvania Railroad wielded so unblushingly in Harrisburg. A bill to protect the Pennsylvania from Gould's maneuver was introduced into the Legislature, passed both houses, and was signed into law by the Governor in a total elapsed time of thirty-four minutes flat. The new law called for the election of boards of directors of railroads chartered in Pennsylvania not as a whole body every year but serially, with one-fifth being elected every year to five-year terms.

The law meant that Gould would have to wait three years, at least, before gaining control, despite owning a majority of the stock. Like the Commodore, Gould knew when he was beaten, and he sold his stock in the Pittsburgh, Fort Wayne and Chicago to the Pennsylvania, which thus became the first of the Eastern railroads to reach Chicago. But Gould managed to snatch something from the débacle and shrewdly recognized that a similar bill in New York State would be an ample substitute for his soon-to-be-extinguished power to print new stock clandestinely, and would further tighten his grip on the railroad against any attempt by the stockholders to have a say in the running of their own property.

The real purpose of the so-called Classification Act—to put managers, not stockholders, in ultimate control of corporations— was apparent to many, and Henry Raymond of the *Times* was outraged by it. "There is pending before the Legislature," he wrote on May 5th, "a brief but important bill—deceptive in language, disgraceful in its history, false in its recitals, pregnant with gigantic mischief; an evidence at once of how much measureless audacity may not dare to ask, and of how much unparalleled venality may not scruple to grant." Regardless of such editorials, however, both the Legislature and the Governor found the precedent of the Pennsylvania law a fig leaf more than ample to hide behind.

The newspapers had suggested that there might be a deal brewing between Vanderbilt and the Erie as early as December 26th and were openly discussing an *entente cordiale* by January 17th. After Judge Ingraham's ruling it was soon clear that there had developed a tacit understanding between the two sides not to work against each other in Albany.

If the lobby and the legislators were counting on receiving rich bribes from the Commodore to do his bidding, they were in for an unpleasant surprise. The Commodore's men in Albany maneuvered them into buying large amounts of Central stock, telling them how it was sure to rise with the passage of the bill in the Assembly. Once they had bought, however, the Commodore had them where he wanted them.

"It is notorious," the New York *Evening Telegram*, a Bennett paper, wrote on April 8th, "that the Albany ring have been heavy purchasers of Central during the last few days, and are now 'long' of this stock to a large amount—the general expectation being that upon the announcement of the report, the stock would take a sudden spring upward. This has proven a false idea; the Street, with that excellent appreciation of the stuff of which legislators are made, having discounted the whole proceedings correctly. . . . [W]ith his immense influence in holding so much stock [the Commodore] can at any time force them to sell at a sacrifice. . . . Thus it will be seen the veteran railroad king has again overreached his annual blackmailers; they are securely caught and have no choice left them what to do, as to retreat is to lose, while to go forward is no gain."

As the *Herald* explained, "The Commodore's friends are determined that the legislative rings shall play no tricks, but shall pass the scrip bill and the consolidation bill . . . before the stock shall be allowed to 'jump.' "[23]

In late April the Assembly passed the two bills, and the price of New York Central rose to an all-time high of 170. With the Senate still to act, some members of the upper house thought that they might try a leaf out of Daniel Drew's book of tricks and short the stock, planning to defeat the bill. The Commodore was unperturbed by this, however, and simply worked the game he had played earlier, only this time backward. "With reference to the New York Central," wrote an admiring *Herald* on April 28th, "it is said that 'the honorable the Senate' went 'short' of it after the passage of the bill by the lower house, expecting by defeating it to make a handsome profit. But the 'old man' stepped in, bought the stock, and has so far encroached upon the margins of 'the honorable the Senate' that their brokers are beginning to call for new installments or threatening the alternative of 'covering.' " On May 1st, Central reached as high as 178 and the Senate hastily passed the two bills.

On May 20th Governor Hoffman signed them into law as Central rose to 189¼. The Governor also signed the Erie Classification Act that day, but the stock of Erie, moving against a sharply rising market, had been weak all year and had tumbled as low as 28¾.

Both Vanderbilt and Gould had gotten what they wanted from the Legislature this time. In response, the market could not get enough of Central and soon sent it over 200 while it treated Erie like poison. But then the Commodore was interested only in running his own railroads. Fisk and Gould seemed to be interested in running everything.

•

Just as the brief age of local railroads had begun to pass when they agglutinated into regional carriers in the 1850's, so now, fifteen years later, railroads were beginning to emerge as national thoroughfares, as symbolized by the race among the eastern roads to reach Chicago. The Erie, however, was at a severe disadvantage in this race against both the New York Central and the Pennsylvania. "The Erie is an impoverished, debt-laden institution," wrote the *Herald* in early January, 1869, "which can hardly hope to compete with more direct lines in the effort to divide the trade of the trans-Mississippi country. Its broad gauge, which it still insists upon preserving, thereby isolating itself from the great continental network of railways, is a further disadvantage."[24]

Gould's solution to the problem of the Erie's broad gauge was to lay a third rail so that either gauge could use the Erie tracks, but this would have been an expensive—and in all likelihood dangerous—stopgap. The third rail was to prove far more useful on Wall Street as an excuse to justify further issues of stock than for hauling the traffic of the West.

The Erie's ramshackle condition, both financial and physical, seems not to have greatly occupied Gould's time, despite his frequent protestations to the contrary in the newspapers. He was still far more interested in playing the game than in running a railroad. Despite Gould's genius, perhaps because of it, his search for his fortune through the short cut of speculation was to cost both him and the Erie dearly.

His activities were always much less in evidence than Fisk's. The latter seems never to have said "No comment" in his life (he kept elaborate scrapbooks of all his newspaper clippings) while Gould spent his time behind the scenes devising corporate strategy, plotting a means to get the Erie through to Chicago, negotiating deals, and developing new tactics to use on the Street. "Jay Gould is the complement—the foil of James Fisk, Jr.," wrote Fowler. "He is a short, slight man, with a sable beard, a small, bright, introverted eye, and a cool, clear head. His forte is planning, and he represents the man of thought as Fisk does the man of action, in the firm of Fisk and Gould. He is the engineer, with his hand on the engine-lever, while Fisk is the roar of the wheels, the volume of smoke from the stack, the glare of the head-light, and the screaming whistle of the locomotive."[25]

No description of Gould at this time failed to mention his stature, his eyes, or his silence. "While you speak," wrote *Harper's Monthly*, "he listens, and looks at you with eyes which freeze and fascinate."[26]

Fisk, on the other hand, was large, lively, and voluble. He was given to saying exactly what was on his mind and doing "all his deeds, both the good and the bad, in the broad open light of the day" as a song written after his death would put it. It was easy not to admire Jubilee Jim, as the press began to call him, for he had many characteristics that were not admirable. But it was much harder not to like him and nearly impossible not to be amused by him.

Fisk's interests and activities covered an extraordinary range. He had bought a controlling interest in the Narragansett Steamship Company, which ran the *Providence* and the *Bristol* between New York and Fall River, Massachusetts. He fitted up the two elegant paddle wheelers in fine style, even installing a canary in each stateroom and giving the little birds such names as Jay Gould and General Grant. He had his tailor design an "admiral's" uniform and would often wear it when he went down to the dock to see his boats off. Further adorning this and other costumes was a stickpin with a five-carat diamond. A cartoonist's delight, this diamond became Fisk's personal symbol and as emblematic of its owner and his persona as, in a later age, would be FDR's jaunty cigarette holder.

Not content with railroads and steamships, Fisk, who always loved the stage, also bought Brougham's Theater, which he renamed the Fifth Avenue, and even leased the Academy of Music on 14th Street, where the Con Ed Building is today, the city's largest and most prestigious house until the opening of the Metropolitan Opera in 1883. But the costs and hazards of producing grand opera and filling so large a theater proved too rich even for Fisk's gambler's blood, and he soon let the lease lapse.

Then, in December, 1868, Fisk and Gould bought the city's other opera house, known as Pike's, on the northwest corner of 23rd Street and Eighth Avenue. Samuel N. Pike had built his theater the previous year, and it was widely regarded as one of the handsomest in the city.

Pike's Opera House held 2,600 people and had 6 proscenium and 27 dress-circle boxes. Its stage measured fully 70 by 80 feet and, with a temporary floor, the auditorium could be transformed into a ballroom accommodating 600. Pike had hoped that all this opulence would draw people as far west as Eighth Avenue, for he had built his theater "in defiance of the managerial sentiment that no theater can do well that is not situated on Broadway."[27]

Pike was wrong, and the theater did poor business from the start. In less than a year he was more than ready to sell, and Fisk and Gould together bought the theater for $820,000. It was widely assumed that the Erie Railway, and not its president and controller, had bought the building, and an anonymous Erie investor (who admitted to having bought the stock at 60) lamented in a letter to the *Herald* that the only "upward tendency" that could now be expected in Erie was among the "pretty ankles" of its new chorus line.

In fact, the theater was owned by Fisk and Gould personally. But if the Erie did not own the theater, Fisk thought that it would make a splendid corporate headquarters for the railroad. The building had ample office space, and this space the pair leased to the Erie Railway for the very handsome sum of $75,000 a year. Before the company could occupy its new offices, however, they had to be altered to suit the taste of its controller and landlord. Workmen started in February, and after six months and $250,000 (more than ten times the total net profits of the company the previous fiscal year) they were finished.

The façade of Pike's Opera House, soon renamed the Grand Opera House by Fisk and Castle Erie by the press, was quite restrained by the standards of the day, but Fisk had other ideas about the new Erie offices within. When they were finished, they dazzled everyone who saw them. "There are but few places," said one of the New York papers after its reporter had taken a tour, "wherein so rich a *coup d'oeil* could be presented as that of the main offices of the Erie Railway Company. . . . The carved woodwork, the stained and cut glass of the partitions, the gilded balustrades, the splendid gas fixtures, and, above all, the artistic frescoes upon the walls and ceilings, create astonishment and admiration at such a blending of the splendid and the practical. . . . Mr. Fisk, who planned and has superintended the arrangement . . . has certainly reason to be proud of the result, there being nowhere in this country or in Europe anything of the kind to compare with these splendid rooms."[28]

Fisk's own office featured not only the gaudy patterned wallpaper and wall-to-wall carpeting then so much in vogue but a desk raised on a dais and chairs that were rumored to be held together with golden nails. (Judge Barnard was so taken with the chairs at the new Erie offices that he ordered a set just like them for his own dining room, graciously permitting the Erie to pick up the tab.) Throughout the offices cartouches emblazoned with the seemingly royal cipher ER adorned the walls and woodwork.

The reporter was fascinated by the safe, "which has cost over $30,000. It is seven stories high, each totally unconnected, and is built upon a solid foundation of granite. Rising to the very roof of the main building, this immense safe is so constructed that were the Grand Opera House to be burned to the ground, the safe would stand. It is reared within the house, but in no wise is connected to it." The basement, moreover, housed "very large and complete printing offices," a feature that must have wryly amused the Commodore when he read of it.

"Throughout the new offices," the thoroughly awed reporter continued, "are the most complete arrangements for the comfort of those who will occupy them. The managers have a dining room, the employees have theirs, and a *chef de cuisine* of acknowledged capacity will provide their daily meals. Dumb waiters will go from the kitchen to every floor. In short, nothing has been overlooked in rendering these new offices as commodious as they are magnificent."

This corporate Xanadu would be Fisk's headquarters for the rest of his short life, and he reveled in the new nickname that the newspapers bestowed on him when he moved in: the Prince of Erie.

Having established himself at Castle Erie, Fisk began to buy up the adjoining buildings on both 23rd and 24th streets. He established elaborate stables on 24th Street for his horses, among the handsomest in the city, and arranged for Josie Mansfield to acquire the money

CASTLE ERIE

with which to buy a brownstone at 359 West 23rd Street, just a few doors down from Castle Erie, and "all the accessories that wealth and refinement could suggest were heaped in this palatial apartment with a reckless profusion."[29] He soon moved in with her.

Fisk took the ceremonial aspects of a princely life seriously. George Templeton Strong—who disapproved of much in his voluminous diary but could never bring himself altogether to disapprove of Fisk—wrote that on New Year's Day the Prince of Erie "made calls in a gorgeous chariot drawn by four high-stepping horses, with four smart footmen in flamboyant liveries. When he stopped before any favored house, his mamelukes descended, unrolled a carpet, laid it from the carriage steps to the door, and stood on either side in attitudes of military salute, while their august master passed by."[30]

As soon as the Erie Railway had moved into its new headquarters, Fisk sent for the local police precinct captain. The Prince of Erie said that he assumed that neighborhood people in need often came to the captain's attention and that he should send them over to the Opera House if they needed rent money or a bag of coal or a ticket home on the railroad. A steady stream of supplicants began to flow through Castle Erie, and few went away empty-handed. Fisk made a habit of handing the money he received for attending a directors' meeting over to his clerk to be given to the next worthy case that walked in the door.

Jubilee Jim lived his life in the unremitting glare of publicity and would have had it no other way. But his endless charities were always strictly private.

Though the Erie Railway had not gotten into the theater business, at least officially, it did augment its position in the ferry business, buying two new ferries to convey passengers from its terminal in Jersey City to its new pier at the foot of 23rd Street. Fisk characteristically named these two boats the *Jay Gould* and the *James Fisk, Junior.* They featured portraits of their namesakes at each end of their grand saloons, an adornment that Charles Francis Adams thought "converted noble steamers into branch galleries of a police office."[31]

When the city failed to grant a franchise for what Fisk regarded as adequate public transportation to connect this new ferry service with points inland on 23rd Street, the Erie provided it gratis, running a line of cabs, painted white with red wheels and embellished with the word "FREE!" in blue, from the Hudson piers past the opera

JIM FISK'S OFFICE AT THE GRAND OPERA HOUSE   *Courtesy of The New-York Historical Society, New York City*

house and on to the Fifth Avenue Hotel on Madison Square, in the center of town.

As if his multifarious business and theatrical activities were not enough, Fisk spent much time suing nearly everyone in sight and in picking fights in the newspapers, a technique that would soon become a standard publicity gimmick. So complex did Fisk's legal entanglements become that he hired full-time a lawyer whose sole function was to keep him abreast of the various lawsuits that were pending in the various city and state courts.

As the *Herald* stated, "Fisk, Jr., is a very active man, the active, energetic man of the age, indeed, and finds time enough, in addition to running all our railroads, theaters, steamboats and jails, to sue everyone for libel. We recommend that this energetic genius give five or ten minutes of his time to the Erie Railroad."

CHAPTER TWELVE

The Raid on the
Albany and Susquehanna

FISK was in fact paying close attention to Erie affairs. For all his grandstanding and theatrics, he was always an efficient, well-organized administrator, who kept several secretaries occupied transcribing his dictation and orders as he handled the day-to-day affairs of what was, for all its troubles, still one of the country's largest and most-important corporations.

In the summer of 1869 the Erie Railway, through its president and controller, attempted to gain control of the Albany and Susquehanna Railroad. This road was in many ways a miniature of the Erie, both in the sort of country through which it passed and the vicissitudes it had endured in the course of its construction. Running from the Hudson River at Albany to the Susquehanna at Binghamton, it covered 143 miles through hilly, thinly populated farming country with few towns of any significance.

Chartered in 1852, it had been from its beginning the creature of Joseph H. Ramsey, "at once the originator, president, financial agent, legal advisor, and guiding spirit of the enterprise."[1] Construction had begun the following year with a million dollars in capital, which had been raised by individual subscription to its stock by people living along its right-of-way, who could only benefit from the cheap transportation it would provide. But work had to be suspended in 1854 when the money ran out.

The New York State Legislature passed a special act allowing the towns along the way to subscribe to the stock, and the city of Albany loaned the enterprise $1,000,000, taking the first mortgage bonds of the company. Work began again in 1857 and the little road slowly made its way through the hills and valleys of the western Catskills. Eight times bills giving the railroad special aid passed the Legislature and six times the Governor of the day vetoed the aid bills. In the end the state would contribute only $750,000 toward its construction costs.

By 1868 the Albany and Susquehanna was once more out of money, and it was still not finished. The last 22 miles to Binghamton had yet to be built. And these 22 miles were through the most difficult terrain of all, involving not only numerous grades but a tunnel fully 2,200 feet long 15 miles east of Binghamton near Harpursville. Ramsey, desperate to get his dream finished at long last, went to Wall Street in hopes of raising the needed capital, and it responded on terms that were, not surprisingly, very favorable to the lenders. All the Albany and Susquehanna had to offer by way of securities were some of its unsold second-mortgage bonds and 8,000 shares of forfeited stock (stock that had been subscribed to but not paid for in full within the allotted time period).

Azro Chase provided the Albany and Susquehanna with $50,000, taking second-mortgage bonds at 70 and receiving an option on 300 shares of the forfeited stock at 20. David Groesbeck, a well-known Wall Street broker (two years earlier he had been the first broker on the Street to install a stock ticker in his office, and Daniel Drew had long been one of his most important customers), loaned the company $560,000, taking as collateral, but not buying, second-mortgage bonds also at 70 to protect his risk. He was given an option to buy the bonds anytime within the next eighteen months at 80 and to buy 2,400 shares of the forfeited stock at 25.

Finally, the Albany and Susquehanna was finished, and on January 12th, 1869, it formally opened to the public. It had already been in business for some time, of course, running from Albany to as far as it reached, and it had been showing a steady increase in its net earnings as the road made its way westward. In the last fiscal year it had earned $227,818.79 in net operating revenues. But the Albany and Susquehanna was still a tiny affair, a holdover from a period in railroad history that had already passed. It owned altogether only 17 locomotives and 214 cars, while the Erie that year had 317 engines and 6,343 cars running over its many hundreds of miles of tracks.

What interested Gould in the Albany and Susquehanna, now that it was completed, was not its insignificant local traffic, but the strategic connections it made. Possession of Ramsey's railroad would make the Erie a direct competitor of the New York Central for the traffic running between Albany, Buffalo, and points west, with all the possibilities that would mean for giving the Commodore grief. The bridge over the Hudson at Albany, which Vanderbilt had used, or rather not used, so adroitly a few years earlier in his quarrel with Henry Keep, linked the Albany and Susquehanna directly with the New England market. Given the Erie's proximity to the Pennsylvania coal fields, its burgeoning traffic in coal (over a million tons that year), and New England's fast-growing appetite for the great fuel of the steam age, the value of the Albany and Susquehanna to the Erie and to Gould was obvious.

Ramsey, "a little, grey-headed, sallow faced gentleman, weighing about 115 pounds, with a very bright eye,"[2] was perfectly well aware of the threat to his railroad from the Erie, but his dominance of the corporation he had founded and built was no longer unquestioned. In the seventeen-year struggle to complete the road he had made many enemies, and seven of the fourteen seats on the board of directors were now held by men opposed to him, most notably Vice President Walter S. Church. Ramsey had already made it plain that at the next election one side or the other would have to go, saying that the railroad could not operate with a stalemated board.

It was this division on the board that gave Gould his opportunity, for Ramsey's opponents were looking around for allies in the coming contest and soon found a powerful one in the Erie Railway. Church and Gould agreed to make common cause. Gould began to buy up Albany and Susquehanna stock, but the market was a very thin one. Regularly quoted but seldom traded, in the low 20's, there was little floating supply, and Gould's buying soon sent the price soaring. The outstanding stock of the railroad was largely in the hands of its directors and other investors who lived along its right-of-way, or was held by the towns along the way, whose commissioners acted as trustees for the citizens.

Together with the dissident directors, Gould had a large but not controlling interest, and it was soon clear that the stock that was held by the towns would prove decisive in the struggle for the company. The law that had made it possible for the towns to buy the stock in the first place was very specific about the terms under which they could sell it: at par or above and for cash only. Gould sent emissaries to the various towns and secured several hundred shares at par. But he was afraid that Ramsey, inevitably hearing about what was going on, would start bidding for the town stock as well, driving the price to heaven only knew what heights above par.

Gould and Fisk decided to try another tactic, and invited the town commissioners to come to New York City as guests of the Erie Railway. Once they were in the big city, Gould and Fisk entertained them lavishly and housed them at the Fifth Avenue Hotel. There, on Sunday, August 1st, Gould and Fisk made the commissioners an offer. If they would agree to vote as Gould and Fisk wished at the upcoming annual meeting, the Erie Railway would agree to buy their stock at par as soon as it had control of the company. Fisk and Gould, well and expensively counseled at law, must have known that this deal was unenforceable, for the law specified that the commissioners could not sell their votes or their proxies to anyone. But the town commissioners, apparently, did not know this, for the trustees for 4,500 shares of stock accepted the offer.

If Fisk and Gould were up to their usual tricks, Ramsey was not above trying a few himself, for he also often failed to distinguish between his own interests and those of the company he headed. (When he had run for Congress a few years earlier, he had handed out no fewer than 3,000 free passes to voters along the way.) The subscription books of the company had never been closed, as 12,000 of the authorized 40,000 shares had never been issued. As long as the stock was selling below par on the open market there was no interest in this unissued stock, of course, but with the struggle for control of the company hanging in the balance, Ramsey decided to buy a large amount of it, more than enough to secure his continuance in office.

He smuggled the subscription books out of the railroad's headquarters one day, and at a meeting at his home he and some friends subscribed to 9,500 shares. The company charter required a deposit of 10 percent, and Ramsey borrowed the needed $95,000 from David Groesbeck, giving him $150,000, face value, in Albany and Susquehanna equipment bonds as collateral. These bonds, however, did not belong to Ramsey, but rather to the company. The president had simply removed them from the treasurer's care and hypothecated them for his own convenience. Then, to make sure that no one could make use of the same idea, Ramsey hid the subscription books in a tomb in the Albany cemetery.

On August 3rd, the Erie presented the stock it had bought from the various towns to the treasurer of the company for transfer, the transfer books being scheduled to close on August 7th, a month before the annual meeting. The treasurer, a strong Ramsey man, felt that he had no choice but to transfer most of the stock, but he balked at any he could find an excuse to balk at. On the next day a judge in distant Owego enjoined the transfer of seven hundred shares from the town of Oneonta to the Erie, but Thomas G. Shearman, dispatched on a flying trip there, managed to get the injunction dissolved. The next day the ever-faithful Judge Barnard granted an order compelling the transfer of the Oneonta stock and, while he was at it, suspended Ramsey from the board and enjoined the voting of the stock optioned to Chase and Groesbeck.

When Barnard's orders arrived at the Albany and Susquehanna offices, an uproar ensued as "the offices of the company swarmed with indignant directors and opposing counsel; angry words passed, loud threats were uttered; the suspended president was informed that his presence was undesired, and the unsuspended vice president showed a strong disposition to assume also the duties of treasurer in so far as these involved the entering of transfers and the issuing of certificates of stock."[3]

Everyone realized that control of the transfer books meant control of the company, and a brawl erupted between some of the state capital's most respectable citizens as they fought for physical possession of the vital ledgers. The police had to be summoned, and they finally managed to impose "an angry truce."

Church decided to call a meeting of the board for the next morning. With Ramsey suspended, he would chair the meeting, and the board would be aligned seven to six in favor of the Erie. He proposed to replace the treasurer at this meeting with one who would transfer the disputed stock and thus secure control for the Erie faction. Once this was accomplished, the annual meeting itself would be reduced to a merely confirmatory exercise.

The next morning, just as the board was settling down to act on the vice president's intentions, a Ramsey attorney appeared and served the vice president and three other members of the Erie faction with judicial orders suspending them from the board as well. With all these suspensions the board now lacked a quorum and thus could not act at all. The rival factions and their rival judges had managed, more or less accidentally, to legally decapitate the Albany and Susquehanna Railroad, and no one at all was now in charge.

Informed of the latest developments by telegraph, Thomas G. Shearman knew just what the Albany and Susquehanna needed in the present emergency: a receiver. He drew up papers appointing Charles Courter of upstate Cobleskill, already a member of the Albany and Susquehanna board and an Erie man, to be receiver along with Fisk. Shearman's papers, of course, required a judge's signature, and Barnard, unfortunately, was in Poughkeepsie, seventy-five miles up the Hudson, where he was visiting his fast-failing mother. A frantic telegram was sent to him saying, "Come to New York without fail tonight."[4]

Receiving the telegram, Judge Barnard was faced with the agonizing choice of remaining at the bedside of his dying mother or coming to the aid of his friends in Erie. He caught the next train to New York.

By 10:30 Friday night everything was in order, and Fisk was able to catch the eleven-o'clock train to Albany to take personal charge of the situation the next morning. Accompanying him was "a select bodyguard of directors, friends and lawyers"[5] and, incidentally, a few of the Erie's thugs in case some muscle was needed.

The Albany newspapers had been expecting his arrival and were delighted with the prospect of having Fisk in their city, for he was almost guaranteed to provide first-class copy. On August 7th, the Albany *Evening Journal*, pretending to an intimacy with Erie affairs it could hardly have had, declared authoritatively that it was "plain that the real head of their party could no longer remain in the background. It was therefore decided to bring James Fisk, Jr.—he of the blue coat and brass buttons—to the front, and let the blazing glare of his immense diamond pin dazzle and bewilder the rural Albanians."

In the event, the *Evening Journal* was to be disappointed in Fisk's sartorial accouterments, reporting sadly that "the regalia of his office as Commander of the Sound Steamers and Grand Generalissimo of the unsound railroad which runs through fire and water along the Southern Tier was not on."

Fisk showed up at the Albany and Susquehanna offices on Albany's waterfront at eight Saturday morning to take possession, backed by his Erie guards and lawyers. He was met at the door by John W. Van Valkenburg, the superintendent of the Albany and

Susquehanna, who informed him curtly that a receiver, Robert H. Pruyn, had already been appointed by Supreme Court Judge Rufus W. Peckham (the father of the U.S. Supreme Court justice of the same name) sitting in Albany, and that therefore Fisk's services would not be required. Peckham's order establishing a receivership, as it happened, antedated Barnard's by a few minutes, and Van Valkenburg would not allow Fisk to take charge, although he was willing to admit him to the outer office. Fisk said that he intended to take possession of the railroad if it required "millions of money and unlimited number of men,"[6] and Van Valkenburg, not easily intimidated, hoped in turn that Fisk would have a good time trying.

Fisk ordered his "boys" to storm the office, but Van Valkenburg's own troops, far more numerous and on home ground, made short work of them. Fisk found himself unceremoniously heaved out onto the street like a sack of yesterday's trash.

No sooner had he picked himself up out of the dust than he was arrested. He followed his captor peaceably to the local police station only to discover to his chagrin that the man was not a policeman at all but only an employee of the Albany and Susquehanna masquerading as one. Jubilee Jim then returned to the railroad's offices to find that Pruyn, backed by ten lawyers, had now appeared on the scene, and with the rival receiver a mood of considerable civility had also arrived.

Fisk had telegraphed to New York for judicial reinforcements from Judge Barnard, and until they arrived he did not have much choice but to return the courtesy. In any event, he was a naturally genial man and a thoroughly good loser. He praised Van Valkenburg for his forcefulness, telling him that there was a place for him in the Erie anytime he wanted it, and when Ramsey's principal lawyer, Henry Smith (who also happened to be the Albany County District Attorney), arrived, "Receiver Pruyn claimed the honor of introducing him to his friend, Mr. James Fisk, Jr., which ceremony was performed with that suave courtesy which so eminently characterizes our distinguished fellow citizens." Having claimed that honor, Mr. Pruyn then politely requested of Henry Smith an introduction to Mr. Fisk. "Railroad wars," deadpanned the *Evening Journal*, "establish novel rules of etiquette."[7]

Smith, making small talk in this ridiculous situation, remarked to Fisk that staid Albany was not used to such goings on.

"Well," replied Fisk with his habitual lack of regard for the truth, "I am. This is the twenty-sixth or twenty-seventh raid I have engaged in."[8] To settle the matter without further violence, however, Fisk offered Ramsey single combat in a game of seven-up, a popular card game, winner take all.

As the standoff wore on through the hot August afternoon, "the lawyers assembled, and grave efforts were made by all parties to maintain composure and be friendly and genial, which succeeded to a good degree. The hours passed in talking over matters between each other, private consultations, jokes and business."[9]

Finally, Fisk received word of Barnard's latest actions, and his favorite judge had not disappointed him. Barnard had vacated Peckham's order naming Pruyn receiver and summarily enjoined Pruyn, the Sheriff of Albany County, the Albany police, and all railroad employees from interfering with Courter and Fisk in pursuit of their duties as receivers. To back this up, he issued a writ of assistance, a piece of judicial process that dated back to the time of James I and had seldom been used since.

"The writ," explained the Albany *Argus* to its readers, "is little known and rarely used, except in the last extremity; but it is very potent and is equivalent to giving the sheriff power . . . [by] commanding him to call upon the whole county as a *posse comitatus*, if need be to enforce the writ."[10]

Barnard, in fact, was simply ahead of his time, for the sheriff's posse would soon be well known on the frontier, and in the next century would become quite indispensable to the plots of countless Hollywood westerns.

More interesting even than Barnard's issuance of so arcane a legal instrument was the means of its dispatch to Albany, for it was sent by telegraph, perhaps the first use of electronic communication for this purpose. But the Sheriff of Albany County refused to act on a writ that necessarily lacked the usual seals and signatures to guarantee its authenticity, and the stalemate continued.

Finally both sides agreed that nothing more could be accomplished that day, and they established a truce for the remainder of the weekend, agreeing "to rest on their arms till nine o'clock Monday morning, each receiver leaving a personal representative in the office."[11] Fisk took the train down to New York. He returned to Albany by the night boat Sunday, now armed with duly executed writs from Judge Barnard. But Monday morning did not find him any closer to his goal of control of the Albany and Susquehanna Railroad. Injunction or no injunction, Van Valkenburg would no longer even let Fisk into the outer offices of the road, and the Sheriff of Albany County declined to organize a *levée en masse* of the citizenry to enforce the rights of the Erie Railway and the writs of a New York City judge. Albany was strong for Ramsey, who lived there, and it had heard more than enough about the Erie and this corpulent denizen of the fleshpots of Gotham to want any part of either.

Fisk did his best to change public opinion. He had written Edmund Savage of Albany a letter and distributed copies to the newspapers, where it was widely printed. "Can anyone suppose that we want the Albany and Susquehanna road for its business between here and Binghamton?" he asked. "No; we are not so foolish. We want it as a means of communicating with every city and town and hamlet of New England that today we are isolated from. We wish to pour out the wealth brought over the Erie Road, in your city and on your docks, for transportation eastward. We would make Albany the great terminus of one long line of road—the distributing point for the North and East."[12]

Fisk's promise to make Albany an important rail center was a serious one. Because of the Erie's crippling broad gauge, a defect it shared with the Albany and Susquehanna, it would have no choice but to break bulk at Albany on the way to New England. The New York Central could, and increasingly would, treat Albany as a whistle-stop. The Commodore could hardly have been happy about the prospect of another trunk road in Albany, the Erie above all. And while Fisk was raising the bogeyman of the Commodore one more time, he was probably not far from the mark when he wrote of the Albany and Susquehanna that "the interest of the Erie is to run it; the interest of the Central is to discontinue it."

But public-relations campaigns take time, and Fisk was fast running out of that commodity. Van Valkenburg had dispatched a fresh raft of injunctions, which according to the *Argus* had been "flying around in a promiscuous manner,"[13] from Judge Peckham on the 8 A.M. express to Binghamton, putting railroad employees on notice that they were to pay no attention to Erie demands for control.

Then Fisk, mulling things over at the Delavan House, suddenly realized his mistake: the Erie had launched its assault against the wrong end of the line. Albany was the enemy's strongest point; it was at Binghamton, in Erie country, that he would find the soft underbelly of the Albany and Susquehanna.

As Adams noted admiringly, "A party to a conflict . . . who operates by steam is at a manifest disadvantage when acting against one who dispatches writs by telegraph."[14] As Van Valkenburg's express train sped down the tracks, Fisk turned its flank by getting Barnard to send one of his "electro-writs," as Adams called them, to Binghamton in seconds.

Accepting the writ as genuine, the Sheriff of Broome County, where Binghamton is situated, seized the Albany and Susquehanna terminal at 2 P.M. in the name of the Barnard receivers and managed to secure three of the four locomotives in the yard. The fourth made good its escape when an alert crew figured out what was going on and switched the Sheriff's approaching locomotive off onto another track and then fled down the line, where it was soon "making good time for Albany."[15]

Half an hour later an Erie engine, the *Roswell McNeill*, named after the Erie's rolling-stock superintendent, was attached to what had been the afternoon train to Albany and prepared to move down the line and seize control of each station as it went. Aboard were Sheriff Browne of Broome County and H. D. V. Pratt, newly appointed superintendent of the Albany and Susquehanna by orders of receiver Fisk. Also aboard were about twenty Erie employees, who in all probability were somewhat bewildered by all these goings on but were happy enough to join the party for the fun of it.

Van Valkenburg, meanwhile, aware of events in Binghamton, had ordered all regular trains on the line to halt at the nearest siding and mounted a special train with 150 men commanded by Henry Smith. "They took a good supply of flour and beef with them," reported the *Herald*, delighted to have such a red-hot story in the midst of the August doldrums, "and appeared more like men on a military expedition than a civil mission." The *Herald*, to be sure, was helping along this martial atmosphere as best it could with such headlines as "THE LATEST FROM THE SEAT OF WAR."[16]

Smith's train soon set off for Binghamton, stopping at each station to fortify it with a contingent of men and to instruct the stationmaster as to just who was running the railroad.

The Erie train was doing exactly the same thing from the other end of the line, using Barnard's writ of assistance to cow employees of the Albany and Susquehanna into compliance and leaving an Erie man at each station. The Sheriff of Broome County was so taken with his duties that he continued to perform them even after his power ceased at the county line. At Afton, in neighboring Chenango County, Pratt received a telegram from Van Valkenburg warning him that they proceeded further at their own peril, and they in turn telegraphed Fisk for instructions. The generalissimo, pacing the floor at the Delavan House in Albany, told them to proceed as ordered.

At Bainbridge, still further along the line, they found Smith's train standing on a siding. Nightfall had long since come upon them by this time, and Pratt, who obviously had not grasped the essence of one-dimensional warfare as quickly as Smith, foolishly ordered his train to crawl up the tracks while lookouts peered into the gloom in search of missing rails or other sabotage. The lookouts failed, however, to notice the "frog" that had been attached to the tracks. A frog, in those days when locomotives were still quite small, was a device for remounting rolling stock onto the rails after an accident. Unfortunately for Pratt, they were equally useful for derailing rolling stock, and the Erie train was off the tracks and helpless in an instant.

No sooner had the *Roswell McNeill* come to grief than Smith's train sprang into motion and moved off the siding and onto the main track between the Erie train and its base at Binghamton, cutting it off from all retreat. Fisk's forces had been routed and they had no real option other than surrender. Swiftly put back onto the track by Van Valkenburg's men, the Erie train was taken to Albany, where the spoils of war were greeted by a cheering populace.

Fisk, needless to say, was not ready to give up after suffering so ignominious a defeat, and he soon ordered another train at Binghamton prepared for combat, this time loaded with perhaps as many as eight hundred men. On Tuesday afternoon it steamed out of the Albany and Susquehanna terminal and headed down the line for the tunnel near Harpursville. The long tunnel was the great strategic point in this absurd little war, as both the Fisk and Ramsey forces realized, for it was easily held and necessarily secured all the territory behind it.

In the late afternoon the Erie train arrived at the western end of the tunnel, and the leaders halted it to consider the situation. While the Erie train was packed with men, they were not armed with much more than their fists, and so they were sent into the nearby woods to cut branches for use as clubs. At five o'clock, armed with these bludgeons, a few pistols, and knives, the Erie train started up again, creeping through the gloom toward the far end of the tunnel. There, a rail was found to have been dislodged, but the track was soon repaired and the train emerged and began to round the curve ahead.

Suddenly, to their horror, they saw puffing up the steep grade toward them an Albany and Susquehanna train likewise prepared for combat, loaded with 450 men. The Erie engineer frantically signaled "down brakes" with his shrieking whistle and screeched to a halt, but the only response from the enemy train was to pour on the steam, its oversized stack belching smoke and cinders.

"In vain," wrote Adams, "the Erie conductor jumped off his train and gesticulated like a madman; in vain the Erie engineer tried to back out of the way; the curve was here so sharp and the incline up which it was necessary to back . . . so great, that it was instantly evident, not only that the Albany people wanted a collision, but that their wish was to be gratified."[17]

Because the Erie train had stopped and the Albany train could not make much speed up the line's steepest grade, the collision, when it came, was not catastrophic. The cowcatchers of the two engines were demolished and the headlights smashed, while the Albany locomotive was partially derailed. Otherwise the two trains and their passengers were unharmed. The Albany men piled off as soon as their train halted and assaulted the enemy. Although Fisk's troops outnumbered their opponents by perhaps as much as two to one, they broke at once and fled precipitately over the hill and back toward the other end of the tunnel, while their train, its engine straining every seam and pouring out smoke and steam, clawed its way frantically back up the grade and into the blessed darkness of the tunnel, out of harm's way. At the other end of the tunnel once again, the Erie army stopped to reconnoiter and catch its breath.

They knew that the Albany train would soon be remounted on the tracks and then be upon them. At least it would no longer have the advantage of surprise, and the Erie men rallied to defend their end of the tunnel.

When the Albany train appeared "the conflict was reopened with great fury. The Erie men, occupying their own ground, had no intention of giving it up. . . . The Albany men, flushed with success, attacked vigorously. Pistols were used, with stones, clubs and fists."[18] The battle raged for some time, but having little if any leadership, it was really more a riot than a battle. Finally, as dusk crept in, a noise was heard over the din, the sound of distant drums. The state militia had been called out to quell the disturbance, and the 44th Regiment, on the march from Binghamton, was arriving at the scene. The combatants, faced with arrest, immediately began to melt into the gathering night, and the Albany train withdrew to the far end of the tunnel.

THE BATTLE FOR THE ALBANY AND SUSQUEHANNA *Courtesy of The New-York Historical Society, New York City*

Considering the number of men involved and, in all likelihood, the amount of alcohol consumed, the casualty list was astonishingly small; only eight or ten men had been shot, some others suffered "bruises more or less severe,"[19] and one man had a fractured skull. No one had been killed.

If the effects upon the combatants had been minimal, the effect upon the body politic was not, and the state government took stern action. The State Comptroller, the highest public official present in Albany, had been alerted by David Dudley Field as to what was happening and he wired Governor Hoffman, who was vacationing at West Point. The Governor returned at once to Albany and took no uncertain charge of the situation.

He threatened to declare the Albany and Susquehanna to be in a state of insurrection, subjecting it to martial law, unless these offenses against the public peace ceased forthwith. Both sides, probably somewhat stunned by what they had managed to work, immediately agreed to the Governor's appointment of Major General James McQuade, Inspector General of the State Militia, to be superintendent of the Albany and Susquehanna until the whole matter could be settled in the courts.

Peace returned all along the line, and by Wednesday night a *Herald* reporter visiting the Albany police headquarters in search of a story could write that "this evening revealed a blissful state of repose. A dim light was burning in the passage, which was under the charge of a small dog, and in one of the rooms the only official on duty was sleeping as soundly as the mosquitoes would permit."[20]

•

On September 7th the annual election of the Albany and Susquehanna board of directors was held on schedule. Fisk was again on hand and "was arrayed in his usual fancy style, and, with his speckled straw hat and blue ribbon, looked as gay and frisky, and almost as Fisky, as when he hops about in his regimentals on the wheelhouse of a Bristol steamer."[21] Also on hand was David Dudley Field, who had been lured from his summer vacation near Springfield, Massachusetts, only when the Erie agreed to deposit a fee of $10,000 into his New York bank account.

Ramsey had also brought in the big guns and had the young J. P. Morgan on hand as his chief advisor. The subscription books that Ramsey had entombed for safekeeping were meanwhile exhumed and returned stealthily by means of a basket lowered from a back window.

As the time approached for the election, the room filled with lawyers, stockholders, employees, process servers, and men who were either proxy holders or thugs depending on the observer's point of view. When the proceedings got under way "a perfect meteoric shower of suits, injunctions, and receiverships that has not been surpassed in any of the Erie Wars"[22] instantly reduced the meeting to chaos. Ramsey, Henry Smith, and the company treasurer were arrested for having stolen the subscription books. In the end two separate elections were held, with one election backing Fisk and the other Ramsey. The Albany and Susquehanna remained under the control of General McQuade as the dispute once more returned to the courtroom.

There, the Ramsey side, under the guidance of Morgan, managed to get the case tried not in New York City or even Albany but in the rural fastness of Delhi, New York, before a Supreme Court judge who was safely on their side. He decided for Ramsey right down the line, damning Fisk and the Erie for misconduct on every point at issue. The judge's opinion was to be reversed by the Court of Appeals on every point except the crucial one of who won the election. But by that time it was academic. As soon as the first opinion was handed down, and the Ramsey side returned to power, they took J. P. Morgan's advice and leased the road to the Delaware and Hudson Canal Company, effectively removing it from the Erie's clutches.

As far as Wall Street was concerned the Albany and Susquehanna war was a minor skirmish off in the wilds of upstate New York. But the legal profession took the whole matter much more seriously, for nothing could have demonstrated more clearly that something was terribly wrong. As former United States Attorney General Jeremiah Black wrote, "A moment's attention to this will . . . show that the confusion, misapprehension, and total failure of justice which took place in these cases, while they could not possibly have happened in any other country, could scarcely have been avoided in New York . . . all parties were fighting under the ensign of public authority. It was judicial power subverting order and breaking the peace; it was law on a rampage; it was justice bedeviled; in one word, it was the New York Code in full operation."[23]

Harper's Weekly fretted about the future of New York unless it cleaned up its judiciary. "If scenes of anarchy are to be avoided, if

New York is to retain its preeminence as the commercial metropolis of the country, if foreign capital is to be retained here, something must be done to prevent, in the future, the unseemly abuses of power into which certain of our state judges have been betrayed in the past."[24]

Although Governor Hoffman was a product of Tammany Hall (the only elected Mayor of New York ever to reach higher office, Hoffman had won the governorship with the help of an avalanche of fraudulent votes), he was beginning to have higher ambitions still. With an eye cocked toward the 1872 presidential election, Hoffman was seeking to distance himself from his political background. In his annual message to the Legislature in January, 1870, he called for the abridgment of the powers of judges in ex parte proceedings. But the Legislature was in no mood for reform and took no action.

If the Legislature again blocked any meaningful reform of the law, however, the lawyers, like the brokers before them, could act on their own, and the early months of 1870 saw the establishment of the New York State Bar Association. William Maxwell Evarts, another former United States Attorney General, lamented in a speech at the organizing meeting how New York's growth had caused the old restraints to decay. He remembered a time when "for a lawyer to come out from the chambers of a judge with an *ex parte* writ that he could not defend before the public, would have occasioned the same sentiment towards him as if he came out with a stolen pocket book."[25]

This speech was widely published in the press and occasioned a wide debate about the ethical responsibility of lawyers. David Dudley Field, the subject of much vituperation for his association with Fisk and Gould, was saved from an official inquiry by the new Bar Association only when Evarts himself intervened. But Field was adamant regarding a lawyer's ethical duties. "A lawyer is responsible," he wrote to Samuel Bowles in a widely printed exchange of letters, "not for his clients, nor for their causes, but for the manner in which he conducts their causes." He insisted: "I have not knowingly defended [Fisk and Gould] in a single wrongful act. I am assured by them, in the most solemn manner (this much I am permitted to say) that they have never appropriated to their own use one dollar's worth of the Erie Company's assets."[26]

The Bar Association would do much to improve the standards of behavior by both lawyers and judges in the next few years and would be a major force in cleaning up the New York State judiciary and its procedures. But these lawyers and judges had still to deal with the law as it was written. And the law was written by the Legislature.

"There can be no safer rule for a lawyer to follow," wrote George Ticknor Curtis, a distinguished lawyer and historian, about the Albany and Susquehanna imbroglio, "than to assume it to be right to do for any man what the law allows to be done."[27]

•

Despite this latest fiasco, the Erie and its directors still had their defenders. On August 17th the *Herald* printed a letter, signed "Independent," which said that "the Erie directors are now the best abused men in the country; but the time will soon come when the truth will be spoken and they will be regarded the ablest railroad managers on the continent. The time is not far distant when the Erie Railway stock will be [at] par and its owners will receive good dividends."

This letter quite possibly was part of a public-relations campaign. But if it was genuine, one can only hope that "Independent" made up in patience what he lacked in prescience. The stock would never reach par, and the wait by the Erie stockholders for dividends was to be a long one. There would be one issued in 1873, but the one after that would not be forthcoming until 1942.

Conspicuously absent from the battle for control of the Albany and Susquehanna, especially considering how greatly his immediate interests were involved, was Commodore Vanderbilt. The Commodore, as it happened, was in nearby Saratoga Springs, then at the height of its glory as a fashionable summer resort. He was there to take the waters, indulge his passion for first-class horseflesh, and preside over a conference to settle the details of the consolidation of the New York Central and Hudson River railroads.

The Commodore, it turned out, was also up to something else. His wife, Sophia, had died in August of the previous year. Although she had been a shadowy, even reclusive, figure for many years, long lost in the glare of her remarkable husband, Vanderbilt missed her after a fashion and did not fancy living alone in the house on Washington Place with only servants for companionship. On August 21st he slipped off to London, Ontario, and secretly married Miss Frank Armstrong Crawford, a divorcée from Mobile, Alabama. The Commodore was seventy-five, his new bride thirty. When the story leaked out, as it did almost immediately, the country's newspapers surrendered as one to an orgy of bad puns about "Vanderbilt's last and most notable consolidation."[28] Given the difference in their ages it is not surprising that the New York clubs and upper-class brothels were filled with far less restrained commentary.

Like Sophia, Frank Crawford was a close relative of the Commodore, being his first cousin twice removed, but she had a much stronger personality than her predecessor and considerable diplomatic skills. The *New York Times* described her as "tall and queenly in form, and beautiful in features";[29] the *Herald* demurred, saying that "she is said to be talented and highly accomplished, though not very beautiful."[30]

To the Commodore's old age she would bring companionship at home, an understanding of the rewards of charity, and at least an introduction to the comforts of religion. She is even supposed to have given him the only book he is known to have read other than the Bible, John Bunyan's *Pilgrim's Progress*.

Also largely absent from the struggle for the Albany and Susquehanna was Jay Gould. To Gould the fight to gain control of a small upstate railroad, however useful it might have been to the Erie, was a side issue, for his first love still consumed him. All year he had been quietly planning his next move in the great game, and as summer faded away, Gould made ready. The unhealthy little man with the sunken, glittering eyes was poised for a strike at the very heart of the financial system itself.

Gould was out to corner gold.

Chapter Thirteen

Black Friday

WHILE sudden squalls are a common feature of Wall Street's financial meteorology, no one was prepared for the hurricane that was conjured up by Gould and that swept through the Street on Friday, September 24th, 1869. While its effects would be mostly transitory, even in some ways salutary, the sound and fury of its passage would not be exceeded or even equaled until the great crash of 1929 brought the old order on Wall Street to an end some sixty years later.

It is not known when Gould first conceived the idea that gold might be successfully cornered, but he began to act on it not long after Ulysses S. Grant's inauguration as President in March, 1869. Over the next six months, while he would never himself so much as set foot in the Gold Room, where the metal was traded, he would be by far the most important financial force operating in it.

As Henry Adams, who first wrote the gold panic's history, noted, "Of all financial operations, cornering gold is the most brilliant and the most dangerous, and possibly the very hazard and splendor of the attempt were the reasons of its fascination to Mr. Jay Gould."[1] It would be hard to exaggerate the centrality of gold in the financial system of the mid-nineteenth century. It was lawful money in all countries, and Great Britain, still by far the world's leading industrial, commercial, financial, and maritime power, had been on a pure gold standard since 1821. The Bank of England, the world's de facto central bank, stood ready to buy and sell unlimited quantities of gold for pounds sterling at a fixed rate. This meant that the pound was literally as good as gold and that sterling and gold were the sole mediums of international exchange.

Most countries of commercial importance were either on or moving rapidly toward some form of the gold standard. The United States, however, was not among them because of the lingering effects of the Civil War. While the war had had the result of greatly simplifying the country's monetary system, its financial demands had forced the national government to pay part of its bills with printing-press money, greenbacks as they were called from the color of ink used to print them.

Until the war, currency in circulation in the United States was in the form of bank notes issued by state-chartered banks and backed by their deposits. They circulated at values that reflected both the perceived financial soundness of the issuing bank and also the distance of the transaction from it. The farther away the issuing bank, the only place they were guaranteed redeemable at par for lawful money, the less the notes would buy. The federal government's only contribution to the nation's money supply was to mint coins, including gold coins at the value of twenty dollars to the ounce.

At the end of 1861, by which time it was evident that the Civil War would be both protracted and expensive, the government suspended specie payment, that is, it stopped paying its bills in gold. The National Banking Act established nationally chartered banks that were empowered to issue notes backed by government bonds held in their reserves, and it drove the state banks out of the currency business with a prohibitive tax on its issuance. The Treasury had already begun to issue its own non-redeemable notes. At first the government required by law that its new notes circulate at par with gold. It was soon recognized that this requirement, because bad money drives out good, would only have the effect of driving all gold coins out of circulation almost instantly. This section of the Legal Tender Act was soon repealed; what was not repealed was the requirement that contracts specifying payment in gold could be satisfied, at par, with greenbacks. This obscure provision—obscure because it was always ignored—was one of the key elements in Gould's audacious scheme.

The government had issued a total of $400,000,000 in greenbacks by the end of the war. While the struggle raged, their value relative to gold fluctuated with the fortunes of the Union army. Just prior to Gettysburg, it took 287 greenback dollars to buy 100 gold dollars. As the Confederacy slowly collapsed during the last two years of the war, the value of the greenback dollar slowly rose, and, with the war's end, gold traded in a range of 30 to 45 percent over greenbacks.

To accommodate the market for gold and greenbacks, an efficient system was devised for trading them. In 1862 the Gold Room was organized for this purpose right next door to the Stock Exchange, providing speculators with an unmatched opportunity to gamble. These speculators received a good deal of adverse publicity. They were called "General Lee's left wing in Wall Street,"[2] and Abraham Lincoln publicly wished that "every one of them had his devilish head shot off." But the opprobrium that was heaped upon the gold traders for their lack of patriotism affected their activities not in the slightest. For the lucky—or the skillful and determined—there was just too much money to be made.

In 1866 the Gold Exchange Bank was organized to provide a clearinghouse, and it greatly facilitated trading, which by 1869 was averaging $70,000,000 a day. Much of that amount was what Fisk called "phantom gold," gold bought on margins so thin as to seem nearly incredible today. In his testimony before the House committee that investigated the gold panic, Charles J. Osborn said that "if a man has a thousand dollars, he can go and buy five millions of gold, if he feels so inclined."[3]

While that might be somewhat of an exaggeration, Gould was certainly telling the truth when he testified that "a man with $100,000 of money and with credit can transact a business of $20,000,000."[4]

Here was another element that made a corner in gold seem both feasible and attractive to Gould. The president of the Erie Railway had resources both personal and corporate that greatly exceeded $100,000, and yet there was not $20,000,000 in real gold in private hands in New York City. Gould, testifying later, thought that there was perhaps $14,000,000 in gold certificates and about $3,000,000 or $4,000,000 in gold coin available to the market on the day of the panic. After all, there was not much reason for anyone actually to hold gold, with all its inconveniences. Asked who did hold it that day, Gould replied that some banks did and that "there are always lots of old fogies who keep gold to look at."[5]

In addition to his other financial resources, Gould had recently acquired control of the small Tenth National Bank, along with Fisk and some of his Tammany friends. The bank would prove invaluable by providing certified checks without Gould's having to provide the cash to back them. On the day before the panic the bank would provide no less than $25,000,000 in these certified checks.

Greenbacks did not rise to par after the war because the government, caught up in the politics of cheap versus sound money, made only feeble efforts to return to a gold standard. And there were certain important uses to which greenbacks could not be put. Even the government that issued them wanted gold, not paper, and required that the payment of tariffs and customs duties, its main source of revenue until the First World War, be made in the precious metal. American foreign trade, of course, was conducted entirely on a gold basis.

The fact that gold was the only money acceptable in the international market presented New York merchants, who totally dominated American foreign commerce, with a very practical problem. These merchants, most of whom would not have dreamed of speculating, were habitually short of gold, a transaction they had to conduct through the Gold Room. The reason was that when a merchant sold abroad he was paid in gold, but there was always a period of time between when the deal was made and when payment was received. If the price of gold were to decline in this interval, the merchant would lose money. To prevent that, he sold short in the Gold Room as much gold as was owed him. Then, if the price declined, he would make as much on his short position as he lost on the gold that was coming to him. If, on the other hand, gold went up in price, he would lose on the short and make it back on the metal crossing the Atlantic. In either case the profit on his business deal was locked in.

This use of the market by merchants to protect their investments, called hedging, is one of the primary, indeed essential, purposes of any commodity market. The presence of these merchants in the gold market must have been still another element that attracted Gould. Not only were they likely to have assets far in excess of the usual speculating riffraff that operated in the Gold Room, and thus be far more worth the squeezing, but their very respectability made them more vulnerable. With valuable reputations to protect, they would be far more inclined to settle up quietly rather than run the risk of being involved in a public default, however temporary. And, not being speculators accustomed to the bluff and pose of the great game, they might prove to be more easily intimidated by Gould.

So Gould saw his opportunity and decided to take it. Risking comparatively little of his own money, he could buy gold contracts that amounted to far more than all the gold in private hands that could be brought into the New York marketplace. Since many men of wealth, in the ordinary course of their business, would be short of gold, they and any speculators caught in the net could be squeezed until their pips squeaked. And, because contracts made in the Gold Room—which, of course, specified settlement in gold— were unenforceable at law, there was a convenient escape hatch. If things went badly awry, Gould could simply repudiate any con- tracts he found uncomfortable to fulfill and, in Fisk's airy words, "nothing [would be] lost save honor."

There was one very large "if" between Gould and the successful accomplishment of a corner in gold. In the vaults of the Subtreasury at the head of Broad Street there was stored more than $100,000,000 in gold. The federal government could break any attempted corner in the metal with the dispatch of a single telegram from Washing- ton. Before Gould could hope to corner gold he had to suborn the government into active cooperation or, at least, into benevolent inactivity. To be sure of doing that, Gould needed the President of the United States in his pocket.

•

Gould had never met the President, so he set out to make the acquaintance of the sad-eyed, reticent man who had striven so hard to save the Union and who had been rewarded for his success with its highest office. Gould sought out Abel Rathbone Corbin, an aging lawyer, speculator, and fixer-about-town, who had one priceless asset. The previous year he had married Grant's middle-aged spin- ster sister and was thus at least a quasi-member of the President's inner family. Corbin had moved with his new wife to 37 West 27th Street, just off fashionable Madison Square. The President and Mrs. Grant often stayed there when they visited the city.

Gould, who had bought $7,000,000 in gold during April, 1869, while gold was rising from 130 to 137, called upon Corbin a number of times, beginning in early May, and propounded to him a scheme for both increasing the prosperity of the country and, incidentally, helping the freight revenues of the Erie Railway. It all hinged on the price of gold. If gold was expensive in terms of greenbacks, Gould

THE GRAND CENTRAL DEPOT While Gould speculated on Wall
Street, the Commodore built the the largest railroad station in the world,
a "ferruginous palace" that covered four acres.

argued, farmers in the Middle West would be able to sell their crops in Europe for less than their competitors (notably Russia, a major grain exporter until 1917) and still make a profit. They would ship their crops east, and the Erie Railway would get its share of the traffic.

Gould was arguing, with considerable logic, that what was good for Middle Western farmers and the Erie Railway, cheap money, was good at least in the short term for the country. But, Gould cautioned Corbin, if the government were to step up its regular gold sales, or attempt to force the price of gold down to par with greenbacks, or even, God forbid, go back on the gold standard, then the crops would rot in the fields, the railroad boxcars would lie idle, and depression would stalk the land.

Corbin listened to this argument and agreed to help convince his brother-in-law of its soundness. To ensure Corbin's enthusiasm for the project, Gould offered to buy for his account $1,500,000 in gold on no margin at all. Corbin accepted this largess provided that the gold be put in his wife's name. He testified later that he took Gould's offer only to help ensure his wife's future. He, after all, was an old man and might not be around long to provide for her. It is not likely that either the Congressmen who heard this testimony or the people who read about it in the papers believed a word of it. The deal was just too transparent a bribe. It meant that for every $1 rise in the price of gold, the Corbins stood to profit by $15,000 without having invested a cent.

On June 15th the President passed through New York on his way to a great "peace jubilee" in Boston. It was arranged that the President and Mrs. Grant would travel from New York to Fall River, Massachusetts, by the Narragansett Line steamer *Providence,* and then go on to Boston by train. The owner of the Narragansett Line was Jim Fisk.

The Grants spent the day at the Corbins', and it was there that the President was first introduced to Gould. When it was time to depart for Boston, the President, Mrs. Grant, and Gould went by carriage to the Narragansett pier, where they were met by "Admiral" Fisk in full regalia. A newspaper reported that Fisk, "in a blue uniform, with a broad gilt cap-band, three silver stars on his coat sleeves, lavender gloves, and a diamond breast-pin as large as a cherry, stood at the gangway, surrounded by his aides, bestarred and bestriped like himself."[6] One can only wonder what Grant, once so careless of his appearance in army uniform and now so fastidiously clothed by Brooks Brothers, thought of Fisk's getup.

The Grants were installed in the *Providence*'s bridal suite, which had been well supplied with the President's beloved cigars and buckets full of iced bottles of champagne. About nine o'clock, as the *Providence* made its way up Long Island Sound, the President was escorted down to dinner. To keep him company a number of notables from the city's business community, including David Dudley Field's brother Cyrus, were there along with Gould and Fisk.

Fisk fed the President a sumptuous dinner, followed by whiskey and cigars, while Gould tried diplomatically to sound Grant out on his views regarding economics and the government's gold policy. He outlined his plan to ensure the country's prosperity and was very unhappy when Grant replied, according to Gould, "that there was a certain amount of fictitiousness about the prosperity of the country, and that the bubble might as well be tapped in one way as another."[7] Grant, it seemed, was a sound-money man, and Gould testified later that the President's remark "struck across us like a wet blanket."

Despite this setback, Gould kept up gold purchases and continued to try to cultivate the President. On his return to New York from the peace jubilee, Grant accepted an invitation from Fisk to attend a performance of Offenbach's *La Périchole* at the Fifth Avenue Theater. Grant was cheered when he entered Fisk's private box and again when he left, and it was widely noted that Fisk and Gould were in close attendance upon him. (Josie Mansfield had been banished for propriety's sake to a box on the other side of the theater.) Gould could only have been pleased by the press reports, for surely the next best thing to having the President in your pocket is to have everyone think you have him there.

Gould called on Grant at the Corbins' at least three times in the course of the summer, making a pest of himself to the point where Grant, who tolerated a lot for a man in his position, told Patrick Hussey, who tended the door at the Corbins' house, not to be so quick to admit him. He complained to Mrs. Grant that "Gould was always trying to get something out of him."[8]

In the meanwhile, the post of Assistant Treasurer in New York fell vacant. As the Assistant Treasurer's job was to run the New York Subtreasury, any order from Washington to sell gold would have to be executed by whoever held this post. Gould obviously wanted someone he could control. Even ten minutes' warning of an order to sell gold might mean the difference between success and disaster. At first Gould, through Corbin, lobbied for the appointment of Robert B. Catherwood, the son-in-law of Corbin's first wife. But when Catherwood proved reluctant to make a deal with them, they switched their efforts to General Daniel Butterfield. Butterfield already had strong support from others, including A. T. Stewart, whose palatial mansion was just being completed at Fifth Avenue and 34th Street, and who had been Grant's original choice to be Secretary of the Treasury.

Butterfield had had a successful career in the Union army until an overfondness for army politics had gotten him in trouble. Even so, in later years he was awarded the Congressional Medal of Honor for his actions at the Battle of Gaines's Mill, and his statue stands today on Riverside Drive, not far from the tomb of the President he served better in war than in peace. Curiously, Butterfield is least remembered for what is by far his best-known accomplishment, for he was the composer of "Taps."

Shortly after Butterfield's appointment on July 1st, he allowed Gould to make him a loan of $10,000 with no collateral, an obvious impropriety even then. And he appears to have allowed Gould to open a gold account for him for which he, like Corbin, put up no margin.

The following year, when Fisk was asked if he and Gould had tapped the telegraph wires to learn the government's intentions, he replied, "Tap the wires? Nonsense! It was only necessary to tap Butterfield to find out all we wanted."[9]

●

As the summer continued the Grants traveled. No one spent any more of summer in Washington than could be helped, and anyway the White House was being redecorated in Mrs. Grant's high Victorian style and was largely uninhabitable. The first family made a progress through such fashionable watering holes as Newport, Saratoga, and, their favorite, Long Branch, New Jersey, passing often through New York on their way to and fro. Corbin continued to press the case for cheap money with his brother-in-law while Gould assembled a pool to bull the price of gold and maintained his attempts to corrupt people in power. He wrote General Horace Porter, the President's military secretary and nearly constant companion, that he had opened a gold account in his name in the amount of

$500,000. Porter replied to this out-of-the-blue communication: "I have not authorized any purchase of gold and request that none be made on my account."[10] But apparently he never informed Grant of the attempted bribe.

Although the pool members were able to force the price of gold as high as 140 on July 27th, they could not keep it there. It fell sharply the next day to 135⅞ because real market forces were working against them. The country's foreign trade tended to run increasingly in surplus as summer advanced and American produce was sold abroad.

This meant that all summer gold moved the other way, flowing into New York and driving down the price of gold in the Gold Room to an annual low in September, when shipment of agricultural products peaked and merchants carried their largest short positions. Summer, it was the received wisdom on the Street, was the best time to short gold, and this, Gould knew full well, made it the best time to set a bear trap. But it also meant that Gould had his work cut out for himself keeping the members of the pool in line. Indeed, several defected and went over to the short side. By August 21st the price had dropped to 131⅝.

Gould also continued to work to give the impression, if he could not bring about the reality, that the administration in Washington agreed completely with his ideas of how to ensure the prosperity of the nation. To do this Gould pulled off one of the first great public-relations coups in history: he planted an editorial in the *New York Times*. Henry J. Raymond, who probably spent more time in a state of high dudgeon than was good for him, had died in early summer of apoplexy at the age of only forty-nine, and the new editor was John Bigelow, a pompous man who had been Minister to France during the Civil War.

Gould had Corbin write an article expressing the notion that gold should be allowed to rise freely in price for the good of the country and had James McHenry deliver it to Bigelow. McHenry was a successful British entrepreneur who controlled the Atlantic and Great Western Railway and was, at this time, a close ally of Gould. Gould had selected McHenry as the messenger because McHenry knew Bigelow, who was one of that large class of Americans who were impressed by everybody and everything European.

Bigelow fell for this completely. It was common practice for papers to run editorials that expressed the views of the government (today they would be attributed and called op-ed pieces). But Bigelow made no attempt to ascertain if these really were the views of Grant or anyone else in the administration, or even why they were being delivered by a foreigner. He simply took McHenry's word for it and ordered the piece run as it was, double-leaded to lend it even more authority. The *Times* financial editor, C. C. Norvell, saw the piece in galleys and immediately smelled a rat. He toned it down somewhat and took out the double leading, but it ran on August 24th and could only have helped to bolster the impression on the Street that the Grant administration was entirely prepared to stand by while Gould manipulated the gold market. (Bigelow, understandably, did not last long at the *Times*.)

On September 2nd President and Mrs. Grant passed once more through New York, this time en route from Newport to Saratoga, and they breakfasted with the Corbins. The Middle West was having a banner crop year, a fact that Corbin no doubt pressed upon his brother-in-law as they ate together in the dining room. Grant, apparently, was now ready to accept the logic that Corbin had been pushing so hard all summer. At any event, before Grant left for Saratoga that morning he wrote a letter to Secretary of the Treasury George S. Boutwell, instructing him not to make any irregular sales of gold without consulting him. The President told Corbin of this, for Corbin left the table and informed Gould, who, unbeknown to the President, was lurking in the hallway.

Gould had been waiting patiently for the time to strike. Clearly the time had now arrived.

•

The pool began to buy gold in earnest, and by the middle of September they held contracts amounting to many times the total quantity of gold physically present in New York City outside of government hands. Gould himself testified that he had held perhaps $25,000,000, but Russell A. Hills had $7,000,000 and James Ellis had nearly as much, Edward Woodward had $18,000,000, H. K. Enos and E. K. Willard had $10,000,000 each, and Charles Quincy $14,000,000.[11]

Gould noised it about that the government was in the matter so deep that there was no possibility that the Treasury might sell gold before the matter was completed. James B. Hodgskin, a broker who served as the head of the Gold Room's arbitration committee, which settled any disputes that arose there in the course of business, testified that by the middle of the month it was common knowledge on the Street "that the parties who . . . were manipulating the gold market had in league with them pretty much everybody in author- ity in the United States, beginning with President Grant and ending with the door-keepers of Congress."[12]

On September 13th, Gould adroitly seized yet another opportu- nity to demonstrate publicly his close relationship with the Presi- dent. The Grants were once more in the city, this time on their way to Washington, Pennsylvania, where they were to stay with some relatives of Mrs. Grant. Gould offered the President the use of an Erie Railway private car for the journey to Pittsburgh, and the Presi- dent naïvely accepted the free ride in the nineteenth-century equiv- alent of the corporate jet. It would be Grant's tragedy as a politician that he, a naturally honest and utterly straightforward man, was so slow to learn just how duplicitous others were capable of being.

By September 15th, the price of gold had risen to 138, and the shorts must have been feeling the pinch. They were, after all, re- quired to put up the greenback equivalent of their gold borrowings, and as the price advanced they had to deliver more and more cash. But then the price backed off a bit, and Gould began to get nervous, a nervousness he manifested only in his habit of tearing pieces of paper into ever smaller bits, littering the office with homemade confetti. He was afraid that the numerous, and powerful, sound- money men on Wall Street were putting considerable pressure on Treasury Secretary Boutwell to narrow the spread between green- backs and gold, and that Boutwell, who was made far more of willow than of oak, might bend to their demands. He decided to get some insurance and nearly ruined himself in the process.

Gould went to Corbin and had him write the President a long letter detailing still again all the arguments for allowing gold to rise in price unimpeded by government action. Because Washington, Pennsylvania, was remote, eighteen miles beyond Pittsburgh and the telegraph, it was decided to dispatch the letter by messenger. Fisk—very much the personnel director as well as the controller of the Erie Railway—was asked to provide a good reliable man, and he was happy to supply one W. O. Chapin, who took the letter from Corbin as well as a letter of introduction and caught the morning train to Pittsburgh. When he arrived there late in the evening, he hired a horse and buggy and drove through the night to Washing- ton.

Arriving the next morning, he was told that Grant and General Porter were out on the lawn playing croquet. A servant went out and informed Porter, who came into the house and took the letter of introduction, read it, and, when the President entered, handed him Corbin's letter. Chapin asked if there was any reply, and Grant said that there was not. So the messenger left and as soon as he reached Pittsburgh telegraphed to Castle Erie that the letter was "Delivered. All right."[13]

But matters were anything but all right. Porter, curious, asked Grant who the messenger had been. Grant was surprised at the question because he had assumed that he was just the local postman taking advantage of an opportunity to meet the President, but Porter assured him that he had come all the way from New York.

Suddenly, Grant realized that he was being bamboozled. No one, he knew, and certainly not Corbin, was going to take the trouble and expense of sending a private messenger on a twenty-four-hour journey through the wilds of Pennsylvania simply in order to deliver an already familiar lecture on economics. Corbin could only be up to his eyeballs in some sort of speculation, and if Grant wasn't careful a scandal might erupt that could bring his presidency crashing down in ruins before it had fairly begun. He went into the library, where his wife, coincidentally, was writing a letter that very minute to Mrs. Corbin, and, in Mrs. Grant's word, "dictated" to her.[14]

Grant was not, in any ordinary sense, a henpecked husband, but neither did he very often order his wife to do something. It is a measure of the seriousness of the situation he had finally realized himself to be in that he did so now. Mrs. Grant wrote to Mrs. Corbin, "Tell your husband that my husband is very much annoyed by your speculations. You must close them as quick as you can!"[15]

•

In New York, Gould, in receipt of Chapin's telegram, decided it was time to bring matters to a head, and for that he needed Fisk. One of the mysteries of the gold panic is when and to what extent Jim Fisk became financially involved. He was more than willing to help his friend hobnob with the President, but he was much more cautious about committing his own capital to an enterprise he thought risky in the extreme. Gould did not really need Fisk's money, however. What he needed at the climactic moment was the histrionic talent that Fisk possessed in such abundance and which Gould himself so utterly lacked.

Gould assured Fisk that all was in hand, telling him that "this matter is all fixed up. Butterfield is all right. Corbin has got Butterfield all right, and Corbin has got Grant all right."[16] Fisk called on the Corbins and was assured by the President's sister herself: "I know there will be no gold sold by the government; I am quite positive there will be no gold sold; for this is the chance of a life time for us; you need not have any uneasiness whatever."[17] Fisk was convinced. While he had grave doubts that gold could be cornered honestly, "the scent of corruption"[18] was enough to lure him in.

Representative James A. Garfield, who headed the House committee that investigated the gold panic the following year and who one day, briefly, would be President himself, was deeply steeped in classical learning (he had once devised a particularly elegant proof of the Pythagorean theorem). In the committee's report he wrote of Fisk's entrance into active participation now that he was sure that Grant was in on the plot. "He joined the movement at once," Garfield reported, "and brought to its aid all the force of his magnetic and infectious enthusiasm. The malign influence which Catiline wielded over the reckless and abandoned youth of Rome, finds a fitting parallel in the power which Fisk carried into Wall Street, when, followed by the thugs of Erie and the debauchees of the Opera House, he swept into the Gold Room and defied both the Street and the Treasury."[19]

By the end of the week Fisk would hold gold contracts that according to his testimony amounted to between $50,000,000 and $60,000,000. He recruited his own network of brokers, such as his old partner William Belden and Albert Speyers—neither of whom had much reputation on the Street before the panic or any at all afterward—to act for him entirely separately from Gould's brokers. He loudly proclaimed that he would wager any part of $50,000 that gold would be up to 145 or 150 or whatever point he was currently aiming at.

Jim Fisk knew how to be a public bull. When William Worthington Fowler sought him out to get his opinion on the future of gold that week, Fowler encountered him outside the Opera House, in the act of handing a lady up into a carriage.

"Gold!" replied Fisk to Fowler's inquiry. "Gold! sell it short and invite me to your funeral."[20]

The other members of the pool also increased their purchases. Henry Smith, Gould's partner in the brokerage firm of Smith, Gould and Martin, held about $50,000,000. The price of gold began to move inexorably up. On Monday it closed at 137⅜. On Tuesday it nudged ahead to 137½, but on Wednesday, when Fisk himself appeared in the Gold Room for the first time, it soared through the 140 level to close at 141½, while the by now vast short interest squealed in pain.

The shorts included nearly everybody who was anybody on Wall Street, with the conspicuous exceptions of Drew and Vanderbilt. Fisk testified, and no one contradicted him, that the list began with Jay Cooke, the country's most prominent banker, thanks to his efforts on behalf of selling war bonds, and "probably went through two hundred and fifty houses. In fact, it included nearly every firm in this country of any magnitude whatever."[21] These prominent, highly respectable, and mostly very savvy brokers and bankers had not closed out their short positions earlier because they could not believe, apparently, that anyone would be so brazen or so foolhardy as to attempt a genuine corner in gold. Rather, they had viewed it as a mere bull movement that would soon run its course, after which real market forces would reassert themselves and drive the price back down.

Secretary Boutwell was bombarded by telegrams from important Wall Streeters, many of them Republicans and heavy contributors to the party, demanding that the government take action to break the corner.

On Wednesday afternoon, in this atmosphere of increasing frenzy, Gould received an urgent message from Corbin. Mrs. Grant's letter had arrived. Gould called on Corbin late that evening. Garfield described the scene in his report: "Shut up in the library, near midnight, Corbin was bending over the table and straining with dim eyes to decipher and read the contents of a letter, written in pencil, to his wife, while the great gold gambler, looking over his shoulder, caught with his sharper vision every word."[22]

Corbin, frightened down to his toenails, wanted out then and there. His stock-in-trade was his brother-in-law, and he desperately wanted to be able to assure Grant that he had no interest in gold whatever. But he also wanted his profits. He asked Gould to take the gold off his hands and give him a check for the difference between the 133 at which the gold had been bought and the 141½ it had closed at that afternoon. Gould turned this down but offered to give Corbin his check for $100,000 if he would agree to stay in and shut up. "Mr. Corbin," Gould told him, "I am undone if that letter gets out."[23] In the event, Gould neither handed over the check nor did Corbin release the letter, which, after all, would have ruined him as much as Gould.

But Gould knew, as did nobody else on the Street except, probably, Fisk, that the game was up and it was time to cut and run. While Fisk continued to buy, Gould became a heavy net seller. "My purchases were very light," Gould testified regarding his actions on Thursday. "I was a net seller of gold that day. I purchased merely enough to make believe that I was a bull."[24] Despite Gould's secret sales, the price of gold continued to edge higher, closing at 143⅜ as volume exploded. It had been far above average all week, but on Thursday the Gold Exchange Bank cleared $239,000,000, well over three times the normal daily volume.

On Thursday evening, many members of the pool assembled at the Opera House to plan their moves for the next day. Fisk suggested that a list of everyone known to be short be drawn up and published in the next morning's newspapers together with a blunt warning to settle before 3 P.M. at 160 or be prepared to settle the following day at 200. Someone pointed out that that might very well constitute evidence of conspiracy under the laws of New York State, and the idea was dropped.

•

The next morning dawned clear and pleasant, the sort of September day that justifies fall's reputation for having New York's finest weather. And it was as clear as the weather to all who had even a bowing acquaintance with Wall Street that Friday, September 24th, was likely to prove a day to remember. Gould went downtown for the first time in the affair, which until then he had handled from Castle Erie, well connected to Wall Street by telegraph. Gould and Fisk arrived in the Street each in a manner that might have been expected of him. Gould probably took public transportation and slipped in a back door while Fisk arrived at the front door in an open carriage flanked by a pair of actresses blowing kisses at the assembling multitudes.

The pair set up their command post in the back office of William Heath & Company. (Heath complained later that they did not even bother to ask permission.) Erie Railway guards were assigned to watch the door. Broad and Wall streets, always crowded on business days, were already densely packed, and trading on the street started long before the official ten-o'clock opening.

From the start the volume was enormous, although just how enormous will never be known, for the Gold Exchange Bank never managed to settle its clearings for that day. Fisk instructed Belden and Speyers, in effect, to buy all the gold that was offered, and the price quickly climbed to 145. By 10:30 Butterfield telegraphed to Boutwell that the price was 150.[25] The New York *Herald* the next day reported that "it was a desperate battle between two hosts of gamblers, whose minds were quickened by incessant plots, whose hearts were cold and their greed rapacious. Gold, Gold, Gold was the cry."[26]

The action in the Gold Room itself was confusion compounded by terror and greed. Brokers screamed and gesticulated, some cooling themselves occasionally at the fountain of Cupid that gurgled so incongruously in the middle of the room. The indicator, a device that showed the latest price of gold, moved frantically, trying to keep pace with the action. Indeed, Garfield reported that it, and its many duplicates in financial centers around the country, could not keep pace. "The complicated mechanism of these indicators," Garfield explained, "is moved by the electric current carried over telegraph wires directly from the Gold Room, and it is in evidence that in many instances these wires were melted or burned off in the efforts of operators to keep up with the news."[27] As brokers and bankers in these distant cities clustered around the telegraph wires to get the latest reports, commerce all but stopped from Boston to San Francisco. For two brief hours, the Gold Room was the scene of virtually the only financial action in the whole United States.

It is not hard to understand why, for money was in thrall. It was not wheat or pork bellies that Gould and his allies were seeking to control. It was gold, legal tender throughout the world, the very stuff and symbol of wealth itself.

Outside the Gold Room, on Broad Street, matters were no less uproarious. "Broad Street was thronged by some thousands of men . . . and within an hour staid businessmen, coatless, collarless, and some hatless, raged in the street, as if the inmates of a dozen lunatic asylums had been turned loose. Up the price of gold went steadily amid shouts, screams, and the wringing of hands."[28] So great did the commotion become that a Brooklyn regiment was ordered to assemble at its armory in case it should be needed to restore order, though the soldiers would presumably have had to commandeer a ferryboat in order to effect a timely crossing of the still unbridged East River.

At Heath & Company matters were somewhat more orderly. Gould sat on one side of the room quietly giving sell orders as they were needed and tearing up paper into confetti, while Fisk, coatless

THE GOLD ROOM, SEPTEMBER 24TH, 1869 Matters were a good deal
more chaotic than the artist managed to convey. *Courtesy of the Union
Club Library*

and looking "like a bull badly baited, puffing and blowing at a great rate,"[29] was on the other shouting buy orders. Meanwhile Willard and Smith and other members of the clique were leading a steady parade of shorts into a private office and threatening 200 gold if they did not settle while the settling was good, as many of them chose to do.

Still, there was confusion even among the clique. Gould's brokers, such as Carver & Company and Lockwood & Company, were instructed to sell but under no circumstances to sell to Belden and Speyers or anyone else acting for Fisk. Even so, in the uproar they sometimes inadvertently did so, and Willard screamed at them at one point, "Goddamn it! you are selling right back to the clique brokers."[30]

At 11:20 Butterfield telegraphed that gold was at 158.

E. C. Stedman, not only a broker but the poet laureate of Wall Street, remembered the day:

> Zounds! how the price went flashing through
> Wall Street, William, Broad Street, New!
> All the specie in the land
> Held in one ring by a giant hand,—
> For millions more it was ready to pay,
> And throttle the Street on hangman's day.
> Up from the Gold-pit's nether hell,
> While the innocent fountain rose and fell,
> Loud and higher the bidding rose,
> And the bulls, triumphant, faced their foes.
> It seemed as if Satan himself were in it,
> Lifting it,—one per cent a minute. . . .

What was going on was perhaps the greatest bear panic in history, and, as Jim Fisk said, "There is no fright as great as the fright in Wall Street when the bears become panicky. Burnt brandy won't save 'em, for the very reason that they have sold what they have not got."[31] The price of gold was shooting upward not because there was so much buying but because, relative to demand, there was almost no selling. The clique were the only sellers and they were unloading as much as possible privately, while Fisk was doing his very considerable best to make it seem that they were large buyers. Men who had made comfortable livings for years on the Street confronted the prospect of imminent ruin.

Speyers was running around the Gold Room like a madman shouting that he would take any part of five millions at ever higher prices. At 11:40 Butterfield telegraphed Washington that gold was at 160 and moving upward still. But Butterfield must have known that Washington was about to move, for Gould soon found out that Joseph W. Seligman, Butterfield's broker, was quietly selling gold, a move he would have made only with inside information. Speyers was anything but quiet in his buying, screaming that he would take $5,000,000 in gold at 160. But there were no sellers.

Then James Brown, of James Brown & Company, and certainly no part of the clique, suddenly, firmly, shouted, "Sold!"

Like a hysteric after a slap across the face, the market came abruptly to its senses, the terrible psychology of panic broken in an instant. The price that had ratcheted up point by point all morning now plummeted with equal speed. While Speyers, a fool—which is precisely why Fisk had chosen him—was still trying to buy more at 160, gold was being sold freely for 140 not ten feet away from him.

Ironically, the much-dreaded, long-prayed-for telegram from Washington was sent at almost the same moment that Brown had made its dispatch unnecessary, 11:42 to be exact, and arrived in Butterfield's office minutes later. The Assistant Treasurer was ordered to sell $4,000,000 in gold, but the need for the order had already been obviated. At noon Butterfield could telegraph Washington that gold was at 140 and falling.

Brown, who must have been one of the coolest people on the Street, had needed great courage to sell short into the teeth of such a buyer panic. He was, after all, short of gold already. Anger, apparently, had helped. "We had transactions . . . on our books," he explained to the House committee some months later, "running from the time when gold was at 133, and we had paid, paid, paid through that infernal combination that was entered into up to 144 and the question arose with us: 'Is this thing to be perpetuated? Are we to stand by and be flayed by this unscrupulous party. . . ?' "

By early afternoon a mood almost of listlessness had settled over the Street. "For the remainder of the day," reported the *Herald*, "the Gold Room and all the approaches thereto were like the vicinity of a great fire or calamity after the climax has passed. A sudden quiet and calm came over the scene. The brokers, hoarse with shouting earlier in the day, were gathered in groups comparing notes and talking in subdued tones. Each few minutes the hammer of the presiding officer called the assemblage to order, and gold was bought or sold 'under the rule' for the account of some defaulting bull or bear."[32]

Gould and Fisk, their work done, left the Street about 1:30, heading for the Opera House, which would serve very well in the next few days as a fortress against the injured and outraged. Fisk seemed cheerful enough, being overheard to remark that "these are high old times."[33] But Fisk described Gould as being so drained that "there is nothing left of him but a heap of clothes and a pair of eyes."[34] At the afternoon call of the New York Stock Exchange, Speyers stood up and said, "I understand threats have been made of shooting me. I am ready to be shot." No one took him up on the offer, but he was roundly hissed by everyone present.[35]

To the press Gould would only say, "I regret very much this depression in financial circles, but I predicted it long ago. I was in no way instrumental in producing the panic." Fisk noted with mock peevishness that "a fellow can't have a little innocent fun without everybody raising a hulloo and going wild."[36]

•

While the panic was over there were a good many pieces that needed picking up. Fisk described the cleanup as being a case of "each man drag out his own corpse,"[37] and Gould and Fisk did their best to make it as difficult as possible. They got the judges to issue a slew of injunctions, no fewer than twelve on Monday, September 27th, alone. Asked about them, Hiram C. Rogers, Assistant Cashier of the Gold Exchange Bank, said, "Oh, yes; they came in there by the hat full, until finally we did not know what to do. We were enjoined against performing almost every act."[38]

Confusion was just what Gould and Fisk wanted, and they sowed it so effectively that the bank did not manage to get back into operation until November 22nd, and then only with the mess more swept under the rug than straightened out. Fisk repudiated the contracts that had been made for him by Belden and Speyers, who both went broke, although Belden's losses were made good by Fisk and Gould. The Tenth National Bank, which had been swooped down upon by federal bank examiners the very day of the panic and found to have certified checks for far more than was on deposit to cover them, also escaped more than censure, for the practice was not then illegal.

Corbin's reputation, such as it was, lay in ruins. Grant would no longer give him the time of day, and he had been exposed as that saddest of creatures, the fixer who couldn't even fix. He and his wife, their circumstances reduced, moved to Jersey City. As for Butterfield, saved from malfeasance by the force of circumstances if not conscience, he managed to escape largely unscathed, taking care to resign before the congressional hearings could make it seem as though he were doing so under pressure.

A major question is whether or not the clique made money. The *Herald*, for one, had no doubt of it, reporting the next morning that "Satan sits complacently upon the unholy spoils,"[39] but historians are by no means so sure. If $100,000,000 in gold had been bought at an average price of 135 and sold for an average of 150, the profits would have amounted to $15,000,000. But matters were hardly so tidy as that. For one thing Gould did not settle the last suit generated by the gold panic until 1877, and there were hundreds of suits in all.

When he was asked by the congressional investigation what had happened to the clique's profits, Fisk replied that they had gone "where the woodbine twineth," a phrase that immediately caught the fancy of the entire country. Woodbine, another name for honeysuckle, was often grown around outhouses to help mask the smell. In our more technological and less euphemistic age, Fisk might have said "down the toilet."

The confusion so deliberately and successfully created by Fisk and Gould cannot be unraveled from a distance of a hundred years. While it will never be known for sure whether or not Gould and Fisk made money in the gold corner, it certainly secured forever their places in the popular imagination as titans in the great game. Only two years later, Black Friday, as September 24th, 1869, was immediately dubbed, had already taken on mythic proportions, and the London *Times* wrote that "the attempt to 'corner gold' in that terrible week was so near complete success that it appeared to the imagination of Wall Street like the defeat of Hannibal or Napoleon—a victory of Fate over Genius."[40]

What is equally certain is that the Gold Panic's immediate direct effect upon the stock market and consequently its indirect effect on the Erie Railway was disastrous for the Erie and eventually for its two leading lights as well.

Black Friday did not have many long-lasting effects on the Street. Because it was a buyer panic, it did not herald a period of economic depression. It was, rather, essentially a flash in the pan, however brilliant the flash. But its long-term effects upon government policy were considerably greater.

As Garfield, the soundest of sound-money men, wrote in his report, "So long as we have two standards of value recognized by law, which may be made to vary in respect to each other by artificial means, so long will speculation in the price of gold offer temptations too great to be resisted."[41]

Jay Gould, who in all likelihood was completely indifferent, had at least made the politics of returning to the gold standard very much easier, if only by providing so spectacular an example of the consequences of not doing so.

CHAPTER FOURTEEN

President Gould and Colonel Fisk

IF the victims of Black Friday were primarily small houses and individuals, there was nonetheless one major casualty on the Street: Lockwood and Company, the largest stockbrokerage house in New York, headed by Legrand Lockwood. A major speculator in railroads, Lockwood was treasurer of the recently merged Lake Shore and Michigan Southern line, which ran between Chicago and several of the burgeoning cities in Michigan and Ohio. The Lake Shore had recently snapped up the small Buffalo and Erie Railroad, which ran between those two cities, thus providing a link between the Lake Shore and both the New York Central and the Erie. This gave the Lake Shore great leverage in the race to Chicago.

Lockwood and Vanderbilt had seemed to be moving closer together for some time, and it was widely assumed that there was an "understanding" and perhaps even a consolidation in the works between the New York Central and the Lake Shore. But Lockwood, with the worst possible timing, got greedy and overplayed his hand. He made a sudden deal with Jay Gould that called for the Erie to begin actually laying down the much-talked-about third rail to accommodate standard-gauge rolling stock. Gould announced the issuance of $5,000,000 in convertible bonds to pay for it, the first issuance of Erie bonds in years to be publicly announced in advance.

This agreement, Lockwood thought, would make it possible for him to play Vanderbilt off against Gould.

The Commodore was not about to let himself be whipsawed by Lockwood or anyone else, and he suddenly threw all the Lake Shore stock he had been buying onto the market on Saturday, September 18th, driving the price from 106 to below par. The following week, as the gold corner culminated, credit tightened fearfully on the Street, and the speculative railroad stocks declined steeply in consequence. Not even the mighty New York Central was exempt on Wednesday as Gould tightened the screws in the Gold Room and Vanderbilt went to Albany to see about the consolidation with the Hudson River Railroad.

"On the 22nd," the *Herald* later reported, "just after the New York Central had been called at the morning board, and while the president was passing to the next stock on the list, there was an outcry at the rear of the room. Central had broken; no one could tell why. It rallied temporarily and then broke again, falling in a few days about sixty [points]."[1]

Vanderbilt ordinarily owned his stocks free and clear and had no concern about any temporary drop in price that resulted from speculative shenanigans by the likes of Gould. Lockwood, who had borrowed heavily on his Lake Shore holdings, was not in the same invulnerable position, and the fortunes of both Lockwood and Company and its senior partner were intimately bound up with the price of Lake Shore stock and the value of the gold contracts it had been brokering in large numbers in the Gold Room.

In the turmoil that engulfed the Street in the week that followed Black Friday, railroad stocks fell across the board by about 25 percent from their recent highs. The price of Erie had recently risen sharply on the announcement that the days of the printing press were over and that the stock would conform to the New York Stock Exchange rule and be registered. But, in the wake of the panic, Erie fell back from 38 to 27, while Lake Shore declined from 98 to 76. This was too much for Lockwood. His firm had been left holding the bag on many gold contracts, and on Wednesday, September 29th, Lockwood and Company was forced to suspend business.

Vanderbilt, seeing his opportunity, moved immediately to take it. He borrowed $10,000,000 from the great London banking house of Baring Brothers on the security of his Hudson River Railroad stock, and with this money behind him bought 70,000 shares of Lake Shore, 20 percent of the total outstanding, and enough for control.

Before long the new president of the Lake Shore and Michigan Southern Railroad would be son-in-law Horace F. Clark, while two of Vanderbilt's most trusted lieutenants, Augustus Schell and James H. Banker, were vice president and treasurer and members of the new board of directors.

The Commodore and the New York Central were through to Chicago, and he had done it at the fire-sale prices that had resulted from Jay Gould's speculations in gold. The Erie Railway was now the only one of the three New York City trunk lines to remain a regional carrier, hemmed in by the New York Central to the north and the Pennsylvania to the south. It is no wonder that the *Herald* reported the next day that a "grim smile"[2] could be seen on the statue being erected in Vanderbilt's honor in what had formerly been St. John's Park.

•

St. John's Park had been developed in the 1820's in the once swampy area west of Broadway and south of Canal Street known as Lispenard's Meadow. It had been one of Trinity Church's many successful exercises in urban planning and for the next few decades had been among the city's most fashionable residential areas. Then, as the city expanded uptown, the Lower West Side fell increasingly to commerce, and the park's wealthy residents began to flee northward to Washington Square, Gramercy Park, and Fifth Avenue. By the 1860's the area was solidly commercial, and the once fine houses surrounding the beautiful green had declined into boarding establishments and tenements.

The only prominent person to remain in St. John's Park was John Ericsson, the designer of the *Monitor,* who stubbornly continued to live there until his death in 1889. "All around the residence of Ericsson," William Croffut remembered, "were aristocratic mansions in a state of decay—mansions of thirty or forty feet front with vast parlors turned into tenements or cheap stores, and porches once imposing with their half-moons of radiating glass above the doors and long, narrow windows of many-shaped glass flanking them, with doors now smudged and crippled and the handsome windows broken. The house of the great inventor was about the only one in good condition."[3]

In 1866 the Commodore bought the park for $1,000,000 and ripped out its two hundred trees preparatory to building a depot to handle the Hudson River Railroad's freight business. At some point it was decided that the west pediment of the new depot, facing Hudson Street, should be adorned with a monument honoring the Commodore. Whoever had the idea (and it might even have been the Commodore himself), it was certainly grand enough, and the *Herald* noted that "it is not so prodigious as the Pyramid of Cheops, nor so lofty as the Colossus of Rhodes, but it will do."[4] The whole pediment of the building, 31 feet high and 150 feet long, was to be filled with what amounted to Vanderbilt's biography, written in 100,000 pounds of bronze.

A central niche held a statue of Vanderbilt twelve feet high and weighing four tons, while on his left was depicted his career in ships, beginning with his first periauger and including the *North Star,* in which he had toured Europe, and the *C. Vanderbilt,* which he had donated to the country in defense of the Union. On his right the short history of railroads was laid out in similar high relief.

Opinions on the artistic quality of the monument were sharply divided. George Templeton Strong, getting old and crotchety, thought the whole thing vulgar beyond belief. Vanderbilt "is a millionaire of millionaires," he wrote in his diary when the work was unveiled. "And therefore we bow down before him, and worship him, with a hideous group of molten images, with himself for a central figure, at a cost of $800,000. These be thy Gods, O Israel!"[5]

Still, he couldn't resist making a pilgrimage of sorts to the shrine, although it did not improve his opinion of it. "It's a 'mixelaneous biling' of cogwheels, steamships, primeval forests, anchors, locomotives, periaugers . . . railroad trains, wild ducks (or possibly sea gulls) and squatter shanties, with a colossal Cornelius Vanderbilt looming up in the midst of the chaos, and beaming benignantly down on Hudson Street, like a *pater patriae*—draped in a dressing gown or overcoat, the folds whereof are most wooden. As a work of art, it is bestial."[6]

Horace Greeley, personally fond of Vanderbilt and less stuffy than Strong, only lamented that the artist, the now largely forgotten Ernst Plassman, had failed to capture the essence of the Commodore's physiognomy, which Greeley thought to be among the "noblest" in the country. The *Times,* for its part, ignored its artistic aspects but noted approvingly that it "will bear his proud and impressive personality and his famous name down through the generations and the centuries indefinitely."[7]

But the *Herald,* which took a wider view of the bronze and its purpose, was not so sure. "The objection that this 'bronze' is only a monument to the achievements of a private citizen is of no force," it noted; "for in truth the 'bronze' is a monument of the greatest material inventions and enterprises of the nineteenth century. In other words, this beautiful work is a monument of the genius and progress of the age, and in this light it will be a valuable legacy to posterity. The [Central] Park is the place for it, because this monument should not be lost, and we know of no other place on the island where there is any security for its preservation."[8]

No one took Bennett up on his suggestion, but his fears for its future in New York's continuing and turbulent development proved all too true. Just as Lispenard's Meadow had given way to St. John's Park and the park in turn to a railroad depot, so the depot itself fell before the automobile, and the area became the Manhattan approaches to the Holland Tunnel. In the flood tide of reaction against all things Victorian that so marked the early twentieth century, no one thought the Vanderbilt bronze worth preserving, so this incomparable artifact of its time and place was junked. Only the central statue survives, now fittingly placed high in front of the crowning glory of the railroad age, Grand Central Terminal, looking out upon the heart of the great city that the Commodore did so much to create.

The Vanderbilt bronze was formally dedicated on November 10th, 1869, and virtually all the leading officials of the city, state, and federal governments were there. Mayor A. Oakey Hall delivered the principal address.

While the official ceremonies took place uptown, some unofficial ceremonies were taking place in the gallery overlooking the Long Room of the Stock Exchange, as brokers amused themselves by burlesquing both the Commodore and his monument. A "statue" was to be unveiled and one of the assembled brokers rose to deliver the dedicatory address, but before he could do so he was "served" with an injunction, the server being then hauled off "to an unknown fate."

The orator delivered a speech on the Commodore's love of watered stock. Vanderbilt, he said, in the words of the *Herald*'s paraphrase, "was originally a waterman, and had made water the 'Central' idea of his life. Formerly men had been made to see double by other liquids besides, but the Commodore had made the grand discovery that water, simple and pure, in the hands of a financial genius, possessed the extraordinary power not only of making one see a thing double, but also of making the thing itself double."[9]

THE UNVEILING OF THE VANDERBILT BRONZE   *Courtesy of The New-York Historical Society, New York City*

The statue was then unveiled, revealing a "hideously ugly broker in a wig and mask," one arm across his chest, while the other, wearing a boxing glove, held a watering can labeled "Central 207," the price—it had been announced ten days earlier—at which the New York Central was to be consolidated with the Hudson River Railroad. The statue unveiled, the assembled brokers joined in a tribute to the Commodore sung to the tune of "John Brown's Body":

> His watering machinery as yet has never failed,
> And to show our gratitude to him this statue's now unveiled.
> Before Jim Fisk, Jay Gould and Co. his courage never failed,
> As he goes driving on.[10]

The Commodore at this point in his life was rapidly becoming a living monument, regarded with awe by nearly everyone, although, as the *Herald* wrote, "there is nothing ministerial in his conversation or bearing." Indeed, the *Herald* thought that "he is a jovial companion and a lover of a good game of whist, a good dinner, a good cigar and a bottle of good old port. He dresses plainly, generally in black, and has a weakness for white cravats" (a fashion that had gone out of daytime use by 1850 and survives today only in the utmost evening formality of "white tie").[11]

Despite the high regard with which he was held on Wall Street, Vanderbilt seldom went downtown in person anymore, preferring to handle matters from the office on West 4th Street next to his stables. But in the days following the Gold Panic he visited the Street a couple of times, helping to steady it by his mere presence and causing as much of a commotion as a modern-day rock star. As any great celebrity must, he had learned the trick of never stopping to talk in public but rather moved steadily onward, "scattering nods here and there as he progressed through the crowds, but studiously avoiding conversation with acquaintances."

"Central's coming up, Commodore," a young man yelled to him as he moved along.

"Top o' the heap still, my boy," agreed Vanderbilt cheerfully as he headed toward his downtown office at Bowling Green.[12]

•

Unfortunately for the brokers, they had plenty of time to play in the autumn of 1869, for business was way down. The previous October, as Gould maneuvered Uncle Daniel toward catastrophe, a total of 2,362,027 shares had traded on the Stock Exchange, but this year as the shock waves caused by the Gold Panic reverberated through the market, only 447,911 shares changed hands. Even trading in government bonds—the mainstays of widows and orphans rather than speculators—shrank by more than half. The worst-hit group of securities were the speculative railroad stocks. In December of that year only 95,091 shares of railroad companies were traded during the entire month, less than one-tenth the amount of the previous December.[13]

The panic had caused a wave of personal bankruptcies, and among those it hadn't ruined it had certainly induced a decided caution. The little guys, always present in large numbers at the height of a bull market, had withdrawn from Wall Street in droves. "One very important cause of the present depression," said the *Commercial and Financial Chronicle*, "arises from the fact that the class of smaller operators have been thus mulcted by a minority of wealthier speculators; and it is not easy to see how there can be any important revival in these operations until a new class of dupes have been drawn into the market."[14]

If the public's interest in Wall Street had much diminished, its interest in Fisk and Gould had redoubled, and their names, unknown a year and a half earlier, were now familiar to everyone in the country who read a newspaper. Shortly after the panic the *Herald* sent one of its reporters, George Crouch, to Castle Erie at Fisk's invitation.

Fisk, apparently, wanted his version of events to be recorded, but he must have been much disappointed by what finally appeared on October 8th, for Crouch crowed about bearding in their den "the great gorilla of Wall Street, the gold-gobbling Gould; the amphibious what-is-it? or 'ring'-tailed financial orangutan otherwise known to naturalists and the world at large as the 'irrepressible Jim Fisk, Junior.' "[15]

Crouch's interview took place in the middle of the night, and he described the circumstances in the best melodrama style. "Time:—near midnight. The representative of the *Herald* discovered in the depths of a capacious armchair, cushioned with fawn-colored morocco, embossed with the gracefully entwined initials 'E.R.' in gold. A sliding panel moves slowly in its grooves and the portly form of the Prince of Erie oozes as slowly and silently through the aperture. The Prince is gorgeously arrayed in costly velvet, the sheen of priceless diamonds and the glare of his trebly refined gold surround him with a radiance before which the very gas jets wink and blink and 'pale their ineffectual fires.' "

Fisk complained bitterly to Crouch that he and Gould had been quite innocent of any wrongdoing and that it was Corbin who was to blame for everything. Fisk said that he felt trapped like "a tiger in a menagerie" and that public opinion made it impossible for him to leave that ultimate in gilded cages, the Grand Opera House. Fisk was now, according to Crouch, "alarmed at the increasing fury of the honest bark of that most faithful of watch dogs, public opinion."

Feeding stories to reporters and expecting their editors to swallow them whole clearly did not work well, given the results with George Crouch and the *Herald*. But Gould and Fisk, ever resourceful, soon had a better idea: they hired George Crouch and employed him as what was quite probably the first corporate public-relations expert. Although he apparently did not leave the *Herald* immediately or tell Bennett about his new connection, the age of the flack had dawned.

In December, 1869, Crouch wrote a highly laudatory article, which was printed in the New York *World* (a strongly Democratic paper sympathetic to William M. Tweed) under the title "Another Chapter of Erie," and which was soon issued as a pamphlet. Before long he was turning out pamphlets and articles supporting the Erie Railway and its management, laying on the flattery with a trowel. In one piece he unblushingly wrote that Fisk and Gould "will deserve a bronze memorial apiece—one at New York and the other at San Francisco, where the western terminus of the Erie is destined to be located at no distant date."[16]

In March, 1870, he testified on the Erie's behalf before a committee of the New York State Assembly, claiming, presumably with a straight face, to be the owner of five thousand shares of Erie stock. Reporters were very poorly paid at this time (and as a consequence often took bribes from politicians—not to mention railroad managers—to look the other way). The *North American Review* had complained that there was only one journalist in all New York, other than the newspaper owners and their families, who was paid a living wage.[17] Undoubtedly Crouch had received a considerable increase in pay when he left the *Herald*, but it is altogether unlikely that he had acquired anything like the fortune that five thousand shares of Erie represented.

On January 17th, 1870, the Erie Railway issued its annual report for the fiscal year that had ended the previous September. It was the first full year under the management of Gould and Fisk, and interest in the report was intense. Almost certainly written by George Crouch, it was printed in newspapers around the country.

Gross revenues on the Erie, according to the report, were up a healthy 16.3 percent to $16,721,500 while total operating expenses actually declined by more than 4.4 percent. Still, when interest on the bonds had been paid there was none left over for a dividend on the stock, which now totaled 780,000 shares. Horace Greeley, for one, was unimpressed with this performance. "Alaska has a tropical climate," he sneered in the *Tribune* on January 21st, "and strawberries in their season. The Borgia was a saintly, much slandered martyr of a woman. The Devil is white. Mr. Jay Gould shows how *admirable, successful and economical* is his management of the Erie Railway." As far as Greeley and a good many others were concerned, it was a matter of no dividend, no deal, for all the fine words in the world couldn't make up for the lack of a return on the capital of the long-suffering shareholders.

The report argued with some justice, however, that the Erie was in such a state of disrepair when Gould became president that he was forced to spend large sums to repair and upgrade the right-of-way—finally beginning to install the steel rails that Drew had talked about for so long—and to pay for maintenance that had been deferred for years. The money spent on maintaining the right-of-way that year had increased by more than 25 percent, at least according to the report, which was, of course, prepared by Gould and not certified by independent auditors.

In addition, the report stated that the Erie had added seventy-seven engines and more than a thousand freight cars to the rolling stock, while retiring much older equipment. And the Erie had begun to replace the old, vulnerable, and expensive-to-maintain wooden trestles with new iron ones, including a six-hundred-foot span across the Susquehanna at Binghamton.

There can be no doubt that under Gould and Fisk the Erie at least began to recover from the years of utter neglect it had suffered under the previous regimes. Gould cared no more about the stockholders' interests than had Drew, but he was a much more intelligent and farsighted man. He must have known, as he would subsequently demonstrate with the Union Pacific and other roads, that a prosperous railroad is a far more powerful weapon to use on Wall Street than a derelict one. Gould would never pay the detailed attention necessary to get the Erie's finances really under control or institute the sort of strong, hands-on, cost-conscious management techniques of William H. Vanderbilt that had helped make the Commodore's railroads so profitable. Indeed, Gould often could not even spare the attention or the money to pay his workers on time.

The *Herald*, in its characteristic enterprising way, sent a reporter up the Erie line all the way to Buffalo and back to examine matters for himself. He agreed "that no matter what Fisk and Gould may do in Wall Street they have done much of substantial service for the Erie Railway." The anonymous reporter—bylines were still many years away—talked to numerous people, all as anonymous as himself, who praised the Erie under its new management fulsomely. "In New York," he wrote from upstate, "the Erie management is more widely known by connection with the recent gold conspiracy, but here in Buffalo its fame rests principally upon the genius and enterprise of its guiding spirits. 'While Drew had charge of the road,' remarked a leading flour merchant to your correspondent, 'I would not send a single barrel of flour over it, much more risk myself on it. I did my business with the Central, but now that the Erie is in good hands I send all my stuff over it.' "[18]

So favorable were the *Herald*'s articles that it is hard to escape the suspicion that George Crouch had a hand in them. It is possible, if he had already left the *Herald*'s employ, that he bamboozled the reporter assigned to the story, who would not yet have learned to beware the clutches of the professional public-relations man. More likely, he was still working for the *Herald* and sold the whole idea of the trip to Bennett or to Bennett's son, who was assuming more and more responsibility at the paper, without bothering to tell him of his new connection with the Erie, and wrote the articles himself. Their style, not that there is much, is similar to articles known to have been written by Crouch.

Whatever the truth, about the only caveat in the whole series of articles is in the concluding sentences: "It is fair to say that there is nothing strained in the interesting report made by Jay Gould to the stockholders. If he succeed in declaring a dividend one of these fine days everybody will believe him. The report is satisfactory enough but a dividend would be still more so."

If there was much in Gould's annual report that was disingenuous, simply false, or just omitted, it was no different from many others in that respect. New York State railroads were required to file an annual report with Albany, but there was no requirement that these reports be audited. There were as yet no recognized standards to which annual reports were expected to adhere, for the certified public accountant had not yet been invented. The *Commercial and Financial Chronicle,* which catered to brokers, who had a considerable interest in timely, accurate, and inclusive financial information, noted that the managers of corporations had no self-interest whatever in providing it. Just the opposite, they had every reason to bury any mistakes or embarrassments as deeply as possible. And inside information was personally useful to management, especially on Wall Street, only so long as it remained inside.

In December, 1868, Gould and Fisk had undertaken to negotiate a new lease arrangement between the Erie and the United States Express Company. Before taking any corporate action, however, they personally sold the stock of the express company short and only then announced that the company would have to pay $500,000 more per year to use the Erie's facilities. The express company immediately balked at this considerable increase, and so the Erie Railway abruptly canceled the lease and announced that henceforth it would handle its own express business. On this news the stock of the express company fell from 59 to 43, allowing Gould and Fisk to settle their short contracts at a considerable profit.

Then, after going long the stock, they compromised with the express company, publicly announced the settlement, and watched with satisfaction as the stock promptly climbed back up into the 60's.[19]

"The one condition of success in such intrigues," noted the *Chronicle,* "is secrecy. Secure to the public at large the opportunity of knowing all that a director can know of the value and prospects of his own stock, and the occupation of the 'speculative director' is gone. There will be some difficulty in effecting this in detail, but it can be substantially done with great simplicity. Let it be made the duty of the officers of every railway company to publish all its financial statistics in a clear, intelligible form, as soon as they can reasonably make them up. The full balance sheet of the road, showing the sources and amounts of its revenues, the disposition made of every dollar, the earnings of its property, the expenses of working, of supplies, of new construction, and of repairs, the amount and form of its debt, and the disposition made of all its funds, ought to be made up and published every quarter."[20]

These eminently sensible ideas, which today are taken entirely for granted, were quite new when proposed by the *Chronicle* in

May, 1870. At that time, other than railroad and canal companies, there were hardly any public corporations in existence, and not a single industrial concern was listed on the New York Stock Exchange.

By the end of the century fast-multiplying industrial companies would need more capital than could possibly be raised within a single family or by subscription, as the railroads' original capital had been largely raised. They were forced to turn to Wall Street for the money, and there a new breed of bankers, epitomized by J. P. Morgan, raised the required capital in the by then far larger open market. It was these underwriters who first imposed the discipline of both periodic and inclusive financial reports. It was Wall Street, intimately familiar with human frailty, that required the accountants to certify these reports.

•

Fisk's non-railroad activities continued unabated as he sought outlets for his inexhaustible energies. In early 1870 he enjoyed his first theatrical smash hit, an extravaganza entitled *The Twelve Temptations*. It more than compensated for its dearth of plot by its huge cast and spectacular special effects. It featured sumptuous costumes, a waterfall, and even chorus girls juggling balls of fire. Made of sulphur and magnesium, they sent sparks and cinders flying in all directions, frequently burning the performers, sometimes seriously. *The Twelve Temptations* was exactly Jim Fisk's idea of theater, and New Yorkers heartily agreed, flocking to see it for months, often twice, for Fisk maintained two chorus lines—one all blondes, the other brunettes—and alternated them.

The night of the grand opening, Fisk gave a party that left the *Herald*, for one, agog. "In the course of human events," it said the next day, "many things . . . happen such as dynasties being overturned, monarchs dethroned and republics established; but such a reception as that given last evening by the Prince of Erie, at his princely palace, the Grand Opera House, is without precedent in the historical annals that make centuries notable and men's lives sublime."[21] Although most of the performance was canceled (in order, it was piously explained, to avoid running over into the Sabbath) no one seemed to mind, and the party went on, Sabbath or no Sabbath, far into the night.

Nor were the guests just the usual rich and political riffraff that Fisk so often associated with. "Such a select, refined and fashionable assemblage," gushed the *Herald*, "is rarely gathered together in this city. Congressmen and ex-Congressmen, Governors and ex-Governors, Mayors and ex-Mayors, Judges and ex-Judges, millionaire merchants, men eminent in the learned professions, artists and art critics and last, but not least, gentlemen of the newspaper profession who were especially largely represented. Private boxes, parquet and dress circle shone with the bewitching smiles of the loveliest ladies of New York. Altogether there has never been gathered together a more discriminating and intelligent assemblage on any similar occasion in this city."

Not content with running a great railroad, overseeing a large theatrical enterprise, and being the Admiral of the Narragansett Line of steamers, Fisk still had time for more, and his eye fell on the bedraggled Ninth Regiment of the New York State Militia. The Ninth had fallen on hard times since the end of the Civil War, and its muster roll was down to a mere three hundred, threatening its future existence as an independent unit. When its colonel retired, the regiment's lieutenant colonel, Charles R. Braine, realized that what the Ninth needed was an angel, someone who could breathe new life into the regiment by supplying it with money for new uniforms, an improved band, and a recruitment drive. Colonel Braine thought that Fisk was just the man for the job, and Fisk entirely agreed. On April 7th, Braine stood aside while Admiral Fisk added the title of Colonel of the Ninth to his list of purchased honors.

Fisk's military experience had consisted entirely of smuggling cotton while avoiding insofar as possible all contact with armed forces. Therefore, while he immediately began a period of intense study, he had no choice but to leave it to Braine to give the orders that put the regiment through its complex evolutions. The first parade under Fisk's nominal command, held on April 13th, was at best an unimpressive affair, but the next one, held a month later, was a different story.

A vigorous recruitment drive, fueled by cash bonuses and no little encouragement of Erie Railway employees, had swelled the ranks, and Fisk had supplied everyone with handsome new uniforms of dark blue trousers with wide gold stripes down the sides and coats of the same color decorated with dark red epaulets and gold lace trim. For himself Colonel Fisk had ordered up a uniform that, at least according to the newspaper accounts, cost as much as $5,000. Wearing it, according to the *Herald,* Jubilee Jim "looked for all the world like a pleased school boy let out of school to play soldier. He shook hands with his intimate friends, nodded at mere acquaintances and smiled at everybody in general. He had his natty soldier cap cocked to one side, his kids [i.e., his gloves] were as white as somebody's 'milk-white steed' and his moustache was waxed until the ends looked stiff and strong enough to run a soldier right through the body. This was how he appeared in the *role* of a colonel. Fearful of disarranging his toilet, however, he stood still and smiled—while his lieutenant did all the work."[22]

Asked by a reporter if the Ninth Regiment had a motto, Fisk revealed his attitude toward soldiering with his usual forthrightness by suggesting that "The last in the field and the first off" would do nicely.

Following up on their new motto, the members of the Ninth concluded their dress parade by marching down Eighth Avenue to the Grand Opera House, where they attended a special performance of *The Twelve Temptations*. The whole affair went off splendidly except for the fact that after the performance, as Colonel Fisk and his "staff" walked through the lobby of Castle Erie, a "sharp attorney's clerk" suddenly pounced and served Fisk with a summons. Enraged, Fisk "threw it down on the marble tiling, spelled mad dog backwards and told the attorney to go to where it is not said the 'woodbine twineth.' "

Fisk had hired a new bandmaster for the regiment and gave him *carte blanche* to assemble a first-class band. He soon turned the Ninth's into what was universally acknowledged to be the biggest and best brass band in the country, and at the end of May the band had a chance to display its capacities, for Colonel Fisk threw a ball in the regiment's honor at the Academy of Music on 14th Street. The ball, catered by Delmonico's, was as well attended as the opening of *The Twelve Temptations* had been and equally well reviewed. "In all respects," declared an impressed *Leslie's Illustrated*, "the affair was a success and, in spite of the ideas entertained in certain quarters of the 'eccentricities' of the celebrated colonel of the Ninth, the tone of the reception was strictly 'orthodox.' The spirit of the ball was intensely respectable, while the details were intensely regal."[23]

Regal, perhaps, but the *Herald* felt that some of the ladies were dressed "in styles that modesty does not tolerate in good society."[24] Fisk, with regard to his own appearance, joked that he was ordering a curved musket for himself, the better to fit his rotund shape.

•

Fisk was not the only one on Wall Street to indulge himself in extracurricular activities at this time, for even the Commodore had taken up a new interest. Early in 1870 Victoria Woodhull and her sister, Tennessee Claflin, moved to New York. This pair of genuine American originals—ardent feminists, one a candidate for President, advocates of "free love"—fascinated, titillated, and scandalized Victorian society throughout the middle years of the nineteenth century. Now, they announced, they intended to open a Wall Street brokerage firm and began operations in a rented parlor of the Fifth Avenue Hotel. After receiving backing to the extent of at least $7,500 from the Commodore, they opened a proper office at 44 Broad Street in the heart of the business district.

It is hard to imagine today just how oxymoronic the phrase "lady broker" sounded to the Victorian ear, for the presence of women in business and the professions, except in the most menial capacities, was quite unknown. The rough and tumble of Wall Street was thought to be very nearly as unsuitable a place for women as a pool hall or even a battlefield. It would be fully another hundred years before a woman would hold a seat in her own name on the New York Stock Exchange.

Quite possibly Vanderbilt backed the Claflin sisters to please his new wife, who had strong feminist leanings, or perhaps the whole idea just amused him, for he had a keen sense of humor. At first the "lady brokers" were such a tourist attraction that their office was choked with gawkers and they were forced to put up a sign saying, "All Gentlemen Will Please State Their Business and Then Retire at Once"; before long, however, to the astonishment of many, they were making a success of it. But the Claflin sisters, far more inspired flibbertigibbets than real crusaders, soon tired of Wall Street and moved to England.

If the Commodore was backing the Claflin sisters, he was also paying close attention to other matters, and in the spring of 1870 he precipitated a rate war with the Erie and the Pennsylvania railroads. As the competition to acquire western connections and thus secure as much of the Chicago traffic as possible had heated up, the agreement that had existed, at least in theory, among the three roads since 1863 became ever more ignored. Finally the Commodore, the "Colossus of Roads"[25] as the *Herald* called him, decided he had had enough and declared open hostilities. "The doughty Commodore," it reported on June 7th, "yesterday flung down the gauntlet by notifying President Gould that all arrangements hitherto existing between the New York Central and Erie lines are to be considered null and void."

The *Herald*, on learning of the outbreak of war, sent a reporter scurrying over to the Commodore's office to hear from the great man himself what the *casus belli* was. Vanderbilt greeted the reporter politely and, not surprisingly, threw all the blame for the situation on the other roads. "The New York Central, the Pennsylvania Central and the Erie Railways," he explained, "had entered into an arrangement seven years ago, establishing similar rates of passenger and freight charges, which had been strictly adhered to by the New York Central but had been repeatedly deviated from by the other roads. It had been found utterly useless to make any compact or arrangement with the controllers of the Erie, for the reason that they would violate any and every such compact or arrangement within twenty-four hours."

Asked how he intended to respond to the challenge, Fisk replied, "Why, Sir, we intend to fight. Vanderbilt has begun this thing, and we intend to come up squarely to the scratch and take care of our road to the best of our ability."

At first there was more talk than action in the new rate war, and the newspapers began to suspect that it was all for purposes of speculating on Wall Street. The *Herald* even reported that the Erie was being deliberately manipulated in London in order to induce selling in New York, but predicted, quite incorrectly it proved, that the stock would "see a remarkable advance in the price before the close of the year."[26]

On June 17th, however, Central broke to 98⅝ as passenger fares to Chicago were reduced from $20 to $15, and the rate war seemed to be on in earnest. But a week later the *Herald* reported that it still seemed largely confined to the price of shipping livestock. The Central had started it by slashing the rate per carload from Buffalo to New York from $120 to $100 in early May and three weeks later had followed up by cutting the rate again to $40. Then, on June 25th, the Commodore was surprised when the Erie, which had been content up to then to follow the Central's lead, had suddenly cut the rate to a purely nominal $1 a carload.

Vanderbilt, doubtless feeling that he could afford such suicidal rates far better than Gould, immediately followed suit. He soon noticed that something very strange was happening. While the Central's tracks were choked with car after car carrying cattle, to the exclusion of its other traffic, the Erie's cattle traffic was way below normal. Before long, the Commodore—who became nearly apoplectic with rage—learned that Gould and Fisk, acting on their own account, had bought all the cattle in the Buffalo market, some 6,000 head, and were happily shipping them to New York at the Commodore's expense and there selling them at a handsome profit.

Vanderbilt grimly held on to the new rate the rest of the summer until it could inflict some harm on the Erie as well (and, quite coincidentally, give New Yorkers a break on their meat bills), but the Commodore was disgusted at himself for being so easily hornswoggled and resolved "never [to] have anything more to do with them blowers."[27]

As the fall, with its heavy agricultural shipments, neared, both sides tired of the game, and the war wound down to a few skirmishes. On August 10th the *Herald*, on top of things on the Street as usual, noticed that "certain brokers were purchasing very heavily of the New York Central, Lake Shore and Erie, and the Street, taking the hint at the last board, began to buy also, the effect being a decided scare to the 'shorts,' who in covering their contracts by purchases for 'cash' rendered the market very buoyant and fairly active. It transpired that the orders to buy originated in great part from Saratoga [where Vanderbilt was staying and] where the leading speculators who cluster around the Commodore were given the point that the rival trunk lines were to bury the hatchet in expectation of a heavy transportation business this fall in connection with the extensive crops of the West and that a harmonious schedule of advanced freight rates would be agreed upon."

A new agreement, as ephemeral in the event as the old one, was soon hammered out. The cost of shipping cattle from Buffalo to New York went up to $140 a carload. "The great war," *Leslie's Illustrated* sadly reported, "which for some months has been raging between the New York Central and the Erie Railroads, greatly to the benefit of forwarders, has been brought to a close, the opposing hosts under the leadership of the mighty Vanderbilt on the part of the Central and the great Fisk on that of Erie are gradually withdrawing from the field, both equally beaten. Recognizing each other's prowess, the late opposing generals propose, like other great powers, to enter into a treaty of peace that will bring about a combination of all the great railroad corporations in the country—that the people may be plundered and fat dividends declared."[28]

Other than a few flurries caused by the rate war and a couple of false reports about the Commodore's health that were successfully planted with the newly established Associated Press, Wall Street remained notably quiet that summer. On August 8th the New York Stock Exchange even went so far as to officially cancel the afternoon board so that everyone could go out to the Lower Bay and watch the America's Cup race being run that afternoon. Even when there was nothing so exciting as a yacht race on hand, the brokers did not feel they needed the Exchange's permission to desert the Street in search of sport; on July 30th the *Herald* reported that "the Stock Exchange was almost empty yesterday afternoon, the boys having gone down to Long Branch to be in good time for the [horse] races."

•

Although it would soon be eclipsed by Newport, in 1870 Long Branch, New Jersey, was the country's most fashionable seaside resort. Grand hotels, including the Continental, which at 1,200 rooms was the world's largest, lined the boardwalk, and even President and Mrs. Grant had taken a cottage there for the summer that year. Only a short trip from New York City, Long Branch was an exciting place, with its mix of fashion, politics, bathing, and gambling. Jim Fisk found it quite irresistible. Scenting profit as well as pleasure, Fisk had organized a boat run from New York to Sandy Hook, a short railroad trip from Long Branch, laying on the *Plymouth Rock*, which had cost him $94,000. At 345 feet long, she had 32 private suites, her own brass band, and dozens of canaries.

Fisk was hardly content merely to enjoy Long Branch's many pleasures by himself, and he decided that the resort would make a perfect place for the Ninth Regiment to hold its summer bivouac. With the help of the local government, Fisk temporarily established "Camp Jay Gould" on some undeveloped land in the town, and on August 20th the Ninth, now six hundred strong, arrived for a week's summer training. "As they are to feed at the hotels . . ." the *Herald* noted drily, "they bring no rations with them, encumbering their knapsacks, but fill them with white pantaloons, white gloves, and other dilettante adornments of holiday soldiers."[29]

On Sunday, August 21st, Colonel Fisk dutifully led his men off to church. "It is said," reported the *Herald*, "that it is the first sermon he has heard in nine years. He was greatly moved by the unusual sensation and shed tears. It was better than a play to him."[30]

Having rendered unto God, the Ninth Regiment and its colonel prepared to do the same for Ulysses S. Grant, and held a parade in Long Branch the next day that was to be reviewed by the President. The President, however, left town in order to avoid having to shake hands with a principal architect of the Gold Panic. Nonetheless the *Herald* was distinctly impressed with the whole proceedings and headlined its story THE DRESS PARADE OF THE GORGEOUS NINTH—COLONEL FISK SUBLIME. Fisk had obviously been taking his store-bought colonelcy more seriously than most people had thought he would, for the *Herald* reported that "the magnificent Fisk, in all the grandeur of gold and bullion, and the five thousand dollar uniform which so well sets off his imposing figure, commanded in person and gave highly satisfactory evidence to his friends of having crammed himself full of military knowledge."

CHAPTER FIFTEEN

God's Expressman

WHILE Fisk was spreading his boundless energies among a dozen pursuits, Gould was hoarding his very limited ones for the defense of their corporate empire and was now fending off the most serious threat to their control of the Erie since they had come to power two years earlier. The patience of the English stockholders, long tested, was wearing dangerously thin.

By 1870 fully 450,000 of the 780,000 shares of Erie stock outstanding were held by English investors. But the power over the Erie's corporate affairs that that stock should have given them remained firmly in the hands of Jay Gould, for the stock had not been officially transferred on the company's books, and until it was the new owners could not vote it. In the fall of 1869 a committee was formed in London that represented 190,000 of these shares through the banking house of Bischoffscheim and Goldschmidt. The committee sent Joseph L. Burt to New York to authorize its New York agent to demand the transfer of the stock to the names of two of its members, Robert A. Heath and Henry L. Raphael. When the agent left 16,770 shares at the Erie offices, however, Gould flatly refused to transfer them. The agent soon left 60,000 more shares for transfer and again demanded that they be registered on the company's books in the names of their rightful owners' authorized representative, this time taking legal action to compel the transfer.

By this time Gould was more than ready to handle a legal challenge, for he had arranged for John Nyce of Milford, Pennsylvania, an Erie stockholder of no importance whatever, to sue Fisk, as controller, and Justin D. White, the Erie treasurer, to prevent them from doing what they had no intention of doing in any event, transferring the stock. Through no coincidence, the case came up before Judge Barnard, and he, of course, immediately appointed a receiver to hold the stock. Further, he empowered the receiver, one James H. Coleman, to employ his own counsel and pay that counsel out of the assets in his care, and he enjoined the English stockholders from even trying to get the stock transferred.

While the stock was thus locked up in legal limbo, Gould continued to vote it as he saw fit, electing three safely pro-Gould directors in the annual election in October, 1870, by a vote of 304,938 to 3,000.[1]

The English shareholders, brought face to face with the New York judiciary, went into federal court. Confronted with this threat, Fisk and Gould could not have been more polite or less helpful. "Contrary to expectation," reported the *Herald,* "no difficulty was experienced in serving the Erie officials with notice of the suit instituted by Burt's bondholders. Learning that the papers were ready, Fisk dispatched a member of his legal staff to the United States Marshal's office for the purpose of escorting the deputy to the Erie stronghold. Fisk and Gould received the bearer of Burt's challenge to legal combat with the utmost good humor and courtesy, and, the ceremony of serving over, the Colonel entertained the deputy marshal at lunch. His Erie-pressible amphibiousness, the admiral of the Narragansett navy and Colonel of the Ninth was advised to array himself in full militia uniform, as in that martial garb he could have defied the majesty of the civil law, but he magnanimously declined, saying, 'If these Britishers prefer that their share of the earnings of the road shall be eaten up in lawsuits instead of being distributed in dividends, I can't help it.' "[2]

Finally, in July, 1871, more than a full year after they had started, the English shareholders obtained a judgment in their favor from the United States District Court. But it would be December of that year, after still another annual election, before Gould would run out of legal maneuvering room and be forced to turn the stock over to the people who owned it. The legal battle cost the English stock-holders $25,000.

The British, meanwhile, also sought to get the New York State Legislature to repeal the Classification Act, which gave Gould such a tight grip on the company and sent Burt to Albany to testify on their behalf. On March 23rd, 1870, Gould likewise testified before the Assembly committee holding hearings. He did not address the merits of his case, however (not that there were many), and instead confined his testimony largely to appeals to the chauvinism and bigotry that were such prominent elements of the American psyche in the later years of the nineteenth century.

If the Classification Act were to be repealed, Gould piously and incorrectly predicted, "Bona fide owners are to have no voice, and the board of directors to manage the affairs and administer to the wants of this great corporation is to be made up in the dingy office of a Jew banking-house in London."[3]

The legislators, using the excuse of the threat of foreign owner-ship, refused to repeal the Classification Act, and while Gould's testimony may have helped marginally in bringing about this result, one Assemblyman candidly told Burt that he might have done bet-ter had he "brought $20,000 to smooth the way."[4]

Though Gould was still able to maintain his iron grip on the Erie by his skillful use of the courts and the Legislature, the railroad's financial and strategic position was going from bad to worse. The Commodore's splendidly managed New York Central and the now thoroughly aroused Pennsylvania Railroad were steadily taking more and more of the western traffic.

The Erie's broad gauge, steep grades, and inadequate facilities increasingly exacerbated the situation. While the New York Central was now beginning to quadruple-track its line, the Erie main line still had seventy miles of single tracking as late as the middle of 1871.

Gould sought to improve the Erie's finances by issuing con-solidated mortgage bonds to replace the myriad of earlier debt is-sues. But the Scarlet Woman, whose "draggled skirts . . . [had] always had a fascination,"[5] had finally peddled her charms once too often on Wall Street, and the new paper had no takers, except Gould himself, who took $3,000,000 at 60. Gould was finding out that it was getting harder and harder to manipulate the judgment of Wall Street's fast-growing and ever better self-patrolled free market.

His partner in Erie affairs, meanwhile, was finding out that the most private of matters can come to dominate the most public of lives. His beloved Josie Mansfield was acting exactly as everyone, except Fisk, would have expected. Even that least introspective of men must now and then have wondered, as did the *New York Times*, "whether fate has yet quite done with James Fisk, Jr."[6]

•

Jim Fisk had moved into Josie Mansfield's establishment sometime in 1869, supplying her considerable appetite for luxury in every way he knew how. "While acquainted with Mr. Fisk," Josie told a reporter when their affair had become the talk of the town, "I was always supplied with silks, wines, food and everything that I could desire; but he would never allow me any freedom."[7] It does not seem to have occurred to her that being free and being kept are mutually exclusive conditions, and certainly nothing Fisk could give her stayed her affections from wandering.

One of Fisk's side enterprises was the Brooklyn Oil Refinery Company. Its principal owner was Mrs. Edward H. Stokes, but it was managed and controlled by her son, Edward S. Stokes. At Stokes's request, Fisk had made a substantial investment in the business and saw to it that the Erie Railway transported the crude oil from Pennsylvania to the refinery at low rates, shipped its products at equally favorable rates, and purchased its own considerable needs for oil and kerosene there. With this backing, Stokes's company should have been a most successful enterprise, but Stokes, it turned out, was too unstable to make a success of anything.

Edward Stiles Stokes had been born in 1841 into one of New York's richest and most distinguished families. His parents soon moved to Philadelphia, where his mother's family lived, and it was there that he grew up and went to school. Stokes was about average height but, weighing only 140 pounds, was "very wiry and active on his feet" and had been a good gymnast in his youth. He was always notably active, even frenetic. "In conversation he talks quickly and to the point and hurries his affairs through as rapidly as possible."[8]

The *Herald* noted that Stokes "manifested great energy and business tact. He had one great fault, however. His blood was hot, and being of a nervous, sanguine temperament he was liable at any moment to break out when he deemed himself imposed upon or outraged. He had always been sensitive to an insult and quick to resent an injury."[9] Indeed Stokes could never seem to accept the

EDWARD S. STOKES *Courtesy of the Union Club Library*

blame for anything and perceived all who questioned his motives or actions as enemies.

His uncle, James Stokes, who lived in great style on Madison Square, had long thought his nephew unreliable and was "unwilling"[10] that his own children should associate with him. Nonetheless, he had lent him a great deal of money out of regard for his own brother, which money was never repaid.

If Stokes was immature and possessed of a violent temper, he could also be extremely charming, and Fisk, no mean judge of character, was quite taken with him at first. He was also undeniably handsome. A *Herald* reporter described him as being "a gentleman of about twenty-eight years of age, of slender but sinewy build, with dark eyes, dark hair and a charming black mustache. He was dressed in the height of fashion and looked to be a man of the world, perfectly self-possessed and well bred, and wearing in his face an expression of savoir faire which takes well with the female sex."[11]

Unfortunately for Fisk, Stokes's looks took all too well with Josie Mansfield. "Miss Mansfield," wrote McAlpine, "while she had no real love or passion for Fisk, had received him as her lover, for his money. But Stokes she really loved; or if love be too exalted a word to use in connection with a woman so worldly and designing, it is safe to say that she entertained for Stokes an ardent passion."[12]

Soon Stokes was calling regularly at the house Fisk had provided, being waited on hand and foot by the servants whose wages Fisk paid, and doubtless being welcomed to the bed of Josie Mansfield, a privilege that Fisk thought should be his alone.

Despite having partners in the business, Stokes treated the Brooklyn Refinery as being entirely his and helped himself to cash whenever he needed it to maintain his luxurious lifestyle. Fisk, always the businessman, would not put up with this and demanded that Stokes make restitution.

While Fisk could be briskly businesslike when it came to the Brooklyn Refinery, he was far less able to deal with Josie's passion for Stokes, for he was still enthralled by her. Finally she made it plain she wanted him to move out, and he did so. Certainly he had moved out by the middle of 1870 and set up his own establishment at 313 West 23rd Street, right next to the Opera House. Far less imposing than Josie Mansfield's house down the block, Fisk's New York home was only four rooms and simply furnished. Like so many people with a compulsive need for the limelight, Jubilee Jim, backstage, had simple tastes and simple needs.

Fisk, perhaps in hopes of winning Josie back, kept her supplied with money for a while, and continued writing her a series of letters. These letters, which in the early days of their relationship had been full of jokes and affectionate references, became more and more anguished as matters deteriorated.

"But what do you think," he wrote her on October 1st, 1870, "of a woman who would veil my eyes first by a gentle kiss, and afterwards, night and day, for weeks, months, and years, by deceit and fraud, to lead me through the dark valley of trouble, when she could have made my pathway one of roses, committing crimes which the devil incarnate would shrink from, while all this time I showed to her, as to you, nothing but kindness both in words and actions, laying at your feet a soul, a heart, a fortune, and a reputation, which had cost, by night and day, twenty-five years of perpetual struggle, and which, but for the black blot of having, in an evil hour, linked itself with you, would stand out today brighter than any ever seen upon earth."[13]

Despite the syntax, the rough power of Fisk's expression and the pain in these letters are all too evident. But Josie Mansfield ignored Fisk's emotional distress, for no sooner had she received this letter than she brazenly wrote to him asking for a settlement that would allow her to keep up the lifestyle that had been provided up to that point by her former lover.

Poor Fisk, driven into the third person by her naked greed, stonily refused. "Had she been the same proud-spirited girl that she was when she stood side-by-side with me," he wrote on October 4th, "she would not have humbled herself to ask a permanency of one whom she had so deeply wronged, nor would she stoop to be indebted to him for a home, which would have furnished a haven of rest, pleasure and debauchery, without cost, to those who had crossed his path and robbed him of the friendship he once felt."[14]

Perhaps to take his mind off Josie Mansfield, Fisk threw himself more deeply into the affairs of the Ninth Regiment, and that spring decided it was time to take the Ninth on the road. The previous autumn the *Herald* had admitted that "the fact is undeniable that the battalion has steadily improved in drill and discipline since the Prince of Erie assumed command. The Ninth is now inferior to none of our city regiments."[15] Fisk decided to show it off to his friends in Boston.

He selected Bunker Hill Day, Saturday, June 17th, as a suitable occasion and wrote the Mayor of Boston asking for permission to parade in the Common and hold a religious service there on Sunday, June 18th. He was flatly refused. The request, wrote the Boston *Advertiser*, "marks a new era in the history of effrontery."[16]

While the Common belonged to the city of Boston—whose establishment wanted no part of Fisk—the streets were under the control of the Governor, and he granted permission for the Ninth to parade and to hold a religious service in the open air on Sunday, as well as to participate in the ceremonies at Bunker Hill in nearby Cambridge on Saturday.

At five o'clock on Friday the Ninth Regiment departed for Boston on board the *Newport* of the Narragansett Line. "They were all fine fellows, in their way," wrote the *Herald* of their departure, "and presently a corpulent, gold-slashed form crossed the gangway. This was James Ulysses Fisk, Jr., the hero of a hundred lawsuits, the boldest stock waterer, the grandest ballet master and opera bouffeist in America and the most magnificent holiday colonel in New York. The hawsers were let go and the large sound steamer *Newport* dropped out into the stream."[17]

When the steamer arrived in Newport, Rhode Island, the regiment piled onto a special train to take them to Boston, but it was soon discovered that their august colonel had forgotten his sword on the steamer and the train had to back up so he could retrieve it. When they finally pulled into Boston a holiday atmosphere was abundant, and the regiment's lead cornetist, Jules Levy, broke into "Auld Lang Syne," to the delight of the crowd that had come to greet them, for the Ninth's brass band was known to be without peer. While the cornetist was the absolute master of his instrument (Fisk paid him $10,000 a year), as a recent immigrant from London he had not yet mastered the political nuances of American martial music and followed up his first selection with the considerably less well-received "Dixie."

Despite this minor gaffe the entire weekend was a great success for both Fisk and his regiment. If the Boston establishment did not care for Jubilee Jim, the ordinary people of the city thought he and the Ninth were terrific and cheered the concert to the skies. And the "holiday Colonel" had obviously been doing his homework, for it was Fisk, not Lieutenant Colonel Braine, who bawled the orders that put the Ninth through its evolutions at the Bunker Hill ceremonies.

Sunday, unfortunately, brought heavy rain, and the Ninth's outdoor religious service, which had caused so much trouble, had to be held in a Boston theater. After the service the Ninth boarded a train and returned to the *Newport,* where they were served a sumptuous supper featuring an "oleaginous lobster salad" as the steamer got under way.

All was well in sheltered Narragansett Bay, but as the *Newport* rounded Point Judith and met the more open, choppy waters of Block Island Sound "the vessel heaved viciously and so did the lobster salad."[18] The members of the Ninth Regiment proved to be as bad sailors as most soldiers, and spent a miserable night on the storm-tossed vessel as it made its way back to New York.

The next morning dawned clear and bright, however, and the Ninth returned in triumph through Hell Gate to its native city. "When off Fort Schuyler," the *Herald* reported, "the band commenced playing as if nothing had happened, and from thence to New York the progress of the *Newport* and the Ninth was one continued ovation.

"At Whitestone the population rushed out on their lawns and down to the banks, waving flags and handkerchiefs. The river steamers blew their whistles energetically, the heavily laden ferryboats resounded with cheers, and with all possible impromptu demonstration riparian New York welcomed her returning braves."[19]

•

Fisk threw himself ever more strenuously into Erie affairs as well, but the situation for the railroad was growing steadily worse. The suit of the English stockholders was slowly moving through the U.S. District Court, and no one thought that Gould and Fisk would prevail there as they might have been expected to in the New York courts. On May 7th Erie stock jumped up from its all-time low of 21 to 25 on rumors that Gould would have to enter the market to buy stock with which to pay off the English. A week later Erie was all the way up to 31 and Wall Street was awash in stories "that a change in the management of the road was near at hand, and that a man with a great railroad name was coming quietly in to rescue this unfortunate road from the sore travail it has been in for years."[20]

Even their long hold on the New York courts had been shaken, for the usually faithful Judge Barnard ruled on May 13th against the Erie Railway on its suit to recover the money it had paid Commodore Vanderbilt in the settlement with Drew. Barnard obviously felt he could not afford to make an enemy of the Commodore, even in the interests of the Erie, and ruled that he could find no fraud on the part of Vanderbilt.

On May 17th, the New York *Sun* reported, Jay Gould was seen at the Fleetwood races with the Commodore. "These worthies had a long conversation. They may have been talking horse, but it was probably iron horse. At any rate they were both too much engrossed with the subject under discussion to pay attention to the racing."[21]

A week later, on May 24th, a *Herald* reporter caught up with the Erie's putative rescuer. "They say you are already negotiating with Fisk and Gould," the reporter said to Vanderbilt.

"Well, they say many things, sonny, besides their prayers," replied the Commodore. "God knows somebody ought to take hold of the Erie Railroad; but I'm not breaking my heart about it."

"Wall Street will believe nothing else, Commodore," said the young reporter.

"Just like Wall Street," said Vanderbilt, giving the journalist a wink. "There are some smart young men down there that can get people to believe anything. It pays sometimes."

That evening the reporter caught up with Fisk and Gould, who were busily conversing and "pacing quickly across the tesselated pavement" in the lobby of the Fifth Avenue Hotel. The lobbies of the great hotels were busy and public places in the days before the telephone, for people tended to congregate there to get the latest news and swap gossip.

Both seemed distracted. "Fisk knit his brows and blinked his eyes repeatedly; Gould fiddled with his eighteen-carat gold chain and stroked his raven beard. Something was on the tapis. It was hardly another injunction, for Fisk only smiles when such a subject is on his mind; but he smole no smile last evening."

Asked about the "painful rumor implying that the days of his glory were over," Fisk was abrupt.

"Why, lookee here," he said, "the Erie road is all right and wants no help from nobody. We wouldn't trust Vanderbilt as far as we could throw him, and this thing is all a Wall Street trick, nothing more." For once the Commodore and the management of the Erie were in agreement, and nothing came of the rumors. But they persisted all summer.

That summer, another rumor swept through New York: Jim Fisk had been shot and killed. The story was entirely false, but it caused Horace Greeley, who often made up in self-righteousness what he lacked in humor, to remark in the *Tribune* that as Fisk's "hand was against every man's" his supposed death had occasioned no sense of loss. This prompted a letter from Richard Grant White, which Greeley, much to his credit, printed in the *Tribune* a few days later.

"In commenting on the report that he had been shot," White wrote, "you speak of him as a man whose hand is against every man's, one whom nobody ever cared for living, or mourned when he was supposed to be dead. Now, I do not know Mr. Fisk, never held any communication with him, never even saw him. Of the nature or justifiability of his operations, I can say nothing, because I know nothing. But I was sorry to see these remarks, because I do know of at least one person whom he cared for, and who should remember him living or dead. In the height of the gold panic, when it might reasonably be supposed that any man who was but moderately interested in the issue would be entirely and nervously absorbed in his own affairs, Mr. Fisk found time and had the nerve and the inclination to write a letter to a friend of mine for the sole purpose of serving a woman—a woman old and poor. The fact impressed me when I learned it at the time of its occurrence, and I refer to it now, because it seems to me that a man who under such circumstances could do such an act, cannot be quite the Ishmael of his kind, or quite deserve to be held up as one whom no one should care for living, or will mourn when dead."[22]

Richard Grant White was a most distinguished man, the country's foremost Shakespearean scholar (and the father of the architect Stanford White). While Greeley was famous for being oblivious of the world around him—he often walked right by lifelong friends on the street—even he should have been able to see that Fisk, for all his rascalities and perhaps because of them, had won a place in the hearts of the ordinary people, if not in those of their moral mentors.

Like the movie stars of a later age, Fisk filled the lives of people with vicarious excitement and glamour through the endless newspaper accounts of his corporate battles, his theatrical triumphs, his personal scandals, and his magnificent ostentation. Fisk never lost any of his instinctive common touch, which the population responded to always, perceiving him as one of their own who had somehow gotten to play with the big boys. Even George Templeton Strong, ever ready to find fault, wrote on hearing of Fisk's actual death, "What a scamp he was, but what a curious and scientifically interesting scamp!"[23]

•

When Jim Fisk accepted the colonelcy of the Ninth Regiment he surely never expected to face anything more difficult or unpleasant than choosing among possible uniforms. When asked if he could even ride a horse, he likened himself to an Erie locomotive because, he said, "I always have a tender behind."[24] But in July, 1871, the Governor called out the Ninth and a number of other New York regiments to help keep the peace among the warring Irish immigrants from New York's teeming slums.

It has been the tragedy of the Irish people through the centuries to be cursed with the longest racial memory on earth. No quarrel or wrong, it seems, however ancient, can be forgiven or forgotten or even settled, and in consequence these mindless disputes have exacted a continuing toll of Irish blood. The Battle of the Boyne, which ended the hopes of the Catholic King James II to regain the English throne at the end of the seventeenth century, has been murderously fought again and again by each generation.

"The story of the battle of 1690," wrote the *Herald* on July 9th, 1871, three days before the celebration of its anniversary, "is one that would be but little mentioned outside of Ireland were it not that the combat has been renewed on almost every anniversary of its happening with a ferocity and pertinacity which profess to find their inspiration in the different forms of Christianity—Catholic and Protestant."

In 1870 the Protestant Orangemen from northern Ireland had held a parade in New York to celebrate the long-ago victory over the Catholics, and the far more numerous immigrants from southern Ireland had been caught unaware. They hardly had time to do more than throw garbage at the marchers and their hated colors and slogans. But they had every intention of being ready the following year, and it was widely feared that a major riot was inevitable if the parade was held.

On July 10th, Superintendent of Police John Kelso announced that the police were ready for anything, and most people felt that the Orangemen had a right to march. "Toleration is one of the first necessities of untrammelled union among men," wrote the *Herald* on the 9th, "and where a body of religionists or others break no law it is the clear duty of the governing powers to protect them from molestation, idiotic though they may be." But the continuance in office of the Mayor and most other New York City officials depended on the votes of the recently naturalized Irish immigrants, and the Mayor ordered Kelso to forbid all parades.

At once a deep, visceral outrage at what was perceived as knuckling under to constituent pressure swept through New York. "The Green above the Red, White, and Blue," the *Herald* called it, denouncing Mayor Hall. "The leading papers, without regard to politics, opened on him and his advisors," wrote Joel Tyler Headley the following year, "with such a torrent of denunciations that they quailed before it. Processions of all kinds and nationalities were allowed on the streets and to forbid only one, and that because it was *Protestant,* was an insult to every American citizen."[25]

Governor Hoffman, with a bad case of Potomac fever and a presidential election coming up the following year, quickly perceived another opportunity to distance himself from his Tammany Hall roots and issued a proclamation. "I hereby give notice that any and all bodies of men desiring to assemble in peaceable procession tomorrow, the 12th inst., will be permitted to do so. They will be protected to the fullest extent possible by the military and police authorities. A police and military escort will be furnished to any body of men desiring it, on application to me at my headquarters (which will be at police headquarters in this city) at any time during the day."[26]

July 12th dawned clear and hot, one of many such days in a summer notably hot even by New York standards. In the fashionable areas of the city, matters were much as normal, and George Templeton Strong, walking home to Gramercy Park for lunch, noted that "children were playing on shady spots of sidewalks, ladies in lovely flowing summer robes [were] fanning themselves at parlor windows or on balconies, little tradesmen [were] pursuing their vocations."[27]

In the poorer sections tension was mounting rapidly, and "early in the morning sullen groups of Irishmen gathered on the corners of the streets."[28] For a while it seemed there might be trouble at Harper & Brothers on Franklin Square—*Harper's Weekly,* and especially its great cartoonist, Thomas Nast, were vehemently anti-Irish—and Superintendent Kelso sent fifty policemen down to guard the building.

The Orangemen were to meet at Lamartine Hall at Eighth Avenue and 29th Street. From there they were to march down to 23rd, turn east to Madison Square, and then march down Broadway as far as Union Square. In the event only about seventy or eighty showed up to march (behind a banner that read AMERICANS! FREE MEN!! FALL IN!!!), but they were to be protected by thousands of soldiers and police. The parade was to be headed by mounted police followed by platoons of policemen on foot, the Seventh Regiment of the Militia, more police, and only then the Orangemen. To their left the Ninth and to their right the Twenty-second regiments were to guard their flanks, while the Eighty-fourth and Sixth regiments brought up the rear, followed by still more police.

Fisk had been at the Ninth Regiment's armory at Eighth Avenue and 26th Street all morning when he left to go down to the Opera House to telegraph orders from the Governor to the Erie ferries to stop running. The Governor had heard that troublemakers from New Jersey were headed across the river in large numbers and was determined to prevent their adding to his problems. Because of the hot weather, Fisk had left his uniform coat and sword at the armory. When he had finished his business at Castle Erie and run back up the avenue, the regiment was already forming up for the parade, and he did not have time to retrieve them. Wearing only his white summer uniform trousers and a shirt, Colonel Fisk borrowed a sword and prepared to lead his men down Eighth Avenue.

The avenue was densely packed with Irish, many of whom had come from other areas of the city, and every window and rooftop was filled with spectators. As soon as the march began, a shot rang out from one of the windows, and curses, garbage, and stones began to rain down upon the soldiers and the Orangemen. The crowd surged forward, but the mounted police forced them back, spurring their horses up onto the sidewalks and clubbing anyone within reach right and left. "Pistol shots were now heard to crack up and down the street."[29]

When the head of the parade reached 24th Street it was halted while the police cleared the way ahead. Suddenly a shot rang out from a second-story window of the building on the northeast corner of Eighth Avenue and 24th Street and struck a soldier of the Eighty-fourth Regiment farther up the avenue. "In an instant a line of muskets was pointed at the spot, as though the order to fire was expected. One gun went off, then, without orders, a sudden, unexpected volley rolled down the line of the Sixth, Ninth, and Eighty-Fourth Regiments."[30] A second volley was fired "straight into the face of the crowd."[31]

"In a moment," the *Herald* reported, "the scene of the parade was changed to a fearful battlefield. The multitude, ringleaders and all, took to their heels, white with fear, and rushed up the cross streets, leaping into cellars and unfinished houses, crowding behind door-steps or falling flat on their faces in the gutters." Colonel Fisk was somehow caught in this "rush of the mob and pushed and mauled about the gutter."[32] His ankle was severely dislocated in the melee and he hopped into Mr. Parke's Bakery at 309 Eighth Avenue, between 26th and 27th streets, where a doctor was summoned.

The scene outside was frightful. "The street and pavement were littered here and there with dead bodies of men and women, some of whom had fallen with outstretched hands in the stiff perfor-mance of immediate death, while others, uttering low moans, clenched at the warm stones, and gazed in helpless agony for relief. Blood trickled everywhere. A man was seen leaning from a second story window in the act of vomiting blood. Purple streams flowed from his nose and forehead and ran in a rill to the curbstone."[33] The *Herald* reporter noted "five men dead in a heap . . . a little girl face down in the gutter, the back of her head blown off."

Then, as if nothing had happened, "the music struck up again from the different bands, and the whole procession leaving its dead still on the street, marched in the direction of Madison Square."[34]

For a while silence enveloped the scene of the massacre, save only for the moans of the wounded. Slowly a new sound gathered strength as people set about the grim task of identifying and dealing with the bodies. The strange, unearthly wail known as keening, by which untold generations of Irishwomen have mourned their dead, began to fill the air. Altogether forty-seven people had been killed, including two soldiers of the Ninth and one policeman. Eighty-three had been wounded.

"After a little while," reported the *Herald*, "carts and furniture wagons were impressed by the police, and one after another the warm but lifeless bodies were laid in these vehicles—the heads towards the tail of the cart—and they moved over towards Broadway and passed the line of hotels carrying melancholy and panic every-where they appeared."

The living began to gather in knots on the street corners, now thirsting for revenge. Someone must have remembered Jim Fisk hobbling into the bakery, and a crowd gathered in front. "The damned son of a bitch is in here," Fisk remembered hearing. "Let's go in and get him out and kill him!"

"Hang him!" shouted another.[35]

Apparently the prospect of being hanged not only concentrates

THE ORANGE DAY RIOT, JULY 12TH, 1871   A strangely lifeless depiction, with Colonel Fisk nowhere to be seen.

the mind wonderfully, but performs miracles of physical recupera-
tion as well. Fisk was up and out the back door in a second, his ankle
not stopping him from heaving his considerable bulk over five
fences and making his way out onto 27th Street through a basement
passage. He entered another across the street and finally made it all
the way to 29th Street, where, hearing shouts, he crawled into still
another basement window and encountered an Irishman likewise
lying low.

Fisk, who prided himself on having the right costume for every
occasion, traded clothes with the Irishman and made his way to
Ninth Avenue in his new disguise. There he spied a hansom cab
that—typical Fisk luck—had Jay Gould as a passenger. Hailing it
frantically, he began to clamber aboard while Gould, thinking some
ruffian was about to rob him, yelled to the driver to move on
quickly.

Once he realized who it was, however, Gould greeted his friend,
who was nearly hysterical, and took him to the Hoffman House, a
fashionable hotel at 26th Street and Fifth Avenue. But Fisk feared
that he might yet be a target for revenge and left immediately for
Long Branch, still dressed in his bartered rags. There he checked into
a suite at the Continental Hotel.

Despite the carnage that had resulted from a near total lack of
leadership and discipline, the newspapers treated the whole affair as
a triumph of order and liberty over the rabble. The *Herald* headlined its story EXCELSIOR! and roundly congratulated everyone involved. But the newspapers had a field day with the Colonel of the
Ninth and his misfortunes. *Harper's Weekly* even printed a long
piece of magnificent doggerel called "The Flight of Fisk."

> His comrades' voices rent the air—
>   "For ankle smashed what speed it is!"
> They shouted *"Ce n'est pas la guerre,*
>   *Mais c'est superbe,* indeed it is!"[36]

Fisk at first ignored all the laughter and told reporters what had
happened with his usual forthrightness. Later he tried to deny the
whole story of his escape and pointed to his stomach as exhibit A
in his defense.

"Look at me!" he told Clara Morris, the actress. "I look like a
sprinter, don't I? If you just could see me getting into that uniform.
. . . It takes two men's best efforts, while I hold my breath to clasp

my belt—and they say I climbed that high fence! Say, I'd give five thousand dollars down on a nail if I had the waist to do that with!"[37] But he had climbed it.

As might be expected of him, however, he knew how to recuperate in style, for the next day a reporter for the New York *Sun* found him at the Continental Hotel in Long Branch "sleeping on the sofa . . . wrapped in a dressing gown. A pretty young lady was fanning him; a small Negro was standing by ready to wait upon him at a moment's notice. The air was fine; everything had an air of ease and contentment."[38]

•

If Fisk had made a fool of himself with his martial ineptness, he soon had a chance to redeem his reputation in the eyes of the public when the Chicago fire broke out on October 8th. This immense conflagration burned over three square miles of the center of the city during the course of 27 hours, destroying 18,000 buildings, killing at least 300 people, and leaving 90,000 homeless.

The entire world, ever more tightly knit together by the telegraph and undersea cables, was appalled by the destruction, and donations from everywhere poured in to help. The New York Stock Exchange gave $20,000, A. T. Stewart $50,000, Tiffany's $1,000 (while its clerks contributed $135 of their own money). Even Queen Victoria donated $2,500 out of her own purse.

On October 10th a notice appeared in the *Herald* and other papers.

October 9th, 1871

The Erie Railway Company will receive and forward, free of charge, any and all contributions which the citizens of New York may be disposed to contribute for the relief of the sufferers by the disastrous fire in Chicago.

Contributions of food and clothing especially called for. Donations may be sent to the Erie Railway Depot, foot of 23rd Street, New York, where they will be packed and forwarded at once, free of charge, by fast trains.

Jay Gould
President

Just as he had galvanized Boston to help the soldiers at Antietam nearly ten years earlier, Fisk now galvanized New York and the Erie

Railway to help Chicago. The Erie printed 30,000 leaflets asking for donations and had them distributed by the police. Fisk hitched two of his finest carriage horses—"splendid, fiery, satin-coated aristocrats"—to an express wagon and placed a sign on its side saying "Contributions Received Here for Chicago."[39] Then, with the horses "prancing and curvetting their way from door to door, Mr. Fisk [stopped] wherever a beckoning hand appeared at a window. And bundles of clothing, boxes of provisions, anything, everything that people could give, he gathered up with wild haste, and brief, warm thanks, and rushed to the express offices for proper sorting and packing."[40]

That night at Castle Erie, "with the exception of Col. Fisk's private office all was wrapped in darkness." A *Sun* reporter found Fisk at the center of activity as he issued orders for the train's departure the next morning. "We must be moving here in New York," he told the reporter, "or these people will starve to death. Crackers and cheese will keep a man alive you know. I propose to fill this train up to its full capacity tonight. I expect five cars of supplies on the *Bristol* from Boston and have ordered a barge to go along side at seven o'clock."[41]

The next morning, Fisk was at the ferry slip at West 23rd Street, overseeing the loading of the packages for shipment over to the Erie terminal at Jersey City. One of the packages, a box of dried codfish, was addressed:

> For the Mayor of Chicago, Ill.
> per Jas. Fisk, Jr.
> God's Expressman[42]

That seen to, Fisk hopped aboard the tugboat *Houston* and went across the river. "The scene at the depot was exciting," the New York *Sun* wrote. "There were crowds of Erie men working like beavers, loading the cars, there were crowds of lookers on cheering the workers. . . . At the head of the train stood the locomotive 'James Fisk, Jr.,' steaming away seemingly impatient to be off."[43]

At that time locomotives could not safely run at top speed for more than about an hour without stopping, so fresh locomotives had to be stationed and ready all along the line. Fisk returned at once to the Opera House to coordinate this, telegraphing up the line to fire the boilers of the fresh engines one by one as the relief train approached. " 'Click click' went the instrument," wrote the *Sun* reporter, who stayed with Fisk all day, "and one could imagine swarthy men applying torches in engines fifty, a hundred or more miles away waiting to seize the train and rattle on."

For all their undoubted good intentions, Fisk and Gould were hardly blind to the publicity potential in all this, and aboard the train was their public relations man, George Crouch.

With the Erie tracks cleared, the train hurtled up the line at speeds that reached sixty miles an hour and averaged almost forty, pausing only to switch engines while George Crouch telegraphed the latest position and running times. From Susquehanna, Pennsylvania, Crouch telegraphed that people were "attempting to throw bundles on board as we whisk past. Goods are piled up at the principal stations awaiting the next train. We are now over the heaviest grade and can make still better time on the Susquehanna Division."[44]

From Elmira, Crouch wired that "dense crowds were collected at Binghamton, Owego and Waverly, notwithstanding the rain. Handkerchiefs waving God speed were seen from every cottage and shanty. Contributions were waiting at every station." These bulletins and the running times between stations were printed in all the newspapers and posted at Castle Erie and at the company's downtown ticket office at 241 Broadway. Crowds gathered to read them and to cheer on the Erie train that had captured the imagination of the entire country and set a new speed record between New York and Buffalo, ten hours and fifty-five minutes.

With Jim Fisk driving his express wagon pulled by high-stepping horses all around town and George Crouch telegraphing the latest from the special train as it sped westward, the Erie's relief of Chicago was not only an act of genuine charity, it was a public-relations triumph. While it was a corporate effort, it would be Fisk, not the poor Erie Railway, that received most of the credit for it from the people. "Their fancy was caught," Clara Morris remembered, "by the picture of the be-diamonded Jubilee Jim placing himself and his valuable horses at the service of the terror-stricken, homeless Chicagoans."[45]

Although in fact he never left New York, in the minds of the public it would always be Jim Fisk himself who had flown to the aid of the stricken city.

CHAPTER SIXTEEN

The Murder of Jubilee Jim

THE relief of Chicago served, briefly, to deflect public attention from the Erie's corporate troubles, as well as from Fisk's personal problems. No one seemed to notice, for instance, that because of the Erie's broad gauge and lack of direct access to Chicago, the relief train had to break bulk in Buffalo, and the supplies were actually delivered to the burned-out city by Commodore Vanderbilt's standard-gauge Lake Shore line.

On October 10th, 1871, the annual meeting of the Erie was held and Fisk, Gould, and Frederick Lane, the corporate counsel, all resigned their positions and stood for reelection in order to demonstrate their supposed popularity with the stockholders. They were reelected unanimously, receiving the votes of more than 335,000 shares. Of course anyone paying the slightest attention knew that this was just so much window dressing, for Gould was still managing to delay turning the stock of the English shareholders over to them.

On October 14th, the case was back in court once more, and Fisk was personally in attendance. "He was dressed within an inch of his life," the *Herald* reported the next day, "and, probably, nearer. . . . His moustache, to be sure Napoleonic, stood out at least three inches from each side of his attractive face."

When court was recessed for the day Fisk was overheard to say to the opposing counsel, "Gentlemen, we had better meet and endeavor to settle this matter, because all earthly possessions fade away."[1] Fisk, usually as irrepressible as ever in public, must have been feeling the heat as never before. His friends in high places were in terrible trouble and less and less able to help him and the Erie.

•

On May 31st, 1871, Mary Amelia Tweed, daughter of State Senator William M. Tweed, had been married at Trinity Chapel, just off Madison Square (the church, still there, is now the Serbian Orthodox Cathedral). Her father, whose favorite of his many titles was Grand Sachem of Tammany Hall and who didn't mind a bit being referred to in the newspapers as "the Boss," gave his daughter a lavish wedding, and hundreds of presents were given to the bride and displayed for one and all, including reporters, to ogle. Jim Fisk had given a frosted silver ice dish and Jay Gould a silver nutpick. Tiffany's had sent an ornate writing desk.

Altogether the newspapers estimated the haul to amount to $700,000. While this figure was certainly a wild exaggeration—$70,000 was probably a lot more like it—still it was an impressive display for the daughter of a man whose fortune had been "made in politics, by a few short years' occupancy of moderately-salaried offices."[2]

The *Herald* thought there had never been anything like it. "Tammany Hall, in her oriental splendors," it wrote a few days later, "throws British royalty completely in the shade, and 'the Boss' is fast approaching the magnificence of the Great Moghul. . . . Seven hundred thousand dollars! What a testimonial of the loyalty, the royalty and the abounding East Indian resources of Tammany Hall! Was there ever any democracy to compare with this democracy, in glory, power, and equal rights, under the sun? Never. And it is just the beginning of the good time coming."[3]

But the *Herald* was wrong, and Mary Tweed's wedding was in fact the imperial sunset of the so-called Tweed Ring. A few weeks later a disgruntled former city employee handed George Jones, publisher of the *New York Times*, solid evidence of who had stolen what from the city's government in recent years, and on July 22nd he began to publish it. Neither government nor American journalism would ever be the same again.

That New York City's government in the middle of the nineteenth century was corrupt is beyond dispute. What is seldom noticed, however, is that government up until this time had always been corrupt. Since the days when modern political administration had first begun to evolve in the courts of medieval kings, people had sought political offices of "profit and trust" far more for the profit than for the trust involved, and government, like the army and the church, had always been one of the main means up the economic, and therefore social, scale.

In fact, what is most remarkable about New York City's government in the mid-nineteenth century is not that it was corrupt but that it was able to govern at all. The city's population had been doubling every ten years as a small seaport had turned into a great sprawling metropolis. Not only did services have to be provided to new neighborhoods as the city relentlessly expanded uptown, but the list of the services that were thought to be the obligation of the city expanded as well. Street lighting, public schools, sewers and water mains, and police and fire departments were all introduced in the middle years of the nineteenth century.

Perhaps the greatest problem faced by the government of New York City, however, was that it was a creature of the state. Its officials could exercise only those powers that the state government chose to give them, and the New York State Legislature was not likely to give up any more control over the country's largest and richest metropolis than it had to. New York City, after all, was a prize worth the keeping. The city's taxable income in 1866 had been 18 percent larger than that of the whole state of Pennsylvania, the union's second-most-populous state.

With economic opportunities abounding in the new industrial age, government, except at its very highest levels, and often even then, tended to attract the second-rate. The *North American Review* thought that "the supremacy in the Common Council of pickpockets, prize fighters, emigrant runners, pimps, and the lowest class of liquor-dealers, are facts which admit of no question."[4] A year earlier the *Review* had thought that "the majority of this board is about equal, in point of experience and ability, to the management of an oyster-stand."[5]

Indeed, City Hall was a foul-smelling den, as full of loafers as a pool hall. On the way to the Council Chamber, wrote a reporter in 1866, "we pass many open doors . . . through which we see idle men with their feet upon tables smoking cigars. There are few buildings in the world, probably, wherein the consumption of tobacco in all

WILLIAM M. TWEED   *Courtesy of The New-York Historical Society, New York City*

its forms goes on more vigorously during business hours than the City Hall of New York. Smoke comes in clouds from many rooms, and the vessel which Mr. Thackeray used to call the 'expectoratoon' is everywhere seen."[6]

The Mayor had little control over the government he ostensibly headed. What power was not retained in Albany was spread around among the Board of Aldermen, the Board of Councilmen, and numerous independently elected officials. They all presided, if that is the word, over an ever-expanding bureaucracy largely peopled with their friends, relations, and political associates.

While political corruption in New York State is usually associated with New York City, the Democratic party, and Tammany Hall, the Republicans were little if any better. Always dominant upstate, they had managed to gerrymander the Legislature so thoroughly that they seldom lost control of it. It was Boss Tweed who wrested the state government from Republican control and gave New York City its first responsible—to be distinguished from honest—government.

In the decade before 1868, about 9,000 immigrants a year were naturalized in New York City. After that date about 40,000 a year were herded into Barnard's and Cardozo's courtrooms and made citizens and Democratic voters. In 1868, the city's Mayor, John Hoffman, was elected Governor with the help of these votes and a good many more besides. In twenty districts of the city Hoffman's vote exceeded the total number of voters registered. One man was found to have registered 128 times.[7] In 1870 the Democrats obtained solid working majorities in both houses of the Legislature.

Tweed pushed a new city charter through that Legislature, a charter that gave the Mayor a four-year term and the power to appoint and remove most city officials. For the first time in the city's history it was effectively able to govern itself. Much altered at the time of the formation of Greater New York in 1898, Tweed's charter remains essentially the basis of New York City government to this day. Even George Templeton Strong, who hated politicians regardless of party, was forced to admit of Tweed that "were he not a supreme scoundrel, he would be a great man."[8]

But Tweed was a scoundrel, as were most politicians at that time and not a few in our own, and profited handsomely from his government positions while he and his associates raised the art of political corruption to new heights. While he was never a "boss" in the later political sense of the term, for he never possessed absolute control but rather shared it with numerous others, he made a most convenient symbol. Horace Greeley in the *Tribune*, the *Times*, *Harper's Weekly* and its merciless cartoonist Thomas Nast, all acted as though Tweed were the fount of all that was wrong with New York government.

The Old New York City Courthouse, universally known as the Tweed Courthouse, is forever the symbol of municipal corruption. Located just north of City Hall, it was begun in 1859 with a budget of $250,000 and wasn't completed until 1873 (by which time Tweed himself was in jail), at a cost, as near as anyone can figure it out, of about $12,000,000. By way of contrast, the Houses of Parliament in London, which cover eight acres and had been built twenty years earlier to house in unmatched splendor the central political institution of the richest nation on earth, had cost only $10,000,000.

Handed the smoking pistol by the disgruntled civil servant, the *Times* made the most of it. In lurid headlines day after day it detailed the nefarious doings of the city's politicians. With the *Times* leading the way the other newspapers as well were soon baying at their heels, and every day brought fresh revelations.

Conspicuously absent from all this was the *Herald*. Perhaps suffering from a bad case of journalistic sour grapes, the *Herald* tried to ignore the scandal at first and, when it could no longer do so, accused the *Times* of pursuing a vendetta. On September 8th the editor called the *Times* "a paper of English cockney proclivities, which might as well be published in some wild district in Wales for any interest it possesses in the eyes of Americans. . . . It has been by times in the pay of all parties and of all cliques, and if found today denouncing the corruptions of Tammany, it is simply because Tammany has failed to rate its friendship at the amount at which it values itself."

If that were true the *Times* must have rated itself pretty highly even then, for George Jones reported being offered a bribe of $5,000,000 to suppress the story. The *Herald* soon got over its snit and joined the fray.

In almost no time the Tweed Ring was in total disarray. Citizens committees formed, notably the Committee of Seventy headed by Henry G. Stebbins, and public meetings were held. Officials resigned and some fled to Europe. The Mayor, A. Oakey Hall, and the City Chamberlain, Peter Sweeny, were forced to resign from the Union Club before scandal could taint that august body, and Sweeny soon departed for Canada (although he wrote the newspapers that he had gone there—in December—only for reasons of health).

On October 27th Tweed himself was arrested and held on a million dollars bail, which was immediately supplied by Jay Gould and others. In early November the Republicans returned to power in the State Legislature by a landslide, and probity, decorum, and circumspection swept through New York courthouses and legislative halls.

It did not go unnoticed by either journalists or politicians that for the first time an independent newspaper had brought down a political organization. Suddenly the potential of the mass media to be the political watchdog of the nation was manifest.

•

By January 7th, 1871, Fisk had given up trying to come to terms with Stokes or to win back Josie Mansfield, and he had his rival arrested on a charge of embezzlement in connection with the Brooklyn Refinery Company. Stokes, as secretary of the corporation, had taken $250,000 in corporate funds, justifying his action by explaining that "the treasurer had done the same."⁹ As with Samuel Bowles, Fisk had taken pains to time the arrest carefully, and Stokes had to cool his heels in jail overnight. The next day the judge released him, saying that the company had not been legally organized as a corporation and was only a partnership; as a partner, Stokes was entitled to withdraw funds.

Stokes immediately counterclaimed for $200,000 against Fisk on a charge of malicious prosecution, but Fisk compromised the suit and bought out Stokes's interest in the company. In all these proceedings Josie Mansfield was a willing witness against Fisk, testifying that he had planned the ruin of Stokes from the beginning.

Just when everything appeared settled, Stokes tried to renew his suit for malicious prosecution, claiming it had not been satisfactorily adjudicated. Stokes and Fisk agreed to take all disputes between them to a referee, Clarence A. Seward. Seward ruled that Stokes had no claim on Fisk except for his imprisonment on the embezzlement charge, and awarded Stokes $10,000 for that. Stokes took the money and signed a release. But once again, Stokes's essential paranoia becoming ever more evident, he changed his mind and sought to reopen the case, this time claiming fraud on the part of Fisk and threatening to introduce as evidence the letters that Fisk had written to his former mistress. Fisk rushed into court to prevent their publication and tried to negotiate their return at the same time.

His friends, knowing that the letters were quite innocent and contained nothing that had not already entered the public domain by way of innuendo and rumor, urged Fisk to publish them himself and thus destroy Stokes's primary weapon against him. But he would not allow it.

Fisk replied to them, "You may laugh at me, but I tell you I can't put up on a signboard some of the purest thoughts that ever stirred me, and let the world laugh at me. They may curse me for this, and damn me for that, and ridicule me for something else—but, by the Lord, this is my *heart* that you want me to make a show of, and I won't."[10] While there is a whiff of apocrypha about this statement, which was widely printed in the papers at the time of his death, it undoubtedly reflects what Fisk, in his anguish, felt.

The battle with Stokes and Mansfield was fairly joined, and Stokes was forced to spend $38,000 he could ill afford in these lawsuits. Josie Mansfield, meanwhile, cheered on her new lover from the sidelines as well as the witness box. Asked by a reporter if she thought Fisk was insane, she replied, "It's more than possible." Then, knowing just where to stick the knife, added, "The disease is hereditary in the family. His father was insane."[11]

On October 18th Fisk asked Judge Pratt, who sat in the Brooklyn district of the Supreme Court, to grant an injunction forbidding any publication of what the *Herald* called "the fatal letters, which are like a pillar of fire by night and a column of smoke by day to the redoubtable Fisk."[12] The fact that Fisk, notoriously open about his private business, was fighting so hard to keep the letters out of the newspapers only intensified the public's interest in reading them, but the judge granted a temporary injunction. On October 27th Josie Mansfield sued Fisk for $40,000, claiming that he had had that amount of her money in his care and had not returned it.

Assistant Sheriff Joel Stevens called on Fisk at Castle Erie to arrest him, and Fisk was prepared. Asked if he had bail in the amount of the suit, Fisk replied, "I am like a department of odds and ends, always put to some good purpose," and hauled a bail bond in the correct amount out of his desk and gave it to Stevens. "I have been besieged all day by friends who wanted to go my bail," Fisk told him, bragging as usual. "I guess I could give bail for $200,000,000 if necessary." Then, business attended to, Fisk produced a handful of "flor de fumas."

"Take a cigar, Joel," the Colonel jovially offered.

Stevens gratefully helped himself. "I always like to smoke after performing a disagreeable duty," he told Fisk, lighting up.

"Oh, that's not disagreeable," Fisk said. "The majesty of the law must be respected and virtue always has its own reward."

The words stuck in Fisk's mind, for he was fond of using high-sounding phrases without bothering unduly about what they meant. Later, as the *Sun* reporter who had listened to all this was leaving Fisk's office, he heard the Colonel "issuing orders with the same rate of speed that the Chicago relief train travelled over the Erie road," and all the while muttering to himself, "Virtue has its own reward" over and over again.[13]

A month later Fisk, Stokes, and Mansfield were back in court to argue the merits of Stokes's case. Stokes had offered to return the letters for $15,000, and while Fisk had accepted this offer and paid the money, Stokes had reneged and refused to part with them, seeking to have this matter, as well, reopened. Fisk had had Stokes arrested on a charge of blackmail and the case had been taken to a grand jury.

All these penny-dreadful details and accusations delighted the public, who followed every twist and turn of the case in the newspapers. Josie Mansfield created quite a stir among the spectators when she appeared in court on November 26th. The *Herald* reporter was once again knocked off his feet by her "pearly white skin, [and her] dark and very large lustrous eyes, which, when directed at a judge, jury or witness have a terrible effect."

He described her clothes in lavish detail: "Her delicate white hands were encased in faultless lavender kid gloves and over her magnificent tournure of dark hair was perched a jaunty little alpine hat, with a dainty green feather perched therein. Her robe was of the heaviest black silk cut *a la Imperatrice* and having deep flounces of the heaviest black lace over Milanese bands of white satin. At her snowy throat the only article of jewelry on her person, a small gold pin, glistened and heightened the effect. Her hair was *a la Cleopatre* and a superb black velvet mantle covered her shoulders. Sitting there, this superb woman was the impersonification of coolness and proud disdain as she looked every now and then with fiery glances of contempt at the agonized Fisk."[14]

For a woman to be compelled to appear in court as a witness at all regarding such charges was scandalous enough. To sweep in dressed in this gaudy getup could only have titillated all who saw or read of it. Nor did she bother to conceal her affections. When her eyes weren't "having a terrible effect" on judge and jury or heaping ocular contempt upon Fisk, they were firmly fixed on Edward Stokes. "Stokes looked so handsome," wrote the reporter, "that Mrs. Mansfield found it quite impossible to take her eyes off his face."

Josie Mansfield was examined by Fisk's lawyer for fully three hours, and according to the *Herald* reporter, whose sympathies are not hard to discern, "the Falstaffian Fisk [was] routed horse, foot and dragoons by the late partner of his joys." In fact, Fisk's lawyer made mincemeat of her, and she came across as a money-hungry tramp in her testimony printed in the *Herald* and other newspapers. The judge put the case over until January 6th, 1872, after the Christmas holidays.

On that day, the judge, far less bowled over by Josie Mansfield's charms than the *Herald* reporter had been, found for Fisk and dismissed the suit. When court was adjourned, Stokes sent "the Cleopatra of the Erie Railroad"[15] back to her house with her cousin and went downtown to Delmonico's at Broadway and Chambers Street for lunch with his lawyers.

During lunch Stokes was joined by Judge Barnard, who brought him the entirely unwelcome news that the grand jury had acted to indict him on Fisk's charge of blackmail and that a bench warrant was out for his arrest. Stokes went white. He rose from the table without saying a word and went uptown to West 23rd Street to inform Josie Mansfield of what had happened. Then he called on Fisk at the Opera House. But Fisk had already left Castle Erie in order to call on a Mrs. Morse at the Grand Central Hotel, and Stokes, apparently, was told that he might find Fisk there. Mrs. Morse had been staying at the hotel with her two children and her mother, at Fisk's expense, since her husband, an old friend, had drowned in an accident the previous year.

Stokes hailed a cab and went down to the hotel at Broadway and 3rd Street, arriving there before Fisk did. The Grand Central, soon to be renamed the Broadway Central to avoid confusion with the Commodore's new train station far uptown, was one of the leading New York hotels of the time, having been opened only the previous year in the heart of the shopping district.

While the pulse of New York never stilled, it slowed on Saturday afternoons, a time, according to the *Herald*, when "New York's great thoroughfare presents the pleasantest sight." This particular

Saturday was like most others. "Men of business were walking leisurely homeward, troops of ladies were lingering among the glories of the shops, stately carriages lined the curbstones waiting the pleasure of their mistresses, and the color and sound of life were more subdued and harmonized than at busier hours of the day. The rumble of the vehicles was not so noisy, for the heavy drays and trucks had done with their incessant dragging hither and thither, and had left Broadway, going home through the by-streets."[16]

Stokes must have learned that Fisk had not yet arrived, for he went up to the parlor floor to wait for him at the head of the ladies' staircase. A few minutes after four o'clock, Fisk arrived at the ladies' entrance and walked toward the stairs that led to the parlor floor. Stokes, concealed, waited at the top.

"Come along," Stokes was heard to mutter to himself, oblivious at this point of everything but the compelling whispers of his paranoia, "I have got you now."[17]

Fisk started up the staircase. "I saw Edward Stokes at the head of the stairs," he told the coroner a few hours later. "As soon as I saw him I noticed he had something in his hand." It was a gun.

The realization that he was about to die must have rushed through the swift mind of Jubilee Jim Fisk like a sudden gust of wind through winter trees. The gun barked out and the ball thudded into Fisk's abdomen. The blow knocked him over backward and he tumbled down the stairs. He rose immediately and a second bullet passed through his left arm, doing little serious damage but knocking him down once more.

Stokes turned and walked down the corridor, throwing the gun under a sofa in one of the empty parlors. He then went to the hotel's office and told the man in charge that someone had been shot.

"Yes," said one of the hall boys who had seen him lurking at the top of the stairs, "and you are the man that did it."[18] The hotel doctor was summoned and a boy was sent flying over to the Mercer Street police station, while Stokes calmly sat and awaited their arrival.

Stokes was taken to the station but was soon transferred to the Tombs, where he was held without bail. All night he paced his cell, lighting cigar after cigar and then flinging them away unsmoked. "What do you think," he asked the policeman stationed outside his cell at one point, "is the man seriously injured?" He continued to pace and mutter.

At first it seemed that Fisk might not be badly hurt. He rose from

THE MURDER OF FISK   *Courtesy of The New-York Historical Society,
New York City*

the floor a second time and walked up the stairs under his own power and was taken to Parlor 215. It did not take the doctor long to realize otherwise. The bullet that had struck him two inches below the rib cage on the right side had angled downward deep into the gut beyond the reach of the longest probe. An autopsy would reveal that Fisk's intestine was perforated in four places. Today, with antibiotics and modern surgical techniques, such a wound would most likely present few problems in an otherwise healthy man, and Fisk was extraordinarily robust. But in 1872 it was a death sentence, for peritonitis was inevitable. "Although hope was expressed by those at the bedside," the *Herald* reported the next day, "not much was felt outside the door." Fisk asked that his wife, Lucy, be summoned and that David Dudley Field be called so he could write his will.

The coroner arrived to take an ante-mortem statement. "Do you believe you are about to die?" the coroner asked.

"I believe I am in a critical condition," Fisk answered.

"Have you any hope of recovery?"

"I hope so," Fisk said, wiping out most of the evidentiary value with his characteristic optimism, for ante-mortem statements must be made in anticipation of death. Once his will had been written (he left everything to his wife except for $3,000 a year for his parents and similar bequests to his half-sister and Mrs. Morse's two daughters), Fisk was given a large dose of morphine and went to sleep. He never really regained consciousness.

•

The news of the assassination reverberated through New York. "Never since the memorable night that Abe Lincoln was shot," wrote the *Herald* the next day, "was there such excitement. . . . In the street cars, in the hotels, everywhere throughout the entire city nothing was talked of but the attempted assassination."

Within an hour of the shooting, newsboys were running up and down the streets with copies of the *Evening Telegraph* and other papers. "Extra!" they shouted. "Shooting of Jim Fisk!"[19] A crowd gathered at the Grand Central Hotel, and the police had trouble maintaining order. It was much the same throughout the city. "There was a general rush for the hotels," the *Herald* reported, "and when the incredulous had made themselves positively certain they hurried away to tell their friends, who wouldn't be satisfied with such a report, but came down themselves in person to test its truth and swell the crowds in the corridors of the hotels. The scene at the Fifth Avenue Hotel was simply indescribable. As soon as ever the news of the shooting reached the clubs the members adjourned to the hotel as to one common center." Rumors flew in all directions, and "poor Fisk was reported to have received every known wound which it was possible for him to have received without getting his immediate quietus."[20]

Brokers poured into the Fifth Avenue Hotel, and its hallway was "converted into a lively stock market on a small scale." While they felt "a kind of sympathy for the man who had been shot down in the prime of his life in cold blood," brokers have always been a notably unsentimental bunch when it comes to acting on news likely to affect the great game. A *Herald* reporter heard one of them say that "Erie is sure to go up now, anyhow." And he was right, for when the Stock Exchange opened on Monday morning, Erie shot up to 35¼.

But, if the brokers could take a dispassionate attitude, the ordinary citizens of New York did not. "They remembered that he had once been a poor, toiling lad who had wrought his success out of hard, earnest effort; that his steps upwards, while decked with a gaudy, semi-barbaric show, were marked by strong traces of liberality and generosity of spirit that threw for the time the faults of his nature in the shade."[21] The rage against Stokes's cowardly, irrational act ran deep through the city's population. Rumors abounded that a lynch mob, and even the Ninth Regiment itself, was on the way to the Tombs to work swift justice. Superintendent of Police John Kelso took these rumors seriously enough to dispatch 250 additional policemen to guard the already well-defended prison against any attack that might arise, and sent four policemen to guard Josie Mansfield's house.

She heard of the shooting from a *Herald* reporter who called at her house to get her reaction. At first she refused to believe it. "The shooting is a fact," the reporter told her. "I am astonished that you have not heard of it. The city is alive with the excitement it has caused."

Josie had no trouble assessing the situation: "I wish it to be distinctly understood," she said, "that I am in no way connected with the sad affair. I have only my reputation to maintain." One can hardly help wondering what reputation she had in mind. Later, when the news had had time to sink in, she was distraught over her future prospects, if not over her former lover's death or her present one's incarceration. "Oh, dear me!" she wailed to a *Sun* reporter, "I do wish I had never had anything to do with the affair."[22]

As the news spread, Jubilee Jim's friends made their way to the Grand Central Hotel. Jay Gould arrived early, his eyes red, and stayed the night. Fisk's servants came to tend to him, and one told a reporter, "Ah, they may well talk of him who did not know him, but to those who were about him there never lived a kinder or a better man."[23] Colonel James Fisk, Jr., had been no hero on the battlefield, or even Eighth Avenue, but he was a hero to his valet.

Jay Gould and the others waited in the outer room as the doctors came and went and Fisk continued to sleep. Gould's chair was pushed up against the wall, and he sat there "composed but anxious for a long time." Then, even that most self-controlled and seemingly unemotional of men cracked under the strain. The tears welled up in his eyes, and, with his head in his hands, Gould wept "unrestrainedly with deep, audible sobs."[24]

At 6:20 in the morning Mrs. Fisk arrived from Boston, near hysteria, but Fisk could not be roused. Slowly his pulse became more rapid, his breathing shallower. Finally, "at a quarter before eleven the soul of James Fisk, Jr., sped from its earthly tenement and he lay stiff and lifeless."[25]

The people who had been waiting in the outer room came in to take a last look.

Not many minutes after Fisk's demise a woman, very plainly dressed, appeared at the door to Parlor 215 with a small child in tow. She was turned away by the guard who had been posted by the hotel, but she would not be deterred. "For six months," she said, "he has kept me and my child from starvation, and I have never seen his face. I want to look upon my noble benefactor."[26]

Fisk's body was transferred to a coffin, and preparations were got under way to move it back to his house at 313 West 23rd Street. Before he was moved, however, a man walked down the hall and into Parlor 215, as "clerks made way for him deferentially." The coffin had been closed, and he motioned for it to be reopened. "The newcomer," wrote the *Herald*, "looked long and earnestly at the pallid features and the sightless eyes that stared up at him. Unforbidden tears welled up and slowly trickled down his cheeks and with bowed head and clasped hands William M. Tweed looked down on all that remained of his friend. It was a scene mournful beyond measure. Whatever his other failings Tweed has a great good heart."[27]

Gould, interviewed at the Opera House, was distraught. "I cannot sufficiently give expression to the extent I suffer over the catastrophe," he told the *Herald* reporter. "We have been working together for five or six years and during that time not the slightest unpleasantness has ever arisen between us. He was genial in his habits and beloved by all who had any dealings with him."

Gould, whose idea of an evening's entertainment was reading in his library at his new house at 576 Fifth Avenue, also thought that Fisk had been settling down rapidly. "Since the dissolution of whatever tie has existed between him and Mrs. Mansfield," he said, "he has been a changed man. He had ceased to practice many of the old habits of which he has been accused, and was in every sense becoming what all who loved him desired he should be. His old associations were being rapidly broken up, and if he had lived some time longer a complete reform would have taken place in his whole conduct, though I do not for an instant say that his improprieties were so heinous as they have been generally represented to be."[28]

•

The next morning the body was taken to the Opera House next door to Fisk's house and, dressed in his $5,000 uniform as Colonel of the Ninth Regiment, prepared for public viewing in the lobby. A crowd had been gathering since early morning and by the time the doors opened at eleven o'clock the crush was immense, filling the streets, while boys had climbed the lampposts to observe the scene from the cross arms. The *Herald* estimated that the number "could not have been less than one hundred thousand," but that seems an impossibly high figure. Certainly "the jumble of cars, stages, drays, trucks, and men and women was fearful."

It was immediately obvious that all who wanted to see Jim Fisk for the last time could not do so, as the viewing time allowed was only three hours, but about 20,000 forced their way in, although the police at least once had to resort to nightsticks to keep order at the door of the Opera House. "The ladies who ran the gauntlet," reported the *Herald,* "did so in the face of every difficulty, and on emerging from the crowd and gaining the sidewalk their appearance was more picturesque than flattering. Many of them had torn clothes and dishevelled hair, but curiosity triumphed over every obstacle, and they were rewarded for their perseverance by gaining the entrance to the building."

Outside the Opera House the vehicles for the cortège were lined up, the hearse, it was widely noted, being parked in front of Josie Mansfield's house, where the shutters were closed and the blinds drawn. At two o'clock, the troops of the Ninth Regiment assembled, and the cortège began to make its way toward the old railroad station at 26th Street and Fourth Avenue, which was soon to be converted into the first Madison Square Garden. Although Jim Fisk's military exploits had bordered on the nonexistent, he received a military funeral that New York would not see the likes of again until General Grant himself was buried there thirteen years later.

"As far as the eye could see along 23rd Street," the *Herald* reported, "the sidewalks were lined with people closely packed, and the occupants of the houses along the street, with many invited friends . . . occupied the windows." When it reached Madison Square, where thousands stood to catch a glimpse, the procession turned up Broadway and then east on 26th Street to the railroad station, where "the multitude that surrounded the spot was immense, and filled not only the avenues but all of the streets like a black, restless sea."

The coffin was placed aboard a private car and the car hauled up to Commodore Vanderbilt's new Grand Central Depot by horses, where it was hooked onto the New York, New Haven and Hartford train that would take Jim Fisk home to Brattleboro. Five thousand people waited at Grand Central to see the coffin go by, and this crowd would be repeated at every station along the way. There were a thousand people at Stamford, five hundred at Bridgeport, seven hundred at Hartford. At grade crossings and villages across half of New England, small knots of people stood and waited in the January cold in order to pay their last respects to the Prince of Erie.

Five thousand people came out at midnight to meet the train at Brattleboro, and the town's citizens raised $25,000 to commission from Larkin Mead—the sculptor of the statue of Lincoln in Springfield, Illinois—a monument for the grave of their most famous native son. The monument, carved in Italy, featured an obelisk supported by four female figures representing the Erie Railway, the Narragansett Line, the Muse of Music, and Commerce.

Almost at once tourists, seeking souvenirs, began to chip away at it, chiseling off most of the fingers and toes. A few years earlier Fisk had contributed to the fund to build a fence around the cemetery, although he said he didn't see much use in it. "The fellows that are in," he noted, "cannot get out, and those who are out do not want to get in."[29]

All across the country, preachers and guardians of the public morals, such as Henry Ward Beecher in his Sunday sermon at Plymouth Church, had denounced Fisk and called his murder a fitting end to a rascal's life.

"Yet I say," Beecher thundered in his righteous wrath, "to every young man who has looked upon this glaring meteor, and thought that perhaps integrity was not necessary, 'mark the end of this wicked man, and turn back again to the ways of integrity!' " Those who would write the first histories of the time were Beecher's intellectual heirs, and took their cue from Beecher and his ilk. Of course, like most intellectuals, it never occurred to them to ask the opinion of the man on the street.

For the ordinary people would have none of this cant. They remembered Fisk's generosity, not his knavery, his unstudied kindness, not his equally unstudied buffoonery. The Victorians would remember Jim Fisk for the rest their lives, and the overwhelming majority of them thought kindly of him.

When the *Herald* printed a sermon by the Reverend J. S. Willis of the 17th Street Methodist Episcopal Church that was much the same in tone as Beecher's, Bennett was astonished at the hundreds of letters that poured into the *Herald* defending Fisk, and he printed many of them.

"We should not judge too harshly of James Fisk," wrote Colonel J. G. Dudley. "He was a creature of circumstances—a legitimate fruit of the state of public and private morality existing when he began his career. He found legislatures corrupt and he purchased them; he found judges venal and he bribed them; he found a large part of society fond of vulgar display, dash and barbaric magnificence and he gratified the taste of that portion of society. How much further he could have gone on in this course, if the assassin's bullet had not suddenly put a stop to it, no one can tell; but the closing scenes of his death-bed condoned for much of the waywardness of his life. . . . He made ample provision for his aged parents and sister, and munificently remembered the children of those who had befriended him when he needed friends. Let the mantle of charity cover his sins—and may it be long before his counterpart appear to dazzle and vex the world again."[30]

•

Jim Fisk's estate amounted to less than a million dollars. It had never been his aim in life to accumulate great wealth, and he had

"LIKE A BLACK, RESTLESS SEA" 100,000 New Yorkers turned out for the funeral of Jim Fisk. *Courtesy of The New-York Historical Society, New York City*

spent money and given it away as fast as it came in (he had given the Ninth Regiment $11,000 only two days before his death). Many of his possessions were auctioned, including his canaries; the bird named Jay Gould was sold for $8.50 while Commodore Vanderbilt fetched $6.50. Mrs. Fisk, who inherited most of her husband's estate, took bad investment advice and soon lost most of it. But Jay Gould saw to it that she was never in want.

Stedman would note, doubtless accurately, that "had Stokes been an illiterate laborer he would have dangled in a noose two months later."[31] But Stokes was not an illiterate laborer. While most of the family wanted nothing to do with their black sheep, they had no desire to see him swing from a gibbet either.

They hired the best criminal lawyers in New York, who in the first trial won a hung jury, no small accomplishment given the evidence and public opinion. Charges of jury tampering were widely bandied about. His second trial resulted in a conviction for murder, and Stokes was sentenced to be hanged on February 28th, 1873. But the conviction was set aside, and a third jury found him guilty only of manslaughter. He was sentenced to serve four years at Sing Sing and did so.

Stokes lived the rest of his life in New York, socially ostracized but not impoverished, dying at the age of sixty in 1901.

For Josie Mansfield life was less kind still. With no great family behind her and her only real asset a rapidly wasting one, her fate was to live too long. No one in New York would associate with her after the murder, and she fled to Europe, where she lived for the next quarter century. In 1891 she married an American expatriate, Robert L. Reade, the alcoholic brother-in-law of Viscount Falkland, but divorced him when he was declared insane a few years later.

Returning to this country penniless, her fifteen minutes of fame long over, she settled with her brother in Watertown, South Dakota, about as far from the lights of Broadway as it is possible to get. When he died in 1909 she had to move elsewhere. Somehow she made her way back to Europe, her hair now white, her always ample figure long gone to flab. In Paris once again, she lived on and on, until, at the age of eighty-three, a fall caused her death on October 27th, 1931.

Sixty years earlier, half the population of a great city had turned out to see the funeral of the man who had loved her and whom she had wronged. In this new era into which she had lingered, it seems that only a reporter for the *New York Times* noticed the hearse and the three mourners walking behind it as they made their way through the rain to the cemetery on Montparnasse.

CHAPTER SEVENTEEN

The Fall of Castle Erie

LONG afterward people would say that had Fisk lived he and Gould would never have lost control of the Erie. "The majority of the Board of directors . . . were enemies of Gould," the *Sun* reported, "and were desirous of forcing him from the Presidency. But they were nearly all warm friends of Col. Fisk, and out of respect to his wishes they suffered their opposition to lie dormant until after his death. Stokes's bullet killed Jay Gould's power at the same time it took away Col. Fisk's life."[1]

In fact this was only romanticizing the dead. Gould had been struggling with the ever more desperate situation of Erie's rulers for months before Fisk died, and he knew that only a radical restructuring of the management could hope to save his control of the company in the new political atmosphere.

Ironically, just as control of the Erie was beginning to slip from his grasp, Gould's stewardship was beginning to produce real improvement in the earnings. The gross for the year ended September 30th, 1871, had been $17,168,005 and expenses totaled $12,446,355, leaving a gross profit of $4,721,650. Interest on the mountain of debt gobbled up $3,908,603 of that but still left a net profit of $813,047, far more than the Erie had ever earned before in a single year.[2] If one added in the fact that a five-month-long strike in the Pennsylvania coal fields had severely curtailed the railroad's highly profitable coal traffic, it began to look as though the Erie might at long last be starting to deliver on its economic promise.

The *Commercial and Financial Chronicle,* no friend of Gould, nonetheless noted that since "we have so often been obliged to rebuke the financial managers of the Erie Railroad . . . it is really a pleasure to find reason for a less harsh criticism." The *Chronicle* was especially impressed with the fact that Gould had managed to reduce the Erie's fuel costs from twenty-two cents a mile in 1867 to only ten cents a mile four years later.[3] Gould even announced that a dividend on the preferred stock would be resumed, and was hopeful that a dividend on the common would not be far behind.

None of this was enough to impress Wall Street. Erie stock remained mired in the low 30's, and the consolidated mortgage bonds still had no takers other than Gould himself.

In late November, 1871, Gould had called on several prominent brokers to ask for their ideas. William Butler Duncan, a partner in the major Wall Street firm of Duncan and Sherman, was unequivocal in his advice. "Gould," he said, "there is but one thing that can help Erie out of its troubles, give it credit, and enable you to sell your bonds abroad and get money."

Gould, all ears, asked what Duncan had in mind.

"Change the Board of Directors, and put in some strong names that people have confidence in!"[4]

Gould had also sought the advice of Levi P. Morton, already prominent on Wall Street and later to be Governor of New York and Vice President under Benjamin Harrison (his house, long given over to commerce, still stands on the northeast corner of Fifth Avenue and 42nd Street). Morton had agreed completely with Duncan and suggested several names for the new board. On December 11th, Gould wrote to Duncan and Morton with a proposal:

> Gentlemen:—Acquiescing in the importance of a reorganization of the Board of Directors of the Erie Railway by associating with the best railway and financial talent in the country in its management, I propose as follows:
> First.—To procure the resignation of the present Board, and to substitute the following-named gentlemen: Jay Gould, August Belmont, J. S. Morgan, Erastus Corning, representing the New York Central; James F. Joy, representing the Michigan Central Railroad; Horace F. Clark, representing the Lake Shore Railroad; William Butler Duncan, representing the Atlantic and

Great Western Railroad; Levi P. Morton, Moses Taylor, Edwin Eldridge, John A. Stewart, Thomas A. Scott, John Jacob Astor, L. M. Von Hoffman, E. D. Morgan; George Talbott Olyphant, representing the Delaware and Hudson Canal Company; John Ewen, representing the Pennsylvania Coal Company; Asa Packer, representing the Lehigh Valley Railroad Company.

In order to secure permanency to this board, and to avoid merely speculative control, I would further propose that Messrs. Bischoffscheim, J. S. Morgan, and Sir John Rose be a committee to procure irrevocable proxies from the owners of a majority of stock; . . . The permanent organization of the company to be selected by Messrs. William Butler Duncan, Levi P. Morton, and myself.

> Yours respectfully,
> Jay Gould[5]

Gould's proposed new Erie board, a veritable who's who of the American financial and railroad establishment, would certainly have revived Wall Street's confidence in the Erie and its securities. Duncan and Morton approved wholeheartedly and agreed to help get the necessary agreements. Armed with an irrevocable proxy for the 280,000 shares of Erie owned or controlled by Gould, Duncan set off for England to sell the idea to the English shareholders represented by Heath and Raphael and by Bischoffscheim & Goldschmidt.

Gould was confident that the scheme would be adopted, but he had a plan in case the old board objected. "If there should be any trouble . . ." Gould said, "I will facilitate an act of the Legislature repealing the Classification Act, and order an immediate election."[6] The Classification Act, which had served Gould and Fisk so well, was now to serve Gould once more, by its death if necessary. Gould would soon find, however, that events were moving too swiftly for him to have much control over them.

Absent from Gould's proposed new board, of course, had been Jim Fisk. Whether Fisk had known of Gould's plans to reshape the board of the Erie is not certain, and many of Fisk's friends always maintained that he was double-crossed by Gould, whose reputation as the "Mephistopheles of Wall Street" began at this time. But that seems most unlikely. Fisk so often acted the clown that it is easy to forget he had been nobody's fool; it is most improbable that he had been oblivious of what was going on in the very next room.

Certainly Fisk had known that the old regime was doomed, for a week before his death he had resigned as vice president and controller—although not from the board—a fact that was never publicly announced. The Prince of Erie had already renounced his throne when Stokes ended his life.

•

Besides the long-suffering English stockholders, there were many others hopeful of wresting control of the Erie from Gould for their own purposes. One of these was the Englishman James McHenry, of the grandly named but actually diminutive Atlantic and Great Western Railroad. McHenry had built his railroad, which ran from Salamanca, New York, to Dayton, Ohio, using the Erie's broad gauge. It had originally been intended to exploit the new traffic in oil from the Pennsylvania oil fields and to provide a link between the Erie and the Ohio and Mississippi Railroad, which ran a broad-gauge line as far as St. Louis. McHenry and Gould had long been allies in the race for western connections and other matters. But the Pennsylvania Railroad had been gaining more and more of the oil traffic, and the Atlantic and Great Western seldom earned enough money to do more than pay the interest on its considerable debt.

When the Ohio and Mississippi Railroad converted its tracks to the standard gauge in 1871, the Atlantic and Great Western, with the broad gauge it could not afford to change, was left as little more than an appendage to the Erie and had little choice but to play ball with that railroad's management. But McHenry quarreled bitterly with Gould and decided that if he was to prosper he had to get Gould out of the Erie and put men in who were friendly to him. Hardly for the last time in corporate history, David decided to take over Goliath. To do that McHenry needed the help of someone intimately familiar with the American power structure, and he decided that General Daniel E. Sickles was just the man.

Sickles was an eccentric such as only the nineteenth century could have produced. Born in New York in 1825 he studied for the law but drifted into politics, where, with his passion for conniving, he soon found a natural home. A Congressman by 1857, Sickles caused a national sensation when, in Lafayette Park in full view of the White House, he gunned down Philip Barton Key—the son of Francis Scott Key and District Attorney for the nation's capital—for having an affair with his wife.

Sickles pleaded temporary insanity, the first time in legal history such a defense was attempted. He got away with it, too, for the jury found him not guilty. Having resumed his seat in the House, he further titillated Victorian sensibilities by taking his wife back to his bed and board. Apparently she decided she preferred the grave, for she soon committed suicide.

When the Civil War broke out, Sickles raised a regiment of volunteers in New York and soon rose to the rank of brevet major general. No one ever doubted Sickles's courage but many doubted his military common sense. At the Battle of Gettysburg he seriously compromised the integrity of General Meade's line by advancing his troops on his own authority to a small rise where they "stuck out like a sore thumb" and were exposed to enemy artillery fire. Just how exposed they were was soon evident when a Confederate cannonball took off Sickles's right leg. As he was carried away on a stretcher, he lit a cigar to prove to his troops that he was still breathing; he was eventually awarded the Medal of Honor. The General donated his shattered leg bones to the Smithsonian, where in later years he visited them regularly.

After the war, President Grant appointed him ambassador to Spain, then a most important diplomatic post. While ambassador, Sickles had a well-publicized affair with Isabella II, the deposed— and allegedly nymphomaniacal—queen.

Sickles and McHenry had known each other for some time when they met again in London in the fall of 1871. McHenry made Sickles an offer: get Gould out of Erie and he would pay him $100,000. Sickles immediately applied for leave from his job as ambassador to Madrid and sailed for New York.

Sickles hoped to accomplish his task by using the suddenly law-abiding courts, but he soon saw that an approach through the law, even if successful, would be too slow for his purposes, so he fell back on the tried-and-true system of bribery. To help him in this task he had George Crouch. Realizing the fast-collapsing position of Fisk and Gould, Crouch had decided to jump ship and left his job at the Erie soon after the triumph of the Chicago relief train. He sailed for his native England, where he offered his services to the English stockholders and to McHenry. He was soon back in New York, where his intimate knowledge of the personalities of the Erie board members would prove invaluable.

Besides McHenry and the English stockholders, Gould had increasingly to contend with the newspapers. In the new atmosphere engendered by the fall of Tweed at the hands of the *New York*

Times and *Harper's Weekly,* the newspapers were in full cry, and the mighty *Herald,* slow to get on the reform bandwagon and now playing catch-up, attacked the management of the Erie in a series of thunderous editorials.

"There is no citadel of fraud," wrote the *Herald* on March 1st, 1872, "no matter how strongly garrisoned and entrenched, that will not yield in time to the incessant and well-directed blows of an independent and powerful journal. . . .

"We virtually say to foreign investors that if they send their money to the United States they must run the risk of confiscation. The owners go to the Legislature and find that the [Erie] Ring has purchased its members. They entreat the courts only to learn that the servants of the Ring wear the ermine. They appeal to Albany and discover that the pen of the Governor obeys the Ring as readily as the timid Faust when he wrote his name in blood at the command of Mephistopheles. . . .

"Tammany was an ulcer: Erie is a cancer. It must be rooted out, and at once, and we must make it impossible that it can ever grow again upon our body politic."

The *Herald*'s first priority was the repeal of the Classification Act, which was then before the Legislature. Reports of its impending passage had sent Erie stock up from 33 to 36, but the *Herald* was taking no chances, for there were numerous reports of large sums of money changing hands in Albany.

"We do not believe that this impudent and undisguised attempt to bribe and corrupt the present Legislature as the notoriously venal Legislatures of 1869 and 1871 were bribed and corrupted, will succeed. Since those years the terrible exposure of the Tammany frauds and the fate of the unfaithful public officers who were implicated in them, stand forth as a warning to the legislators whose fingers are itching for the money of the Erie Ring. They may go the way of their predecessors if they will, it is true; but in the road now stands a signpost with a fettered hand pointing in the direction of Sing Sing. They have seen how a mighty combination can be broken to pieces, despite its influence and wealth, and how readily, when the exposure comes, the fellow conspirator turns into the informer and the accuser."[7]

This, indeed, was Gould's biggest problem. The Erie board of directors had been perfectly happy for Gould and the executive committee to run the company while the board itself met seldom and perfunctorily. Now, in the frenzy of reformation that had seized the Legislature and the courts, the members of the board began to fear that they might be held personally liable for their failure to guard the interests of the stockholders. "Every man for himself" was the new order of the day. General Sickles exploited this fact and approached members of the board to offer them inducements to desert Gould. As always in the Erie Wars, silver bullets proved to be most effective. Indeed, Sickles soon learned that Frederick A. Lane, the Erie's general counsel and one of Gould's closest confidants, was busily trying to make a separate deal with McHenry to deliver the Erie board to him.

McHenry and the English stockholders were prepared to pay out large sums to the directors and others because they expected to make big profits in Erie stock when Gould was deposed as president, and had been buying in the market. Timing was crucial, as the stock had to be purchased before the coup could be executed. As early as February 29th, Crouch was cabling McHenry to ask, "Have you bought all you want?"[8]

Before long he had the agreement of several members of the board, who were paid at least $30,000 each for their perfidy. There were at the moment two vacancies (the seats that had been held by Tweed and Fisk), and the directors agreed to fill these slots with men friendly to McHenry and the Atlantic and Great Western Railroad. Then, rather than vote Gould out themselves (as so often among Victorians, the board cared more about appearance than fact), the board members agreed to resign one by one, their places to be taken by McHenry men one by one until they constituted a majority of the board and they could vote Gould out of office.

There were two problems. One was that men had to be ready to step into the vacant places on the board and fill the office of president until the Classification Act was repealed and new elections could be organized. Sickles, with the help of S. L. M. Barlow, a very prominent attorney who lived in state at 1 Madison Avenue, soon had the new board ready to go. The new directors included William R. Travers, long an ally of Leonard Jerome on the Street, and Colonel Henry G. Stebbins. Stebbins at this time was both the chairman of the city Department of Parks (and a major force behind the continuing creation of Central Park) and the chairman of the Committee of Seventy dedicated to reforming the city government in the wake of the fall of the Tweed Ring. A man of immense energy, he had once been president of the New York Stock Exchange and a sitting Congressman at the same time. Everyone agreed that Stebbins was a symbol of unquestioned integrity and that his name would give the new board an undeniable appearance of "reform."

For the new president of the Erie, the McHenry forces chose General John A. Dix, another symbol of rectitude. Dix had had a long and distinguished career in government already and would go on to be elected Governor of New York the following November.

The second problem was arranging for the board to meet in order to effect the coup d'état against Gould. The bylaws of the company, which had been rewritten to suit the president, read that the board was to meet only at stated times unless called into special session by the president of the company. Gould, needless to say, had no intention whatever of summoning the board, for he knew that conspiracies were hatching all around him.

One evening in late February Lane called on Gould and told him, "There is a great conspiracy against you, and you are being sold out of the Erie management." Lane told Gould the details as to who had taken McHenry's and the English stockholders' money to change sides. "They are counting on me," Lane assured him, "but I shall remain true to you, and they have not money enough to change me."

Gould, recalling this conversation later, remarked that "I took [this] with a slight discount, knowing Lane very well."[9] Gould was right to do so, and Lane would find $67,500 of McHenry's money ample inducement to switch sides.

•

A few days later a meeting of the executive committee was called to handle some business regarding the Erie's strained relations with the Atlantic and Great Western Railroad. The executive committee now consisted of Gould, Lane, Homer Ramsdell, and O. H. P. Archer, who had replaced Fisk as vice president. Gould knew that he could count only on his own vote at this meeting and fully expected one of the others to submit a resolution calling for a meeting of the full board. Gould knew how to handle this.

"I had the resolution confirming the Atlantic and Great Western settlement ready, called the meeting to order, put the resolution, passed it, and adjourned the meeting so quickly that before they could get their resolution ready the meeting was over and I was off; so the effort failed. I don't know who made the motion to adjourn. I thought I heard it. Then I thought I heard a good many 'ayes,' and declared it carried."[10]

Thwarted, nine members of the board, a clear majority, wrote Gould a letter and demanded a meeting of the board.

> Erie Railway Company
> New York, March 8, A.D. 1872
>
> Mr. Jay Gould, President Erie Railway Company:
> Sir:—The undersigned, Directors of this company, having witnessed with deep regret the growing distrust which pervades the community in regard to its management, deem it their duty to request you to call a meeting of the Board, with a view to the consideration of such measures and to the transaction of such business as may be deemed necessary. Prominent among the embarrassments are its finances and a general want of confidence in the credit of the company. Impressed with the responsibility which rests upon us, we regard this call for a meeting as an imperative duty, and therefore respectfully request that, in compliance with our by-laws, you convene the Board at a meeting to be held on Monday, the 11th day of March, at 12 o'clock.

Gould claimed never to have received this letter, although he may simply never have opened it, knowing full well what was in it. The next day, having had no reply from Gould, who remained incommunicado in his office and refused to see them, the same nine members of the board asked the vice president to call a meeting, and he did so. Gould thought he knew how to handle this threat too. Obtaining an injunction against the irregular meeting from Judge Daniel P. Ingraham, he called in the police and, as further insurance, the famous "thugs of Erie" commanded by Tommy Lynch.

On the morning of Monday, March 11th, Lynch showed up at the Opera House with a hundred men. A law that Tweed had pushed through the Legislature in 1870 gave railroad presidents the right to swear in "special police" for duty on railroad property, and Gould promptly did so, giving Lynch's dockside ruffians the legal status of deputy sheriffs.

The *Herald* described Tommy Lynch: "His pantaloons were considerably too short, his shirt of no decided hue, his hair unkempt and his coat and hat of a dirty, shaggy brown."[11] If his appearance was unprepossessing, the menace he presented was very real. One of the directors asked him what he was doing at the Opera House and

Lynch replied that he was a "candidate for a brakeman's position."
"Brakeman on what?" the director asked.
"On people's noses, if they ain't careful," Lynch replied.[12]

Gould, once he had sworn in Lynch's gang, thought matters were fully in hand and departed for Wall Street. He counted on Tommy Lynch, with his thugs, and on lawyer Thomas G. Shearman, with Judge Ingraham's injunction, to prevent any illegal meeting of the board. It was a fatal mistake on Gould's part, for despite his bullying approach, Lynch throughout these proceedings kept a close eye on which way the wind was blowing. He never gave Gould the whole-hearted support he needed if he was to survive. Shearman, whom the *Herald* described as being only "a little bit of a man with gold spectacles,"[13] would do his best, regardless of his utter disdain for the goon squad Gould had left as his main support.

Lynch's men made themselves at home, spitting freely on the marble floors and burning holes in the velvet carpets of Castle Erie with their cigar butts. Police Captain Joseph Petty soon arrived with seventy policemen and orders from Superintendent Kelso to admit no one to the building but members of the board and bona-fide employees of the company.

The would-be new members of the board, meanwhile, assembled at S. L. M. Barlow's mansion on Madison Square, a few blocks away, and dispatched George Crouch to the Opera House to reconnoiter. Crouch, learning that Gould had gone downtown, reported that the coast was clear, and they then boarded carriages and proceeded along 23rd Street to Castle Erie, where, on Lane's direct orders, they were admitted.

Captain Petty asked the Barlow group to leave, but they refused to do so and were invited to remain by the board. After checking with Kelso by telegraph, Petty allowed them to stay. Kelso himself soon showed up with forty-two more policemen, determined to keep the peace if at all possible. That was beginning to seem more and more dubious, however, for General Dix had asked for and received a contingent of U.S. marshals, which made a third constabulary now on duty inside the Opera House, while outside a large crowd awaited the outcome with mounting excitement.

When Vice President Archer called the meeting of the board of directors to order at noon, Shearman appeared with a Mr. Poucher, one of Gould's clerks. Poucher, holding the injunction that had been granted by Judge Ingraham, approached Frederick Lane.

"Here is a copy of a summons, complaint, affidavit, and injunction," Poucher told Lane formally, handing it over. "And here is the original."

Lane angrily demanded to see the latter.

"Here it is," replied Poucher, holding up the papers. Lane snatched the precious document out of Poucher's hand and, backing up against the wall, held it behind him.

"I want that," shouted Poucher, making a grab for it, but he only succeeded in tearing it. Shearman, meanwhile, tried to pass out to the other members of the board copies of the injunction, which forbade the board to accept the resignation of any directors or from electing or balloting for any members to fill their places. Pandemonium ensued and Shearman realized he needed more help than Poucher and went for the police, returning with forty of them to enforce the judge's injunction.

"The heavy, folding doors [of the board room] were thrown open," the *Sun* reported, "and in they marched. Bedlam broke loose in an instant. All hands jumped to their feet and howled with mingled rage and fury. Wild gesticulations were emphasized with angry words."

"Shearman, what do you want here?" one of the new directors yelled. "Get out! You don't belong here!"

"It is the custom," replied Shearman, mustering all the dignity at his disposal, "for counsel to be present at meetings of the Board of Directors!"

"Can't help it," he was told. "Get out!"

While the police were willing to help with the formal service of the injunction, they were not prepared to physically prevent the board from meeting. "Oh," someone was heard to exclaim through the uproar, "for one hour of Jim Fisk! He'd have a thousand men here if need be and he'd sweep the room like a deluge."[14] But Fisk was not there, and the rebelling board continued to defy Gould's forces.

When the new board members were seated they duly voted to remove Gould as president of the Erie Railway and to install General Dix in his place. Dix, seated in the president's chair, asked one of the U.S. marshals to deliver to Gould the formal notification of his dismissal.

Gould had returned from Wall Street to discover how ineffectual his efforts to prevent the board from meeting had been and had barricaded himself in the president's office, tying the doorknobs of the elegant black walnut double doors together with sash cord. The marshals, with a piece of steel and a wrench, "the only weapons available,"[15] started to batter the door down and finally succeeded in prying it open enough to admit a knife to cut through the sash cord. The U.S. marshals and "twenty to thirty of the friends of the new board poured in"[16] to the president's ornate office, which was already a shambles.

Gould hightailed it out a side door while Shearman bravely stood his ground and screamed for the police. A law partner of S. L. M. Barlow "took him by the coat collar and pitched him away from the door,"[17] while the mob ran pell-mell through the suite of adjoining offices after Gould, who desperately flung chairs and slammed doors in their faces. He finally took refuge in Lane's office at the other end of the Opera House, while the marshals demanded that he open up "in the name of the United States."

One of the marshals, David H. Crowley, knowing this was hardly likely to be effective, soon went around to the hall door to Lane's office and there found poor Shearman knocking for admittance. As soon as Gould opened the door a crack, the marshal leapt at the luckless attorney—who was certainly earning his fee that day— "tackled him, flung him aside and forced his way in in his place."[18] Crowley lunged at Gould, who tried to jump back out of reach, and succeeded in stuffing the dismissal notice into Gould's waistcoat pocket, yelling, "You are served—you are served."[19]

Shearman, picking himself up and dusting off his clothes yet again, looked at the notice and said in surprise, "Why, this is not a writ."

All the hubbub had really been for nothing, for Gould could certainly claim that the notice of an action by an illegal meeting of the board was without legal effect.

At this point the police, responding to the screams for help, showed up at the back door to the office and nearly bludgeoned Crowley senseless before he was able to identify himself as a fellow officer of the law. The uproar continued throughout the afternoon, with Archer and Crouch in possession of the board room (noting, apparently, the inefficacy of sash cord, they secured the doorknobs with brass tubing from a gas lamp). Gould held Lane's office, and Tommy Lynch's men occupied anywhere they liked, moving "into the private offices of the directors, lounging on the handsome chairs

FORCING THE DOOR TO THE PRESIDENT'S OFFICE AT CASTLE ERIE *Courtesy of The New-York Historical*

and cursing in low tones while they chewed and squirted tobacco juice over the brussels carpet."[20]

Despite the confused situation and the ever-present potential for mayhem, there was a great deal of coming and going about the Opera House. General Sickles, who had not been present earlier, showed up, and even Tweed and Sweeny—the latter back from Canada to face the music—put in an appearance.

Sickles and the newly elected directors soon "departed to Delmonico's and other resorts of luxury to sip their Chablis with their oysters and talk over the events of the day,"[21] leaving Crouch and Archer to hold the fort at the Opera House. Meanwhile "a vast crowd of influential businessmen, bankers, merchants and politicians thronged the corridors, reading rooms, and barroom of the Fifth Avenue Hotel, excitedly discussing the ousting of Jay Gould from the presidency of the Erie Road, and predicting all manner of disasters and successes in consequence."[22]

The market itself had no doubt about the future of Erie, for the price rose five points on the New York Stock Exchange. Rumors swept through the city, and Tweed, from his office window, heard one newsboy shouting, "Death of Gould."[23]

At Castle Erie the standoff continued into the evening, and reporters milled around the corridors interviewing anyone willing to talk. "What effect will this have on the stock?" the *Herald* reporter asked Thomas Shearman.

"Why, it'll go down," replied Shearman, anticipating J. P. Morgan's famous market forecast, "if it don't go up."

Even corporate raiders and their targets have to eat, and "a bountiful supper was served to all hands about seven o'clock. The resources of the Erie restaurant were taxed to the utmost to supply the two factions."[24]

Later, while Tommy Lynch's men came and went in the night and those who stayed cheerfully got drunk as they relieved "their watchfulness of Erie's property by frequent libations of vile whiskey,"[25] George Crouch panicked and sent a note to General Sickles.

Erie Railway Co. March 11, 9:20 PM

Dear General:
Gould has a gang of the most desperate ruffians of New York in and around the building. A Tammany gang has just arrived. Trouble is evidently brewing and our force of police is ex-

ceedingly slim. Please take measures at once to reinforce the garrison. The roughs are plentifully supplied with liquor, and are armed to the teeth.

Yours, truly,
George Crouch

Sickles did not respond to this plea and in fact nothing came of it. Gould spent the night locked in Lane's office, considering his unenviable position. Undoubtedly he was aware of the market's reaction to the news of his fall from power at Erie, and this may well have influenced his thinking, for he was still the largest single stockholder and would be a major beneficiary of any further rise. Sometime in the evening he decided to parley and sent Dr. Eldridge, a director who had remained loyal to him, over to S. L. M. Barlow's house. The next morning, as reporters haunted the halls of Castle Erie looking for news, and police, U.S. marshals, and Tommy Lynch's thugs stood around waiting for what might happen, there was much coming and going between offices as the rival factions tried to thrash out a deal.

One of the old directors, asked his opinion by the *Sun* reporter, responded that "there will be a compromise in an hour or so or there will be war to the knife." Then, perhaps thinking his metaphor had been a bit infelicitous given the firepower ranging the corridors, added, "Of course when I speak of a knife I speak of it only in a figurative sense."[26]

Finally, the deal was done. Gould insisted that the meeting held the previous day had been illegal and that a new one would have to be held with him in charge. He came out of Lane's office looking "very pale and scarce able to walk."[27] In the boardroom the old directors were seated at the table when Gould entered the room. "Gentlemen," he said, "I call this meeting to order."

"In an instant," reported the *Sun*, "one could have heard a pin drop." One by one the old directors resigned their seats. One by one the new ones took their places. When the new board was seated, Gould addressed them. "Gentlemen, I herewith resign the office of President of the Erie Railroad Company."

The first act of the board was to accept Gould's resignation. The second was to adopt a resolution:

Resolved, that public notice be given that it is the intentions of this board that the *bona fide* stockholders of this company

GOULD FLEES HIS OFFICE AS THE U.S. MARSHALS BREAK THROUGH *Courtesy of The New-York Historical Society, New York City*

shall at all times hereafter have and be allowed to exercise their
full and absolute right to control the direction of this company,
and that this board will do all in its power to bring about such
a speedy election as shall secure this result, and in view of this
determination it is further

Resolved, that this board does heartily approve of the principles embodied in the act recently reported to the Senate and
Assembly of this State for the repeal of the so-called Classification Act, and for other purposes, and that Messrs. Porter and
McFarland, two of the counsel of this Board, be requested to
proceed to Albany to urge the passage of the act. . . .

Gould then led General Dix to the president's office. "You won't
find things in very good order," Gould told his successor, as he
showed him into the grand but utterly disheveled room.

"Oh, that makes no difference," Dix replied, surveying the
wreckage.

"I am very much obliged to you," Gould responded, determined
not to be outdone in graciousness.

"Not at all, not at all," insisted Dix, bowing low. "I am very much
obliged to you."[28] Then the general settled himself into that "perfect work of art known as the President's chair."[29]

Gould told Tommy Lynch to take his men home and, taking
"another drink of Mr. Gould's whiskey,"[30] they went. The corridors began to empty. "The troubles of the past two days had left
some very decided traces in the gorgeous halls of Erie," reported the
Herald. "The discarded quid of virgin leaf, the relic of one of
Lynch's guerrillas, slept peacefully alongside the stump of a fragrant
Havana which had some hours since graced the lips of some aristocratic director."[31]

Earlier one man had looked around anxiously for a spittoon.
Seeing the tobacco chewer's distress, an Erie employee told him,
"Spit on the floor! Spit on the floor! the jig's up—who cares?"[32]

•

The next day the *Herald,* helping itself to the credit for the latest
developments, was jubilant. "The blow has fallen at last on the Erie
thieves and banditti," it wrote, "and not a fragment of their once
great conspiracy remains to tell of its arrogance, dishonesty and
unblushing effrontery."[33] And it noted in an editorial that Gould's
troubles were just beginning. "The judges who have heretofore

stood his friends will hesitate before they aid him in his present dilemma. This is not the time when they can afford to use the power of the court." Indeed it wasn't, for cries for impeachment were ringing ever louder in the ears of Cardozo and Barnard.

Wall Street was delighted with the turn of events. "The brokers and railroad men," wrote the *Herald* on the 14th, "are . . . jubilant over the general effects of the downfall of Gould. A few months ago the disclosures of the frauds on the city and the apparent vanity of all efforts to oust the Erie Ring had brought European confidence in nearly all American securities, except those guaranteed by the government, to the lowest ebb, and there was the best possible ground to fear that it would soon be impossible to induce foreign capital to aid in the development of our resources. But the overthrow of the Tammany Ring followed so speedily by the downfall of Gould, will, it is claimed, at once restore the credit and the popularity of American stocks on the London Exchange and the Paris Bourse."

The president of the New York Stock Exchange was afraid that McHenry would be little if any improvement over Gould, and urged that new elections for the Erie board be held as soon as possible. The State Legislature obviously had the same fears, for it passed the repeal of the Classification Act on March 16th, 1872, and required that no director of the Atlantic and Great Western Railroad could sit on the Erie board, a development that could only have come as a nasty shock to James McHenry, receiving daily cables from George Crouch.

But McHenry must have been gratified by the action of Erie stock in the market. On the day following Gould's resignation, Erie rose to 40 on large orders from London. The next day the Erie books for the last six years were released, and it appeared that the company was in much better financial shape than had been feared. The market reacted at once, and Erie rose to 44⅜ on the awesome volume of 200,000 shares.

The *Herald*, which had been gleefully anticipating all sorts of awful financial secrets to come tumbling out of Castle Erie as soon as its walls were breached, recovered nimbly. "The cause of [yesterday's] rise," it said on the 16th, "was foreshadowed in the *Herald* in the morning, predicting from what was already known of the finances of the road, that the total liabilities would be much less than what was generally feared to be their extent under the reckless, if not felonious, extravagance of the deposed ring."

On that day Erie stock soared to 47½ before reacting to 45⅜, and volume reached 300,000 shares, not far short of 40 percent of the total stock outstanding. The speculators, who a few weeks earlier would not go near it, now could not get enough of Erie. On March 20th Governor Hoffman signed the repeal of the Classification Act, and the following day the London Exchange declared all Erie stock to be a good delivery. By the 25th Erie reached 60, a price it had not seen since the earliest days of the Gould regime.

"In the Stock Board itself," reported the *Herald* on the 27th, "Bedlam reigned supreme. It was a picture that only Doré could faithfully draw in its intensity—these haggard faces, these bloodshot eyes and the rushing, pushing, crushing and turmoil of the great bull ring. Everyone was yelling 'E-e-r-y' at the top of his voice, buying it or selling it, this world renowned stock. Lombard Street vibrated like an earthquake, and Wall Street, across a trackless sea of three thousand miles, answered back electric-like."

Such volumes could only result from orders far beyond New York, and the *Herald,* which only thirty-five years earlier had been the first newspaper in the world to carry daily stock prices, reported that "it is not exaggerating the facts to say that many of the orders executed in Erie on the New York Stock Exchange today came by telegraph from such remote points as San Francisco in the west and Frankfurt and Berlin in the east. Indeed, two continents were buying and selling this stock.[34]

"The McHenryites," the awed *Herald* continued, "the Jay Gould party and the other several combinations were pygmies in the giant speculations of the populace of two worlds. . . . One thing seems certain, that Erie has been restored to its old pinnacle of fame as the great speculative medium of the Stock Exchange, with the modification that henceforth, with a cable across the Atlantic and the shares distributed over the two continents, its field of patronage will embrace a much wider world."

The Scarlet Woman of Wall Street, quite unintentionally, had brought forth a child, and the global capital market had been born.

"BEDLAM REIGNED SUPREME"   The speculators of two continents bid for Erie. *Courtesy of The New-York Historical Society, New York City*

The End of the Erie Wars

DANIEL Drew was among those who thought they saw opportunity in Wall Street's suddenly renewed infatuation with its Scarlet Woman, and he sold 50,000 shares of Erie short at 55 for delivery before the end of the year. Uncle Daniel offered another 50,000 but found no takers, and he told reporters that he expected to fulfill his contract at 30, clearing $1,250,000. Perhaps it was only his bear's instinct for the down side of the market that prompted his short sale; perhaps it was the cool realization that the Erie's continuing economic troubles hardly justified the market's new evaluation. In all likelihood it was a combination of both. But it is a measure of how far Drew had fallen in the estimation of the Street that it paid no attention whatever to the Great Bear's large and very public bet that the price of Erie would collapse before the end of the year.

" 'Erie' was in every man's mouth and on every man's tongue," said the *Herald* on March 27th, the day Drew took his position. " 'Erie' rang the everlasting changes of chance and wild speculation. To be a broker of good standing it seems necessary to have the lungs of cast iron, the cheek of Satan himself, and the mind of Cagliostro. 'Erie' has played the wanton with thousands of them; has ruined and beggared hundreds of homes and families, and they will still pay court to this fickle courtesan who only smiles for a moment, then to languish into indifference and finally destroy them."

For a while it looked as though Drew were going to take another drubbing in Erie, for in May the stock rose as high as 75⅞, and the former speculative director, on paper, was a million dollars in the hole. Drew's contract, however, still had more than seven months to run, and Uncle Daniel could afford to hang on, waiting for the tide to turn.

On July 9th, the new election for directors, mandated in the repeal of the Classification Act, was held, and the new directors in turn elected Peter H. Watson to take over as president from General Dix, whose tenure had always been thought of as temporary. After the election, reported the *Herald*, "the directors and stockholders wended their way from the gorgeous apartments that once resounded to the laughter of James Fisk, Jr., and the petulant commands of Jay Gould, with radiant faces and satisfied minds, hugging the consoling thought to their bosoms that the dark night of Erie was over and the dawn was at hand."[1]

Soon after the election, the Erie abandoned the Opera House as too expensive and certainly unsuited to the new down-to-business image the company was trying to build. It returned to its old headquarters at Duane and West streets, but despite such modest cost-cutting measures the much-heralded new dawn, alas for the real stockholders of the Erie, proved once again to be a false one.

Even before the election the company's troubles were again mounting. The books of the Erie, which had been released soon after Gould's ouster and which had been thought to show the company in better than expected shape, were now suspected to have been quite thoroughly cooked by the former regime. In early July the Erie sued Gould for $10,000,000, claiming the former president had misappropriated that amount of the company's assets for his own use on Wall Street. Few thought the Erie stood much chance of collecting from Gould, for as things then stood it was a matter of his word against theirs.

The Commodore, meanwhile, chimed in with a suit of his own against the Erie to force it to pay him his guaranteed interest on the Boston, Hartford and Erie bonds that he had taken in the settlement of 1868, that company being once more in bankruptcy.

By August 1st, the *Herald* noted sadly that "Erie seems born to trouble," reporting that "the fortunes of that stock seem to be waning rapidly." The price of Erie tumbled into the 40's, allowing Drew to close his short, reportedly making $500,000 on the transaction. No sooner had Drew pulled in a considerable fortune from the short side of the market than he went over to the long side and now moved to corner Erie.

By the middle of September, the *Herald* was reporting that "foreign bankers doing business in Exchange Place"[2] were behind the action in Erie and that that accounted for the bounce in the price from its August lows. The *Herald* soon learned that it was Drew who in fact was the principal agent behind the corner, and it dispatched a reporter downtown to interview him.

"Well, I have a few 'sheers' of Erie," Drew admitted, using that habitual pronunciation that the newspapers so loved to report. But he denied being involved in any pool. "I ain't in any pool nohow," he said, his veracity about on a par with his grammar. "I never go into a pool with anybody. If I lose money I've only myself to blame for it, and if I make any, why I keep it; that's all."

Drew declined to say who the shorts caught in his net were, but when the reporter suggested that perhaps Jay Gould was one of them, the old man perked up immediately. "I believe," he replied, his gray eyes twinkling happily, that "he is a little short of Erie."[3]

The following Monday Drew cinched home the net. The market had opened quietly, "but Erie," reported the *Sun*, "true to its instincts, came to the rescue when it appeared that the venerable ex-Erie Director had called in his lent-out stock early in the forenoon. This carried consternation into the ranks of the bears, who were compelled to 'shin' around pretty lively"[4] to find the stock they needed to deliver to Drew. Those who happily were long the stock were able to charge as much as $325 for the overnight loan of 100 shares, and 15,000 shares were not delivered in time at all and therefore were bought on the Exchange "under the rule" at the shorts' expense. Three days later Gould and his former brokerage partner Henry N. Smith acknowledged defeat and settled with Drew, paying $800,000 according to the *Herald*, which said only that "the story is given for what it is worth."[5] In all likelihood, this sum represented only what they paid for the shares that had been bought for them when they failed to deliver. If they had sold shares short at 45, their net loss would have been only about $150,000, a pittance by the standards of past operations in Erie.

Smith somehow conceived the débacle to have been Gould's fault and demanded that Gould make up his losses. Gould, feeling that the game was for big boys, refused. "Then I'll get good and even with you before another year!" Smith threatened.[6]

The Erie corner of September, 1872, was only one of three corners that culminated that week in Wall Street's fast-growing market. Modest as it was, it would prove to be Drew's last winning move there. The great game that the Old Man of the Street had played so passionately and so long was about to turn against him for good. And Drew was not the only one to know Wall Street's passion for the last time that day.

In reporting the Scarlet Woman's antics since the ouster of Gould, the *Herald,* which had so faithfully chronicled the Street's fascination with Erie over the years, must have thought her fateful charms eternal. But in fact this was to be her last fling, and never again would the financial district ring with her name while the titans of the Street battled for her favors.

•

While it was business as usual on the Street, the government housecleaning that had begun as a result of Tweed's fall continued. As early as the previous November the new Bar Association had established a committee to investigate judicial behavior in New York City. To no one's surprise, the committee found evidence that the judicial behavior of several magistrates had been a good deal less than exemplary during recent years. Their offenses, it reported to the Bar Association on January 4th, consisted "in the gross abuse of the powers of such judges and the courts held by them, respectively, in the granting of injunctions, in the creating of receiverships and the appointment of receivers and transferring to them vast amounts of property, both of corporations and individuals; in abusing the power to appoint referees and in making excessive allowances to receivers, referees, and others for purposes not justified by law . . . in making improper *ex parte* orders out of court, and in deciding causes and motions without a hearing in court."[7]

The Bar Association petitioned the State Senate to remove the offending judges, McCunn of the Superior Court and Cardozo and Barnard of the Supreme Court, convincingly demonstrating its sincerity by contributing $30,000 to the expenses entailed in doing so. The Senate voted to remove McCunn on July 2nd, and Cardozo resigned from the bench rather than face impeachment proceedings. His son, Benjamin, would devote his life to redeeming the family name in the law.

Barnard refused to cooperate in his own execution. Because he sat on the Supreme Court, he could be removed only by a High Court of Impeachment, consisting of the State Senate and the Court of Appeals sitting together. The court convened on August 19th, not in Albany as might have been expected or even in New York City but rather amid the sporting and social pleasures of Saratoga Springs. The Bar Association itself presented the evidence against Barnard, and the court unanimously voted to remove him from the bench. When Barnard died six years later, among his effects was found that now-mythic staple of corruption in New York government, a little tin box containing close to a million dollars in cash and negotiable securities.

In its earnest and successful pursuit of the "Erie judges" the Bar Association had succeeded in making it plain that the members of the New York City legal establishment, now thoroughly aware of their long-term self-interests, would no longer tolerate the judicial venality that had served so well the short-term interests of many of their clients. Soon the Bar Association was able to reform the procedures under which receiverships and injunctions could be granted and vacated, and pushed through a rule requiring that all motions in a case before the Supreme Court had to be filed in the court where the case had originated.

The people of New York would long refuse to give up their right to elect all judges—only very recently have even Court of Appeals judges come to be appointed—and it would be the 1890's before some of the worst effects of the Jacksonian ideals of the 1840's could be removed from the state constitution. But, while the New York judiciary remains far and away the most convoluted and elaborate in the country, it has long been among the most competent and esteemed as well.

The Legislature would prove to be far more resistant to reform than the courts. To be sure, the ever more intense scrutiny of the newspapers would increasingly circumscribe the room for maneuver of its members. But it remains to this day the fount of political corruption in New York State, many of its members openly and persistently opposed to any effective restraints on their behavior or their opportunities to profit from their offices. In 1874 a stiff provision against bribing public officials was added to the state constitution, where it was safely beyond the reach of the legislators.

•

Gould did not seem much chastened by his misfortune in Erie, and he moved swiftly to recoup with the stock of the Chicago and Northwestern Railroad. The president and several of the directors of Northwestern had been shorting the stock of that corporation with the intention of mounting a bear raid on Wall Street, a move whose continued legality disgusted the *Commercial and Financial Chronicle.* "How these managers can be allowed by law to speculate to the detriment of the property of the stockholders," it wrote, "to sell 'short' the stock of their own road, and then by virtue of their office to adopt a policy calculated to depress the shares at the Stock Exchange is one of the anomalies of modern legislation. Till laws can be passed making such conduct a penal crime, branding such men as felons exposed to fine and imprisonment or other appropriate punishment, the standard of railroad morality can scarcely be raised much above its existing disgraceful depression."[8]

The principal holders of the floating supply of the stock were Horace F. Clark, Augustus Schell, and other members of the so-called Vanderbilt clique, conspicuously excepting the Commodore himself, who did not indulge in such Wall Street shenanigans (although he had no objection to his allies doing so—entirely at their own risk, of course). Uncle Daniel, irresistibly drawn, apparently, to speculating railroad directors, joined the Chicago and Northwestern board in shorting the stock, selling 10,000 shares at 78. Gould, it turned out, was the buyer of those shares, for he had joined with Schell and Clark on the bull side of the market.

It was widely noted that Gould, so long the nemesis of the Commodore in Erie, had been welcomed by the "Vanderbilt party" in manipulating Northwestern. "But speculation," harrumphed the *Herald*, "like politics, sometimes makes strange bedfellows."[9] And so, it turned out, did revenge, for Henry Smith thought he saw an opportunity to get back at Gould by joining with Drew and the Northwestern management in shorting the stock heavily.

On October 31st, the Chicago and Northwestern announced a $10,000,000 issue of convertible bonds, but those potential shares could not play a part in the present contest, thanks to the thirty-day notification rule the Exchange had adopted four years earlier. The price of Northwestern had been inching up steadily all month, and on November 2nd the *Herald* reported that "the corner upon the shorts is tightening daily and the venerable Mr. Drew is learning how it feels to be subjected to the painful experience he has so often compelled others to undergo." He was shortly to learn what it felt like to be on the sharp end of treachery as well, for on November 20th, the *Herald* reported that the bulls had made "a harmonious arrangement with the bear clique in the directory and [they] were prepared to act together."

The next day the price of Northwestern shot up from 83⅜ to 95. All the profits that Drew had made in Erie that year, and much more besides, were now at risk. Henry Smith was in far worse shape, for he was short fully 40,000 shares.

Smith discovered too late that Gould, Clark, and Schell had a rock-solid corner on Northwestern. "In this stock," reported the *Herald*, "the corner had been so carefully and neatly and artistically built up that the victims must either gracefully consent to have their financial throats cut or make one desperate stroke for compromise or revenge."[10]

Smith knew all too well that Gould was unlikely to compromise, but he also thought he saw a way out. He was aware that the Erie Railway had withdrawn its $10,000,000 suit against Gould for lack of proof, and he knew equally well that the books of their old firm, Smith, Gould and Martin, told much about Erie affairs during the Gould and Fisk regime. On November 21st, as the price of Northwestern reached 100, he went to see Gould.

"You must let me have Northwestern," he said, "and let me have it so I can get out of this fix whole." Gould, of course, declined to help his ex-partner, now so firmly in his clutches.

"If you don't help me out of this," Smith warned, "I will turn over the Smith, Gould and Martin books to [S. L. M.] Barlow [the Erie's counsel]—and you know what that means!"

If Gould was perturbed by the prospect he gave no sign of it. "Very well," he told Smith. "Turn them over. I have no objection."[11] As with Drew in 1868, desperation had driven Smith to tip his hand to Gould prematurely.

Smith immediately turned over the books to Barlow. The Erie's counsel and President Watson, overwhelmed with their sudden good fortune, promptly swore out a complaint against Gould before Judge Fancher, newly seated on the Supreme Court, alleging fraud in the tidily precise amount of $9,726,541.26, and asked that Gould be arrested and held on no less than $10,000,000 bail. The judge must have felt that he could hardly hold Gould on ten times the bail that even Tweed had been required to post and issued an arrest warrant that required a mere $1,000,000 bond.

Smith and his allies were counting on Gould's sudden arrest to throw the market into such turmoil that they would be able to wiggle out of their predicament in the confusion. But they were deeply disappointed in that regard. Gould had been handling matters in the brokerage offices of Osborne & Chapin at 34 Broad Street; at ten minutes to three on Friday afternoon a deputy sheriff arrived to arrest him. He surrendered without a fuss, and he, Horace F. Clark, and Augustus Schell proceeded to the police station, where they were immediately met by Gould's counsel in this case, the young Elihu Root. Clark and Schell produced sureties, already prepared in the amount of $500,000 each, and Gould was back at Osborne & Chapin within half an hour. The *Herald* was duly impressed. "He did not seem especially agitated or excited," it reported the next day, "and the entire business of his arrest was transacted within a few minutes and passed off as if it were one of the most commonplace and ordinary incidents of routine official duty."[12]

The market, far from being thrown into turmoil by Gould's arrest, hardly had time to notice before he was back at work putting the screws to the shorts as the screws had never been put before. "A man could not resist a suspicion," the *Herald* reported the next morning, "that for a brief season the operator at the Stock Exchange had been seized with a fit of insanity and was writing simultaneously on thousands of tapes the wild suggestions of a disordered imagination." Drew and Smith, huddled over the tickers, must surely have hoped so, for their doom was written in numbers as the tape recorded the final sixteen transactions in Northwestern that afternoon: 200 @ 110, 300 @ 111, 300 @ 112, 100 @ 116, 200 @ 125, 200 @ 130, 300 @ 140, 500 @ 150, 100 @ 152, 100 @ 155, 100 @ 160, 100 @ 161, 300 @ 160, 500 @ 162, 400 @ 165, and finally 200 bid with no takers.[13]

Wall Street was staggered by the success of the corner. Gould had succeeded, reported the *Herald* the next day, "in making one of the most brilliant and successful strokes of financiering strategy on record in the annals of Wall Street."[14] Gould himself told a reporter that the losses of the bears "will foot up pretty close to twenty millions."[15] Nobody thought that Drew was doing more than putting up a brave front when he told a reporter "Oh! the boys have had a little sport, you see, and I don't blame 'em, even if I had a few 'sheers.' "[16]

That night a reporter for the *Herald* sought an interview with Horace F. Clark, who had made millions from the corner that day, at his house at 10 East 22nd Street in hopes of finding out what was afoot for the morrow. Clark was dressing to go out for the evening but had the reporter shown into his bathroom while he shaved. "Mr. Clark," the reporter said, "I came to see you in reference to the Northwestern corner."

"Northwestern corner?" said Clark, lathering his face. "I don't know anything of the kind. Has there been a corner?" Asked why the price had doubled from par in ten minutes flat, Clark deadpanned that "the only reason I can see is that people have arrived at a just appreciation of the value of the stock." As for Gould's arrest, Clark said that it "was nothing more than a stock-jobbing operation."[17] As Clark left his house that evening, the informal stock market still functioning at the Fifth Avenue Hotel one block uptown quoted Northwestern at 210 bid, 300 asked.

The next day Northwestern opened at 150, down fully fifty

RUINED *Courtesy of the Union Club Library*

points from its previous close, but it soon turned out that this was by no means a break in the corner. Gould and his allies were letting some of the small operators and brokers off the hook at prices they could afford to pay. Nor was this charity on the part of Gould but instead "shrewd and careful mercy."[18] As the *Sun* explained, "This settling with small shorts at whatever they could pay was a good thing for the brokers, and a much better thing for Mr. Gould's party, as it averted failures, and a panic which might have robbed the bulls of the greatest fruits of their brilliant victory."[19]

If the bulls were letting the small fry escape the net, they had no intention whatever of letting the big fish out so easily.

Smith, who had only himself to blame for the fix he was in, was nearly incandescent with rage at his old partner. Shaking his finger at Gould, Smith told him, "I will live to see the day, sir, when you have to earn a living by going around this street with a hand organ and a monkey."

Gould, already long used to vituperation, was unimpressed. "Maybe you will, Henry," he said soothingly, "maybe you will. And when I want a monkey, Henry, I'll send for you."[20]

Uncle Daniel, in his turn, had not only shorted 10,000 Northwestern at 78, but, according to the *Sun*, had sold a call for that much stock at the same price as well and sold further stock short at 91 and 100. While Gould thought that Drew had managed to get out from under about half of that terrible burden, the Old Man of the Street, getting older by the second, still had a long way to go.

On Saturday morning Drew appeared in the offices of Osborne & Chapin and, adopting bluster as a tactic, offered to settle his shorts at 125, producing a check for the requisite amount. "There, boys," he said, "there's the cash you've stolen from me. I hope it will do you good."[21] But Gould wanted the stock, which had gone unsold at 200 bid, not this comparatively paltry sum. Drew had until 2:15 to produce it or the Exchange would buy it for him at whatever price was necessary to obtain it.

At 2:20 that afternoon the vice president of the Stock Exchange, amid excitement unseen since the Gold Panic, rose from his chair and stepped to the desk at the front of the room. A sudden stillness swept over the brokers as he announced that he would buy 3,300 shares of Northwestern common for the account of Kenyon, Cox & Company. "This announcement," wrote the *Sun*, "was followed by a grand howl, not only over the breaking of the storm but because Daniel Drew is the special partner in Kenyon, Cox & Co. and it was supposed that the stock about to be bought in was practically a refusal of Daniel Drew to deliver."[22] The last sale of Northwestern had been at 150, and Vice President Mitchell began bidding at that price "in a vigorous monotone amidst intense excitement and perfect quiet."

"Fifty," said Mitchell, to be greeted with silence, "50½, 51, 51½, 52 . . ."

"Every jump of one per cent counting $3,300 loss for Kenyon, Cox & Co.," wrote the *Sun*, "and the loss made in ten seconds. Every minute added $20,000 to the debt. This went on, amid breathless silence creating a slight flutter, when the stock passed 70 and another more perceptible when it struck 90, but still there were no offers and the work went on."

"Ninety-one, 91½, 92 . . ." Mitchell intoned, "99, 99½, 200."

"Sold!" shouted two brokers at once, and the stock was bought in at 199¾ and 200 as the tension subsided and "the roof echoed vehement yells."

Before the day was over the Exchange would bid Northwestern up to 230 until Drew's remaining shorts were covered; they cost him fully $1,250,000. But first Mitchell, proceeding methodically down his list, announced that he would buy under the rule a small amount of Erie, "whereat the brokers howled and roared with disappointment. They didn't care anything about Erie, what they wanted was blood: Northwestern."[23]

The Erie Wars were over.

●

The Street was full of admiration for Gould and his allies in the "Vanderbilt party." But the Commodore himself was not amused by the linking of his name with Gould's, and on the 26th he wrote the evening New York *Commercial Advertiser* a letter.

> Sir: The recent "corner" in Northwestern has called forth much comment from the press. My name has been associated with that of Mr. Jay Gould and others in connection with the speculation, and gross injustice has been done me thereby. I beg leave, therefore, to say (once for all) that I have not had, either directly or indirectly, the slightest connection with or interest in the matter. . . . The almost constant parade, . . . of my name in association with his seems very much like an attempt to mislead the public, to my injury, and, after the publication of this, ignorance or misinformation can no longer be urged as an excuse for continuing this course.

As for Wall Street speculators, I know nothing about them. I do not even see the Street three times in a year, and no person there has any authority to use my name or to include me in any speculative operation whatever.

C. Vanderbilt
Nov. 26, 1872

The *Sun* immediately sent a reporter hurrying over to 10 Washington Place to find out what all the fuss was about. The Commodore greeted the reporter courteously and showed him into the front parlor, telling him to sit although he himself remained standing. Vanderbilt clearly was in a considerable state over Jay Gould.

"May I ask you," said the reporter, "if you have any especial reason for thinking ill of him?"

"I have had but one business transaction with him in my life," responded the Commodore quite inaccurately. "In July, 1868, I sold him some stock, for which he paid me promptly. I had no reason to be dissatisfied with him on that occasion." That particular transaction, of course, is the very one that the Commodore, in an earlier letter to the press, had denied took place at all and which Gould had sued to have reversed. The reporter understandably enough was a little confused.

"Why then do you distrust him?" he asked.

"His face, sir," said Vanderbilt, getting still more excited, "no man could have such a countenance and still be honest."

The reporter, hardly knowing what to make of this, said, "But surely, Mr. Vanderbilt, you must have some other reason besides that for your opinion."

The Commodore's anger was now at full throttle. "I tell you, sir," he replied, "God Almighty has stamped every man's character upon his face. I read Mr. Gould like an open book the first time I saw him. I did not like to express too strongly an opinion this morning but if you wish to have it now I will give it to you. You have my authority for stating that I consider Mr. Jay Gould a damned villain. You can't put it too strongly."[24]

Asked to comment on the Commodore's sudden and entirely uncharacteristic outburst, Gould suggested that perhaps Vanderbilt was in his dotage. Then he noted that "so far as his criticism of my personal appearance is concerned, he ought in his piety to attribute any defects in that respect to the same Wisdom that bestowed on him his good looks."

Having rather neatly managed to give tit for tat and turn the other cheek at one and the same time, he also very shrewdly put his finger on the real cause of the Commodore's tantrum. Gould, himself only thirty-six years old, noted that "he can no longer go around as he used to and attend to business, and he is feebly envious of those who can. There is a class of rising financiers whom the old man hates. They are young, full of energy, and possessed of modern knowledge and appliances to aid them in their business. The old Commodore is jealous of them. . . . [T]hese young businessmen are rising into financial power which will far exceed the old Commodore even in his palmiest days."[25]

Vanderbilt, as Gould knew full well, was anything but senile. Instead the Commodore simply sensed that he was now in a battle with time. His swift and unromantic mind as sharp as ever, his passion for life undimmed by seventy-eight years, the Commodore knew that one day soon his body must betray him.

Vanderbilt went downtown to Wall Street for the last time in 1873. More and more he left the handling of his railroads to his son William, reserving to himself only the most fundamental corporate decisions. It was he who had decided to issue $40,000,000 in bonds in order to quadruple-track the New York Central, bonds that were snapped up at once on the London market. The quadruple tracking was a gigantic undertaking and amounted to building a whole new railroad alongside the old one. But this characteristically bold move, together with the Central's sea-level route to the interior, gave it a competitive advantage over its rivals that the Central would maintain long after the Commodore's death.

Slowly the circle of his world closed in around 10 Washington Place like a diminishing spotlight. Soon he had to give up driving his magnificent trotters on the Bloomingdale Road and Harlem Lane. He went out to the Union and Manhattan clubs less often and played cards at home instead. His interest in pseudo-sciences—in which the Victorian age, just as our own, abounded—increased as he sought the elixir of life. With physiognomy he had insulted the living Gould; with spiritualism he paid the dead Fisk the highest of compliments, seeking to contact him at a séance one day, hoping, apparently, to discuss the market.[26]

The Commodore had long had a reputation for being close with his money and not much given to charity. Partly this was due to his utter disinterest in playing to the crowd, partly it was a very practical policy for the richest man in the world. "I am sorry for the distress of the people," he told the Reverend Charles Deems, "but if I was to begin that sort of business, my door would be blocked from here to Broadway, and I'd have to call the police to get to my office of mornings."[27]

His charities, therefore, were private and often spontaneous. When he had first come into control of the Harlem line he had gone to inspect the station at 26th Street and Fourth Avenue. There he encountered a woman who had not quite enough money to pay for tickets for herself and her children. The Commodore told the line's assistant superintendent, I. D. Barton, to make up the difference, and the superintendent did so, asking the woman the cause of her troubles. She replied that her husband was out of work and unable to find any.

"What?" said the Commodore, overhearing this. "Can't find work in New York? Your husband must be a fine specimen." But she explained that he had in fact been employed by the Harlem Railroad itself until he had lost his legs in an accident on the line and been let go without compensation.

"Then he'll be my first pensioner," Vanderbilt immediately replied. "And," he added *sotto voce* to Barton, "I hope my last."[28]

Under the influence of his wife and the Reverend Deems, Vanderbilt's charities began to expand. He gave the Reverend Deems a church of his own, the Church of the Strangers on Mercer Street, and insisted that Deems own it personally so that he wouldn't have to put up with any truck from a board of vestry. In 1873 he gave $500,000, the largest single donation to a worthy cause ever given up to that time, to the new and struggling Central University in Nashville, Tennessee. Its name was changed forthwith to Vanderbilt University, and he soon added another $500,000.

In March, 1876, Vanderbilt came down with the first serious illness he had suffered since his railroad accident more than forty years earlier, and stories cropped up on Wall Street more and more frequently that he was dying or dead. After one such rumor in May, a *Herald* reporter called at 10 Washington Place to ask how the Commodore was faring. Mrs. Vanderbilt was in the middle of telling the journalist that he was much better when the Commodore himself suddenly appeared at the head of the stairs in a dressing gown and slippers. The voice he had once hurled effortlessly to the foretops of sailing ships had not lost its note of command. "Even if I were dying," he bellowed at the reporter, "I could still knock all the truth that there is in these wretches who start these reports out of them."[29]

If the Commodore refused to admit to himself that he was dying, the journalists, equipped with the instincts of vultures, knew better, and they set up a watch across the street. Slowly, inch by inch, the Commodore gave ground through the summer and fall, abandoning no territory that could possibly be defended. Early on the morning of January 4th, it was clear that the end was near. His family—he had sixty-three living descendants—gathered around. He asked them to sing his favorite hymn, and the Reverend Deems said a prayer. "That was a good prayer," the Commodore told him, as judgmental as ever, and then, at 10:51 A.M., slipped suddenly from life. He would have been pleased to know that the "Vanderbilt stocks" held steady at the news.

New York City, the nation, and the world took note of the passing of a giant. Flags flew at half staff at City Hall, the New York Stock Exchange, at the Grand Central Depot and the countless lesser stations along the 4,300 miles of Vanderbilt railroads, at the Union and Manhattan clubs, and at Vanderbilt University.

The *New York Times*, which twenty years earlier had called him a robber baron, realized its error. "His one foible of opposition," it said the day following his death, "was an immense boon to the public, for wherever his keen eyes detected a monopoly he pounced down upon the offenders and literally drove them from the rivers. Nor did he, when he had vanquished them, establish a monopoly of his own. His principle of low rates, founded upon acute reasoning, was never violated, so that in every way the public were the gainers. . . . Commodore Vanderbilt never stopped improving, but went on developing, maturing and ripening his system until death called him away from the scene where he had reigned so long without equal."[30]

His body lay in state at 10 Washington Place until the funeral the following Monday. Among the many mourners who followed the coffin down Broadway that morning to the Church of the Strangers was the Commodore's old friend Daniel Drew, now the last leaf on the tree of his generation.

"The lesson to be learned from the life of Vanderbilt," said the *Herald*, "is simple and impressive. Courage in the performance of duty enabled this man to become one of the kings of the earth. The hardy, strong-limbed boy who guided his vessel from ferry to ferry nearly seventy years ago lived to be a ruler of men. He had no advantages in his battle—no political, social, educational aid. It was one honest, sturdy, fearless man against the world, and in the end the man won. There was no poetry, no romance, no illusions in this long, stern, busy life. He was simple and direct in his ways, knowing his mind all the time and ever going to his purpose like a ball from a cannon. In time the world came to his feet, and his old age was one of vast power and ever increasing responsibilities. There are few kings whose will was as potent as that of the simple citizen who goes to rest in the tomb of his ancestors, on beautiful Staten Island, and by the waters of the bay on which he began his extraordinary career so many years ago, and which he loved so well."[31]

His contemporaries had no doubt that Cornelius Vanderbilt had fully lived up to the moral standards he had learned from his mother before the modern world, and the rules needed to cope with it, had been invented by men like the Commodore. And certainly he had vastly exceeded even the high economic aspirations of his own generation, the first to have known the manifold powers of steam. The intellectuals of the succeeding era would find the former insufficient and the latter quite unforgivable.

•

Although the suit by the Erie Railway against Gould had failed utterly in its short-term purpose of breaking the corner in Northwestern and thereby rescuing Henry Smith, the company had every intention of pursuing the case vigorously for its own sake. The long-term threat of the suit to Gould was very real.

Gould's strategy, as always, was to do the unexpected and catch his enemies off guard. As he was amply demonstrating in the legal conflicts that had resulted from the Gold Panic of three years earlier, Gould could use the processes of the law to obfuscate and delay with the best of them. But, less than a month after this suit was filed, he suddenly offered to settle on terms that appeared to be generous. Gould had realized that President Watson was most anxious for a quick resolution and would bargain accordingly. Several conferences between Watson and Gould ensued as they tried to make a deal.

On December 17th, Gould wrote to Watson and formally offered to turn over to the company, in settlement of all claims the Erie had against him, stocks, bonds, and various pieces of real estate (including the Opera House), that Gould stated were "worth more to the Erie Company than the total sum claimed. . . . I do this," he wrote to Watson, "for the sake of peace, because any litigation of such questions is more annoying to me than the loss of the money involved, and because I am sincerely anxious for the success of the Erie Company, in which I have a large pecuniary interest."[32]

That was putting it mildly, for Gould, in addition to his already considerable holding of Erie stock, later claimed to have bought calls on 200,000 shares of Erie at the then market price of 50. Watson turned Gould's letter over to a special committee of the board, with a recommendation that the offer be accepted, and the committee agreed to it if the company could be assured that the property was worth $9,000,000 and might bring $6,000,000 at a forced sale. The board unanimously accepted the offer on December 19th, and, happily counting its unhatched chickens, the company opened a special "reclamation account" on the books with a balance of $9,000,000.

If the Erie board thought it had gotten a good deal, Daniel Drew certainly knew better. "It beats all I ever heard," he said to a reporter. "Just mind what I tell ye. He'll make up the best part o' them nine million they say he's turned over . . . by bullin' its sheers. But nine million? Pooh!"[33]

Wall Street promptly proved Drew right by sending the price of Erie stock up to 62, making Gould's calls worth $2,400,000. But the euphoria soon faded. The property turned over had not cost Gould anything like $9,000,000, nor was the Erie able to realize any such sum. Much of the real estate turned out not to be nearly as free and clear as Gould had promised, and the Erie sued him once more in 1874. By that time the ex-president was in a much better position— and the company in a far worse one, its stock lower than it had ever been under Gould—and he was able to settle matters once and for all with the Erie Railway.

As for the books of Smith, Gould and Martin, Henry N. Smith had taken the evidence for safekeeping to his farm in New Jersey. One day in 1874 persons unknown showed up at the farm and intimidated the caretaker into turning them over. The books vanished, never to be seen again.

Writing only twenty-five years after the events, E. H. Mott, the historian of the Erie Railway, was filled with admiration for Gould's tactical genius if not his moral standards. "What a spectacle then was that! This man, lately reviled by his successors in control of Erie, and standing charged by them, under oath and in sickening detail, before a solemn court, with robbery, embezzlement, and gross violation of a sacred trust, and held in bonds of fabulous amount to answer the charges, which, if proved, would place him in a felon's cell, boldly and confidently dictating terms upon which he would release them from the annoyance of litigation! Terms that included virtually his rehabilitation in the good graces of the company whose treasury he was charged with looting, and whose name and fame they affirmed he had besmirched. Was ever triumph in defeat greater than this?"[34]

The poor Erie Railway was once more in the hands of an incompetent management. Watson and the new board seem to have had a much surer grasp of the shadows of public relations than the substance of economic reality. In 1873 they authorized a dividend on the common stock, the first since 1866 and the last until 1942, but it was not remotely justified by the company's earnings or its capital needs. In September of that year, a major sellers' panic hit Wall Street, and, as usual, the crash foreshadowed a depression. The railroad's earnings collapsed, and Watson's tenure as president soon ended as the company staggered for the third time into bankruptcy, a condition the Erie would know three times more before it disappeared forever as a separate company in the early 1970's. As Victorian moral myths demanded, the Scarlet Woman's old age would be largely a sad and bedraggled matter.

Jay Gould, who had learned much during his days at the head of Erie, would spend the rest of his life on Wall Street, growing richer and more mysterious every year. Principally interested in railroads and communications, especially the Union Pacific Railroad and the Western Union Telegraph Company, he was perhaps the greatest single force in shaping the two industries as they matured in the final quarter of the nineteenth century. But his first love would always be the game itself, although, like an opera star, and for much the same tactical reasons, he often announced his retirement. By 1890 the New York *World* would write that "Jay Gould is the axis upon which Wall Street now revolves. Never was one man's power so great in speculation as now."[35]

Gould bought Lyndhurst, a splendid Gothic house on the shores of the Hudson twenty miles north of New York, and built a vast greenhouse there. As with everything that interested him, he was soon deeply learned in the subject of botany. His yacht, *Atalanta*, was one of the finest of the floating palaces of yachting's greatest era, and he often used her to commute in unmatched splendor between Lyndhurst and Wall Street.

Lyndhurst and *Atalanta* were much more to their owner than simply the baubles of a gilded age. They were Gould's refuges from the world, the only places he could be himself, safe in the bosom of his family, willing to let down the opaque façade he so resolutely maintained in public. When his wife, Helen, not yet fifty, died of a stroke in 1889, he paid more attention to business than ever. But if Gould's will to win remained undimmed, his will to live began to crumble.

His health, always precarious, declined. Unable to sleep he would pace through the night outside his house at 579 Fifth Avenue, tuberculosis now eating away at him. On December 2nd, 1892, with little struggle, he died. He was not yet fifty-seven years old. All his adult life he had done his best to keep the world from knowing the real Jay Gould. Long before his death the legend that had filled the resulting vacuum had overtaken him.

•

The market crash of 1873 should have been the salvation of Wall Street's Great Bear. As it turned out, it was his final ruin. Drew would often visit the Commodore at 10 Washington Place in these days, and the two old men would play euchre together and talk over past times. The story is that Vanderbilt finally converted his friend to his own bullish outlook on life, just in time for the break in the market to sweep away the remnants of Drew's fortune. It seems altogether unlikely, however, that Uncle Daniel would have changed his essential nature so late in the day. More plausibly, like a poker player with a fast-diminishing pile of chips, he let his financial situation overwhelm his instincts. "His genius haunted and hunted him,"[36] an obituary would say of his life. Now it consumed him.

For two and a half years after the panic, Drew evaded disaster with all his old vulpine wiles, but finally some of his creditors forced an accounting. "His answers on the occasion revealed a singular state of things. He kept no books; his transactions he carried in his head, except so far as his brokers had account of them. The 'boys' had got his money—that was all."[37]

In March, 1876, he was finally forced into bankruptcy. With assets of less than $700,000 he admitted liabilities that considerably exceeded a million. The man who ten years earlier had been thought able "to command more ready cash at short notice than any man in Wall Street" had now to admit in his petition to the court that his cash on hand amounted to zero.[38] His house on Union Square was sold to satisfy his creditors, the endowments to the Drew Theological Seminary and Wesleyan University, which he had long promised and met the interest on, would now never be paid.

Drew had long before transferred considerable assets to his son, so his family was not impoverished, but they were no longer among the city's truly wealthy. Drew moved into his son's house at 3 East 42nd Street and, as incorrigible as ever, soon had a stock ticker installed there. He could only dabble in odd lots now, on points given him first by the Commodore and, later, the Commodore's son (who forty years earlier had been Drew's clerk), but it passed the time.

On September 18th, 1879, Uncle Daniel suffered a stroke and died suddenly at the age of eighty-two. The family arranged for a special train of the Harlem Railroad, now only a minor branch of the Vanderbilt empire, to take Drew's body back to Putnam County, from where, a lifetime before, he had set out to make his fortune.

Like the Commodore, he had started with only his brains, his will to win, and a hundred dollars. In the spring tide of opportunity set loose by the industrial revolution, these had been enough to take both men very far indeed. But finally, unlike the Commodore, he had ended with nothing.

Drew was buried next to his wife in the family plot near his son's farm, and a small monument was raised above his grave. Today, weedy and forgotten, the little cemetery is nearly invisible to the traffic that rumbles by on Interstate Highway 684 not fifty yards away. Only on a side road is there a rusting historical marker to tell the passerby, briefly and inaccurately, of Drew's journey through life.

•

The newspapers all ran lengthy obituaries retelling the many legends of Uncle Daniel and the Wall Street he had known and often epitomized. Already he was thought of as some curious relic from a vanished time. In 1875 a label—"Victorian"—had begun to be applied to the era in which he had lived the last half of his life, a sure sign that the time referred to was passing away.[39]

The New York City of his later years, as transient as the New York of his youth, was already changing as electricity began to replace gaslight, as Jews and Italians began to pour into the city's slums and alter and enrich the ambience of the great metropolis, as apartment buildings instead of rowhouses began to shelter the middle class, as the city began to seize the new technology of steel and soar into the sky.

Uncle Daniel's Wall Street had already disappeared. The crash of 1873 had ended the frenzied speculation of the Civil War years. The trading on the Curb and at the Fifth Avenue Hotel had languished in the ensuing depression, and the New York Stock Exchange had used the opportunity to consolidate its power to regulate the Street and the companies that sought to market their securities there. Soon the Exchange was able to require member brokers to trade listed securities only on the floor, where the Exchange could keep an eye on things. It was the Exchange, not government, that first forbade the directors of a listed corporation to be short their own stock and forced them to adhere to specified accounting principles.

By the time of Drew's death the United States was back on the gold standard, with all the financial discipline that implied, and a new bull market had erupted on the Street. In 1883 brokers would see the first million-share day as industrial corporations began to displace railroads from the center of Wall Street's attention. Already an investor could rely on the fact that if a broker was a member of the Exchange his sales pitch, however glib, was not fraudulent. If a security was listed there he knew it represented real assets, however risky, not smoke.

The Street was still no place for fools, nor would it ever be. But the New York Stock Exchange now functioned much like the governor on the steam engine that had brought it all into being. Wall Street's free market could thus continue to work its mysterious way without destroying itself.

Bibliography

IN quoting from these sources (I have by no means quoted from all of them) I have not hesitated to fill in words the Victorians delicately left blank and to correct spelling and punctuation where necessary, but never, I hope, to alter the authors' intentions in any way. I did this to spare the reader from having to cope with the vagaries of Victorian punctuation and from typos that should have been caught a hundred years ago. (Although, given the fact that the newspapers were set by hand—often from handwritten copy—until the invention of the linotype in 1884, it is astonishing how few typos there were. Deadlines were quite as brutal then as now, and in many ways far worse, without radio and television to handle late-breaking news. It is computer spelling-checker programs that recently have allowed late-twentieth-century newspapers to finally attain the standards that were taken for granted by their mid-nineteenth-century journalistic ancestors.)

Scholars who want the unvarnished originals can easily find them via the notes and will, I trust, have no mercy about informing me of any transgressions on my part.

Nearly all these books, pamphlets, magazines, and newspapers can be found in the New York Public Library.

381

NEWSPAPERS

Albany *Argus*
Albany *Evening Journal*
Binghamton *Democrat*
Boston *Herald*
Brooklyn *Eagle*
Commercial Advertiser
Commercial and Financial Chronicle
London *Times*
New York *Evening Mail*
New York *Evening Telegraph*
New York *Herald*
New York *Independent*
New York *Sun*
New York Times
Troy *Daily Times*
Vermont *Phoenix*
Wall Street Journal

PERIODICALS

Adams' Magazine
American Law Review
Appleton's Journal
Atlantic Monthly
Frank Leslie's Popular Monthly
Fraser's Magazine
Galaxy Magazine
Harper's Monthly
Harper's Weekly
Johns Hopkins University Studies in Historical and Political Science
Ladies' Repository
Leslie's Illustrated Newspaper
The Literanian
The Merchant's Magazine and Commercial Review
Municipal Affairs
New York Genealogical and Biographical Record
The New-York Historical Society Quarterly
New York Railroad Journal
Niles Register
North American Review
Proceedings of the American Antiquarian Society
Putnam's Magazine
The Railroad Man's Magazine

BOOKS AND PAMPHLETS

Adams, Charles Francis, Jr. *Railroads: Their Origin and Problems.* New York: G. P. Putnam's Sons, 1878.

———, and Adams, Henry. *Chapters of Erie, and Other Essays.* Boston: James R. Osgood, 1871. A classic work of investigative journalism. The Adams brothers were the Mike Wallaces of their day and indefatigable in the pursuit of their quarry. Unfortunately their personal animus toward both Gould and Fisk made them all too ready to excuse behavior on the part of others that they would have condemned without mercy had it been exhibited by the heads of the Erie Railway. For sheer power of expression, however, these essays can hardly be beat.

Adams, Henry. *The Education of Henry Adams.* Boston and New York: Houghton Mifflin Company, 1918.

Albion, Robert G., with Pope, Jennie Barnes. *The Rise of New York Port, 1815–1860.* Hamden, Conn.: Archon Books, 1961.

Alexander, DeAlva Stanwood. *A Political History of New York State.* Port Washington, N.Y.: Ira J. Friedman, 1969. A reprint of the 1909 edition.

Armstrong, William. *Stocks and Stock-jobbing in Wall Street.* New York: New York Publishing Company, 1848.

Barlow, Francis C., and Field, David Dudley. *Facts for Mr. David Dudley Field.* Albany: Parsons and Company, 1871.

Barrows, Chester L. *William M. Evarts, Lawyer, Diplomat, Statesman.* Chapel Hill, N.C.: University of North Carolina Press, 1941.

Barrus, Clara, M.D. *John Burroughs Boy and Man.* Garden City, N.Y.: Doubleday, Page, 1922.

Bartlett, Irving H. *Daniel Webster.* New York: W. W. Norton, 1978.

Beach, Moses Y. *Wealth and Biographies of Wealthy Citizens of New York.* New York: New York *Sun,* 1845. Beach was the owner of the *Sun,* and this pamphlet, which ran through many editions, purported to give the size and origin of every fortune in New York City over $100,000. While hardly reliable, for it could only have been based on much guesswork, it is sometimes wildly funny as Beach libels everyone in sight at the rate of one sentence per victim. As evidence of the early Victorian passion for money it is without peer.

Berger, Meyer. *The Story of the New York Times.* New York: Arno Press, 1970.

Biography of Zadock Pratt of Prattville, N.Y.

Botkin, B. A. *New York City Folklore.* New York: Random House, 1956.

Boyer, M. Christine. *Manhattan Manners, Architecture and Style 1850–1900.* New York: Rizzoli, 1985.

Brace, Charles Loring. *The Dangerous Classes of New York.* New York: Wynkoop & Hallenbeck, 1872. A vivid, horrifying tour of the vast slums of mid-nineteenth-century New York.

Breen, Matthew P. *Thirty Years of New York Politics.* New York: by the author, 1899.

Bristed, C. Astor. *The Upper Ten Thousand.* New York: Stringer & Townsend, 1852.

Browder, Clifford. *The Money Game in Old New York.* Lexington, Ky.: University Press of Kentucky, 1986.

Burnham, Alan. *New York Landmarks.* Middletown, Conn.: Wesleyan University Press, 1963.

Burnham, Henry, edited by Hemenway, Abba Maria. *Brattleboro, Windham County, Vermont.* Brattleboro, Vt.: D. Leonard, 1878.

Cabot, Mary R., ed. *Annals of Brattleboro 1681–1895.* Brattleboro, Vt.: Press of E. L. Hildreth, 1921.

Carlson, Oliver. *The Man Who Made News: James Gordon Bennett.* New York: Duell, Sloan and Pearce, 1942. There has never been a first-rate biography of this remarkable and very important man. I cannot imagine why, as there have been several of Horace Greeley and Henry J. Raymond.

Clews, Henry. *Fifty Years in Wall Street.* New York: Irving Publishing Company, 1908. Originally titled *Twenty-Eight Years in Wall Street* and published in 1876. Clews evidently felt that his opinion on any and every subject was of deathless interest to the public, for this book runs to better than seven hundred pages. He is highly unreliable regarding matters that took place far from Wall Street, for he was an incurable gossip. But he was a very successful broker and well wired in to what was happening on the Street itself. In reading his memoirs, I find it hard to escape the notion that he must have been nearly insufferably pleased with himself.

Condit, Carl W. *The Port of New York.* Chicago: University of Chicago Press, 1980.

Croffut, William A. *An American Procession.* Boston: Little, Brown, 1931.

———. *The Vanderbilts and the Story of Their Fortune.* Chicago: Bedford, Clarke, 1886. Croffut was a newspaperman all his life. When first approached to write this dual biography of the Commodore and his son William Henry, he asked the Vanderbilt family to read the galley proofs to ensure accuracy and Cornelius II agreed. When Croffut declined to make some of the changes demanded, however, they refused further cooperation. One can only wonder what they objected to as the book is very flattering to both men.

Crouch, George. *Erie Under Fisk and Gould.* New York, 1870.

Curtis, George Ticknor. *An Inquiry into the Albany and Susquehanna Litigation.* New York: D. Appleton, 1871.

Deems, Charles Force. *Autobiography of Charles Force Deems.* New York: Fleming H. Revell, 1897.

Dickinson, H. W. *A Short History of the Steam Engine.* Cambridge, England: Cambridge University Press, 1938.

Dimock, A. W. *Wall Street and the Wilds.* New York: Outing Publishing Company, 1915.

Dix, Morgan. *Memoirs of John Adams Dix.* New York: Harper & Brothers, 1883.

Dodge, William E. *Old New York.* New York: Dodd, Mead, 1880. Dodge was a founder of Phelps Dodge and an uncle by marriage of Edward Stokes. This pamphlet was from a series of lectures he gave at the New-York Historical Society.

Duganne, A. J. H. *Report of the Select Committee.* Albany: C. Van Benthuyson, 1857.

Eames, Francis L. *The New York Stock Exchange.* New York: Thomas G. Hall, 1894.

Earle, Walter K. *Mr. Shearman and Mr. Sterling and How They Grew.* 1963.

Ellis, David, *et al. A History of New York State.* Ithaca: Cornell University Press, 1967.

Field, David Dudley; Field, Dudley; and Bowles, Samuel. *The Lawyer and His Clients.* Springfield, Mass., 1871. What started as a private correspondence soon evolved into an increasingly passionate debate over the ethical responsibilities of both lawyers and journalists. These letters are a window into the thinking of first-class Victorian minds as they wrestled with the serious issues of their day.

Fowler, William Worthington. *Ten Years in Wall Street.* Hartford, Conn.: Worthington, Dustin, 1870. Fowler's witty and informative book was a huge best-seller when it first appeared, selling over 40,000 copies in its first year. Fowler was a grandson of Noah Webster, but his punctuation was deplorable and he seems to have sprinkled commas over his prose like salt over scrambled eggs. I have not hesitated to change it where necessary for clarity.

———. *Twenty Years of Inside Life in Wall Street.* New York: Orange Judd Company, 1880.

Friedman, Lawrence M. *A History of American Law.* New York: Simon and Schuster, 2nd edition, 1985.

Friedman, Milton, and Schwartz, Anna Jacobson. *A Monetary History of the United States, 1867–1960.* Princeton: Princeton University Press, 1963.

Fuller, Robert H. *Jubilee Jim.* New York: Macmillan, 1930.

Goldberger, Paul. *The City Observed: New York.* New York: Vintage Books, 1979.

Gould, Jay. *History of Delaware County.* Roxbury, N.Y.: Keeny & Gould, 1856. Written when Gould was nineteen, this is still the standard history of the area.

Grafton, John. *New York in the Nineteenth Century.* New York: Dover Publications, 2nd edition, 1980. A collection of engravings from popular magazines.

Grodinsky, Julius. *Jay Gould, His Business Career, 1867–1892.* Philadelphia: University of Pennsylvania Press, 1957.

Hadley, Arthur T. *Railroad Transportation—Its History and Its Laws.* New York: G. P. Putnam's Sons, 1886. A wonderfully lucid book, mercifully free of ideology. In it Hadley uncovered an error in David Ricardo's reasoning, which must have been satisfying. He was later president of Yale University and a famous connoisseur of wines.

Halstead, Murat, and Beale, J. Frank, Jr. *Life of Jay Gould.* Philadelphia: Edgewood Publishing Company, 1892.

Harlow, Alvin A. (actually F.).*Old Towpaths—The Story of the American Canal Era.* New York and London: D. Appleton, 1926. I wonder what the publisher tells an author when it manages to get his name wrong on the title page.

Harlow, Alvin F. *Old Bowery Days.* New York: D. Appleton, 1931.

Harris, Charles Townsend. *Memories of Manhattan in the Sixties and Seventies.* New York: Derrydale Press, 1928. Charles Harris is the source of a famous story of the Gold Panic that has James Garfield standing on the steps of the Subtreasury at the head of Broad Street shouting to the multitude: "Fellow citizens! God reigns and the government in Washington still lives! I am instructed to inform you that the Secretary of the Treasury has placed ten millions in gold upon the market!" It's a great story but it doesn't happen to be true. Garfield said something like those words, or at least the God and Washington part, and he said them on the steps of the Subtreasury. But it was on April 15th, 1865, the day Lincoln died. On the day of the Gold Panic Garfield was nowhere near Wall Street and became associated with the events of that day only when he chaired the congressional hearings months later. Harris, as an old man, merged in his memory two events of his youth that were actually widely separated in time but not in space. It is one more example of that bane of the historian's—and lawyer's—existence, the misremembering eyewitness.

Headley, Joel Tyler. *The Great Riots of New York 1712–1873.* Indianapolis: Bobbs-Merrill, 1970. A reprint of the 1873 edition.

Hershkowitz, Leo. *Tweed's New York, Another Look.* Garden City, N.Y.: Anchor Press/Doubleday, 1978. A useful antidote to the usual telling of the Tweed story, although adversarial rather than evenhanded in approach.

Hill, Frederick Trevor. *The Story of a Street.* New York: Harper & Brothers, 1908. A history of Wall Street that manages hardly to mention the fact that a financial market is centered there, as though the author thought it all too vulgar to endure. Very useful for the physical history of the street, however.

Holbrook, Stewart H. *The Age of the Moguls.* Garden City, N.Y.: Doubleday, 1953.

———. *The Story of American Railroads.* New York: Crown Publishers, 1947.

Houghton, Walter E. *The Victorian Frame of Mind.* New Haven: Yale University Press, 1957.

House of Representatives. *House Report Number 31, 41st Congress, 2nd Session.* Washington, D.C.: U.S. Government Printing Office, 1870.

Hungerford, Edward. *Men and Iron, the History of New York Central.* New York: Thomas Y. Crowell, 1938.

———. *Men of Erie.* New York: Random House, 1946.

Jones, Willoughby. *The Life of James Fisk, Jr.* Philadelphia: Union Publishing Company, 1872.

Josephson, Matthew. *The Robber Barons.* New York: Harcourt Brace Jovanovich, 1962. Josephson's research seems mostly to have been lifted from Gustavus Myers. This book has been in print almost since the day it was first published nearly sixty years ago. It is a profoundly dishonest work.

Kip, Frederick Ellsworth, assisted by Hawley, Margarita Larssing. *History of the Kip Family in America.* Privately printed, 1928.

Klein, Maury. *The Life and Legend of Jay Gould.* Baltimore: Johns Hopkins University Press, 1986. The first scholarly, and redeeming, biography of this much vilified man.

Lamb, Mrs. Martha J. *Wall Street in History.* New York: Funk and Wagnalls, 1883.

Lane, Wheaton J. *Commodore Vanderbilt, an Epic of the Steam Age.* New York: Alfred A. Knopf, 1942. The only respectably scholarly biography ever written of this remarkable man. His life cries out for a modern treatment.

Laver, James. *Manners and Morals in the Age of Optimism, 1848–1914.* New York: Harper & Row, 1966.

A Life of James Fisk, Jr. New York: Polhemus and Pearson, 1871.

Lockwood, Charles. *Bricks and Brownstone.* New York: McGraw-Hill, 1972.

———. *Manhattan Moves Uptown.* Boston: Houghton Mifflin Company, 1976. A fascinating and readable history of the physical development of New York City in the nineteenth century.

Lord, Eleazar. *A Historical Review of the New York and Erie Railroad.* New York: Mason Brothers, 1855.

Lowell, James Russell. *James Fisk, Jr., an Epitaph.* Boston: Merrymount Press, 1918. A small-minded sonnet written shortly after Fisk's death.

McAllister, Ward. *Society as I Have Found It.* New York: Cassell Publishing Company, 1890. Perhaps the most pretentious title in the history of the book trade. McAllister was a not very active lawyer by profession, and made himself the arbiter of New York society largely by declaring himself to be so. It was he who coined the phrase "the four hundred." He ruefully admits that had he taken the advice of the Commodore to buy Harlem stock just before the first corner, he would have been rich himself.

McAlpine, R. W. *The Life and Times of Col. James Fisk, Jr.* New York: New York Book Company, 1872. As much cut and pasted as written, McAlpine nonetheless did an excellent job under what must have been a fierce deadline.

McCabe, James D. *Great Fortunes and How They Were Made.* Cincinnati: E. Hannaford & Company, 1871. This book is typical of the money gossip that so enthralled the Victorians.

———. *The History of the Great Riots.* Philadelphia: National Publishing Company, 1877.

———. *Lights and Shadows of New York Life.* Philadelphia: National Publishing Company, 1879. A fascinating tour through the high life and low life of mid-nineteenth-century New York.

McFeely, William S. *Grant.* New York: W. W. Norton, 1981.

Mandelbaum, Seymour J. *Boss Tweed's New York.* New York: John Wiley & Sons, 1965.

Martin, M. J. *Jay Gould and His Tannery.* Scranton, Pa.: Lackawanna Historical Society, 1945.

Medbery, James K. *Men and Mysteries of Wall Street.* Boston: Fields, Osgood & Company, 1870. An excellent book that looked at Wall Street from a wider perspective than Fowler's.

Merriam, George S. *The Life and Times of Samuel Bowles.* New York: Century Company, 1885.

Middleton, William D. *Grand Central . . . the World's Greatest Railway Terminal.* San Marino, Calif.: Golden West Books, 1977.

Miller's Guide to New York as It Is. New York: Schocken Books, 1975. A reprint of the 1866 edition.

Minnigerode, Meade. *Certain Rich Men.* New York: G. P. Putnam's Sons, 1927.

Morris, Clara. *Life on the Stage.* New York: McClure, Phillips & Company, 1902. A star in her day, Clara Morris remembered Jim Fisk and his kindness and vivacity when she was still a bit player.

Moscow, Henry. *The Street Book.* New York: Hagstrom Company, 1978.

Mott, Edward Harold. *Between the Ocean and the Lakes.* New York: John S. Collins, 1901. A monumental act of scholarship, the book is as beautiful as it is indispensable to any study of the history of the Erie.

Myers, Gustavus. *History of the Great American Fortunes.* Chicago: Charles H. Kerr, 1910. Myers, a dedicated scholar, was also a dedicated socialist, and his animosity toward capitalism and capitalists alike sometimes led him into factual error and often into misinterpretation and vituperation.

Neill, Humphrey B. *The Inside Story of the Stock Exchange.* New York: B. C. Forbes & Sons, 1950.

Nevins, Allan, ed. *The Diaries of Philip Hone.* New York: Dodd, Mead, 1927. Hone's diaries are indispensable to the study of the New York of his time. They are a window into his world.

———, and Thomas, Milton Halsey, eds. *The Diary of George Templeton Strong.* New York: Macmillan, 1952. Strong was a very witty man, and his diary is much funnier than Hone's although just as valuable.

Northrop, Henry Davenport. *Life and Achievement of Jay Gould.* Philadelphia: National Publishing Company, 1892.

Oberholtzer, Ellis Paxson. *Jay Cooke, Financier of the Civil War.* New York: Burt Franklin, 1970.

O'Conner, Richard. *Gould's Millions.* Garden City, N.Y.: Doubleday, 1962.

Ogilvie, John Stuart. *Life and Death of Jay Gould and How He Made His Millions.* New York: J. S. Ogilvie, 1892.

Parton, James. *Famous Americans of Recent Times.* Boston: Ticknor and Fields, 1867.

———. *How New York City Is Governed.* Boston: Ticknor and Fields, 1866.

Peskin, Allen. *Garfield.* Kent, Ohio: Kent State University Press, 1978.

Phillips, R. D. *Drew of Putnam County, N.Y.* Unpublished manuscript in the New York Public Library, Local History and Genealogy Collection.

Pierce, Frederick Clifton. *Fiske and Fisk Family.* Privately printed, 1896.

Plumb, J. H. *England in the Eighteenth Century.* Harmondsworth, England: Penguin Books, 1963.

Pratt, Sereno S. *The Work of Wall Street.* New York: D. Appleton, 1910.

Robbins, Michael. *The Railway Age.* London: Routledge & Kegan Paul, 1962.

Roosevelt, Theodore. *New York.* New York: Longmans, Green, 1895.

Rosenberg, Nathan, and Birdzell, L. E., Jr. *How the West Grew Rich.* New York: Basic Books, 1986.

Simmons, Martin. *Union Club of the City of New York.* New York: Union Club, 1986.

Smith, Arthur D. Howden. *Commodore Vanderbilt, an Epic of American Achievement.* New York: Robert M. McBride, 1927.

Smith, Matthew Hale. *Twenty Years Among the Bulls and Bears of Wall Street.* Hartford: J. B. Burr & Company, 1870. Still another description of the Street in the great bull market of the 1860's. Matthew Hale Smith was both a Congregational minister and a lawyer—a frightening combination—as well as a well-known writer and lecturer.

Snow, Alice Northrop, with Snow, Henry Nicholas. *The Story of Helen Gould.* New York: Fleming H. Revell, 1943.

Sobel, Robert. *The Big Board.* New York: Free Press, 1965.

———. *The Curbstone Brokers.* New York, Macmillan, 1970.

———. *Panic on Wall Street.* New York: Macmillan, 1969.

Spann, Edward K. *The New Metropolis.* New York: Columbia University Press, 1981.

Stedman, Edmund Clarence. *The New York Stock Exchange.* New York: Stock Exchange Historical, 1905. Stedman made his living on Wall Street as well as by writing. His poetry was very popular at the time but has been largely forgotten since.

Still, Bayrd, ed. *Mirror for Gotham.* New York: New York University Press, 1956.

Stokes, Anson Phelps. *Stokes Records.* New York: Privately printed, 1910. Anson Stokes was a first cousin of Edward Stokes.

Stokes, Isaac Newton Phelps. *The Iconography of Manhattan Island.* New York: Robert H. Dodd, 1915. I. N. P. Stokes was also Edward Stokes's first cousin (and Anson's brother) and a successful architect. This huge work, in six oversized fat volumes, is necessarily the cornerstone of any study of the physical development of the great city Stokes loved so much.

Sturgis, Henry S., *A New Chapter of Erie.* Erie Railroad, 1948. A brief account of the Erie's fifth trip through bankruptcy, 1938–1941, by one of the principals involved. Some of the debt piled on in the 1840's under Benjamin Loder still haunted the Erie.

Swanberg, W. A. *Jim Fisk: The Career of an Improbable Rascal.* New York: Charles Scribner's Sons, 1959. A vivid book whose usefulness is much diminished by the lack of source notes.

Tanner, Hudson C. *"The Lobby," and Public Men from Thurlow Weed's Time.* Albany: George MacDonald, 1888.

Thompson, Holland. *The Age of Invention.* New Haven: Yale University Press, 1921.

Train, George Francis. *Young America in Wall-Street.* New York: Derby & Jackson, 1857.

Trollope, Anthony. *North America.* Philadelphia: J. B. Lippincott, 1862.

Unger, Irwin. *The Greenback Era.* Princeton: Princeton University Press, 1964.

United States Senate. *Report of the Committee Upon the Relations Between Labor and Capital and Testimony Taken by the Committee.* Washington, D.C.: U.S. Government Printing Office, 1885.

Walling, George W. *Recollections of a New York Chief of Police.* New York: Caxton Book Concern, 1887. A good example of all too many nineteenth-century memoirs. His "recollections" were greatly helped by back issues of the *Herald,* for he copied from them verbatim for pages at a time.

Warren, Charles. *The Supreme Court in United States History.* Boston: Little, Brown, 1926.

Warshow, Robert Irving. *Jay Gould.* New York: Greenberg, 1928.

————. *The Story of Wall Street.* New York: Blue Ribbon Books, 1929.

Wharton, Edith. *A Backward Glance.* New York: D. Appleton-Century, 1934.

White, Bouck. *The Book of Daniel Drew.* Garden City, N.Y.: Doubleday & Doran, 1930. Uncle Daniel would have approved. In 1905 an article in the *Tribune* announced that a memoir written by Daniel Drew in his old age had turned up in a trunk in an attic in Putnam County. Five years later, this book, based on the "memoir," appeared and has been in print more or less ever since. The Drew family at the time maintained that the book was a fraud, and indeed it is highly unlikely that a man of marginal literacy would have turned to the dubious solace of the pen in his old age. The putative memoir itself has never been made public doubtless because it never existed. Like Clifford Irving's hoax of the 1970's regarding Howard Hughes, *The Book of Daniel Drew* is in fact a first-rate historical novel masquerading as autobiography. Bouck White did his homework, and where his specific facts can be checked they are usually accurate. His interpretations are another matter.

White, Trumbull. *The Wizard of Wall Street.* Philadelphia: John C. Yorston, 1893.

Wilson, Rufus Rockwell. *New York: Old and New.* Philadelphia: J. P. Lippincott, 1903.

Winter, William. *Other Days.* New York: Moffat, Yad and Company, 1908.

Writers Project, WPA, State of New Jersey. *Entertaining a Nation.* Long Branch, N.J.: City of Long Branch, 1940.

Notes

PROLOGUE
The Great Game

1. New York *Herald,* December 22nd, 1870. All quotes in the Prologue are from this issue.

CHAPTER ONE
The Rise of Wall Street

1. Edmund C. Stedman, *The New York Stock Exchange,* p. 20.
2. William W. Fowler, *Ten Years in Wall Street,* p. 81.
3. James K. Medbery, *Men and Mysteries of Wall Street,* p. 21.
4. See R. D. Phillips, "Drew of Putnam County, N.Y."
5. R. W. G. Vail, "Random Notes on the History of the Early American Circus" in *Proceedings of the American Antiquarian Society,* vol. 43, part 1, April 19th, 1943.
6. New York *Herald,* October 31st, 1869.
7. Henry Clews, *Fifty Years in Wall Street,* p. 117.
8. Stedman, p. 170.
9. Medbery, p. 169.
10. Stedman, p. 102.
11. Quoted in the Reverend J. McClintock, D.D., "Daniel Drew, Esq., of New York," in *Ladies' Repository,* September, 1859.
12. *New York Times,* September 20th, 1879.
13. Richard B. Kimball, "The Career of a Great Speculator," in *Frank Leslie's Popular Monthly,* December, 1879.
14. Medbery, p. 23.
15. William Armstrong, *Stocks and Stock-jobbing in Wall-Street,* p. iii.
16. Medbery, p. 7.

17. Fowler, p. 41.
18. *Ibid.,* p. 24.
19. *Ibid.,* p. 20.
20. *Ibid.,* p. 40.
21. Robert G. Albion, *The Rise of New York Port, 1815–1860,* p. 154.
22. William A. Croffut, *The Vanderbilts and the Story of Their Fortune,* p. 83.
23. Kimball, see note 13 above.
24. McClintock, see note 11 above. *Harper's Weekly,* April 27th, 1867, lifted the description whole without attribution, plagiarism being then taken entirely for granted. Phrenology was at the height of its popularity in these decades.
25. Clews, p. 156.
26. *Ibid.,* p. 119.
27. Fowler, p. 125.
28. Stedman, p. 171.
29. Fowler, p. 127.
30. Clews, p. 122.
31. Fowler, p. 125.
32. *Ibid.,* p. 126.

CHAPTER TWO
The Great Boom Town

1. William Torrey, "Reminiscences of an Old Man," *Adams' Magazine,* vol. 2, no. 6 (1892). William Torrey happens to be the present author's great-great-great-grandfather.
2. Figures are from Charles Lockwood, *Manhattan Moves Uptown,* p. 14.
3. Quoted in Alan Burnham, *Landmarks of New York,* p. 6.
4. *Ibid.,* p. 3.
5. Robert G. Albion, *The Rise of New York Port, 1815–1860,* p. 386.
6. Lockwood, p. 173.
7. William E. Dodge, *Old New York,* p. 52.
8. Allan Nevins, ed., *The Diaries of Philip Hone,* p. 202.
9. *Harper's Weekly,* August 14th, 1869.
10. *Harper's Monthly,* June, 1856.
11. Anthony Trollope, *North America,* p. 218.
12. Edith Wharton, *A Backward Glance,* p. 55.
13. *Ibid.*
14. Trollope, p. 205.
15. Ernest Duvergier de Haurame, *Lettres et notes de voyage;* quoted in Bayrd Still, *Mirror for Gotham,* p. 187.
16. James D. McCabe, *Lights and Shadows of New York Life,* p. 135.
17. Quoted in Lockwood, p. 129.
18. Quoted in Burnham, p. 203.
19. Lockwood, p. 240.
20. Figures extrapolated from Carl W. Condit, *The Port of New York,* p. 25
21. I find it hard to believe too, but the fact is recorded in J. H. Plumb's *England in the Eighteenth Century,* p. 26.
22. Arthur T. Hadley, *Railroad Transportation,* p. 24.
23. *Ibid.,* p. 8.
24. Allan Nevins and Milton H. Thomas, eds., *The Diary of George Templeton Strong,* vol. I, p. 282.
25. *Ibid.,* vol. III, p. 4.
26. Nevins, p. 722.
27. *Ibid.,* p. 756.

28. Nevins and Thomas, vol. I, p. 108.
29. Hadley, p. 65.
30. *Ibid.*, p. 17.
31. Joseph E. Hedges, "Commercial Banking and the Stock Market Before 1863," in *The Johns Hopkins University Studies in Historical and Political Science*, series LVI, no. 1, p. 31.
32. Quoted in Burnham, p. 3.
33. Figures from *The New-York Historical Society Quarterly*, April 1970.
34. Wharton, p. 2.
35. Quoted in Lockwood, p. 254.
36. *Herald*, January 3rd, 1869.
37. I. Pray, *Memoirs of James Gordon Bennett and His Times*, p. 228.
38. *North American Review*, April, 1866.
39. London *Times*, January 9th, 1872. Shoddy was a cheap fabric made from reclaimed wool, first manufactured in 1838. "Shoddy aristocracy" was soon a stock phrase for the *nouveau riche* and their pretensions. It was through this metaphor that "shoddy" first entered the language as a synonym for poorly made.
40. George F. Train, *Young America in Wall Street*, p. 209.
41. John Sterling, "The State of Society in England," quoted in Walter E. Houghton, *The Victorian Frame of Mind*, p. 183.

CHAPTER THREE
The Commodore

1. New York *Herald*, August 7th, 1876.
2. William A. Croffut, *The Vanderbilts and the Story of Their Fortune*, p. 11
3. Stewart H. Holbrook, *The Age of the Moguls*, p. 4.
4. *Herald*, October 3rd, 1869.
5. Croffut, p. 18.
6. *Ibid.*, p. 36.
7. *Herald*, January 5th, 1877.
8. *The Merchant's Magazine and Commercial Review*, January, 1865.
9. *New York Times*, January 5th, 1877.
10. *New York Genealogical and Biographical Record*, 1976.
11. Croffut, p. 25.
12. *Ibid.*, p. 28.
13. Wheaton J. Lane, *Commodore Vanderbilt*, p. 34.
14. James Parton, *Famous Americans of Recent Times*, p. 384.
15. *Niles Register*, November 12th, 1825.
16. Quoted in Lane, p. 43.
17. Quoted in *ibid.*, p. 136.
18. *Harper's Weekly*, March 5th, 1859.
19. Croffut, p. 20.
20. Matthew Hale Smith, *Twenty Years Among the Bulls and Bears of Wall Street*, p. 121.
21. *Ibid.*, p. 119.
22. Quoted in Henry Clews, *Fifty Years in Wall Street*, p. 383.
23. Smith, p. 124.
24. *Herald*, October 13th, 1869.
25. *Ibid.*, June 5th, 1859.
26. The weekly poker game at the Union Club, in which the Commodore is known to have participated, continues to this day. Without question it is the oldest established, permanent (non-floating) poker game in New York and quite probably the world.
27. Croffut, p. 45.

28. Quoted in Lane, p. 109.
29. *Times*, January 5th, 1877.
30. Quoted in *The Railroad Man's Magazine*, February, 1910.

CHAPTER FOUR
The Early Skirmishes

1. Quoted in Wheaton J. Lane, *Commodore Vanderbilt*, p. 207.
2. Allan Nevins, ed., *The Diaries of Philip Hone*, p. 1280.
3. James K. Medbery, *Men and Mysteries of Wall Street*, p. 9.
4. *Ibid.*, p. 247.
5. To be technical, a "monopoly" is always of supply. A monopoly of demand is properly a monopsony, a word even rarer than the economic condition it denotes.
6. Edmund C. Stedman, *The New York Stock Exchange*, p. 23.
7. William W. Fowler, *Ten Years in Wall Street*, p. 33.
8. Quoted in Edward Hungerford, *Men and Iron*, p. 120. The branch line was never built.
9. *Ibid.*, p. 124.
10. Allan Nevins and Milton H. Thomas, eds., *The Diary of George Templeton Strong*, vol. II, p. 331.
11. Quoted in Gustavus Myers, "History of Public Franchises in New York City," in *Municipal Affairs*, vol. IV, 1900.
12. Fowler, p. 205.
13. *Ibid.*, p. 204.
14. *Ibid.*
15. New York *Herald*, April 23rd, 1863.
16. Quoted in *ibid.*, April 24th, 1863. A pothouse was a cheap bar.
17. *Ibid.*, May 6th, 1863.
18. *Ibid.*, May 9th, 1863.
19. Fowler, p. 207.
20. Stedman, p. 174.
21. Fowler, p. 208.
22. Stedman, p. 175.
23. *Herald*, June 29th, 1863.
24. Fowler, p. 208.
25. Henry Clews, *Fifty Years in Wall Street*, p. 108.
26. *Ibid.*
27. Quoted in Lane, p. 107.
28. *Herald*, July 13th, 1863.
29. Quoted in William A. Croffut, *The Vanderbilts and the Story of Their Fortune*, p. 72.
30. *Ibid.*, p. 71.
31. *Ibid.*, p. 81.
32. Quoted in Hudson C. Tanner, *"The Lobby," and Public Men from Thurlow Weed's Time*, p. 223.
33. Croffut, p. 80.
34. Quoted in Lane, p. 205.
35. Croffut, p. 75.
36. Stedman, p. 178.
37. Clews, p. 114.
38. *Ibid.*, p. 113.
39. Croffut, p. 77.
40. Fowler, p. 351.
41. Clews, p. 114.
42. Fowler, p. 355.

43. Croffut, p. 79. A panel game was a scheme popular in brothels. A panel was fitted into the wall near the clothes hooks. While the customer was otherwise engaged, the panel was slid back and the man's wallet removed from his trousers.
44. Clews, p. 115.
45. Croffut, p. 79.
46. *Fraser's Magazine,* May, 1869.

CHAPTER FIVE
The New-York and Erie Rail Road

1. William W. Fowler. *Ten Years in Wall Street,* p. 356.
2. Quoted in Edward Hungerford, *Men of Erie,* p. 46.
3. Quoted in *ibid.,* p. 39.
4. See E. H. Mott, *Between the Ocean and the Lakes,* p. 69.
5. Quoted in *ibid.*
6. *New York Railroad Journal,* July 1st, 1843.
7. Quoted in Mott, p. 408.
8. *Ibid.,* p. 56.
9. *Ibid.,* p. 86.
10. *Ibid.,* p. 463.
11. New York *Herald,* December 18th, 1847.
12. Quoted in Mott, p. 358.
13. Quoted in *ibid.,* p. 348.
14. Binghamton *Democrat,* November 17th, 1848.
15. Mott, p. 91.
16. *Herald,* May 15th, 1851.
17. *Ibid.,* May 14th, 1851.
18. Quoted in Mott, p. 93.

CHAPTER SIX
Uncle Daniel's One-Stringed Chinese Lyre

1. Figures from E. H. Mott, *Between the Ocean and the Lakes,* p. 484.
2. Figures from Robert Sobel, *The Big Board,* p. 79.
3. James K. Medbery, *Men and Mysteries of Wall Street,* p. 277.
4. *Ibid.,* p. 253.
5. London *Times,* January 9th, 1872.
6. Edmund C. Stedman, *The New York Stock Exchange,* p. 147.
7. Medbery, p. 146.
8. *Fraser's Magazine,* May, 1869.
9. William W. Fowler, *Ten Years in Wall Street,* p. 439.
10. Quoted in Wheaton J. Lane, *Commodore Vanderbilt,* p. 236.
11. Fowler, p. 439.
12. *Ibid.,* p. 441.
13. New York *Herald,* August 2nd, 1865.
14. *Ibid.,* September 6th, 1865.
15. *Ibid.,* March 30th, 1866.
16. *Ibid.,* January 16th, 1867.
17. William A. Croffut, *The Vanderbilts and the Story of Their Fortune,* p. 83.
18. Quoted in Lane, p. 221.
19. *Documents of the Assembly of the State of New York, Ninetieth Session,* pp. 184, 207.
20. Fowler, p. 494.
21. Arthur T. Hadley, *Railroad Transportation,* p. 16.
22. *Fraser's Magazine,* May, 1869.

23. Mott, p. 140.
24. Stedman, p. 198.
25. Charles Francis Adams, Jr., and Henry Adams, *Chapters of Erie*, p. 13.
26. Mott, p. 142.
27. *Ibid.*, p. 143.
28. *Herald*, October 9th, 1867.
29. *Ibid.*, October 10th, 1867.
30. *Ibid.*, October 9th, 1867.

CHAPTER SEVEN
A Formidable Pair

1. William W. Fowler, *Ten Years in Wall Street*, p. 482.
2. *Ibid.*, p. 480.
3. Alice N. with Henry N. Snow, *The Story of Helen Gould*, p. 61.
4. New York *Sun*, January 8th, 1872.
5. New York *Herald*, November 7th, 1869.
6. *Sun*, January 8th, 1872.
7. R. W. McAlpine, *The Life and Times of Col. James Fisk, Jr.*, p. 15.
8. *Ibid.*, p. 16.
9. *Herald*, November 7th, 1869.
10. Clara Morris, *Life on the Stage*, p. 308.
11. *Herald*, November 7th, 1869.
12. McAlpine, p. 24.
13. Quoted in W. A. Swanberg, *Jim Fisk: The Career of an Improbable Rascal*, p. 15.
14. McAlpine, p. 24.
15. *Ibid.*, p. 27.
16. *Ibid.*, p. 28.
17. Quoted in *ibid.*, p. 41.
18. *Sun*, November 28th, 1880.
19. Quoted in Clara Barrus, *John Burroughs Boy and Man*, p. 143.
20. United States Senate, "Report of the Committee of the Senate upon the Relations between Labor and Capital and Testimony Taken by the Committee," p. 1063.
21. Quoted in Barrus, p. 145. In fact, Gould was eleven months older than Burroughs.
22. Quoted in George J. Clarke, "Jay Gould in His True Light," *The Literanian*, vol. 1, no. 3.
23. Robert Irving Warshow, *The Story of Wall Street*, p. 100.
24. U.S. Senate, p. 1063.
25. *Ibid.*, p. 1064.
26. *Ibid.*
27. *Ibid.*, p. 1065.
28. *Herald*, July 20th, 1853.
29. Quoted in Maury Klein, *The Life and Legend of Jay Gould*, p. 30.
30. Quoted in Henry Davenport Northrop, *Life and Achievement of Jay Gould*, p. 38.
31. The version of the tannery episode given in Klein, pp. 45–61, is followed here.
32. *Herald*, March 23rd, 1860.
33. McAlpine, p. 45.
34. *Ibid.*
35. James K. Medbery, *Men and Mysteries of Wall Street*, p. 166.
36. McAlpine, p. 46.
37. *Herald*, January 18th, 1871.
38. Fowler, p. 482.
39. Snow, p. 115.

40. *Ibid.*
41. William A. Croffut, *An American Procession,* p. 281.

CHAPTER EIGHT
The War Breaks Out

1. William W. Fowler, *Ten Years in Wall Street,* p. 496.
2. New York *Herald,* February 5th, 1868.
3. Quoted in Henry Clews, *Fifty Years in Wall Street,* p. 125.
4. Charles F. Adams and Henry Adams, *Chapters of Erie,* p. 16.
5. *Ibid.,* p. 17.
6. *Herald,* February 8th, 1868.
7. Quoted in *Leslie's Illustrated Newspaper,* May 2nd, 1868.
8. Adams and Adams, p. 17.
9. *Herald,* February 20th, 1868.
10. Adams and Adams, p. 18.
11. Clews, p. 130.
12. Adams and Adams, p. 159.
13. David McAdam, *et al.*, eds., *History of the Bench and Bar of New York,* p. 164.
14. Jeremiah S. Black, untitled article, *Galaxy Magazine,* March, 1872.
15. Allan Nevins and Milton H. Thomas, eds., *The Diary of George Templeton Strong,* vol. IV, p. 202.
16. *Ibid.,* p. 264.
17. Edmund C. Stedman, *The New York Stock Exchange,* p. 200.
18. *Fraser's Magazine,* May, 1869, p. 574.
19. *Leslie's Illustrated Newspaper,* November 28th, 1868.
20. *Herald,* February 20th, 1868.
21. *American Law Review,* October, 1868. Most of the legal details in this chapter come from this issue.
22. *Ibid.,* p. 46.
23. Fowler, p. 499.
24. William A. Croffut, *The Vanderbilts and the Story of Their Fortune,* p. 91.
25. *American Law Review,* October, 1868.
26. *Ibid.*
27. Stedman, p. 202.
28. Fowler, p. 500.
29. *Ibid.,* p. 499.
30. Croffut, p. 91.
31. Fowler, p. 501.
32. Clews, p. 139.
33. Fowler, p. 501.
34. *Ibid.*
35. *Herald,* March 14th, 1868.
36. Fowler, p. 502.
37. *Harper's Weekly,* April 17th, 1868. The details of Fisk and Gould's Hudson crossing are all from this issue.

CHAPTER NINE
Fort Taylor

1. New York *Herald,* March 14th, 1868.
2. *Ibid.,* March 15th, 1868.
3. *Ibid.*
4. *Harper's Monthly,* May, 1868.

5. *Herald,* March 17th, 1868.
6. *Ibid.*
7. *Ibid.,* March 15th, 1868.
8. *Ibid.,* March 17th, 1868.
9. Charles F. Adams and Henry Adams, *Chapters of Erie,* p. 43.
10. William W. Fowler, *Ten Years in Wall Street,* p. 505.
11. William A. Croffut, *The Vanderbilts and the Story of Their Fortune,* p. 95.
12. Adams and Adams, p. 57.
13. *Ibid.*
14. *Leslie's Illustrated Newspaper,* November 28th, 1868.
15. Adams and Adams, p. 34.
16. *Herald,* May 27th, 1868.
17. Adams and Adams, p. 45.
18. *Herald,* March 19th, 1868.
19. *Ibid.,* March 21st, 1868.
20. *Ibid.,* March 25th, 1868.
21. *Ibid.,* April 5th, 1868.
22. *Ibid.,* March 20th, 1868.
23. Quoted in Adams and Adams, p. 54.
24. *Fraser's Magazine,* May, 1869.
25. *Herald,* March 21st, 1868.
26. *Ibid.*
27. Quoted in *ibid.,* March 3rd, 1868.
28. *Commercial and Financial Chronicle,* March 7th, 1868.
29. Adams and Adams, p. 48.
30. *Chronicle,* March 7th, 1868.
31. Allan Nevins and Milton H. Thomas, eds., *The Diary of George Templeton Strong,* vol. II, p. 218.
32. Hudson C. Tanner, *"The Lobby," and Public Men from Thurlow Weed's Time,* p. iv.
33. *Ibid.,* p. vi.
34. *Herald,* March 28th, 1868.
35. *Ibid.,* March 30th, 1868.
36. Adams and Adams, p. 49.
37. *Herald,* April 15th, 1868.
38. *Ibid.*
39. Adams and Adams, p. 50.
40. *Ibid.,* p. 51.
41. *Herald,* April 5th, 1868.
42. Adams and Adams, p. 53.
43. *Herald,* April 20th, 1868.
44. Henry Clews, *Fifty Years in Wall Street,* p. 134.
45. Albany *Argus,* April 21st, 1868.
46. Adams and Adams, p. 54.
47. *Herald,* April 21st, 1868.
48. Adams and Adams, p. 55.
49. Fowler, p. 504.
50. Quoted in Clews, p. 138.
51. *Herald,* March 18th, 1871.
52. Fowler, p. 507.
53. Adams and Adams, p. 41.
54. Quoted in E. H. Mott, *Between the Ocean and the Lakes,* p. 161.
55. Fowler, p. 506.

CHAPTER TEN
The Embarrassment of Daniel Drew

1. George Crouch, *Erie Under Gould and Fisk*, p. 29.
2. *Commercial and Financial Chronicle*, October 31st, 1868.
3. *Ibid.*
4. *Ibid.*, August 8th, 1868.
5. Charles F. Adams and Henry Adams, *Chapters of Erie*, p. 63.
6. *Chronicle*, October 31st, 1868.
7. William W. Fowler, *Ten Years in Wall Street*, p. 507.
8. Henry Clews, *Fifty Years in Wall Street*, p. 140.
9. *Ibid.*, p. 141.
10. *Ibid.*
11. *Herald*, November 1st, 1868.
12. *Chronicle*, November 14th, 1868.
13. Clews, p. 142.
14. *Ibid.*
15. *Ibid.*
16. The conversation between Fisk and Drew is recorded in Fisk's affidavit, published in the *New York Times*, November 19th, 1868.
17. Clews, p. 146.
18. Adams and Adams, p. 71.
19. *Times*, November 23rd, 1868.
20. Clews, p. 144.
21. Adams and Adams, p. 74.
22. *Ibid.*, p. 73.
23. Clews, p. 144.
24. *Herald*, November 18th, 1868.
25. *Ibid.*, November 19th, 1868.
26. *Commercial Advertiser*, November 20th, 1868.
27. London *Times*, November 13th, 1868.
28. *Chronicle*, October 31st, 1868.
29. Quoted in E. H. Mott, *Between the Ocean and the Lakes*, p. 163.
30. Adams and Adams, p. 71.
31. *Ibid.*
32. Quoted in *Herald*, November 21st, 1868.
33. *Ibid.*, December 1st, 1868.
34. James K. Medbery, *Men and Mysteries of Wall Street*, p. 344.

CHAPTER ELEVEN
Castle Erie

1. *New York Times*, November 26th, 1868.
2. Charles F. Adams and Henry Adams, *Chapters of Erie*, p. 85.
3. New York *Herald*, November 25th, 1868.
4. *Ibid.*, November 26th, 1868.
5. *Ibid.*
6. *Ibid.*
7. Adams and Adams, p. 84.
8. *Times*, December 6th, 1868.
9. Quoted in Adams and Adams, p. 89.
10. Quoted in *Times*, December 7th, 1868.
11. Quoted in *ibid.*, December 11th, 1868.
12. Quoted in Wheaton J. Lane, *Commodore Vanderbilt*, p. 259.

13. Quoted in George S. Merriam, *The Life of Samuel Bowles*, p. 94.
14. Quoted in W. A. Swanberg, *Jim Fisk: The Career of an Improbable Rascal*, p. 88.
15. Quoted in *The Railroad Man's Magazine*, February, 1910, pp. 147–150.
16. Figures from the *Commercial and Financial Chronicle*, March 20th, 1869.
17. *Chronicle*, April 3rd, 1869.
18. Figures from E. H. Mott, *Between the Ocean and the Lakes*, p. 484.
19. *Herald*, January 5th, 1869.
20. *Ibid.*, January 21st, 1869.
21. *Ibid.*, January 20th, 1869.
22. *Ibid.*, February 5th, 1869.
23. *Ibid.*, April 10th, 1869.
24. *Ibid.*, January 9th, 1869.
25. William W. Fowler, *Ten Years in Wall Street*, p. 483.
26. *Harper's Monthly*, May, 1870.
27. *Leslie's Illustrated Newspaper*, January 18th, 1868.
28. Quoted in Mott, p. 426.
29. *Herald*, January 18th, 1871.
30. Allan Nevins and Milton H. Thomas, eds., *The Diary of George Templeton Strong*, vol. IV, p. 340.
31. Adams and Adams, p. 94.

CHAPTER TWELVE
The Raid on the Albany and Susquehanna

1. Charles F. Adams and Henry Adams, *Chapters of Erie*, p. 141.
2. New York *Herald*, March 12th, 1872.
3. Adams and Adams, p. 153.
4. Quoted in W. A. Swanberg, *Jim Fisk: The Career of an Improbable Rascal*, p. 95.
5. Adams and Adams, p. 153.
6. *Ibid.*
7. Albany *Evening Journal*, August 7th, 1869.
8. *Ibid.*
9. *Ibid.*
10. Albany *Argus*, August 7th, 1869.
11. *Ibid.*
12. *Herald*, August 11th, 1869.
13. *Argus*, August 7th, 1869.
14. Adams and Adams, p. 161.
15. *Herald*, August 9th, 1869.
16. *Ibid.*, August 8th, 1869.
17. Adams and Adams, p. 166.
18. *Leslie's Illustrated Newspaper*, August 28th, 1869.
19. *Herald*, August 12th, 1869.
20. *Ibid.*
21. *New York Times*, September 8th, 1869.
22. General Francis C. Barlow and David D. Field, *Facts for David Dudley Field*, p. 219.
23. Jeremiah S. Black, untitled article, *Galaxy Magazine*, March, 1872.
24. *Harper's Weekly*, February 12th, 1870.
25. Quoted in Barlow and Field, p. 218.
26. David Dudley Field, et al., *The Lawyer and His Clients*, pp. 9, 12.
27. Barlow and Field, p. 348.
28. Troy *Daily Times*, August 23rd, 1869.
29. *Times*, September 17th, 1869.
30. *Herald*, October 3rd, 1869.

CHAPTER THIRTEEN
Black Friday

1. Charles F. Adams and Henry Adams, *Chapters of Erie*, p. 114.
2. Quoted in Ellis Paxson Oberholtzer, *Jay Cooke, Financier of the Civil War*, vol. II, p. 141.
3. House of Representatives, *House Report Number 31, 41st Congress, 2nd Session* (hereafter cited as Garfield), p. 113.
4. *Ibid.*, p. 148.
5. *Ibid.*, p. 135.
6. Adams and Adams, p. 116.
7. Garfield, p. 3.
8. *Ibid.*, p. 246.
9. *Harper's Monthly*, May, 1870.
10. Quoted in Richard O'Conner, *Gould's Millions*, p. 98.
11. Garfield, p. 8.
12. *Ibid.*, p. 35.
13. *Ibid.*, p. 444.
14. William S. McFeely, *Grant*, p. 325.
15. Garfield, p. 252.
16. Quoted in Robert Sobel, *Panic on Wall Street*, p. 144.
17. Garfield, p. 174.
18. *Ibid.*, p. 7.
19. *Ibid.*
20. William W. Fowler, *Twenty Years of Inside Life in Wall Street*, p. 528.
21. Garfield, p. 180.
22. *Ibid.*, p. 11.
23. *Ibid.*, p. 256
24. *Ibid.*, p. 13.
25. *Ibid.*, p. 330.
26. New York *Herald*, September 25th, 1869.
27. Garfield, p. 15.
28. Charles T. Harris, *Memories of Manhattan in the Sixties and Seventies*, p. 48.
29. Garfield, p. 202.
30. *Ibid.*, p. 214.
31. Quoted in Fowler, p. 152.
32. *Herald*, September 25th, 1869.
33. Garfield, p. 92.
34. *Ibid.*, p. 262.
35. *New York Times*, September 25th, 1869.
36. Both quotes in Robert Sobel, *The Big Board*, p. 93.
37. Garfield, p. 176.
38. *Ibid.*, p. 217.
39. *Herald*, September 25th, 1869.
40. London *Times*, January 9th, 1872.
41. Garfield, p. 90.

CHAPTER FOURTEEN
President Gould and Colonel Fisk

1. New York *Herald*, January 1st, 1870.
2. *Ibid.*, September 30th, 1869.
3. William A. Croffut, *An American Procession*, p. 105.
4. *Herald*, September 3rd, 1869.

5. Allan Nevins and Milton H. Thomas, eds., *The Diary of George Templeton Strong*, vol. IV, p. 259.
6. *Ibid.*, vol. IV, p. 260.
7. *New York Times*, September 2nd, 1869.
8. *Herald*, September 24th, 1869.
9. *Ibid.*, November 11th, 1869.
10. Quoted in *ibid.*
11. *Ibid.*, October 3rd, 1869.
12. *Ibid.*
13. Figures from *Commercial and Financial Chronicle*, January 1st, 1870.
14. *Ibid.*, January 8th, 1870.
15. The article, most unusually, is known to be by George Crouch. Bylines were still years in the future so this article is unsigned. But Fisk wanted to establish that he was on familiar terms with Corbin, so later he had the *Herald* reporter watch from his carriage as he entered the Corbins' house on East 26th Street, then had the reporter sign an affidavit to that effect. The reporter who signed the affidavit was George Crouch, and the affidavit is reproduced in the article.
16. George Crouch, *Erie Under Gould and Fisk*, p. 17.
17. *North American Review*, April, 1866.
18. *Herald*, February 6th, 1870.
19. James K. Medbery, *Men and Mysteries of Wall Street*, p. 168.
20. *Chronicle*, May 14th, 1870.
21. *Herald*, February 6th, 1870. George Crouch might well have been the author of this article as well.
22. *Ibid.*, May 14th, 1870.
23. *Leslie's Illustrated Newspaper*, June 11th, 1870.
24. *Herald*, May 28th, 1870.
25. *Ibid.*, June 7th, 1870.
26. *Ibid.*, June 14th, 1871.
27. Quoted in Wheaton J. Lane, *Commodore Vanderbilt*, p. 259.
28. *Leslie's Illustrated Newspaper*, August 27th, 1870.
29. *Herald*, August 20th, 1870.
30. *Ibid.*, August 22nd, 1870.

CHAPTER FIFTEEN
God's Expressman

1. New York *Herald*, October 10th, 1870.
2. *Ibid.*, April 12th, 1870.
3. Quoted in George Crouch, *Erie Under Fisk and Gould*, p. 143.
4. Quoted in Maury Klein, *The Life and Legend of Jay Gould*, p. 117.
5. James K. Medbery, *Men and Mysteries of Wall Street*, p. 213.
6. *New York Times*, October 10th, 1869.
7. *Herald*, January 18th, 1871.
8. *Ibid.*, January 7th, 1872.
9. *Ibid.*
10. Anson Phelps Stokes, *Stokes Records*, p. 57.
11. *Herald*, January 18th, 1871.
12. R. W. McAlpine, *The Life and Times of Col. James Fisk, Jr.*, p. 329.
13. Quoted in *ibid.*, p. 406.
14. *Ibid.*, p. 409.
15. *Herald*, October 14th, 1870.
16. Quoted in McAlpine, p. 311.

17. *Herald,* June 18th, 1871.
18. *Ibid.,* June 20th, 1871.
19. *Ibid.*
20. *Ibid.,* May 25th, 1871.
21. New York *Sun,* May 18th, 1871.
22. Quoted in McAlpine, p. 437.
23. Allan Nevins and Milton H. Thomas, eds., *The Diary of George Templeton Strong,* vol. IV, p. 409.
24. Quoted in *Sun,* January 10th, 1872.
25. Joel T. Headley, *The Great Riots of New York, 1712–1873,* p. 294.
26. Quoted in *ibid.,* p. 295.
27. Nevins and Thomas, vol. IV, p. 370.
28. Headley, p. 297.
29. *Herald,* July 13th, 1871.
30. Headley, p. 302.
31. *Herald,* July 13th, 1871.
32. *Sun,* July 14th, 1871.
33. *Herald,* July 13th, 1871.
34. *Ibid.*
35. *Sun,* July 15th, 1871.
36. *Harper's Weekly,* August 5th, 1871.
37. Quoted in Clara Morris, *Life on the Stage,* p. 311.
38. *Sun,* July 14th, 1871.
39. *Ibid.,* October 11th, 1871.
40. Morris, p. 34.
41. *Sun,* October 11th, 1871.
42. *Ibid.,* October 12th, 1871.
43. *Ibid.,* October 11th, 1871.
44. Quoted in the *Herald,* October 11th, 1871.
45. Morris, p. 34.

CHAPTER SIXTEEN
The Murder of Jubilee Jim

1. Quoted in New York *Herald,* October 15th, 1871.
2. Brooklyn *Eagle,* quoted in W. A. Swanberg, *Jim Fisk: The Career of an Improbable Rascal,* p. 222.
3. New York *Herald,* June 2nd, 1871.
4. *North American Review,* July, 1867.
5. *Ibid.,* October, 1866.
6. *Ibid.*
7. DeAlva S. Alexander, *A Political History of New York State,* p. 216.
8. Allan Nevins and Milton H. Thomas, eds., *The Diary of George Templeton Strong,* vol. IV, p. 394.
9. Quoted in E. H. Mott, *Between the Ocean and the Lakes,* p. 490.
10. *Ibid.,* p. 421.
11. *Herald,* January 18th, 1871.
12. *Ibid.,* October 19th, 1871.
13. New York *Sun,* October 27th, 1871.
14. *Herald,* November 26th, 1871.
15. *Ibid.,* November 26th, 1871.
16. *Ibid.,* January 7th, 1872.
17. Testimony of Thomas Hart at the coroner's inquest. Quoted in R. W. McAlpine, *The Life and Times of Col. James Fisk, Jr.,* p. 356.

18. Quoted in *ibid.*, p. 336.
19. Quoted in *Herald,* January 7th, 1872.
20. *Ibid.*
21. *Ibid.*
22. *Sun,* January 9th, 1872.
23. *Herald,* January 8th, 1872.
24. *Ibid.*
25. *Ibid.*
26. *Sun,* January 10th, 1872.
27. *Herald,* January 8th, 1871.
28. *Ibid.*
29. Quoted in Mott, p. 491.
30. *Herald,* January 21st, 1872.
31. Edmund C. Stedman, *The New York Stock Exchange,* p. 249.

CHAPTER SEVENTEEN
The Fall of Castle Erie

1. New York *Sun,* March 12th, 1872.
2. Figures from *Commercial and Financial Chronicle,* December 23rd, 1871.
3. *Ibid.,* December 30th, 1871.
4. Quoted in E. H. Mott, *Between the Ocean and the Lakes,* p. 181.
5. *Ibid.,* p. 180.
6. Quoted in *ibid.*
7. New York *Herald,* March 9th, 1872.
8. Quoted in Mott, p. 197.
9. Quoted in *ibid.,* pp. 186, 187.
10. Quoted in *ibid.,* p. 187.
11. *Herald,* March 13th, 1872.
12. *Ibid.*
13. *Herald,* March 11th, 1872.
14. *Sun,* March 12th, 1872.
15. *Ibid.*
16. *Herald,* March 11th, 1872.
17. *Ibid.*
18. *Sun,* March 12th, 1872.
19. *Herald,* March 11th, 1872.
20. *Ibid.,* March 12th, 1872.
21. *Ibid.*
22. *Sun,* March 12th, 1872.
23. *Herald,* March 13th, 1872.
24. *Sun,* March 12th, 1872.
25. *Herald,* March 12th, 1872.
26. *Sun,* March 12th, 1872.
27. *Ibid.*
28. *Ibid.*
29. *Ibid.*
30. *Ibid.*
31. *Herald,* March 13th, 1872.
32. *Sun,* March 12th, 1872.
33. *Herald,* March 12th, 1872.
34. *Ibid.,* March 17th, 1872.

CHAPTER EIGHTEEN
The End of the Erie Wars

1. New York *Herald,* July 10th, 1872.
2. *Ibid.,* September 14th, 1872.
3. *Ibid.,* September 20th, 1872.
4. New York *Sun,* September 24th, 1872.
5. *Herald,* September 27th, 1872.
6. Quoted in E. H. Mott, *Between the Ocean and the Lakes,* p. 209.
7. Quoted in McAdam, *et al.,* eds., *History of the Bench and Bar of New York,* p. 198.
8. *Commercial and Financial Chronicle,* November 30th, 1872.
9. *Herald,* November 25th, 1872.
10. *Ibid.,* November 23rd, 1872.
11. Quoted in Mott, p. 210.
12. *Herald,* November 23rd, 1872.
13. *Chronicle,* November 23rd, 1872.
14. *Herald,* November 23rd, 1872.
15. *Ibid.*
16. *Ibid.* Of course a few "sheers" was exactly what Drew did not have.
17. *Ibid.*
18. *Ibid.,* November 25th, 1872.
19. *Sun,* November 25th, 1872.
20. Quoted in *New York Times,* December 13th, 1892.
21. Quoted in *Herald,* November 23rd, 1872.
22. *Sun,* November 25th, 1872.
23. *Ibid.*
24. *Ibid.,* November 27th, 1872.
25. *Ibid.*
26. Wheaton J. Lane, *Commodore Vanderbilt,* p. 310.
27. Quoted in *ibid.,* p. 313.
28. Quoted in *The Railroad Man's Magazine,* February, 1910.
29. *Herald,* May 11th, 1876.
30. *Times,* January 5th, 1877.
31. *Herald,* January 5th, 1877.
32. Quoted in Mott, p. 212.
33. Quoted in *ibid.,* p. 213.
34. *Ibid.,* p. 213.
35. New York *World,* November 26th, 1890.
36. *Frank Leslie's Popular Monthly,* December, 1879.
37. *Ibid.*
38. *Herald,* March 14th, 1876.
39. It was, coincidentally enough, E. C. Stedman who first used the word in this sense, in the title of an anthology, *Victorian Poets.*

Index

About the Author

JOHN STEELE GORDON was born in New York City into a family long associated with Wall Street; both his grandfathers held seats on the New York Stock Exchange. He has worked in publishing and political public relations, serving as assistant New York State press secretary in the presidential campaign of Morris Udall and as press secretary for Congressmen Herman Badillo and Robert Garcia. Mr. Gordon has published several articles in the *New York Times* and is the author of *Overlanding*. He lives in New York City and North Salem, New York.